A SENSE OF BELONGING

Margaret Thomson Davis has lived in Glasgow from the age of three, except when evacuated during the war. She is the author of fourteen previous novels, an autobiography and over two hundred short stories.

Also by Margaret Thomson Davis

The Breadmakers
A Baby Might Be Crying
A Sort of Peace
Scorpion in the Fire
The Prisoner
The Prince and the Tobacco Lords
Roots of Bondage
The Dark Side of Pleasure
The Making of a Novelist (Autobiography)
A Very Civilised Man
Light and Dark
Rag Woman, Rich Woman
Daughters and Mothers
Wounds of War
A Woman of Property

A SENSE OF
BELONGING

Margaret Thomson Davis

ARROW

First published in Arrow in 1994

1 3 5 7 9 10 8 6 4 2

© Margaret Thomson Davis 1993

The right of Margaret Thomson Davis to be identified as the
author of this work has been asserted by her in accordance
with the Copyright, Designs and Patents Act, 1988.

First published in the United Kingdom in 1993 by
Century, Random House, 20 Vauxhall Bridge Road, London SW1V 2SA

Random House Australia (Pty) Limited
20 Alfred Street, Milsons Point, Sydney,
New South Wales 2061, Australia

Random House New Zealand Limited
18 Poland Road, Glenfield
Auckland 10, New Zealand

Random House South Africa (Pty) Limited
PO Box 337, Bergvlei, South Africa

Random House UK Limited Reg. No. 954009

ISBN 0 09 930501 1

Printed and bound in Great Britain by
Cox & Wyman Ltd, Reading, Berkshire

This book is dedicated with love and admiration to my dear son and daughter-in-law, Kenneth and Arlene Davis, and all good and hard-working teachers everywhere.

Acknowledgements

I'd like to thank the staff at the Mitchell Library in Glasgow who never fail me, plus everyone else who was kind enough to help me out with my research. I feel special mention should be made to the following who gave most generously of their time:

FOR THEATRICAL BACKGROUND:
Paul Groves
William G Differ
Deborah McCaffer
Gordon Irving
The staff of The Citizen's Theatre
Evelyn Hood's play, 'Epitaph For A Hard Man'

FOR GLASGOW BACKGROUND:
The Govan Reminiscence Group
George Rountree's book, *The 1930s – A Govan Childhood*
Ned Donaldson and Les Forster and their book, *Sell and Be Damned*
Ina Thomson for her memories of old Garngad

FOR COUNTRY BACKGROUND:
Hoggie's Angels

FOR TEACHING BACKGROUND:

Ag Weir and Lorna McKie

Mrs Young, Dip. Ed, ITQ. Head teacher of
    Royston Primary School

William Roddie, DCE, DPSE, (Inf. Tech.)
    Headmaster of Abbotsford Primary School

Janetta Bowie's book, *Penny Buff*

Miss Mary Thomson, MA

Jane Hood, ACE

Mrs M Harrison, MA ALA. Principal Librar-
    ian, Jordanhill College

Anne Williamson, FLA

Miss Joyce Moffett, OBE, MALRAM. Dean of
    Women in Jordanhill College

FOR LEGAL BACKGROUND:

Lord Cameron, KT, Kt, DSC, HRSA, FRSGS

Sheriff Frank Lunny, MA, LLB, KHS. Advo-
    cate

Jack Craig, Court Officer

CHAPTER 1

Elizabeth stared at the bedroom mirror as if trying to recognize herself. Despite what had just happened she still looked the same. She was dressed exactly like all the other girls at school in her navy gym slip and long-sleeved white blouse. She had a cap of straight black hair with a fringe covering her brow, large dark eyes and small features that made her look younger than her sixteen years. Nothing revealed how her whole world had turned upside down. At the best of times she had never liked change. She had been sick with apprehension two years ago fearing that Nanny would decide the time had come to move on and find a new job with babies to take care of. After all, her charges at Monkton House in a leafy suburb of Glasgow were no longer dependent on her, with Jason a mature fifteen and twins William and Daniel a lusty thirteen. Perhaps Nanny would have left had it not been for baby Charles coming along and saving the day. Charlie was born on Christmas Day 1927, and now in 1929 at two years of age, had grown into a chubby little boy with creamy hair, soft as thistledown, and eyes like cornflowers. He was Nanny's favourite and had shared her bedroom since birth. Elizabeth adored him too and every night she enjoyed telling him a story before Nanny settled him down. Elizabeth liked to lie in her connecting room and listen to Nanny soothing Charlie to sleep if he woke up during the night. There had been plans to move her to the nursery guest bedroom but she had resisted the idea.

'Elizabeth, you can't have any privacy,' Mother had insisted, but Mother, unlike her, was a very private kind of person. She had even tried to tempt her with a guest bedroom downstairs. Elizabeth refused. The nursery at the top of Monkton'House was her safe familiar world and she had not the slightest desire to leave it.

Father said, 'You can't hide up there for ever. You're not a child any more. It's time you grew up.' But time enough to worry about moving after she had left school. Even so, she could not foresee any reason for objecting to having a room connecting with Nanny's. The spacious day nursery, and the boys' rooms, faced the front of the house and looked down on to Queen's Drive. All the other rooms including Nanny's and Elizabeth's bedrooms faced the back, and looked on to a long garden and Queen's Park beyond. Tradesmen, servants and the occasional gypsies used the back garden gate and Elizabeth often watched their approach with interest from her kneeling position on the chintz-covered windowseat. Gypsies often came with a basket on one arm and a baby on the other and used the baby as a means to elicit sympathy and wheedle scraps of food from the cook. They left secret marks on the back gates to show which places had been soft touches. Nanny had a special hatred of gypsies and would have been angry even at the idea of her watching them. She and the boys had always been hustled away if a gypsy came into sight. To Nanny they represented a wild, undisciplined and dirty way of life, the exact opposite of everything she believed in and tried to instil into her charges, especially Elizabeth. The wicked ways of the gypsies had been so impressed on her in fact, that she had acquired not only a fear of them but a fascination. The ones that came to the back door of Monkton House were a rough but colourful-looking bunch, with their long skirts, large earrings and black tangles of hair. When small, Elizabeth had been glad to be a safe distance from them, in her room under the eaves. Now she didn't feel safe any more. She'd never been so afraid. Yet surely what Vera the nursery maid said to her this morning was only cruel, vengeful lies. She had seen Vera slyly tormenting Charlie and had reported to Nanny the true reasons for Charlie's sobs. Vera had passionately denied the accusation but Nanny asked why Elizabeth should say such a thing if it weren't true.

'Because she's got such an imagination, Nanny. You've said so yourself.'

Nanny couldn't deny this, but she remained suspicious. 'From now on I keep my eye on you, my girl,' she told Vera. 'And if I think you're being in any way unkind to that child you'll pack your bags and leave immediately. Is that clear?'

It was after this incident that Vera got Elizabeth on her own and said, 'One of these days you'll be packing your bags, Miss Smarty. You don't belong here any more than I do.'

'What do you mean?' Elizabeth's voice rose with incredulity.

'And you can sneak on me again if you like. I don't care.'

Vera was ironing Charlie's clothes with much vicious bumping of the iron. She was about the same age as Elizabeth, and as ebony-haired, but she had a ruddy, pimply face, and brows that met in the middle. Elizabeth's skin was clear, her brows wide apart, her eyes large and dramatic.

'I wasn't sneaking,' she protested, 'I was sticking up for Charlie. He's not old enough to protect himself, and you wouldn't listen to me.'

'I was only having a bit of fun with him. You're as straight-laced and po-faced as that dried-up old spinster of a nanny.'

'You're just spiteful and silly.'

Vera gave another thump with the iron. 'I know what I'm talking about all right.'

3

'Then what do you mean, I don't belong here? That's the silliest thing I've ever heard.'

'Ah.' Vera gave her a knowing look. 'But you haven't heard what I've heard.'

'What do you mean?' Elizabeth repeated in exasperation.

'Everybody knows downstairs.'

'Knows what?'

'Mrs Monkton's not your mother, so there!' Vera said with a grimace of satisfaction.

An involuntary laugh burst from Elizabeth's mouth at the same time as her stomach gave a sickening lurch. 'What nonsense. You're a real torment, Vera Hollingsworth. It'd serve you right if Nanny did send you packing.'

Elizabeth clung to Christina Monkton in her mind's eye. She needed the normality of thought to ward off the panic. She saw her mother's pale skin, her stylishly coiffured brown hair, her cool self-contained elegance. Words could not convey how much Elizabeth admired her, and not only for her poise. Christina Monkton was clever too. Not content with being mistress of Monkton House, not even with being on the board of her husband's building firm, she had started a business of her own buying and selling property and land. Her husband built houses, churches, offices, extensions, whatever was called for in the construction line, including maintenance. They worked more or less in partnership, although as far as Elizabeth could gather the partnership was not always harmonious. Her father was the more emotional of the two. He had a temper that could boil over in angry accusation. In contrast, the more angry her mother became the colder, more withdrawn she appeared. Elizabeth had liked to think she was a mixture of both, sometimes withdrawn and enigmatic, sometimes wildly emotional. Nanny called her a dreamer as well and accused her of having too much

4

imagination for her own good. Nanny was like Mother in a way, Elizabeth sometimes thought. Not in looks, of course. Nanny had long hair worn in a heavy bun and she had a strong, long-nosed face. There was an air about her, however, that was similar to Christina's, a coolness, a dignified distancing. Elizabeth never gave up trying to get close to both, but never felt she succeeded despite her hugs and kisses and protestations of undying love.

'Control yourself,' or 'Behave yourself,' Nanny would sharply command. 'You're untidying my hair,' or 'You're crushing my apron,' or 'It's time you grew up, you're supposed to be a lady.'

Mother would murmur, 'Yes, all right, dear,' and gently disentangle herself.

To please both women she tried very hard to control her eager displays of affection, but it wasn't easy. Her attempts at control were like a pain constantly gnawing at her. There was also the distress of failure to get close to them, when she did succumb to passionate attempts. Now, as often as not, she just imagined successful scenarios instead of risking failure. She imagined love shining out of eyes instead of wary withdrawal, she felt the warmth in loving hugs, instead of stillness and stiffening away. It wasn't that either Nanny or Mother was unkind, or at least she didn't think they meant to be. Nanny was as kind as her prim perfectionist nature allowed. It was understandable that she became impatient with a child who was so unlike her own nature, Elizabeth thought. When she was small, Elizabeth had been excitable and clumsy and sometimes dropped things or upset her cup of milk, or cut herself and dripped blood on the clean nursery floor. Nanny never smacked her, but her thin tight mouth and stiff body expressed her disapproval and annoyance in no uncertain terms. Often Elizabeth wished Nanny would smack her − it would at least be some show of emotion and physical contact.

Mother was for the most part scrupulously fair. There were a few occasions when she'd obviously favoured the boys. Elizabeth overheard Father reprimanding her about it, but Mother had said, 'I suppose it happens in all families. It's difficult to treat everyone exactly the same when each individual is so different.' Elizabeth had seen the truth of this. The boys were different from each other, or at least Jason was different from the twins. Jason was talented and musical – already he could play the piano almost as well as Mother. He would sit for hours at the piano oblivious of everyone and everything but his music. She loved to listen to him and watch his total absorption, his khaki-coloured hair sliding forward over his face. William and Daniel had short dark hair and were more interested in rugby, football, jujitsu and judo. They were more like Father, who had a burly broad-chested build, and had practised not only judo and jujitsu but boxing in much of his spare time.

'Too much,' Mother complained.

Sometimes Nanny and Mother had disagreements over Elizabeth. Nanny used to insist on tying every lock of Elizabeth's hair in a piece of rag to make it curl. It had always been an agony to sleep in such a headful of tightly screwed-up hair. Recently Mother had allowed her to have it cut and remain in its natural straight condition. There had been one of Nanny's and Mother's little battles over this. They were both women of strong minds, but Mother had the power on her side. Although on many occasions she found it impossible to wield. The nursery was Nanny's domain and she knew how indispensable she was there. Indeed she was the rock on which the whole house depended. Every time Mother was away on business, it was Nanny who supervised the running of the house. If anyone was ill it was Nanny who nursed them.

When Cook was ill, for instance, it was Nanny who

6

not only looked after her but took over the household cooking. Daisy the scullery maid admitted that she 'wasn't half glad' when Cook returned to duty. Mrs Bishop was fussy enough, but Nanny was a perfectionist.

'She had me scrubbing nooks and crannies down here I never knew existed,' Daisy wailed. This was one reason nursery maids came and went so often and were increasingly hard to find. Vera Hollingsworth's days, Elizabeth felt, were numbered. As well as her recurring waves of panic at what Vera said she experienced pangs of guilt at having, as Vera put it, sneaked on her to Nanny. Vera poking and jabbing a finger into Charlie's plump frame could have been meant in fun, but it had made Charlie cry. Elizabeth wondered, however, if Charlie's distress was the only reason she had spoken to Nanny. She had this terrible need to please people, especially Nanny and Mother. Sometimes she felt there was nothing she wouldn't stoop to, to gain their affection or even just their attention. She tried to see herself fulfilling some altruistic task after she left school, thinking that would please and impress them, especially Mother. At first she'd thought of being a doctor and had spent many hours daydreaming about how she'd save Mother's life. Even Father had fallen in need of her tender care and miraculous ministrations. The boys too had their turn, she'd saved all of their lives, and been rewarded by protestations of eternal love and gratitude. Then Nanny, ever down to earth and realistic, had pointed out aspects of doctoring that she would not be suited to.

'You a doctor!' she'd scoffed. 'You'd either faint or panic at the first sight of blood. You've never been any use in an emergency.'

It was true that she became intensely anxious if anyone else was upset and if she saw anyone physically injured she couldn't bear it, she felt the injury more than they did. So being a doctor was out.

A missionary was equally squashable.

'You miles away in Africa.' Nanny shook her head. 'What next? You'd be homesick for your mother before you even got there.'

Then Elizabeth had the brilliant idea of teaching. She could live at home with a job like that. She'd never need to leave Mother or Father. Teaching, that was the thing. The mere idea filled her with joy and hope. She could teach in the Gorbals, where Mother owned so much property. Mother had tried to help the young people there by giving boys premises for a gymnasium, and girls a place for a club of their own. She had also created a holiday house for deprived children in one of her farm properties outside of Glasgow. She thought Mother would be pleased at her wanting to help the children by teaching them, and so she was. Even Nanny showed some interest and approval.

'Yes . . . You're good with children,' she admitted. 'Charlie enjoys you telling him stories.'

She couldn't start training at Jordanhill until she was eighteen. She'd need a group of Highers, and was studying for passes in four subjects. It was very hard going because she wasn't clever like the boys, who seemed to sail through all their examinations. Nevertheless she'd never been so happy in all her life.

Her father teased her about her prospective career, and her mother viewed her ambition with guarded approval. Elizabeth's sensitive antennae picked up a shade of disappointment in her mother's attitude, but that was nothing new. She'd always known that Mother would have preferred her to be properly ambitious and hard-headed enough to go into the family business, or start a business of her own. Christina had long ago resigned herself to the fact that Elizabeth had not the right temperament for success in the cutthroat business world. Disappointment could not be denied, however.

8

'Are you sure that is what you wish to do, Elizabeth?' she'd asked.

'Oh yes, Mother.' Elizabeth was breathless and wide-eyed with excitement. 'I've definitely made up my mind.'

Her mother shrugged. 'Very well, if that's what you've decided. Your father and I will enquire into how you go about getting the training and qualifications you'll need.'

'I'm glad something's been settled,' Adam Monkton said with a relief that indicated he'd previously been worried about whether she'd ever be suitable for anything. A view sometimes made more obvious by Nanny.

'I don't know how you'll end up. It's well seen . . .' She'd pursed her lips and cut herself short in mid-sentence.

Elizabeth had to ask, 'What's well seen?'

After a few seconds Nanny had said, 'You've been spoiled.'

Elizabeth had to laugh. 'Spoiled? Me? You know fine, Nanny, Mother and Father love the boys far better than me.' She'd said it without rancour, simply as a statement of fact. It wasn't her parents' fault. One couldn't help one's feelings. They did their best to hide them.

'That's as it may be,' Nanny said. 'But your mother and father have always been good to you. You'd do well to remember that, miss.'

It was odd, Elizabeth thought, how often her instincts told her that something was being left unsaid. She could never quite put her finger on why she felt this, but the feeling was always there. Even on her visits to the kitchen she sensed the occasional hint of something not quite right in the way Cook spoke to her. Again, it wasn't what was said, but what seemed left hanging in the air behind the spoken words. Sometimes it was in a look between Cook and Nanny. It consolidated her belief that there was something odd about her, something not quite right, something that people shied away from. It made her shy away from herself.

She escaped in daydreams and fantasies. In her dreams she had been a successful businesswoman like Mother, a beautiful knitter and sewer like Nanny. Sometimes she was a famous actress enjoying the adulation of the crowds. She acted out stories in a dramatic and imaginative way to Charlie. But that was different. She loved children and felt at ease with them. With anyone else she was too easily upset. Vera Hollingsworth had upset her terribly. She wondered if she should tell Nanny. Nanny had always been the one to go to in any crisis or emergency, her common sense cut through fears and made them seem foolish. Elizabeth hesitated to repeat Vera's words, however, they seemed so ridiculous. She tried to forget them but couldn't. On the contrary she became more and more agitated until she felt quite sick and couldn't eat her tea.

Nanny eyed Elizabeth sharply. She and the boys still had tea with Nanny. It was only at dinnertime that Nanny dined alone in the nursery while the rest of the family ate downstairs with Mother and Father if they were at home, or if they weren't having guests. Nanny's meals were always sent upstairs. First thing every morning Sarah the maid took her up a cup of tea. Then Nanny would go through to the bathroom looking very different from her usual smart aproned self, with her hair in a long pigtail over her shoulder, and wearing an old red dressing gown with a tasselled cord.

'Are you sickening for something?' Nanny said. 'Empire biscuits are your favourites.'

Elizabeth hesitated. 'It was just something Vera said.'

'What's she been up to this time?'

Elizabeth half laughed. She felt embarrassed and sick at the same time. 'She said Mother wasn't my real mother.'

10

Nanny's sallow skin visibly paled, her thin mouth tightened. 'You stay there,' she commanded.

Vera was downstairs fetching more toasted tea-cakes – liberally filled with strawberry jam, they were Vera's favourites. After Nanny left the room Elizabeth began to shiver. She wasn't sure if this was because of excitement or fear, or because she was sickening for something. After a while she heard footsteps going to Vera's room and out again and away downstairs. Then Nanny, grim-faced, re-entered the day nursery.

'Well, that's her gone for good. She's been nothing but trouble, that one.'

'Vera?'

'Who else?'

Elizabeth felt guilty and ashamed. 'Maybe I shouldn't have told you.'

'Eat up your tea. You're as skinny as a rake.'

'But, why did she say that?'

'Put it out of your head, do as you're told. Mrs Bishop won't be pleased if you waste her Empire biscuits.'

She hardly dared to ask. 'It wasn't true, was it?'

'Ask no questions and you'll be told no lies,' Nanny said. 'Eat up your tea.'

But eating was now completely out of the question.

CHAPTER 2

The house was full of whispers. She sensed it. Eyes avoided hers. Or they fixed on her with unnaturally wide stares as if desperately willing themselves to look natural. Elizabeth kept assuring herself that any minute she would wake up and everything would be back to normal. She kept telling herself that it was the sheer ridiculousness of what Vera had said that had embarrassed everyone. At other times she dismissed the whole thing as a figment of her over-active imagination. Nothing worked. Panic would suddenly materialize from nowhere and seize her by the throat until she couldn't stand it any more. One day in the cool elegance of the dining room they had just reached the coffee stage when she burst out:

'Please tell me the truth.'

Christina and Monkton exchanged glances, Monkton turned to the boys.

'Isn't this your judo night?'

'I've music practice,' Jason said.

'All right, off you go, the lot of you. Elizabeth, you come through to the drawing room with us.'

Elizabeth's legs barely had the strength to lift her from her chair. By some miracle she reached the drawing room. Up until now it had always seemed a beautiful, welcoming room with its parquet floor, the smell of polish, its rugs and long curtains in modern, geometric design, its broad-armed easy chairs and settee in oatmeal-coloured fabric. Often she'd sat here with the family watching dust motes dancing in the sunshine, happily listening to the wireless or the gramophone or enjoying a game of Monopoly. Now it seemed a strange,

12

alien place. Her parents settled themselves in their usual chairs on either side of the fire. Elizabeth sank down on to the settee. For a minute there was silence except for the click of Mother's cigarette lighter and the tinkling of the pyramid-shaped clock on the mantelpiece.

'We're sorry it's happened like this. We meant to explain to you when you were a bit older and could understand, you're really still a child, Elizabeth,' Monkton said eventually.

Anger came to Elizabeth's rescue. 'I'm sixteen.'

'A very young sixteen. I still don't feel you could appreciate the whole story so I'll just say this, it's true that Christina is not your natural mother. She made a pact with your natural mother when she brought you here as a baby. Christina agreed to be a mother to you in every other way and your natural mother agreed to give up all rights to you.'

Elizabeth plummeted into a void. In the silence that followed she had the sensation that she no longer existed. At last Christina said:

'You've always felt one of the family, haven't you? You've always been treated as such and will continue to be so. This need make no difference. Nothing has changed.'

How like Mother to make such a pronouncement so calmly. She still thought of her as Mother although she now knew this was a lie. She had been living a lie for years. Her whole life was a lie. Anger turned to hatred aimed at Christina, her smoothly waved hair, her elegant clothes, her calm secretive eyes.

'What would you know about how I feel?'

'There's no need to be impertinent,' Monkton said. 'Your mother is only trying to help.'

'She's not my mother.'

'Yes she is, she's your adopted mother and I won't have her upset.'

'*Her* upset. Of course, she's all you care about. Her and your precious boys.'

She instantly regretted her words. They reminded her that she was bereft of brothers as well. It was too much. In a welter of sobbing she rushed from the room. Father made to follow her, but before either of them reached the door, Mother said calmly:

'Nanny's the best one to deal with her.'

Upstairs in the other world at the top of the house, Nanny gave her a cup of hot sweet tea and a valerian tablet and told her to act her age. The tea and the valerian calmed away the sobbing. In between sips of tea she eventually managed:

'That would be a shock at any age.'

'Nevertheless there's no need to go to pieces over it. Think how lucky you are.'

Elizabeth's mouth twisted. 'Lucky?'

Nanny briskly began tidying away Charlie's toys. 'You've a good home here. Many's the one hasn't had half the care and attention you've had. Count your blessings, miss.'

'You've known all the time?' Nanny's tight-lipped silence was answer enough.

'Did you see my real mother?' Elizabeth asked. 'They told me she brought me here when I was a baby.'

'We had a nursery maid then called Etta. She went downstairs and fetched you that night.'

'Why was I fetched here? I don't understand.'

'Put it out of your head, you'll stir up nothing but trouble for yourself and everybody else if you keep worrying away at it.'

'I can't help it.'

'Curiosity killed the cat.'

'I'll die if I don't find out.'

'Some things are better not found out.'

'Wouldn't you want to know if you were me?'

'I mind my own business.'

14

'But this *is* my business.'

'Your business is to be dutiful and respectful to the woman who has always been Mother to you. Your duty is to get your homework done and no more nonsense. How will you ever get your Highers if you don't study? No Highers, no Jordanhill.'

Jordanhill Teacher Training College had receded into nothingness. 'I can't just sit here as if nothing had happened.'

'Nothing has happened.'

'How can you say that? My whole life is turned upside down.'

'Life will go on just the same if you let it.'

Her father came upstairs eventually and it was as much as she could do to prevent another paroxysm of sobbing at the sight of him. She had always loved him and treasured the times they spent together. When he was at home he always made some time for her. He was the only one who had ever been in any way warm and demonstrative. He was the one who would hug her and kiss her and tell her she was the most beautiful creature he'd ever seen. Not that she believed this, of course, but it did her heart good to hear him say it. He was her ideal in a man despite the way one brow pulled down (the result of an old eye injury) and gave him a slightly wicked look. He was tall, broad-chested and aggressive, yet with a warmth that made him capable of great tenderness at times. When she'd been ill, Mother had come to the nursery to discuss with Nanny what must be done for the best, and check that she was as comfortable as possible. She'd stood at the foot of the bed and asked:

'Is there anything I can fetch you from town? Have you enough to read, enough fruit?'

Her father had greeted her with a bear hug and a kiss and then sat holding her hand. Before he left he kissed her again. He tried to kiss her now, but she turned her face away, her hair falling like a dark shadow over her face.

'You behave yourself, miss,' Nanny warned.

'It's all right,' Monkton told her, 'she's had quite a shock.' Then to Elizabeth, 'But it's true what Mother said, nothing's changed. We still feel exactly the same about you.'

And what was that? Elizabeth wondered miserably.

'Perhaps we were wrong in not telling you before, but we had the best of motives, Elizabeth. Although I suppose we dreaded it too, knowing you'd probably take it like this.'

'Adopted mother, you said. Does that mean I'm legally adopted?'

'That was just a figure of speech. There was no need for adoption.'

She looked away, a corkscrew of grief twisting deep into the core of herself. She had to make a sudden desperate effort at cheerfulness to cover her grief.

'Oh well, I don't suppose it matters really.'

Then she changed the subject, but it did matter. She felt frighteningly insecure. Did this mean she had no rights here? Could they change their minds and put her out? Appalling scenarios began flickering across her mind's eye. She saw herself homeless, wandering in the streets, prey to all the wickedness and temptations that Nanny had always said were out there awaiting young girls. Although, the way Nanny told it, it seemed as if it was the young girls who caused the wickedness if given half a chance. Eve in the Garden of Eden being the ruination of Adam and forming the basis of all the corruption and wickedness in the world thereafter was one of Nanny's favourite stories. It was also something darkly hinted at and sometimes called 'intimate relations' that was the root of all evil.

'Don't look at me like that, Elizabeth,' Monkton said. 'It's not the end of the world.'

But it seemed the end of her world. Elizabeth shuddered at the idea of being cast adrift. She had always had such a keen appreciation of security. Sitting in front of the nursery fire with Nanny. Listening to the wind howling outside and glad to be so safe and warm and with somebody so trusted. Surrounded by so many dearly loved familiar things within Nanny's reassuring world. In the drawing room with Mother and Father and the boys, listening to Jason playing the piano. Savouring the closeness, the pleasure, the luxury of it all and the delicious sense of belonging. Now, suspended in a frightening vacuum, she belonged nowhere. She didn't know who she was, or where she'd come from.

'Are you . . .' she managed in a quavering voice, 'my real father?'

'Of course I am, darling.' He reached out for her but she turned away, unsure and untrusting in her misery. He was not the same person any more.

Next day at school she couldn't concentrate on her lessons. She gave every appearance of listening to the teacher, but every now and again the concave feeling would grip her and she'd rapidly be sucked into a nightmare of loneliness and despair.

Unlike the boys' schools, her private school was within walking distance of Monkton House, so she was able to go home for lunch. Mother and Father never came home in the middle of the day. Lunch was sent up from the kitchen to the nursery. Today it was beef and potato pie and bread and butter pudding. Nanny mashed up Charlie's food and told him what a clever boy he was, making such a good attempt at feeding himself – although much of his food seemed to drop off his spoon and on to his chin and bib.

'How did you get on?' Nanny asked

Elizabeth shrugged.

17

'I asked a polite question, miss, I expect a polite answer.'

'All right, I suppose.'

'Don't slouch, sit up straight.'

Elizabeth made a half-hearted attempt to pull back her shoulders but depression had now set in.

'You're in one of your moods,' Nanny accused. 'What you need is a good brisk walk. Take a quick turn round the park before you go back to school.'

'I don't feel well. I think I'll go to bed.'

Nanny was outraged. 'You'll do no such thing, miss, you'll go back to school and that's an end to it.'

'You're the same as all the rest, you don't care about me.'

'Self-pity's unattractive and unladylike and it gets you nowhere. Eat up your pudding.'

Elizabeth lethargically did as she was told. A sulky droop had settled on her mouth and in her eyes storm clouds gathered.

At dinner that evening she knew her gloomy presence was a trial.

She had always struggled so hard to please everyone. Now, however, when it was all the more urgent to do so a perverseness prevented her.

Later in bed, she wept under the blankets at how unlikable she'd been. When Mother had suggested she should invite a few friends round next day, she had dourly replied:

'I haven't any friends.'

Mother had said no more, but she had exchanged a look with Father. William jerked his head in her direction.

'What's up with her?'

'Just ignore her,' Daniel said, 'she's having one of her dramas.' The twins were a strong, vibrantly healthy pair, with iron jaws and rock-hard muscles that any man twice their age might have envied.

'I hate you,' she suddenly burst out at them, before

rushing from the room, 'you're all muscle and no brain.'

The worst of it was they just laughed. Their laughter echoed after her all the way up the stairs. In the nursery, Nanny was sitting in state at the table eating tapioca pudding. She put down her spoon at the sight of Elizabeth.

'What's wrong now?'

'Nothing.'

'Don't you nothing me, miss.'

There was no use hiding anything from Nanny. Thumping resentfully down at the table beside her, Elizabeth confessed. Nanny was furious: rudeness or bad behaviour at mealtimes was a particularly heinous sin in her eyes, and she was a stickler for good table manners. Even Charlie had already learnt to say please and thank you. Elizabeth hadn't been all that much older than him when she'd learnt to say: 'Please may I leave the table?'

'What will your mother think of me?' Nanny said.

Nanny didn't like Mother. Not that she'd ever breathe a word of criticism against her, but she stiffened slightly every time she mentioned Mother's name. Everyone knew, however, that she had a soft spot for the master of the house. A great source of secret merriment to all the children was how Nanny could even blush in Father's presence. The gaunt long-nosed spinster seemed to have another person hiding inside who only became visible in Father's presence. Elizabeth thought it more pathetic and embarrassing than funny. Now every time she thought of Father she felt bitter.

'It's me Mother will think badly of, not you,' Elizabeth said, but she knew what Nanny meant. Bad behaviour was taken as a reflection on Nanny's training. It was the sort of thing that Mother was liable to talk to Nanny about when they'd been young, discreetly of course. Never in front of the children. But Elizabeth was uncannily observant as well as having over-sensitive antennae. She found out most things she wasn't supposed to, or at least she sensed them. Despite the keenness of her apprehension she ached to find the answer to the mystery of her origin. Blushing and with nervously blinking eyes, she suddenly asked:

'Nanny, did my father have intimate relations with my real mother?'

Nanny looked equally agitated and embarrassed. 'She tempted a good man into wickedness. She was that kind of woman.'

'I see. And you knew about her beforehand. She didn't just appear out of the blue when she brought me here.'

'The least said, the soonest mended.'

Nanny didn't need to say any more as far as Elizabeth was concerned. At least not about her father's relationship with her real mother. And she still had to find out who she was.

It occurred to Elizabeth that Mrs Bishop the cook had been here at the time as well. Cook was very elderly, long past retirement age. Perhaps she would not prove as strong-willed and tight-lipped as Nanny.

CHAPTER 3

But Cook wasn't much more forthcoming. She sat at the long scrubbed table switching eggs in a bowl and trying to pretend she couldn't hear.

'Can't you even tell me what she looked like?' Elizabeth loudened her voice because admittedly Cook was a little deaf.

Mrs Bishop relented. She stopped switching and stared into space, remembering. 'She had black hair like yours only thicker, and curly. And she had the same unusual dark eyes with flecks of violet in them like yours.' She returned her attention to the eggs. 'Now, that's all I'm saying. No good will come of you knowing any more than that.'

'Why won't it? Why is everybody so secretive? Haven't I a right to know?'

'It's not my place.'

And so Elizabeth was forced to leave the kitchen with the most important of her questions still unanswered. It was infuriating as well as upsetting. On the surface life ticked over much the same as usual. She breakfasted on porridge, tea, toast and grapefruit marmalade with Nanny every morning. Neither she nor Nanny ever felt like a cooked breakfast except on Sunday.

The boys had eaten first and left earlier because they had further to travel to school. Nanny fed Charlie then too because Charlie always wakened at the crack of dawn. Then Elizabeth and Nanny had breakfast in peace before Elizabeth put on her school uniform coat and brimmed hat, with the elastic securing it under her chin, collected her school case and waved Nanny good-bye. Sometimes she met up with Alice and Muriel

Donaldson who lived further down the drive and they walked the rest of the way to school together. Further on again, sometimes Betty Swanson joined them.

Elizabeth preferred to be on her own because trying to be like the other three girls could be a strain. At the same time it was important that she be 'one of the girls'. Betty Swanson was a special embarrassment the way she was always nudging and giggling when any boys were near. It was from Betty that Elizabeth got her first clue to the nature of the sin and corruption to which Nanny so often referred. Betty had purloined a book from her older brother and smuggled it into the school toilets. She'd shown Elizabeth and the other two girls what she called 'some of the dirty bits'. Elizabeth's mind failed to comprehend the printed words, and being so mystified she was unable to join the excited shrieks and giggles of the others.

'She doesn't get it,' Betty said.

'Get what?' Elizabeth asked.

The others groaned. 'Hasn't anyone told you the facts of life?'

This touched a raw nerve. 'Nobody tells me anything.'

'Well' — Betty lowered her voice — 'it's like this. The man has this thing.'

'What thing?' Elizabeth wanted to know.

'You know.'

Elizabeth was trying to look as if she was joining them in the amusement of the moment, but actually she felt annoyed. Half laughing she shook her head. 'No, honestly.'

'Have you never seen your brothers?'

'I see them every time they're in.'

For some odd reason this statement sent the girls almost hysterical with laughter. They had to clamp their hands over their mouths in case the noise would bring the teacher on playground duty. At last Betty managed: 'With no clothes on.'

Any attempts at laughter were immediately wiped away. A flush of embarrassment stained Elizabeth's cheeks. 'No, of course not.'

'Not ever?'

She shook her head.

'Not even wee Charlie?'

'Yes, but Charlie's just a baby.'

'But you must have noticed.'

Elizabeth's eyes widened with innocence, but she was beginning to see the light. 'Noticed what?'

'His thing.'

She had in fact noticed the peculiar appendage between Charlie's legs and been curious about it. She hadn't dared to mention the peculiarity to Nanny, however. She had long since picked up from Nanny that there was something particularly shameful about the area between the legs. This was indicated by the fanatical degree of modesty Nanny insisted on. Nanny's embarrassment was so intense it was almost an anger. It had been like this, for instance, when she struggled to do her duty and explain that once a month Elizabeth would have to wear sanitary towels. Elizabeth had suffered the misery along with Nanny and hated the whole terrible business. Since that first time the shameful subject had never been mentioned again. Elizabeth had deduced that the purpose of the monthly bleeding was God's punishment for women's original sin. There seemed no other possible reason for it. Now, however, Betty Swanson was about to enlighten her.

'All men have one of them, only men's are much bigger.' More hand-suppressed giggles. 'And their thing fits into the woman's place down there.'

Elizabeth paled. 'You're terrible, Betty Swanson.'

'It's true, cross my heart and make me die if I tell a lie. The man squirts this stuff called sperm into the woman, and that's what makes a baby grow inside her.'

Alice Donaldson overcame her giggles to manage,

'And if a baby's not been made, blood comes away. That's why we bleed every month, the blood's not needed, you see!'

Elizabeth was shocked beyond words. A rush of outrageous scenarios flashed across her mind. Mother and Father doing it. Grandmother and Grandfather doing it (and Grandfather was a minister!). The King and Queen doing it! Father and her real mother doing it! The world turned upside down yet again. Was there no end to the shocks in life? She could think of nothing else for the rest of the day. Lessons and subsequent conversations slid over a surface area of her mind. She blushed deeply at every boy she saw on the street on the way home. In the evening she dined with Mother and the boys – Father was away at a job and wouldn't be back until late. After dinner William and Daniel went into the downstairs drawing room and played the gramophone. Jason disappeared upstairs to play the piano. Mother went through to the morning room because she had some papers she wanted to read through in peace. The morning room was more or less regarded as Mother's room. It was cool and elegant like herself with its muted blue carpet and matching velvet curtains, white walls, a crisp chintz-covered suite and a white bust of Mozart. Elizabeth nervously entered the morning room and stood hovering near the door. Mother raised an eyebrow. She was looking particularly attractive in a silver-grey skirt and matching Schiaparelli jumper that reached down over her hips and had a narrow belt at the waist.

'Yes dear?'

Elizabeth tried to appear casual. 'I can't help being curious, I was wondering who my real mother was, and where she was.'

Mother picked up one of her papers. 'I'd rather not discuss the matter at this stage, Elizabeth. Perhaps when you're older.'

'I want to know now.'

Christina glanced up. 'Elizabeth, can't you see I'm busy? Please go through to the drawing room.'

'I don't see why I shouldn't know. After all, it's my life.'

'Elizabeth!'

Elizabeth felt herself become sullen and moody again. She hated herself for it but could do nothing to stop the rot. 'Everyone has the right to know who their own mother is.'

The air had become noticeably cooler. 'I refuse to be subjected to such questioning. Leave the room at once, Elizabeth.'

As she left Elizabeth banged the door shut. Then in sudden fright at her temerity as well as rudeness, she took to her heels and flew upstairs to Nanny.

Nanny was sitting by the fire darning the boys' school socks. It was a placid scene. The nursery was a snug retreat with the firelight leaping along the brown polished linoleum, dancing on the fire screen and flickering on the toy shelves. There was a fireguard with a flat padded top. Elizabeth went over to sit on it and stare into the fire.

Eventually she tossed her head. 'It's not that I want anything to do with her. If she didn't want me, I don't want her. It's just' – she shrugged to emphasize how little she cared – 'curiosity.'

'Oh yes.' Nanny was intent on her darning. In the silence that followed Elizabeth listened to the gentle puttering of the gas mantles and stared bleakly at the quiver of light on Nanny's bent head. The light picked out a few grey hairs among the dark brown, increasing Elizabeth's depression. Nanny must be at least forty. Mother was thirty-five. Father was as ancient as forty-one. Everybody was getting old. For the first time the thought occurred to her that her real mother might die before she found her. It brought an unexpected rush of panic that made her suddenly burst into tears.

Nanny put down her darning. 'Now, now, we'll have less of this. Tears are for babies, not big girls.'

'What if she dies?'

'Everybody dies eventually.'

'Before I get to know her.'

Nanny tutted and shook her head. 'You're just letting that imagination of yours run away with you.'

'I haven't imagined I've got a real mother.'

'Your mother's downstairs, and lucky you are to have her. Try to control yourself. No good will come of stirring everything and everybody up like this.'

'I'm sorry,' Elizabeth sobbed, 'truly I am, but I can't help it.'

'Yes you can. You're just not trying.'

'You knew all about it. You knew her.'

'No I didn't, not like you mean.'

'But you knew all about her.'

'Yes I did.' Nanny was beginning to lose patience. 'And I'm telling you, miss, she's not the kind of person you'd want to have anything to do with. Now will you take a telling and leave it be.'

'Why, what kind of person was she?'

'Did your mother and father give you any answers?'

'No.'

'Well I can't either.'

'Please, Nanny.'

'I'm sorry, Elizabeth, it wouldn't be right. It's your parents' place to speak to you about this, if they have a mind to. I've said as much as I can.' She picked up the sock again. 'After I've finished these I'll go and fetch you a cup of Ovaltine. Meantime get your books out and concentrate on your homework.'

Elizabeth sniffled as she went to open her school case and spread her books on the table.

'There's a new nursery maid starting tomorrow,'

Nanny said, 'Flossie Matheson. I hope to goodness she turns out better than the last one.'

Nanny eyed Elizabeth's white shirt blouse. 'These cuffs look grubby, I'll get her to wash that, and press your gym slip and tie.' She tutted. 'It's always been a struggle to keep you neat, I don't know what you do with yourself.'

Elizabeth propped her head in her hands and stared gloomily down at her buff-coloured jotter. Then, from nowhere, a wave of determination as well as bitterness came over her. She didn't care what anyone or everyone said. One day, one way or another, she'd find out what she wanted to know.

CHAPTER 4

Gibson's Angels were loading sacks of potatoes on to the waiting lorries. Josiah Gibson was a well-known Glasgow potato merchant and the lorries were lined up in the cobbled yard at the back of his premises in the Gorbals. The Angels, as they were nicknamed, had to deliver the potatoes to the shops and hotels before starting their day's work gathering potatoes from the fields on the outskirts of Glasgow. No one knew how the Angels nickname originated. Farmers said it was because the women were anything but angels. The women themselves claimed they had to be angels to put up with the sour-tempered Gibson, or some of the farmers for that matter. But Josiah Gibson was the worst. A tall reed of a man with hollow cheeks, red-rimmed eyes and steel-rimmed spectacles, he was a pernickety dresser and cleanliness fanatic. His high old-fashioned collars were stiff as a board and his trousers sharply pressed. His raincoat and trilby hat had seen better days, but were also carefully sponged and pressed by the hard-worked maid at Gibson House. He carried a heavy walking stick with which he prodded his female workers. Some days he followed them in the potato fields and cried:

'You've missed a potato there, Jessie.'

Or Mary or whoever, and probed both the potato and the woman with his stick.

He was so mean he never gave his workers any potatoes to take home. It was usual in other parts of the country for the potato pickers to get what was known as a boiling to take home for their evening meal. Josiah, however, watched them like a hawk to make sure they never took one potato – although at the end of the day many a potato had been successfully hidden in bras or knickers.

Today was a chilly September morning and a bank of icy mist lay heavy over the sooty tenement buildings. There was the usual bedlam of noise among the dozen or so women who were carrying the hundredweight sacks of potatoes from storerooms to the vans. The women helped each other to lift the heavy loads on to their shoulders. Then each woman, staggering under the weight, reached the van and heaved her burden on to it. Some of the younger girls, their legs almost buckling under them, marvelled at old Aggie who could move the sacks with little apparent effort and with her clay pipe clamped in her toothless mouth. Once the potatoes were delivered the lorries would take the women to the farms and the picking would begin. As they clambered aboard the lorry Tam the driver was the butt of much ribald shouting. A shy young man new to the job, he suffered acutely at the hands of the women. The more he blushed the worse they tormented him. He was glad when they all piled on to the back of the open lorry and he was able to get started.

Some of the women were dressed in men's coarse trousers and heavy lacing boots, usually their fathers' castoffs. Their trousers were held up by heavy buckled belts or braces. Others wore long black skirts and open-necked shirts. Vividly coloured scarves tied over their heads were knotted at the nape of the neck.

Annalie Gordon shivered. She was glad of the bodies of the other women crowding the lorry. A scarlet scarf made a bright contrast to her mop of black hair and smooth tanned skin. A waistcoat of the same hue topped her long-sleeved white shirt and black skirt. The other women often teased her about her appearance; not because of her beauty, but because she had such a gypsy look about her. Indeed they had long since

29

nicknamed her Gypsy. 'A pair of gold earrings,' somebody said, 'and you'd pass for a gypsy any day.' She'd often put her appearance to good effect and earned some extra cash telling fortunes with cards or tea leaves. Nobody had been surprised when she'd eventually confessed that, in fact, her mother was a gypsy. She'd long since lost touch with her, however. She had not seen hide nor hair of Saviana for years. Not since that time she'd run off with baby Elizabeth. Saviana had insisted that her little 'Darklass', as she'd christened her granddaughter, should be brought up in the gypsy camp.

'My Darklass beauty doesn't belong with the gaujos,' she told Annalie.

Gaujos were non-gypsies. Saviana had also claimed she could give the child a better life on the open road than having it brought up a prisoner of poverty in a place like the Gorbals.

At first she'd asked Annalie to come too, and it was only when Annalie refused that Saviana had stolen the baby and disappeared. With the help of Adam Monkton and some of his labourers she'd tracked Saviana down eventually and got the baby back. Even yet thoughts of Adam Monkton could make her sigh. It was, she realized now, the old, old story. She had been a maid at Monkton House, and the master's son had taken advantage of her. She'd been little more than a child herself when she'd fallen pregnant with Elizabeth. Oh, how she had loved him, and she had believed so passionately and for so long that he loved her. She realized now, however, that she'd been no match for Christina Monkton as an adversary in love. She had once thought that butter wouldn't melt in the mouth of the minister's daughter, who had appeared so quiet, so biddable, so goody-goody when she used to visit Monkton House with her parents, and Annalie, as maid, had served her with afternoon tea. Christina was always making up to Adam's father too. She had known what she was doing there all right because old Mr Monkton had left her shares in his building business. It was a most unusual thing for a woman to get into such a business. It had all been in the papers at the time. Christina had become pregnant by Adam too. Annalie could have forgiven Adam for falling prey to Christina's charms when they were offered to him. Men were like that, she'd discovered. She could even understand him being pressured and emotionally blackmailed into marrying her. His father had taken a stroke after a heated argument with Adam, who had refused to marry Christina at first. As soon as he'd heard of the predicament of the daughter of his best friend and neighbour, the Reverend Gillespie, the old man had insisted in no uncertain terms that a marriage must take place. The argument had been the juiciest titbit among all the servants for miles around at the time. What Annalie couldn't forgive him for was that not only had he fathered subsequent children on Christina, he had refused to leave her. He would have been quite content to keep his wife in Monkton House and his mistress in his love nest in the Gorbals for ever after had Annalie not given him an ultimatum.

'I can't go on like this,' she'd told him, 'you'll have to make a choice. It's either your wife or me.'

Looking back, she could see his difficulties. His wife was on his social level. They had business interests in common as well as a home and family ties and shared responsibilities. He couldn't just throw everything up. It had been a terrible blow all the same. There had been the financial trauma too. She felt she couldn't take money from him any more and he'd been paying the rent of her lovely flat. She'd been so proud of that place and it had been a wrench to give it up.

The worst trauma of all of course had been giving up her baby. She had been determined, however, that

Elizabeth wouldn't suffer for anything that Annalie did or did not do. Elizabeth had been a beautiful child and Adam had always said she was too beautiful to be brought up in a place like the Gorbals, and Annalie had been afraid for her. She couldn't bear her to be ground down with poverty and hopelessness as so many others had been in the slums. That is if she survived the killer diseases that claimed the lives of so many children. Whooping cough, scarlet fever, diphtheria and consumption were all rampant. A fever van was never away from the streets. Elizabeth had just one chance in life and that was to be brought up as Adam Monkton's daughter in Monkton House. Annalie used to have so many dreams for herself, dreams of escaping from the Gorbals and becoming a lady in a fine mansion like Monkton House. It wasn't to be, however. But Elizabeth could have the reality. Even to the very last moment she'd hesitated, unable to carry through her eventual plan. It wasn't until Christina Monkton had said 'Elizabeth will be a lady' that she had found the courage to face the pain of parting with her baby.

She remembered crying out, 'When she wakes up and finds herself in a strange place, she'll be frightened.'

'I'll see that she's comforted,' Christina Monkton assured her. 'She'll settle in no time, don't worry.'

Adam had been away at a job up north at the time, and she'd pleaded with Christina, 'Promise me you'll explain to Adam.'

'Of course,' Christina said.

'Tell him that I'm not doing this because my feelings have changed for him in any way. On the contrary, tell him I'll always feel the same for him. It's just that I want Elizabeth to have a good life.'

'And she will,' Christina said.

Of course it had been naive of her to think that Christina would explain to Adam, but she had been young and still completely innocent of the wiles of people like Christina Monkton. At the time she'd worked at a paper shop, but, overcome with restlessness and unhappiness, had left soon after. She had to have something that would work her so hard she wouldn't have either the time or the energy to think about what she'd done and succumb to the madness of her grief. She had gone from job to job before settling on being a Gibson's Angel. The work was hard and the hours long enough. More than that there was something deeply satisfying about being out in the open country all the time. There was a sense of freedom that suited her. She guessed that it was probably her gypsy blood although of course her father was a very different type. He was a bricklayer by trade and a very steady home-loving person.

The earth was pearled with dew when they reached the field and low fingers of mist still writhed and curled in the morning wind. There always seemed something magical to Annalie about September. The dew was heavier in the morning. It fastened to the gossamer threads of the spiders' webs in the grass and hedges. The morning sun reflected in the gently swaying droplets and vividly reflected and flashed like a string of diamonds. Huge flocks of sparrows chattered and fluttered in the hedgerows. Then they flew off in a cloud to raid the remaining fields of corn.

Sandy drove the digger and it was his job to start at the beginning of a drill and drive steadily down. Revolving metal feet dug out the potatoes, leaving them lying on the surface. Each woman had a carefully measured stent. Hector, the gang boss, was treated with as little respect as Tam or Sandy. He stuck sticks in the earth to mark each stent and if one stent looked suspiciously longer than another he could be pelted by potatoes. As the digger went down the drill, Annalie bent double and started gathering the largest potatoes. Jenny, the next woman, followed picking up the smaller ones. It was backbreaking work and made them sweat like animals, but Annalie had become used to it. At thirty-three she was as tough and fit, if not more so, than many of the girls half her age.

While she worked she thought about her meeting with Geordie the farmer's son that night. He was a healthy hunk of a fellow with strong white teeth in a face as hard and brown as a nut. His eyes were the same colour as the sky on a summer's day, and usually brimming with good humour. The other women said he was a great catch, and that she was lucky.

'If you play your cards right,' big Mary told her, 'you could end up a farmer's wife.'

She believed this could be a possibility but the idea didn't fill her with too much excitement. He was certainly good-humoured but he had his faults as well. He wasn't as parsimonious as Josiah Gibson but he did have an element of meanness. The other women said, 'Och, that's just farmers. They know how to keep a hold of their money all right, but you'd have plenty once you were his wife.'

The thing about Geordie that saddened her most was that his lovemaking was so rough and clumsy. She kept trying to teach him to be more patient and imaginative but he never could restrain himself from acting like a full-blooded bull. She could not help remembering Adam Monkton in comparison. She and Monkton had been so loving and considerate, so passionate yet so gentle with each other. She knew she was a fool to think of a man she hadn't seen for years and with whom there never had been any chance of marriage. A thousand times she'd told herself she must banish Monkton once and for all from her mind. At least now she was able to have a serious relationship with another man. For years because other men could never measure up to Adam Monkton they had never come to anything. If Geordie asked her to marry him she'd say yes. All the other women were envious.

34

'You lucky devil,' they kept telling her, 'it's a chance in a million, especially when he knows you're one of Gibson's Angels.'

If the girls went to the dancing, or to any social event where they would be liable to meet a boyfriend, they pretended they were something else: office workers, shop assistants, domestic servants, anything but the notorious Gibson's Angels whose reputation stretched from one end of Glasgow to the other and far beyond. The Angels in fact had a reputation for toughness, unruliness, bad language, stealing from farmers, and other sins too many to mention. People shied away at the mere sound of their name. Potential boyfriends in particular were snobby and standoffish if they discovered who they were. But Geordie knew who she was and it made no difference.

They were meeting in the South Field which meant she couldn't go home to wash and change first. To get back to the Gorbals meant getting a lift in the lorry, or if later, walking a mile or more to the main road to catch a bus. After having been up since five o'clock in the morning and done a hard and long day's work, this was not something particularly to look forward to. But Geordie also had to get up early, and he too worked hard. As a result she felt it only fair occasionally to meet him on his home ground instead of him having to travel to and from the Gorbals.

He was waiting for her over by the clump of trees, sitting in the shade among the long grass chewing at a green blade. Rooks and starlings were circling high in the sky. He grinned a greeting at her and jerked her down beside him. She grimaced in pain. Her back had not yet recovered from the day's constant bending.

'Watch my back!'

'I'll watch your back and your front if you take all your clothes off.'

With a sigh Annalie lay back on the grass. There

was no breeze, a sultry September haze cloaked the distances, rooks cawed ceaselessly. Then she noticed Geordie fumbling with the buttons of his trousers preparatory to climbing on top of her.

'No,' she protested, struggling into a sitting position.

'What do you mean, no?'

'I don't want you suddenly jumping on top of me.'

'That's what we came for, wasn't it?'

Propping her elbows on her knees, she nursed her head in her hands. 'I can't stand any more of this.'

'What do you mean, you can't stand any more of this?'

He had a loose-mouthed vacant look, and she suddenly realized he wasn't very intelligent. She hadn't had much of a formal education any more than he had. But she'd always wanted to better herself and she'd been, and still was, an avid reader. 'Exactly what I say.'

'But we're going to be married. You know that.'

'No I didn't.'

'It's taken for granted.'

'Not by me.'

'But we've been courting all this time.'

'You never asked me.'

'Well I'm asking you now.'

Here was her chance in a million, she thought, and suddenly knew she couldn't take it. 'I'm sorry,' she said. 'I can't marry you. I don't love you.'

'Don't be daft, we get on so well. We're perfect for each other.'

'Geordie, we're not. Believe me.'

'I'd make you a good man, I'd always work hard and see you were well provided for.'

'I don't love you,' she repeated, 'I can't help it. I'm sorry. Now I don't want to talk about it any more, I'm going home.'

'You're just tired, you'll feel differently tomorrow. Come on, I'll walk you to the bus.'

She thought it best not to say any more, though she felt nothing but irritation when Geordie's big arm clamped possessively round her as they walked.

After she got home and prepared a meal for her father and herself, the old man fell asleep in his chair by the fire. The clock tick-tocked monotonously through the silence. She began to feel panic. Was this what she'd sentenced herself to? Had she to be a prisoner of this backbreaking routine every day, only to come home to more work, then a lonely bed? Surely anything was better than that? But she wept because she could still remember what love could be like. What passion could be like. What a wonderful, joyful experience life could be with the right person. She knew that there would be no need to argue with or try to convince herself if Adam Monkton walked back into her life. She'd fly into his arms, weeping, and laughing, and crying out with joy. Why, oh why, she asked herself for the millionth time, did she still have such impossible dreams about him?

CHAPTER 5

After weeks of cloud and rain the day dawned bright
and clear and sunny. The trees that the lorry trundled
past were still a late summer green, due no doubt to
the excessive wet. Few showed any signs of turning.
Men in the fields had stripped off their shirts and brown
bodies gleamed in the sun. The Angels shouted and
waved at them, and some of the men returned their
greetings. Others just laughed or shook their heads at
the more vulgar humour of some of the women. An-
nalie caught sight of Geordie, his fair head silvered in
the sun, and returned his wave. He had agreed, with
his usual good humour, albeit reluctantly, not to meet
her for a week or two to give her time to get her feelings
sorted out once and for all.

Not a breath of air reached the field as the women
set to work. As the digger went down the drill, some
like Annalie bent double and picked as fast as they
could. Then once their stent was clear they could
straighten up and take a breather. Those who smoked
sometimes managed a few puffs of a cigarette, but only
if Josiah Gibson wasn't around. Some of the more idle
ones took a breather before they started and so were
still picking when the digger came round the next time.

Having just seen Geordie made Annalie start to think
of him again. The first thing she had discovered since
their trial separation was that she did miss him. Or was
it that she simply missed being with a man? She was a
passionate woman and even Geordie's bull-like advances
assuaged some degree of need in her. Sometimes she
ached for love, to feel a man's arms around her, to savour
the sensation of skin touching skin. Of tender caresses,
of deepest feeling being awakened; the joy of giving oneself

willingly, gladly, totally to a man. The thrill of being overwhelmed, lost, saturated with love. These sensations were as necessary and as important to her as the basic needs of life, like food and water and shelter. The denial of love made her suffer as much as with thirst or hunger. Only exhausting herself with hard physical work could go any way to extinguishing the fire in her.

A puff of wind brought smatterings of rain and made Annalie groan. Rain was what all the women hated. None of them had any waterproof clothing and Josiah Gibson had not a scrap of sympathy if they got soaked to the skin.

'A spot of rain never did anyone any harm,' he'd say, 'you're not going to make that an excuse for neglecting the work I pay you good money for.'

In fact he paid them a mere pittance, and if they did take any time off for any reason, whether it was rain or illness, he didn't pay them anything at all. It was also noticed by the women that he made sure that he never stayed out in the rain for more than a few minutes, despite the long raincoat he always wore. But today Josiah was nowhere to be seen. As the wind rose, the rain began lashing like whips, and clothing clung and stung, forcing the women to race for shelter.

Reeking of sweat and wet earth they crowded into the old barn, some of them cursing their lot and wishing Josiah Gibson and his potatoes to hell. Their good humour was soon restored, however, by old Aggie, who kept a mouth organ secreted with her clay pipe in her voluminous black skirts. She fished the mouth organ out, polished it on her sleeve and with foot tapping to the rhythm she proceeded to play a lively Scottish reel. The women had long since found that it was no use sitting around in misery and wretched discomfort in soaking wet clothes. The best thing was to move as energetically as possible to keep warm and give the clothes a chance to dry. So they performed energetic dances to old Aggie's music. Sometimes they stripped off their dripping clothes and hung them up wherever they could to dry while they danced naked to keep warm. Annalie was even more enthusiastic and wild in her movements than the rest. She loved dancing, a talent she'd inherited from her mother. She still remembered the days when Saviana used to make regular appearances in the house and stay for a time before disappearing away on the road again.

'Once a traveller always a traveller,' she used to say.

But during her stay she used to add a touch of magic to the two-roomed tenement flat. One day there would be a knock at the door and there she would be, with her brown skin, her gold earrings, her bold dark eyes and black hair unevenly cut straggling over one side of her face and reaching to her shoulders. She was a colourful sight in her red skirts with flouncing frills of petticoats showing underneath and swishing about as she entered the house. High-heeled buttoned boots beat a tattoo on the floorboards. Her dress had a tight bodice and sleeves puffed to the elbow. Over the long skirts she sported a jodaka or apron of white satin, with two deep side pockets embroidered with floral patterns and coloured threads. She wore massive gold rings in the form of a strap and buckle on one hand and a gold sovereign on the other. Round her neck hung strings of red coral and her gold earrings were crescent-shaped. She would bring gifts: a pair of castanets, a pair of earrings, a frilly petticoat or a bright scarlet skirt.

One of the things she always brought with her was her piano accordion, and many a time she'd played baby Elizabeth to sleep with her haunting gypsy melodies. Or she'd shock Aunty Murn, Father's sister, by her uninhibited dancing. A highlight for Annalie at one New Year's party had been when Saviana clambered up on top of the table and with stamping feet and swirling petticoats did a wild gypsy dance. Her mother had said Annalie had a natural talent for dancing, and nothing pleased her more than for Annalie to join her in one of her abandoned exaltations. Aunty

Murn always said that no good would come of such goings-on. Poor Aunty Murn, she had conscientiously brought up Annalie and her young twin brothers while Saviana blithely came and went. Eddie and Davie were mere boys when they were killed in the war and Aunty Murn had never been the same again. She'd tried to put on a brave face and act as tough as ever but her health had deteriorated. Annalie had been broken-hearted at her death and missed her desperately.

The house wasn't the same without her. The loss had affected Annalie's father too. He'd become quite morbid and seldom spoke to anyone, even Annalie. Of course she supposed he would be brooding about Saviana too. She'd never returned after going off with Elizabeth, not even for Aunty Murn's funeral. The last words her mother had spoken to her, or rather screamed at her, were at the gypsy camp when Annalie had rescued Elizabeth:

'Gaujo, you're no daughter of mine, I disown you from this moment on. You've seen the last of Saviana Lee.'

It looked as if her father had seen the last of Saviana too. It was also as if he had turned his head away from Annalie, because her likeness to her mother was too painful to bear. It made life at home very difficult and dull for Annalie and it felt good to let go and dance on occasions like this. She could have danced without the help of old Aggie's mouth organ. All she needed was a beat to give her the rhythm. As an old poem said about gypsy women: 'Two battered pans together they beat and to this music they rave and leap.'

After the Scottish music, she did one of these uninhibited dances with all the women clapping in rhythm. Eventually when Annalie had thrown herself down in exhaustion, one of the women said:

'You should go in for one of these talent competitions, Gypsy. You'd be sure to win.' The other women took up the cry. 'There's one tonight in Green's Playhouse. Aye, go on, Gypsy, we'll come along and back you up.'

'Dance along with me?' Annalie laughed.

'Don't be daft, to give you a cheer of course, there's a first, second and third prize, you're bound to get something.'

'Do you really think I'll be any good?' Annalie queried uncertainly. It wasn't that she was shy. The thought of performing in front of an audience thrilled and excited her but her pride made her wary of making a fool of herself.

'You're fantastic, hen,' big Mary assured, 'we wouldn't suggest you go in for it if we thought you'd let us down, would we, girls?'

There was a general chorus of 'No fear', peppered with the usual coarse adjectives. Some of the women were like Annalie, who had not a taste for swearing. She had been too well trained by Aunty Murn, who didn't like bad language and wouldn't think twice about giving an offender a clip on the ear. Or instructing them to wash out their mouth. As a result Annalie swore if only truly provoked in anger, and even then only occasionally, despite her hot temper. Others could not utter a word without an 'effing' or a 'bloody' in front of it.

'All right,' Annalie said, her eyes sparkling with anticipation, 'I'll do it.' The gritty rattle of wind-blown rain lashing windows and roof went unheard now as the women planned their evening's entertainment; where and at what time they would meet, where they would sit in the hall, what Annalie would wear, what kind of music she would need.

Green's Playhouse, a super cinema in the centre of Glasgow, boasted a ballroom above, and had been opened for just three years. It was claimed to be the largest cinema in Britain, and had a massive auditorium which seated 4,200 people. It also had a fair-sized orchestra.

'I'll just ask for gypsy music,' Annalie said. 'I don't know the names of anything, but *they* should, it's their job.'

It wasn't until much later when she was at home that panic mixed with her excitement. The thrill of facing an audience was now tempered with the sobering thought that she had no formal training as a dancer other than what her mother had given her. Also she remembered how devastating a Glasgow audience could be to a performer who did not please it. She forced herself to banish such thoughts. To hell with them! If they didn't like her, it only proved how little they knew about dancing. Once on that stage she'd dance with all her heart and soul, and not care what anyone thought.

It was quite late when she met the other women, but they knew the talent competition was not until the interval between the two big pictures of the second house. Once in the foyer they separated, the women going into the auditorium and Annalie being led with the other contestants to the normally forbidden area backstage. Now, despite her early bravado, all her apprehensions returned. Especially when she peeked from behind the giant curtain, and saw the enormous audience packing the hall. She could have died on the spot. Just then, however, the manager appeared and began hustling all the contestants into a queue. From where Annalie was made to stand she could view the first performers. The experience was embarrassing and terrifying. A hopeful stand-up comic got heckled by raucous calls of 'You couldn't make a cat laugh', and 'Away home to your bed', and 'I've heard better jokes at a funeral'. A singer was lustily booed, and worst of all a dancer raised uproarious laughter. Certainly she had tripped and fallen a couple of times, but Annalie's heart went out to her. Then as the curtain went up once more the manager announced:

'Next we have a dancer of a different kind, put your hands together for a gypsy dancer, folks.'

A desperate bravado returned to her aid. I'll show them, she thought, I'll show them!

CHAPTER 6

The music started, but she did not immediately step on to the stage. She began clicking the castanets from the wings, then to the beat of the rhythm she slowly made her entrance, arms raised above her head, body stretched in lascivious grace. The audience fell silent, hypnotized by her hands swaying like a cobra preparing to strike. They were spellbound with the beauty of the thick black hair, the sultry eyes and sensuous figure in its embroidered blouse, tulip-coloured skirt and flouncing petticoats. As the music quickened, people began to clap to the rhythm, but the crackle of the castanets and the stamping of Annalie's feet could still be heard above them all. Until she whirled into a mad finale, then was suddenly still. For a moment or two there was a stunned silence, then a storm of applause and cheering hit the roof. Annalie had never experienced anything like it. She felt intoxicated with delight. Her whole body throbbed with pleasure. Her eyes sparkled, her cheeks gleamed. Later to more enthusiastic applause she was presented with the first prize, a giant box of chocolates. She shared the sweets with the other Angels on the way back to the Gorbals, she was so grateful to them for suggesting she went in for the competition.

They'd barely reached Sauchiehall Street, however, when a car drew up near them at the side of the road, and a man called out to her:

'Here miss, you that did the dance back there, can I have a word for a minute?'

Annalie tossed her hair and was making to walk past him, when he called out again, 'No, this is legit, I'm an agent, I can maybe offer you work as a dancer.'

At first she didn't believe him. She raised a sarcastic brow. 'Oh yes, that'll be right.' But the other women were obviously taking the man seriously and were excitedly nudging her and whispering at her to pay attention.

'Here's my card.' The man, a dapper fellow with a neat moustache and spotted bow tie, stretched an arm from the open car window. 'Come and see me tomorrow afternoon.'

Annalie took the card before the car drove away and disappeared into the night. Under the nearest street lamp, and with the women crowding around her, she read: Maurice Rutherford, Artists' Agent, Charing Cross, Glasgow.

'This could be your big chance, Gypsy,' Jenny said. 'I don't know about you, but I won't be able to sleep tonight for thinking about it.'

Annalie still found it hard to credit. Yet why not? One audience had enjoyed her dancing, why not others? She trembled with joy at the thought. All the way back to the Gorbals she and the other women chattered in breathless excitement about the prospect. In her mind she span beautiful dreams. Only after she was alone in the quiet kitchen in Cumberland Street did the dreams fade and she wondered if anything would come of it. After all the man had only said maybe. Her feelings were like a swing, one minute she was careering heavenwards, the next she was plummeting down.

The kitchen in the two-roomed flat was so small that Annalie had to twist sideways to move about it. Her father had gone to bed in the front room, leaving his newspaper lying on his chair by the kitchen fire. She sat down on one of the spar-backed chairs that crowded round the table, and cupped a hot beaker of tea between her palms. There were two other bigger chairs by the fireplace, one, a leather winged or 'leather-lugged' chair, being her father's favourite. Its leather had a myriad of hairline cracks from constant usage. Here Hugh Gordon would sit, chin sunk in neck, staring bleakly into the fire, smoking his pipe or reading his *Glasgow Herald*. It was his habit to read out bits of the news to Aunty Murn or to anyone who cared to listen. These readings were usually of a dramatic nature, like the unemployment rate breaking the two million barrier or the R101 airship exploding in a ball of flames and killing forty-four of its passengers. The chair opposite her father's was a wooden rocking chair on which Aunty Murn used to sit, as often as not with her hands busy with knitting or darning. A dark green horsehaired sofa sat in front of the bed recess. The sofa was used as a stepping stone for Annalie to reach up to the piled-high mattresses. If it was a very cold draughty night, she would pull the plum-coloured chenille bed curtains across to keep cosy.

The colour of the curtains was about the only thing that her father had allowed her to change since Aunty Murn's death. Admittedly they couldn't afford to refurnish or do anything drastic but she had hoped at least to brighten the place up a bit more, with different coloured paint and more modern ornaments. But no, her father would have none of her newfangled ideas.

'This is my house,' he insisted, 'and it'll stay the way it's always been. That's the way I want it.'

So the black iron fire grate stayed the same, but it was seldom polished with brush and black lead. Its steel edges seldom saw a piece of emery paper. The brass fender and antimacassar-shaped brass fronting to the mantelshelf no longer sparkled with Brasso. Annalie was too tired after a long day in the fields to tackle the extra hard work of polishing the fireplace. At weekends she tried to do some house cleaning, but her heart wasn't in it. Nothing was to her taste. On top of the mantelshelf sat Aunty Murn's fat toby jugs, a rusty old alarm clock, a dish of spills to light the gas mantle and a toffee tin in which the rent money was kept. On the opposite wall above the coal bunker was a high shelf on which perched two china dogs. It always seemed to Annalie there was a look of Aunty Murn about these ornaments. It was the way their heads stretched so high on top of such rigged backs. Their marly-blue and white colour also reminded her of Aunty Murn's favourite wraparound apron.

Annalie sipped at her tea before eventually going over to the sink at the window and washing her cup at the swan-neck tap. Then she laid out her working clothes for the morning. She could ill afford to take time off to go to the agent's office in the afternoon. Still, it would be crazy not to go, just in case. It had never occurred to her before to look for a job as a dancer. For one thing Aunty Murn had made her feel guilty about 'carrying on like a mad thing', or she would warn, 'You'll get like that dirty tinker if you're not careful'. That dirty tinker had been what Aunty Murn had always scathingly called Saviana, although in fact she was a true Romany gypsy and kept herself scrupulously clean. There had been a time when Annalie had been enchanted by her mother and rejoiced every time she returned. It had been her mother who had filled her head with dreams of being a lady. 'That dirty tinker fills your head with fairy tales,' Aunty Murn always said. 'No good will come of it.'

Aunty Murn had never liked Saviana and never understood why Annalie and her brothers loved her so much. Eddie and Davie used to sob every night for a week or more every time their mother disappeared. Often Annalie would join them in their noisy grief. Saviana was such a colourful character, full of songs and stories and wicked enjoyment of their mischief.

But when Annalie was dressed up for Sunday school in her best white pinafore and boots, Saviana would brush her hair and polish it with a silk scarf until it gleamed, and she'd say:

'You're a real lady, so you are, a real lady if ever I saw one, dearie.'

When she'd been a child, Annalie had thought her mother to be not only a warm, loving and caring person but someone with the gift of making magic. Memories of her were not only laced with kisses and cuddles but wafts of heady perfume, the jangle of golden earrings and the dazzle of brightly coloured clothes.

It had been her mother who had filled her head with tales of Cinderellas transformed into princesses and handsome princes always coming to the rescue in times of trouble. Her mother had read her palm. She had only been twelve at the time but she could still remember her mother's husky mysterious voice:

'I see a big house, dearie. You belong in this house, and with a handsome gentleman by your side. Oh, handsome as a prince he is. Yes, and that's where you belong, dearie. I see you as such a fine lady by this gentleman's side, and he loves you more than anyone else in the whole world. You mark my words, it's your destiny to be loved by this man.'

As a little girl she had been hypnotized by her mother's great dark eyes, and she had believed every word. When she'd eventually got a job in Monkton House, and fallen in love with Adam Monkton, she'd believed he was her destiny. It had taken her many long years to realize what a fool she'd been. Now however, she might have come to a real turning point in her life. Tomorrow might mean something really fulfilling and exciting.

She awoke early and worked feverishly. So great was her anticipation of what might happen in the afternoon, she didn't even mind the long walk from the potato fields to the bus. She strode with a will, in her black skirts and lacing boots, and shawl slung round her shoulders.

At home she washed and put on a red coat and knitted beret, and set off to catch a tram into town. She had some difficulty in finding the office at first because the entrance was a narrow close between shops. Upstairs there were various flats. One or two were offices. Another was a tailor's workshop. Yet another was a photographer's. The glass door marked Maurice Rutherford was on the top storey. The door lay half open and Annalie entered with her head in the air but with heart secretly thumping.

'Yes, dearie?' A plump woman with platinum-blonde marcel-waved hair, orange-tinted skin and heavy black mascara sat at a desk at the end of a lobby plastered with large theatre posters and bills, which partly covered very dirty-looking wallpaper.

Annalie looked her straight in the eye. 'I have an appointment with Mr Rutherford, my name is Annalie Gordon.'

'Oh, you're the dancer, dearie? He's expecting you.' She indicated a door.

'Thank you.' Annalie knocked at the door, and on a shout of 'Come in' she entered Rutherford's office room.

She later discovered the rest of the flat was used as his home, and the blowsy blonde was his wife. This room, the biggest in the house and facing the front, was kept for business. It held a flat-top desk, a swivel chair for Rutherford and several other chairs dotted about for clients, a filing cabinet and a drinks cabinet. The walls were covered with posters and framed photographs of artistes. Some were famous like Sir Harry Lauder, Stan Laurel and Charlie Chaplin. As it turned out none of the really famous ones were clients of Mr Rutherford. Annalie regarded this as cheating, giving the wrong impression, but Rutherford maintained that he had as much right as anyone to hang pictures of people he admired. However, he did have quite a few fairly successful artistes on his books. He might have made the really big time, his wife always maintained, if he hadn't been so fond of 'a wee refreshment'.

'Now then, my dear,' he greeted Annalie, 'how about a drink?'

Annalie looked down her nose at him. 'No thank you.'

'You won't mind if I have one, just to celebrate the find. That's you. A real cause of celebration, my dear.' He poured himself a generous glass of whisky. 'Sit down, sit down, my dear, make yourself at home. We're all friends at Rutherford's agency.' He gulped over the whisky and gave an appreciative 'Ahh. Now where were we?'

'You said you might have work for me as a dancer,' Annalie prompted.

Rutherford dabbed at his moustache. Then he suddenly jabbed a finger towards Annalie. 'The very thing, I've got the very thing for you, my dear. The Carlinos!'

Annalie looked puzzled. 'What's that?'

'*Who's* that you mean, my dear.'

'Well, who's that?'

'The most marvellous dance team. A really original act. Never out of work. Here's to them.' He poured another whisky and knocked it back. 'I'm telling you. Never out of work. I can get that act a booking anywhere, and do, my dear, and do.' He blinked at her in such an innocent fashion that Annalie felt slightly suspicious. Yet she was intrigued.

'How would I fit in? A team, you say?'

'Well it was until the accident. It was Anthony and Marie until poor Marie broke her arm, after that things weren't the same. Well to be frank, Marie left. Marie walked out on Tony and there we are, Tony needs a new partner.'

'Me, you mean?'

'Just the ticket. "What a dancer," I told Tony. He'll be here any minute. "What a dancer," I said, "suit you to a tee." Marvellous!'

'I've never danced with a partner,' Annalie said, then added quickly, 'but I've no doubt I could learn given half a chance.'

'Not a doubt, I told him. And of course he'd teach you the routine. You would go down a treat, the pair of you. Just the ticket.'

'Is it gypsy dancing?'

'No. Apache they call it, you'll have heard of it no doubt, my dear.'

'Of course I have.' A light was beginning to dawn, she had indeed heard of it, or rather read about it. It came to her now she'd once actually seen it performed in a silent film. 'That's the one where the woman gets thrown about?'

'Very artistic.' Rutherford fingered his bow tie. 'Really first class. You'll make a great pair. Yes, Anthony and Annalie, I can just see it up in lights. Ah, Tony old son,' he greeted the man who'd just entered the room, or rather made an entrance.

Tony Carlino was of Italian descent, not much taller than Annalie, lean and muscular, with dark fiery eyes and a sleek raven head.

'I was just saying what a marvellous dancer you were. This is Annalie Gordon, another marvel. I'm telling you, Tony, she's just the ticket, what a pair you'll make, I can just see you now. Bloody marvellous. How about a drink to celebrate?'

CHAPTER 7

'You still like it then?' her father asked.

'Oh yes.' Elizabeth smiled but was careful to retain the distance she had built up between them. 'I'll be sorry when I have to leave Jordanhill. I could stay there for ever.'

It had been fortunate that because of the new regulations of 1931, Elizabeth had been able to go straight from school to the college at seventeen. As long as she completed her leaving certificate, she was able to do a three-year course at Jordanhill College. She had been very excited about the course. The prospect of it had gone a long way in taking her mind off brooding about her roots.

She had uncovered one family secret, however. Uncle Simon, her mother's brother, had committed suicide. He had been suffering severe shell shock since the war and had become worse instead of better. Until one day he'd taken an overdose of sleeping tablets. Cook had told her about it – to stop her, as she said, stirring up the past by asking so many questions. 'You'll just put your foot in it. You've done that already, in fact. You've upset your granny and grandpa more than you realize.'

It was a relief in a way to stop nagging at everyone, and subsequently plunging into her moods of depression when people refused to respond. She had been shocked to learn about Uncle Simon – she only vaguely remembered him, although with some fondness. Mostly she stopped her pestering because it was obvious she wasn't getting anywhere. She was only sparking off antagonism and getting upset herself.

The need to have answers didn't completely disappear. At the back of her mind and deep in her heart the ache still remained. Going to Jordanhill did help, however. It was such an adventure in comparison with her previous cloistered existence. Jordanhill was four miles from the centre of the city, a quiet residential district of large houses and secluded gardens. The college was in fifty acres of countryside, at the top of a long winding drive with wooded areas on either side, and sheep grazing in the rolling grassy area in front.

There was a pond and a beautiful walled flower garden. Further on, on a high hillock to one side of the vast college building with its central towers, was the original mansion house. It was now used as a hostel for students who came from further afield than Glasgow, mostly from the Highlands.

The view from the left side of the college was magnificent. On a clear sunny day the River Clyde was like a sparkling silver ribbon and away beyond lay a toytown Renfrewshire. From the high vantage point of the mansion house at the other side the beautiful Kilpatrick hills could be seen.

Trundling along in the tram every day through the busy Glasgow streets, Elizabeth was always thrilled when she reached the college. Admittedly it had been difficult at first because she'd been so shy. She'd felt overwhelmed by the boys as well as girls milling about, although there was a certain amount of segregation, at least in the corridors and on the stairs. The two staircases that rose from the pillared hallway were kept strictly separate, one for males and one for females.

She felt very grateful that Jessie Gallagher had made friends with her, but Mother, Father and Nanny had all thought it was strange that she'd chummed up with a girl like Jessie.

'She seems to come from a very tough background, she's not at all ladylike,' Nanny complained.

Mother shrugged. 'It's not that I have anything

against her. It's just she seems so different from you, Elizabeth.'

She certainly was different in both appearance and nature. Elizabeth was medium in height, although her slim frail build gave the appearance of being smaller. She had neat features, a creamy skin, straight hair with a fringe and a shy, rather timid expression. Jessie was plagued with enlarged pores and the occasional crop of blackheads. Her bright eyes fizzed with laughter. Her hair was thick and blonde and untameable.

Nanny said, 'That hair's peroxide, I'm sure it is. It shouldn't be allowed. It's a disgrace, a girl of her age.' But the really striking thing about Jessie was that she was big. Her bones were big. Her shoulders were broad. Her flesh was ample and bounced a lot. She was a very bouncy kind of person.

Elizabeth thought she was wonderful. Meeting her every day was like a breath of fresh air, a far better tonic than Nanny had ever procured from the chemist. She admired Jessie's supreme confidence in her own abilities and, despite her enlarged pores, blackheads and ungainly size, her own self-worth. Elizabeth felt she would have died if her complexion had let her down to such an extent. Her own physical problems worried her a great deal, her small bosom for instance. The boyish shape of the twenties was old hat now. The latest fashion was for a much more feminine, rounded look. If she could have just a little of Jessie's well-endowed bosom, Elizabeth felt she would have been deliriously happy. Not that she wanted to attract boys herself. She simply longed to be fashionable and sophisticated.

She did secret exercises to try to enlarge her breasts, all to no avail. On one occasion when she'd been desperately over-enthusiastic, she'd strained her chest muscles. She could hardly breathe for the pain, and Nanny forced her to rub her chest every night for a week with Vicks. The pungent smell had caused her acute embarrassment every day at the college. Then there was her hair. Nanny wouldn't hear of her getting a marcel wave. She had thought of growing her fringe long and kirbying it to the side in a kind of loop that would appear something like a wave. Nanny wasn't pleased about that either.

'You're not long past your eighteenth birthday,' Nanny said. 'Time enough when you're twenty-one to change your hairstyle.'

At least she didn't have a daily fight with the brush and comb like Jessie had. Jessie's hair went to the opposite extreme. The more she brushed down her curly mop the more it sprang up as if it had a determined and cheerful life of its own. Such a desperate problem would have made Elizabeth suicidal. But Jessie laughed uproariously every time she caught sight of her head.

'Would you look at that? Never mind, there's worse things happening in China.' This was one of Jessie's favourite phrases, although Elizabeth suspected she knew nothing about what was happening in China.

Elizabeth felt acutely worried about whether or not she and Jessie would manage to get their diplomas. They had both had a terrible struggle with psychology topics, like perception, attention, memory and thought. They both admitted they were completely stumped by logical aspects of definition, hypotheses, inference and commoner fallacies and the nature and ideals of morality. The course on infant psychology wasn't so bad and was the only one that Elizabeth thought might be of real use in primary schools.

Jessie said, as the eldest of a family of ten, she already knew all she needed to know about infant psychology.

Psychology, it seemed to Elizabeth, made life in general a very complicated and serious business. Everybody she came in contact with now seemed to be full of inhibitions, a sense of failure or inferiority, or they were suffering from some sort of suppression or other. Previously she had thought there were just the seven deadly sins she'd read about in the Bible.

'You've to look out for children with emotional difficulties,' she explained to Nanny. 'All their feelings are caused by lack of love, you see.'

'Lack of leatherings more like,' Nanny said, and Jessie was inclined to agree with her.

Nevertheless Jessie flung herself with a will into trying to learn enough to pass her exams.

Jessie came from a room and kitchen tenement flat in Govan and Elizabeth found it hard to visualize the kind of conditions in which Jessie appeared to have been brought up. It was like another world, one which up until now she'd never even heard of, except in a vague missionary sense. She knew that Mother did good work for poor children in the Gorbals. But what it really meant to be poor, she had no idea whatsoever. Until she met Jessie, that is.

Jessie's stories of her home life both fascinated and shocked Elizabeth. Apparently Jessie's house had no bathroom. There was a toilet outside on the downstairs landing and as if it was not bad enough to share one toilet between a family of ten plus Jessie's parents, it was shared with two other equally large families.

'There's always somebody in that lavvy,' Jessie said. 'I remember as a kid I used to sit on the stairs in a queue waiting to get in. We'd all be reading comics and shuffling our bums down one step at a time as the queue moved on. That lavvy seat was never cold.'

Fortunately Jessie's family were all girls. Elizabeth shuddered to think what the sleeping arrangements would be in a mixed family. As it was, it was a mystery to Elizabeth how Jessie was able to study in such cramped circumstances and in the midst of such a crowd. That was one of the reasons why she invited Jessie home. Upstairs in the quiet of her room or in the day nursery they could do their homework and study in peace. Sometimes Jessie laughed and said:

'I feel as if I've never left school. Jordanhill is still like being at school, isn't it? I mean it hasn't the same freedom you'd have at university. I'd have gone to university if I'd been clever enough, but I wasn't. Never mind, there's worse things happening in China.'

What she and Jessie liked best were the practice teaching sessions in schools. Elizabeth especially found this very exciting. Although at the same time it was frightening as it gave her another insight into the poverty of some people's lives. Often she received a real culture shock. She had to go to schools and college in alternate periods of three or four weeks, but came to Jordanhill each week for a methods lecture. Assessment was by a thesis and examination on methods, but much the greater stress was laid on detailed assessment in terms of practical teaching. Both she and Jessie had been allocated to a school in Govan.

On the way to their first teaching practice, Elizabeth noticed a long queue of silent downcast people. The queue stretched from one block of tenements to another.

'What's that queue for?' she asked Jessie.

'That's for the labour exchange. No wonder they look so sad, jobs are awful hard to get these days. We're lucky, you know. Or at least I hope we will be, when we finish our training. My other three sisters that have left school haven't got a job yet. They've been trying everywhere, but my ma says I should get one because I'll have a diploma. I'm not so sure, though. Our milkman's got a degree and the only job he could get was driving that milk lorry. Still, you've got to look on the bright side, haven't you?'

The idea that perhaps they would not be able to get jobs had never occurred to Elizabeth. Being unemployed was another side of life of which she was completely innocent.

57

The Govan School looked an ancient building. It had once been a handsome red sandstone, but fog and soot and other city grime had long since darkened the warm red colour into blackness. Classrooms looked equally ancient and had dreary rows of dual desks, clamped firmly to the floor. There was barely room for Elizabeth to pass to and fro in the narrow passages between them. In each desk was a china ink-well, and each had a hinged lid over the recess in which jotters or books could be kept. The teacher had a larger edition of this type of desk.

The staff room was a cupboard with bare floor-boards, chocolate-painted walls and narrow slits of windows, almost as high as the ceiling. Its noisy radiator seldom worked as it should and the female staff had usually to sit chittering with coats and sometimes even hats on. Complaints to the janitor were all to no avail. The janitor was a power on his own. Among many other duties he ruled the furnace room in the bowels of the school, a place of intestinal pipes, giant cobwebs and an army of mice. It was a place no teacher, or at least no female teacher, dared to go.

On that first day Elizabeth and Jessie had just settled on the settee to eat their lunchtime sandwiches when Miss Rusk entered. A look of outrage stiffened her long drooping features.

'The settee is for the senior staff,' she informed them. 'There are plenty of chairs.'

Jessie said afterwards that it had taken all her time not to giggle. It wasn't as if the settee was anything special. 'A right old saggy worn-out thing,' Jessie said and then added, giggling, 'A bit like poor old Rusky herself.'

The other problem in the staff room was that there *weren't* plenty of chairs. Jessie reckoned that there was about half a chair each, if that. When all of the staff were assembled they had to jam the chairs together and sit buttocks crushed against buttocks. Most of the women had been at the school for years. This worried Jessie.

'Here, we'd better watch out,' she warned Elizabeth. 'We don't want to get stuck in the same place all our lives and turn into sour old maids like them.'

Not that they were all like Miss Rusk. Even she looked more depressed than sour. Miss Dees was quite chirpy. She enjoyed a gossip more than most. She always seemed to be the enthusiastic bearer of some titbit or other. Miss Dellafield was rather pretty with her brown curly hair and gentle brown eyes. As far as Elizabeth could see the look all the teachers had in common was one of harassment. This was only smoothed out during Christmas, or Easter or summer breaks. It was amazing to see the relaxed, different expression at the beginning of each session before the harassment gradually took over again. This, Elizabeth discovered, was, apart from the noise, due more to how the school was run and to the vagaries of Mr Munn the headmaster than to the children. Although it had to be admitted that they could cause problems as well.

The trouble was nothing went to plan or turned out as neat and orderly as it was supposed to. There would be interruptions by the headmaster that could go on too long. Crisis or absenteeism in the staff meant a general shuffle around. The children would be so poor at one subject that too much time had to be spent on it to the detriment of another planned in the timetable.

Crises, especially among the youngest children, could confuse issues. Too much time could be taken trying to tie shoes. Puddles made on the classroom floor had to be cleaned up. Lessons could be interrupted and sidetracked by all sorts of unexpected things that could not be recorded, far less timed in the record book. Only the other day when Elizabeth had been left in charge of primary one, plump, freckle-faced Angus McAndrews had disappeared for a worryingly long time

59

to the toilet. Eventually he reappeared and stood at the open door with his trousers round his ankles to ask: 'Who wipes the bums in this place?'

She had momentarily been taken aback but managed a polite: 'We wipe our own . . . we clean ourselves here. Please return to the toilet, Angus.'

Then there could be the trauma and upheaval of an unheralded visit by one of His Majesty's inspectors. At least, an officially unheralded visit. Unofficially, word of his arrival was trumpeted around by teachers and children alike. Usually it was Miss Dees who first spotted him and sent a warning signal winging along the school grapevine. Then either the teacher in the next room would put her head round the door and call 'HMI' or a child from the next class along would be sent and come prancing excitedly in with the same shout, prefaced only by: 'Please, miss.'

Different inspectors would arrive each time, a ruse, everyone was sure, to try to fox the teachers into thinking that perhaps the male figure looming on the school horizon might be a marauding parent. This certainly never worked in the Govan School where parents were too poor to afford the smart suits and trilby hats usually worn by the HMI. Then of course if a parent came it was usually the mother. On the very few occasions a father had shown face, usually to cause some disturbing altercation, he wore a muffler and a cloth cap pulled aggressivly down over his brow.

Once an 'HMI was spotted, lessons were rapidly reorganized and the same arithmetic, or page of spelling, or reading, was desperately repeated until it was the turn of your class to be inspected. This worked except in the infants' class where they became quickly bored and restless. This led to a dreaded level of noise and subsequent chaos which was well nigh impossible to quell in time, and could lead to downfall for a probationer.

Elizabeth lived in dread of an HMI arriving while she was teaching a lesson, instead of just observing one. She could never make up her mind which subject would be worse. In reading most of the children persisted in using a broad Glasgow U – they called boot something like 'bute'. There was also the habit of adding W to the word our – 'This is the way we wash wur hands'.

When the dreaded day came, she was teaching Religious Instruction. As luck would have it the children were very highly spirited and sang the hymns rather loudly, to put it mildly. During the repetition it was found that instead of the line 'unlike our friends by nature' some were bawling out 'I like my friends by nature' and others 'I like wur friends'.

What made the occasion infinitely more harassing was her personal reaction to this particular HMI.

To begin with she had been taken aback by his height. She guessed that he was at least six feet four inches. He had a lean sinewy body with broad shoulders and narrow hips. His straight hair was khaki in colour and a lock kept sliding forward over his brow. The bluest and most expressive eyes she had ever seen could twinkle with laughter, soften with sympathy, or harden with authority. With one look and one sharp command of 'Quiet!' he immediately quelled a potential riot of noise.

Mr Jack Dawson was his name, and he had a disturbing effect on Elizabeth, far beyond, she suspected, the normal fear and apprehension of any ordinary visiting HMI. Her heart palpitated so much in his presence she was in agony in case he might actually see it through the white blouse and pink smock she was wearing. When he came near her she felt so light-headed, she feared she was going to disgrace herself by fainting. His piercing stare fixed on her as she took a lesson and she heard her voice falter. She cleared her throat several times and willed the colour to stop creeping up from her neck to suffuse her face. She willed him to look at the children instead of staring at her. But the blue eyes remained fixed on her.

When he shook hands with her before leaving she experienced such an exquisitely pleasurable sensation as skin met skin it was as much as she could do to repress a cry of surprise and delight.

By lunchtime he was the talk of the Ladies – the name that distinguished the female staff room from the Gents, which was the male staff room. The whole place was atwitter.

'Did you ever see such a gorgeous man?' Jessie enthused. 'I made eyes to him like mad but he never took me on.'

Elizabeth laughed excitedly. 'I got so breathless, I thought at one point I was going to faint, I really did.'

'Hey, that would have been a good idea. Why didn't you? He would have gathered you in his arms then and carried you off.'

The two girls squealed with delicious hilarity, only to be quelled by a reproachful look and some tut tuts from Miss Rusk.

'Miss Monkton and Miss Gallagher, it seems you fail to realize the seriousness of this matter.'

'What matter?' Jessie asked.

'What kind of impression the HMI had of the content and method of your teaching, and what kind of report he intends to write.'

This was a sobering thought and one that triggered off an urgent and speculative, as well as apprehensive, line of conversation among every member of the crowded staff room.

Elizabeth's head was still buzzing with it all. She was returning along the draughty corridor towards primary one when suddenly she was confronted by the cause of all the commotion.

'Hello, again.' Dawson greeted her with a slow smile that sent peculiar feelings through the most secret parts of herself. She blushed with shame and embarrassment. She thought she managed to smile in return but in her confusion she wasn't sure.

'Are you doing anything special this evening?' Dawson asked.

'No.' The word escaped in astonishment, leaving the others, 'Why do you ask?' hanging in the air between them.

He smiled again. 'Good, then we could perhaps go to the pictures. There's a good one on at the Regal. I'll meet you there at half past seven.' He raised a hand in friendly salute before strolling confidently away.

Elizabeth was left motionless. It was a minute before she could rally enough strength to continue on her way.

CHAPTER 8

'And so Dinky the cat and Gyp the dog became good friends,' Elizabeth told Charlie, 'and lived together and played happily together for ever after.'

'Tell me another story,' Charlie pleaded.

'Not tonight, Charlie. I've to go out.'

Nanny looked into the bedroom then. 'Charlie, it's time you were asleep. And you've your homework to do, miss. You'll never get your diploma if you don't study.'

Elizabeth kissed Charlie goodnight then followed Nanny through to the day nursery. 'I've done my homework and I surely don't need to study every hour of every night of the week. It's as if I've never left school,' Elizabeth added, echoing Jessie's sentiments.

'Who is this man, anyway?'

'I told you, the HMI.'

'What's an HMI when it's at home?'

'His Majesty's Inspector, he's a very important man.'

'Then why is he wanting to take you to the pictures?'

Elizabeth had no answer to this. She had been asking herself the same question ever since Mr Dawson had sprung the invitation on her. She shrugged. 'I don't know.'

'Well I do,' Nanny said. 'That man's up to no good and you're no better if you go out with him. You don't know a thing about him. He could be another Jack the Ripper for all you know.'

'But he's an *HMI*,' Elizabeth gasped.

It was obvious that Nanny had no idea what a lofty position this was and with what awe it was regarded. It was the first time in her life that Elizabeth saw Nanny as less than perfect, wholly dependable and the font of all knowledge. This was yet another shattering occurrence of a most disquieting day.

'He's a man,' Nanny insisted, 'and men are only after one thing. You'll end up like your mother if you're not careful.'

'What's wrong with being like Mother?' Elizabeth asked in astonishment. Christina was another model of perfection. Admittedly the perfection had been somewhat dented by the deceit and the refusal to reveal Elizabeth's true origins, but she'd more or less forgiven her for that. Elizabeth never kept up any grudge or ill feelings against anybody for long. Although she was finding it difficult to regard Father in the same light as before.

'Your real mother I mean.'

'Oh.' Elizabeth flushed and lowered her eyes. 'We're only going to the pictures.'

'Take my word for it, I've got this feeling and my feelings never lie. No good will come of this.'

But already Elizabeth had withdrawn into one of her stubborn moods. She was, after all, nearly nineteen. Why shouldn't she have an evening out on her own, or with a friend? Not that she was totally convinced herself because he wasn't a friend, he was a man. Every time she thought of this inescapable fact she took an attack of palpitations. She kept thinking of all Nanny's cautionary tales of intimate relations. Only now they excited her as well as frightened her. Sometimes she thought she wouldn't go. Sometimes she didn't want to go. But now that she'd taken up a contradictory position to Nanny, stubbornness wouldn't allow her to give in. She brushed her black hair until it gleamed and worried in case her fringe was all right. It was cut in a perfectly straight line but perhaps it was growing a bit long. It was a cold November evening so she donned a powder-blue jersey over her navy skirt. Then she worried about her small breasts. She toyed with the idea of stuffing handkerchiefs in her bra but hadn't the nerve to face Nanny's horror. Nanny would know it wasn't just for fashion's sake she was doing it. She knew that herself now. Fortunately neither Mother nor Father was at home so she was spared their questioning. Not, she suspected, that Mother would have shown much interest. She'd probably have smiled that vague smile of hers and said something like 'That's nice, dear. Enjoy the film.' She wished she could have looked as cool, sophisticated and elegant as Mother, but at least she could wear her new coat. It was a smart navy wool with a squirrel fur collar and slimly tailored, with a swaying fullness of tapered insets at its lower sides and back. A navy cloche hat with two fur pom-poms close to her face at one side, and a pair of navy ankle-strap shoes, finished the outfit.

'That's your Sunday coat and hat,' Nanny accused when she saw her.

Elizabeth's eyes fixed on her feet, she felt keenly guilty.

'Your mother bought you that to wear at church and Bible class.'

'She never said that,' Elizabeth muttered.

'You know perfectly well. Now what will you wear on Sunday?'

'I just want to look my best.'

The twins came into the nursery then. 'Oh ho,' William cried out, 'and where are we off to tonight all titivated up? Got a boyfriend have we?'

Elizabeth blushed a bright scarlet and fastened her eyes on her feet again.

'Away you go and mind your own business,' Nanny commanded, 'I'm talking to Elizabeth.'

'Elizabeth's got a boyfriend,' both boys began to chant, 'Elizabeth's got a boyfriend.'

'Have you nothing better to do than make a fool of

yourself?' Nanny said. 'I thought this was your judo night.'

'On our way,' Daniel said, 'we just came up to collect our judo things.'

'They've been out with girls, and they're younger than me,' Elizabeth complained after the boys had gone cheerfully whistling to their bedroom.

'They're boys – that's different.'

'Why is it different?'

'You know perfectly well.'

She supposed she did. Boys were always different. They were treated differently. They had more freedom. They were loved more by Mother and Father. She clung to stubbornness for strength because she had begun to feel really frightened. 'I'm away.'

'On your head be it,' Nanny said. 'Don't say I didn't warn you.'

He was standing outside the Regal. She spotted him long before she reached the meeting place because of his height.

The Regal in Sauchiehall Street had originally been an ice-skating palace, then it became Hengler's Circus. The building was partly demolished in 1927 and reopened as the Waldorf Palais de Dance, and in 1929 it had undergone another conversion and become the 2,306-seat cinema now known as the Regal.

'Hello, Elizabeth,' he greeted her, with one of the warm slow smiles that she found so devastating. 'May I call you Elizabeth?' Speechless, she nodded. 'You're looking very nice.' Taking her arm, he added, 'By the way, I'm Jack.'

It seemed an incredible impertinence even to contemplate addressing an HMI by his first name. He led her into the foyer then left her for a few minutes while he purchased the tickets. She had never been in the place before, and felt intimidated by its splendour and the smartness of the usherettes in their almost military uniform. They wore tunics with shining brass buttons, neatly pressed skirts, black silk stockings, black highly polished shoes and big Spanish hats. Inside the hall both sides were sumptuously decorated with autumn scenes, topped with clusters of autumn leaves and viewed through archways. Dawson guided her into a back seat.

'Let me help you off with your coat.'

'No, it's all right.' She clung to it, thinking of her undersized bosom. 'I'll just keep it on.'

'You'll get far too hot later on, better take it off now rather than fuss about in the dark.' There was a note of authority in his voice which she automatically responded to. 'That's better,' he said as he relieved her of the garment, folded it neatly and placed it across her knees.

She stole a surreptitious glance down at her breasts to see how they looked, and was somewhat comforted to see that the soft clinging wool of her jersey made the most of the small curves. If she kept her chest stuck out it didn't look too bad. Although to sit puffed out pigeon fashion proved a great strain. Still, she could relax once the lights went out. This however was not to be. She had felt flustered enough just to be sitting beside the HMI, his leg, warm and strong, brushing against hers. She kept shrinking away but never seemed to lose touch with the disturbing warmth of him. But then he suddenly draped one arm across the back of her seat and before she knew how it happened she was clutched tightly against him, her head firmly glued to his shoulder. She sat tilted to one side with heart hammering madly against her ribcage. Her father had on occasion hugged her in the past. He'd also, she remembered, given her a hug of congratulation when she passed her leaving certificate. But none of his hugs, memorable though they were and appreciated though they were, because she so seldom was the recipient of

68

any demonstration of affection, had felt anything like this.

The newsreel flashed on to the screen with the usual blast of music. Somehow Elizabeth's eyes refused to convey any meaning to her brain. Even the big picture did not register and if she'd been asked later she could not have told what it had been about. Her concentration was completely taken up by the assault on her senses of new harassing, yet delicious, feelings, coupled with the confusion of not knowing what to do about them. Dawson's free hand kept straying towards her breasts, awakening in her exquisite physical sensations that stretched far beyond that immediate area. At the same time she knew instinctively this must be wrong. In the first place her Calvinistic upbringing had taught her that if you enjoyed anything there must be something wrong or wicked about it and so you automatically felt guilty. In the second place she was sure that if Nanny or Mother saw her they would be disgusted with her. It was for this latter reason that she kept struggling to push his hand away.

In the interval she felt flustered and ashamed as if everyone in the hall knew what she had even momentarily been allowing. Dawson seemed astonishingly calm and unconcerned.

'Would you like some chocolate or ice cream?' he asked with one of his disconcerting smiles.

'Ice cream, thank you,' she replied faintly.

She was grateful for the cooling quality of the ice cream and the respite the interval gave her. As soon as the lights went down, however, she was plunged into guilt and harassment again, so much so that she glanced furtively around to see if anyone was watching. To her astonishment she discovered that the couples near them in the back row, indeed, as far along the row as she could discern, were locked in passionate embraces. They were actually kissing, although she didn't dare look to see what they were doing with their hands. She was still reeling with the shock of this discovery when Dawson tipped back her head and fastened his mouth over hers. Gently at first, making her close her eyes and melt beneath the soft warmth and wonderment of the first kiss she'd had in her life. Her first real kiss, that is.

The kiss lasted a long time and no sooner had they come up for air than he kissed her again. Elizabeth was secretly harassed at the beginning of each kiss and by the end of it, deeply drowning in pleasure. For a few moments after the lights came up she didn't know where she was. She just sat looking perplexed and helpless, her jersey rumpled up and her hat slightly askew – until guilt and embarrassment came to her rescue and she quickly tidied herself and allowed Dawson to help her on with her coat. She felt shy too and could hardly bring herself to meet his eye. He tucked her arm through his and led her to where he had parked his car.

He hardly spoke a word all the way back to Queen's Drive. Then when he'd reached the house and he'd stopped the car he said gently, 'When can I see you again?'

She smiled but was too shy and confused to think clearly. Too much had happened in too short a time. 'I don't know.'

'Friday?'

She nodded but her eyes turned wide and apprehensive because his arm had gone round her shoulders and he was leaning towards her, apparently with the intent of kissing her. The thought of anyone from the house seeing her was something too terrible to bear.

'No.' She turned her face away. 'I'd better go in. Thank you for a lovely evening.' She struggled out of the car, ran towards the front door and immediately rang the bell.

Sarah the maid opened it as quickly as if she'd been lurking behind it. 'Good evening, Miss Elizabeth.'

Elizabeth blushed and avoided her eyes. 'Good evening, Sarah.'

'Will you be wanting any Ovaltine brought up?'

'No thank you, I'm just going straight to bed.'

Upstairs Nanny called from the adjoining bedroom, 'Is that you, Elizabeth?'

For the first time Elizabeth wished her bedroom wasn't connected to Nanny's.

'Yes, Nanny, I'm just going straight to bed.'

'Have you brushed your teeth?'

'Yes, Nanny.'

'Well don't forget to say your prayers, and to ask God to forgive your sins.'

Elizabeth's cheeks burned in the darkness. 'Yes, Nanny.'

She lay very still in bed and tried to quell the chaos that had been awakened inside her. It was no use. She turned on her side and gave herself up to deliciously wicked thoughts.

CHAPTER 9

She swore Jessie to secrecy. In a way she would have liked the whole of the school to know that she had been honoured by going out with the HMI. Another part of her, however, wanted to hug the knowledge to herself. It had been too precious and too private an experience to be bandied about by all and sundry.

Jessie was different. Jessie was her best friend. It had been difficult to talk at first. The Ladies was always packed at lunchtime and the day after her meeting with the HMI was no exception. They sat buttock to buttock between two wooden chairs which were also shared by Miss Mayhew on one side and Miss Grey on the other. It was difficult enough to move an elbow in order to lift a cup of tea or sandwich to one's mouth. To talk privately was well nigh impossible. The general conversation had concerned the shocking business of Mamie MacAlaster and the chocolate biscuits.

Mamie MacAlaster was in primary seven and the class sook. Every class had certain well-defined types. Two of the most common were the sook and the clype. The clype carried all sorts of information to the teacher, but usually of the incriminating variety about other people. The sook tried to flatter or keep in the teacher's good books. This was usually attempted by bringing presents.

Every day for over a week Mamie MacAlaster had brought Miss Pettigrew a chocolate biscuit, one of the most expensive kind, wrapped in silver paper. Miss Pettigrew was a very refined person with hair in a neat central parting and coiled in an earphone over each ear. She crocheted her long jerseys herself, including the belt that tied neatly round her waist. Her skirts were also modestly and old-fashionedly long and she wore lisle stockings in summer and hand-knitted wool in winter. She had a very delicate stomach and was extremely pernickety about her food.

The chocolate biscuits presented by Mamie had been the one little treat she allowed herself. But coming every day, they seemed an extravagance that conscience could not permit. She had eventually tackled Mamie about this.

'I appreciate your kindness, dear,' she told the child, 'but I'm sure your mummy can't afford to be buying chocolate biscuits every day, especially to give them away.'

'Oh, it's not my mummy who gets them,' Mamie had explained, 'it's my granny.'

'Surely your granny can afford them even less, I know how expensive these biscuits are.'

'Och, my granny doesn't pay for them,' came the cheerful reply.

Miss Pettigrew experienced a stab of apprehension. The awful thought occurred to her that perhaps the old woman had stolen them. There had been the case of Johnny MacVenes' mother who was arrested for shoplifting.

'What do you mean she doesn't pay for them?' Miss Pettigrew wanted to know.

'She works in the biscuit factory,' Mamie explained. 'She brings some home every day hidden in her knickers.'

Miss Pettigrew nearly fainted with horror on the spot. She had tottered next door to Miss Mayhew's class and from there had to be helped to the Ladies and given a glass of water. Her sensibilities had suffered such a trauma, and she was in such danger of being sick, that it had been decided to send her home for the rest of the day.

Elizabeth found it difficult to divert Jessie's attention from this tale. She, like the rest of the staff, was agog at Miss Mayhew's graphic relating of it, and she joined in the howls of horror at the climax of the story. It was while everyone was sympathetically discussing Miss Pettigrew's condition and whether or not she'd be able to return to work next day that Elizabeth managed:

'I didn't get the chance to tell you yesterday, because I'd to rush home and get ready.'

'Tell me what?' Jessie asked.

'Shhh,' Elizabeth warned, and glanced furtively around. Interested now, Jessie leaned her ear nearer.

'The HMI asked me out to the pictures.'

'WHAT?' Jessie yelled out at the top of her voice.

Elizabeth paled. 'Please be quiet,' she muttered through clenched teeth, 'it's supposed to be a secret.'

'Well,' Jessie gasped, but quietly, 'what a turn-up for the book. Tell all, tell all.'

'I can't talk here. Meet me at the front gate after the bell.'

Jessie suddenly bounced up and down on the chair, nearly spilling not only her tea, but Elizabeth's.

'Roll on bell time. I can hardly wait, you lucky devil you.'

Miss Mayhew glared round at her. 'What's wrong with you? You made me spill my tea.'

'Nothing.' Jessie looked as innocent as she was able. 'Sorry.'

After school they met as arranged and walked giggling arm in arm along the street. Elizabeth told Jessie how the HMI had met her in the corridor and invited her to the pictures and how they'd gone to the Regal.

'I bet he bought the best seats,' Jessie sighed. 'And chocolates and everything.'

Elizabeth looked uncertain for a minute. 'It was the back row and we had ice cream in the interval.'

'Here, I've seen what goes on in back rows. Does that mean he kissed and cuddled you?' Jessie's face lit up with pleasurable expectancy.

'Well . . .' Elizabeth hesitated, torn between desire to share her wondrous experience and to hug it for ever to herself.

'Oh, come on,' Jessie pleaded. 'There shouldn't be any secrets between best friends.'

Elizabeth's eyes widened. 'Cross your heart and swear you'll never divulge a word to a living soul.'

Jessie willingly obliged.

'Well, yes he did.'

'Did what? Tell all, tell all.'

They hugged again with the intensity of their excitement.

'First of all he put his arm around me.'

'Whoo!' Jessie gave a delicious giggle.

'Then he . . .' Elizabeth flushed, but too ashamed to mention the hand on her bosom, blurted out instead, 'He kissed me. It was really passionate, just like something you see in the pictures.'

They both let out a squeal of hilarity and Elizabeth managed to add, 'On the screen I mean.'

In response to Jessie's urgings she tried to explain in some detail what it felt like to be kissed by an HMI. Eventually the two girls parted at the corner, Elizabeth to catch her tram home, and Jessie to walk to where she lived locally. Jessie said she was green with envy, especially that Elizabeth was meeting him again.

'I can just see you,' Jessie told her, 'ending up as an HMI's wife and living in another posh house like the one you've got now. Everything comes to those that have. Some folk are just born lucky.' She let out a parting howl of laughter. 'I'll probably end up in a wee single end with ten kids. Never mind, there's worse things happening in China.'

The mention of marriage set Elizabeth's imagination on fire. She could just see herself, first of all floating down the aisle in a white dress and veil. The organ would be playing, there would be a religious ceremony

75

conducted by Grandfather Gillespie. All the girls from the Bible class would be there. Mother and Father and Nanny would be so proud of her. Elizabeth nearly sang out loud on her way home, she felt so happy.

Once home she danced round the nursery until Nanny said she'd be getting a dose of castor oil if she wasn't careful. That would soon cool her down.

Mother and Father were home for dinner that night and after the boys left the room, but before Mother and Father could disappear again, she blurted out, 'I've got a boyfriend', then coloured to the roots of her hair. Even her neck and chest felt burning hot, yet at the same time she was proud and happy.

'Have you, dear?' Mother said in a slightly amused tone.

'Well, well.' Father laughed outright. 'And who, may we ask, is the lucky boy?'

'He's an HMI.'

'Really?' Mother said, and Father turned serious.

'He's not strictly speaking a boy then?'

'His Majesty's Inspector,' Elizabeth explained although nobody had asked. As usual Mother and Father seemed to know everything. 'I don't know what age he is but I suppose he must be a bit older than me. But he's younger than most HMIs,' she added hastily, then for good measure, 'and he's got a car.'

'Is he a local man?' Mother asked.

It occurred to Elizabeth then that she knew very little about him. Not that it mattered. 'I didn't ask, but I'll find out tomorrow. He's taking me out again.'

'When he calls for you, bring him in to meet us,' Father said. 'We'll be here.'

'Oh, he's not calling for me, we're meeting at the Regal.'

'Well, when he brings you home.'

'He might not want to come in.'

'Why not?'

She shrugged. 'I don't know. Will it not seem a bit forward of me?'

'Nonsense.'

Mother said, 'Perhaps it would seem a bit soon, Adam. We don't want to frighten the young man off.'

Elizabeth felt a drag of depression. Mother wanted to make sure they got safely rid of her. Her marriage would be a happy day all round, but for different reasons.

'Nothing might come of it,' she said, suddenly gloomy, 'I've only been out with him once.'

She sensed her mother and father exchange long-suffering looks.

'Anyway,' Mother said, 'have a nice evening tomorrow. Enjoy the film.'

There had been a change of programme from the last time but, for all they saw of it, it might as well have been the same. At the end of the programme Elizabeth once more surfaced in a dazed condition. She felt saturated with love. She was blissfully, gratefully happy, and her feelings were plain to see in her eyes when she gazed up at Dawson.

'You're very sweet,' he told her gently. Then he sighed.

'Why do you sigh?' she asked. 'Aren't you happy?'

People were beginning to get up and push past them, forcing them to move too. He guided her out to the foyer.

'I'm happy when I'm with you.'

Once they reached Monkton House, she plucked up courage to say, 'Would you like to come in for a cup of tea or a nightcap? Mother and Father said it would be all right.'

The moment she spoke she regretted it. He looked so uncomfortable.

'No, I'd better not, Elizabeth. I've an early start tomorrow, quite a bit of travelling to do, and I've still some notes to catch up on.'

'Yes of course. It doesn't matter.'

And it didn't. She kept telling herself that on the next few occasions when she repeated her invitation to visit Monkton House. Not right away, and not last thing at night, but on her nineteenth birthday she had been really disappointed at his refusal.

Christmas Eve too had been a disappointment. She understood of course that he would need to be with his own mother and father at such a family time of year. She tried to understand that the same would apply to the New Year period.

At Easter, Mother and Father had a special tea to which he was invited but he gave another excuse. At first Father had teased her about her young man being shy. Lately though, he began to seem a little annoyed, even suspicious. He began to ask questions. 'Haven't you met his parents yet?'

She had to answer that she had not.

'Why not? Is he ashamed of you or something?'

Elizabeth paled at this terrible thought, and Father, noticing her stricken expression, laughed and said, 'Darling, I was only joking, how could he possibly be ashamed of you? You're sweet and beautiful and he's a very lucky man, but I'm beginning to wonder if there's anything wrong with him. Why don't you ask him outright why he keeps refusing to meet your parents and why he never introduces you to his?'

It wouldn't have mattered really, except she wanted everything normal and all right. She dreaded anything odd or mysterious or different. There was enough of that in her life already. She kept repeating to herself that everything was all right, more than all right. Everything was beautiful and exciting and fulfilling. She lived for the times they were together. In between times were only for existing and dreaming of when she would be with him again. She could hardly credit how lucky she was to have found someone to love so such, and, blessed of all, the good fortune to have her love returned. He had told her he loved her over and over again. He had whispered the words against her lips, her cheeks, her eyes, her ears. Sometimes they would be embracing in the back row of the pictures. Sometimes he would drive her in his car out to the country or the seaside, and they'd kiss and cuddle and he'd whisper sweet words of love to her.

Everything was perfect and yet . . . There were one or two worrying occasions that seemed to indicate that not only did he not want to introduce her to his parents, he didn't want her to meet his friends. Once he'd seen someone wave to him from across the street and he'd hurried her away through the crowd, almost as if he wanted her out of sight.

Jessie pooh-poohed this idea and said it had only been her imagination.

Knowing her imagination, she decided it probably was. He also made her promise to keep the relationship a secret from anyone else in the school.

Jessie said, 'Can you blame him? You know what staff rooms are like. Anyway it might be as much as his job's worth to be friendly with a member of staff, especially a probationer. He's supposed to put in objective reports about you, remember.'

She knew Jessie was right but still she couldn't help feeling – she was proud of him, wasn't he proud of her?

Gradually she became sick with worry. The core of her had been formed from as far back as she could remember with the knowledge that there was something different about her. With that knowledge came the associated belief that there must be something about her to be ashamed of. Now, it seemed, that belief was yet again being confirmed. Before, it had hurt and worried her but these feelings and reactions paled into insignificance compared with what she suffered now.

She couldn't bear Dawson to think badly of her. If

he thought badly of her, if he was ashamed of her, surely he couldn't love her. The thought dropped her into a pit of fear. If he didn't love her he might leave her, not want to see her again. She began looking for signs. She began straining desperately to please him, to ward off the evil hour. She gave him little presents: a hand-sewn handkerchief which Nanny had helped her to make to perfection, a packet of cigars, and on his birthday a more expensive cigarette lighter than she could afford.

She overcame her natural shyness and inhibitions and returned his kisses with equal passion. She even allowed him to fondle her breasts. Then late one evening in the darkness of his car he began an even more intimate caress.

Her instincts were to stop him despite the fact that it was giving her more pleasurable sensations than she'd ever experienced before. Her desperation to please him, however, was stronger than anything else, even than her love.

It was only afterwards when she had returned to Monkton House and was lying alone in bed that she began to worry again.

Would he have lost respect for her because of what she had allowed him to do? She palpitated so much with apprehension she had to sit up in bed.

Next day she found it so difficult to meet Nanny's eyes that Nanny became suspicious. 'What have you been up to, miss?'

'Nothing,' Elizabeth protested. 'I've a headache, that's all, I didn't sleep very well last night.'

She could hardly wait to see Dawson again. In fact the more she thought of the week that was to pass before their next meeting the more agitated she became. She needed him to reassure her, to tell her that he still loved her. No doubt he'd tell her she was just being silly. Any time in the past when she'd ask him:

'Do you still love me?' he'd always smile and say gently: 'Of course I do, silly.'

She tried to be sensible but it was difficult when she was nursing such a terrible secret. She couldn't even tell Jessie what she'd allowed Dawson to do, she was even afraid Jessie would be so shocked she wouldn't want to be friends with her any more.

Eventually her imagination ran away with her to such an extent it was as if Dawson had already despised her and deserted her. She couldn't bear it any longer. Aghast at her own temerity she decided to phone him. She would make some excuse. She just had to hear his voice and know everything was all right. She didn't know his exact address, only that he lived some-where in the Bearsden area. His name was the same as his father's and she soon found it in the telephone directory.

A woman answered the phone and Elizabeth asked, 'Can I speak to Mr Jack Dawson please?'

'I'm sorry,' the woman said, 'he's not here at the moment.'

'Is that Mrs Dawson speaking?' Elizabeth asked.

'Yes,' the woman said.

'Could you tell him that Miss Monkton phoned, please?'

'Very well, I'll tell my husband as soon as he comes in.'

'Oh no, I don't mean your husband,' Elizabeth said, 'I mean your son.'

'I haven't got a son.' The woman's voice had turned cold.

'Oh, I'm terribly sorry,' Elizabeth faltered. 'I must have made a mistake, I must have got the wrong number.'

Her hand was visibly trembling as she put down the phone.

CHAPTER 10

The nursery was quiet and peaceful. The only sounds were the occasional crackling of the fire behind the fire-guard, Nanny's knitting needles and the gentle hissing and purring of the gas mantles. Nanny was sitting in the rocking chair beside the fire and Elizabeth was hunched over the table nearby, head bent low as she wrote her observation notes in her record book. She did so automatically, pen moving as if by its own accord.

'Today the children learned a new verse of the song "Twinkle, Twinkle Little Star". The teacher taught it phrase by phrase . . .'

'Today the children were taught to write the letter j. The letter was written on the board and the children were asked to say what it was. Then they were shown how to write it in three stages. The chief mistake made was crossing the down stroke too low down . . .'

'I think we'll need to get your eyes tested,' Nanny said, 'you're peering far too close to that paper.'

Elizabeth blinked and stretched her eyes wide. She wanted to rush over to Nanny and bury her face in her lap. She longed to cry out, 'For pity's sake, help me.' Instead she said, 'I'm just trying to concentrate.'

This was indeed true. She was desperately hanging on to her school work and her notes, her marking, her preparation. Anything to keep her mind firmly attached to normality.

It would have been bad enough losing her love, being deceived by him, used by him, having such a terrible blow to her self-confidence and self-esteem. But added to all of these things was the knowledge that if it was true what Betty Swanson and the Donaldson sisters had said about how a baby was made — and there was no reason to doubt them — she could be pregnant. Everyone would know what she'd done. Pregnancy also meant the unknown; being trapped in a dark tunnel from which there could be no turning back. Ahead was the mystery, the unknown experience of childbirth. Little jets of panic kept leaping to life inside her.

'During reading from their primers a few of the children persisted in looking up from their books. After some special attention, they learned to follow the reading and could do it quite well before the end of the lesson . . .'

'The children are very interested in pictures, new objects, blackboard drawings and bright colours. They also like to hear what little children in other lands do . . .'

The panic was cascading through her now. She supported her brow with one hand, making her fringe stick up, but she could do nothing with her heart. It was thumping so violently it was even making the table tremble. She kept trying to tell herself she was just having a nightmare. She would wake up and all would be well again. She would be safe. But a black tunnel stretched on with no light at the end of it. No escape. Staring wider-eyed at her record book, she saw nothing.

'Would you like me to get you a cup of Ovaltine?' Nanny asked. Flossie, the nursery maid, was downstairs washing Charlie's clothes.

Elizabeth nodded.

'Cat got your tongue?'

'Yes please, Nanny.'

Nanny stopped knitting, tucked the half-finished royal-blue jersey into her tapestry work bag, and rose with a crackle of apron.

'I hope this teaching isn't proving too much for you.'

'No, it's not the work.' The words slipped out without thought.

Nanny immediately pounced on them. 'Oh, and what is it then?'

Guilt burned hotly over Elizabeth's cheeks. 'Nothing.'

'Don't you nothing me, miss. It's that boyfriend, isn't it?'

Visibly trembling now, Elizabeth lowered her gaze.

'Well?' Nanny persisted. 'Isn't it?'

She received a faint 'Yes' in reply. And then: 'He's married.'

'I knew it!' Nanny cried out triumphantly. 'I knew there was something about that man, the way he kept refusing to put foot in this house. Well, I hope you've learned your lesson, miss, and steer clear of him in future. I'll go and fetch your Ovaltine.'

Their date was for the next evening and she was tempted to go. She needed the comfort and reassurance of being held in his arms. She wanted him to explain, to somehow make everything all right.

She was still struggling with the temptation next day at school when he rang her. The office wasn't at all pleased. Phone calls for staff were severely frowned upon unless they were of the utmost urgency and, being on probation, she wasn't even considered staff. The secretary stayed in the room and Elizabeth was restricted to mumbling a brief 'yes' or 'no' into the receiver.

She said 'no' to his query about seeing her that evening but he pleaded that he wanted to explain. He must see her, he said. And so, under the disapproving eye of Miss Spencer, she agreed and hung up.

The day was long and trying. She forgot how sticky the children's hands always were and how easily the stickiness was transferred to primers and jotters and thence to her own hands. She had forgotten also how uncomfortable and inefficient it was to try and wash in the icy water and rusted sink in the staff room. It was a windy day and for some mysterious reason the children were always noisy, restless and difficult to control on windy days. Even primary one had proved awkward. Alice McPhail and Benny Brown had both wandered out to the toilet and it had been discovered after their return that instead of using the separate toilets for boys and girls, they had both gone to the same one. This crime was discovered when Alice innocently remarked, 'That's a handy wee thing he's got.'

Lunchtime was bleak. The staff room was even colder than usual and the kettle on the solitary ring took ages each time it was put on to boil. Complaints burdened the air, for the headmaster had been particularly interfering, descending on classrooms like an eagle in his bulky black gown to bombard the children with unexpected questions. The children were intimidated by the headmaster's zeal and could not, or would not, answer. This left the teachers feeling frustrated and inadequate. There was no peace in the staff room either. The racket in the playground reverberated inside to such a degree that voices had to be continuously strained to their highest pitch.

By afternoon, Elizabeth felt like screaming. Everything seemed so senseless and trivial compared with the earth-shattering importance of her own problems and the anguish of her meeting that evening with Dawson.

On the way home after school, noting her distraction, Jessie said, 'What's up with you? You're looking more harassed than all the rest of them put together.'

'It's nothing to laugh about.'

'Sorry. Is something wrong then?'

'Promise you won't tell anybody.'

'Cross my heart.'

Elizabeth found her voice. 'I've discovered that Jack Dawson is married.'

'Damnation! Isn't that just like the thing? The handsome ones always get snapped up.'

'I feel terrible.'

'I don't blame you. But not to worry. There's worse things happen in China. You'll get over it.'

'I'm seeing him tonight.'

'To sock him one, I hope. The two-faced rat.'

'He phoned today and talked me into it.'

'Don't be an ass and let him talk you into carrying on with him. There's no future in it.'

'I know.'

'What a nerve, and him an HMI.'

'I'll have to tell . . .' She nearly said 'Nanny' but changed it just in time to 'everyone at home' – Jessie thought it such a hoot, her having a Nanny – 'that I'm going out with you.'

'Sure, sure.'

At the corner Elizabeth felt reluctant to leave her friend. 'I'll let you know how I get on.'

'You tell him what you think of him, the rat. Leading you on like that.'

'I've been practising in my head what I'm going to say.'

'Make sure you say it then. I'll be dying to know how you get on. See you tomorrow.'

'See you tomorrow,' Elizabeth echoed faintly.

Trundling home in the tram she wished she had been able to share her guilty secret with Jessie. At the same time her whole being withered at the thought of anyone knowing how wanton she'd been.

Mother and Father weren't in and Nanny was busy with Charlie. Jason and the twins were nowhere to be seen. They spent more time downstairs now or out with friends than in the nursery and it was becoming increasingly difficult for Nanny to keep track of them. 'Time enough when you're twenty-one to do what you like,' she kept telling them. After Charlie had been settled in bed and had his usual story from Elizabeth she and Nanny dined alone at the nursery table. Elizabeth barely managed to pick at her venison fillet with sloe jelly.

'Eat that up, miss,' Nanny commanded, 'it's one of Mrs Bishop's best recipes. Mind you,' she conceded, 'I think she's been a bit heavy-handed with the red wine. Not to mention the port.'

Elizabeth took this as her cue. 'It's a bit too strong for me.'

'Oh, very well. Eat your junket and cream. That's nice and light.'

'I'm going out with Jessie tonight.'

Nanny's sharp eyes raked over Elizabeth's face, making it sting with heat. 'Are you sure it's Jessie you're going with?'

'I thought it might cheer me up. Take my mind off . . . off other things.'

'Aye . . . well . . . make sure you're back here at a respectable hour. We don't want your mother or father complaining. Have you told them about the mistake you made?'

Elizabeth's heart thumped against her ribcage. 'What mistake?'

'What do you mean – what mistake? Going out with a married man, of course. If that's not a mistake – to put it mildly – I don't know what is.'

'No. I thought I'd just say I'm not going out with him any more.'

'You know what I think of people who tell lies, miss.'

'It's not a lie,' Elizabeth hotly protested, 'it's true, I won't be going out with him any more.'

'I should think not indeed. I told you you shouldn't have gone out with him in the first place. Finish off that pudding or you're not going anywhere.'

No doubt Mother and Father would be as pleased and relieved as Nanny. If only she could escape the nightmare of being pregnant. Maybe it didn't happen every time you did something wrong. The thought raised a tiny flicker of hope. She promised God that she would never never do anything wrong again. Please, God, have mercy on me and spare me this time. Please, God, she kept fervently praying as she ate her pudding and as she got ready to go out. Not that she changed her clothes and 'titivated herself up', to use Nanny's phrase. She was too distracted for such niceties. She just flung on a coat and was absent-mindedly going out without gloves or hat until Nanny called her back and pointed out this omission.

Please God, please God, she silently intoned in time to the clanging of the tram as it carried her to the usual meeting place in Sauchiehall Street. But as soon as she saw him standing waiting outside the Regal, she forgot her own anguish. He look so worried and anxious that her heart immediately embraced him.

'My dear,' he greeted her, 'I'm so glad you've come. Let's drive somewhere quiet so that we can talk.'

The nearest place was Kelvingrove and he stopped the car in the tree-lined avenue that cut through the park. Still grasping the steering wheel in leather-gloved hands and staring straight ahead he said, 'I'm so sorry you had to find out like that. I was going to tell you . . .'

'You should never have asked me out in the first place,' Elizabeth said miserably. 'Why did you do it?'

He took off his gloves and tossed them aside before turning towards her with a sigh. 'I don't know what came over me, I . . . yes I do. My wife is such a forceful, abrasive character and you were so refreshingly sweet and gentle and compliant. I think I must have fallen in love with you from that first moment I saw you in the class looking like a child yourself in your pink pinafore.'

'You must also be in love with your wife or you wouldn't be married to her.'

'I was once. I thought she was the loveliest, wittiest and most intelligent person I'd ever met. It was only much later that I discovered what she was really like. She could have destroyed me with her shrewish temper and sharp tongue if I'd let her. But I didn't. I have fought back in every way I can.'

'Including going out with other women?'

In a gesture of fatigue he put his finger on the bridge of his nose and screwed up his eyes. 'It wasn't like that with you, Elizabeth.'

At the same time as loving him, she felt bitter. 'You, all this time, went on seeing me . . . you even . . .' Flushing, she stared out at the park. It was a pleasant summer's evening although there had been heavy showers earlier and there was still a steady drip-drip from the boughs of the overhanging trees. 'All this time you never told me.'

'I wanted to, but I was afraid of losing you. I knew, you see, that she'd never give me a divorce.'

'How did you know that? Had you asked her?'

'Yes.'

'Because of me?'

'No, my marriage was on the rocks before I met you.'

She assumed from this that there must have been another woman before he'd met her. In romantic stories she'd read, 'heartbroken' had often been used but it had only been a word to her. Now she experienced its true meaning. An actual pain in her chest splintered upwards towards her throat.

'All this time I believed you.'

Suddenly she began struggling to get out of the car, her fight with the handle giving her something safe to concentrate on.

'Elizabeth, please . . .' He got out his side, his long legs quickly catching up with her. She felt his hand warm and firm on her arm. 'There's a seat over here. Please, give me a few more minutes.'

'What for?' she asked, but she allowed him to lead her over to the wooden bench where a statue of Lord Kelvin stared thoughtfully down at them.

'Don't you believe that I love you, Elizabeth?' His

arm went around her shoulder but she shrugged him off, shrinking away as if he'd suddenly developed some infectious disease. Her actions and her tongue were running away with her of their own accord.

'What does it matter what I think or I believe? We've no future, that's all that matters. This is the last time I'll see you.'

'My dear . . .' he said helplessly, leaning forward, head lowered, hands held limply between his knees. 'I'm so sorry, I've obviously hurt you very deeply. I swear I didn't mean to.'

'I'm going to take the tram home.' She rose, in panic that she was about to shame herself with an avalanche of tears.

'Please, at least allow me . . .' he began, rising too.

'No, I don't want you to, goodbye.'

She steeled herself not to run, not to look round, and soon she was far beyond the sound of his voice calling out to her.

CHAPTER 11

'You're a sadist.' Annalie's eyes flung daggers of anger at him. 'You enjoy tossing women about.'

The muscles round Carlino's mouth tightened when he laughed. They drew back thin lips to reveal perfect teeth made all the whiter against a smooth, tanned skin.

'It's the dance, darling, the Dance des Apaches. I didn't invent it. It originated in the working-class cabarets of Paris among the street toughs, if you must know.'

'That's your story.'

'You look wonderful when you're angry. That's why the audience get so excited by our performance. You show such passion. We're wild together. They love it.'

'You go beyond what's artistically necessary and you know it. You broke the last girl's arm.'

He dismissed this with a flick of his hand. 'That was her own fault. This dance needs an acrobatic skill as well as rhythmic ability. She fell like a stone.'

They had just come off the stage after a performance that had brought enthusiastic applause. If it wasn't for the audience appreciation she didn't know how she'd stand the partnership with Carlino. She had become addicted to the applause, the exciting thunder that filled the auditorium after each performance and brought adrenaline careering crazily through her veins. The Royal Princess Theatre, where they were working at the moment, was situated in the Gorbals, within walking distance of her home. The pay wasn't good but at least it was better than the pittance that Josiah Gibson had doled out.

Now, however, they'd got bookings for a summer season which meant travelling around to several different halls and living in digs, mostly seaside towns. This would inevitably mean that she would be in Carlino's company more often, something she felt uneasy about. She knew, of course, that she was the envy of every woman in Glasgow who'd seen the show and admired Carlino's fierce looks and the passion he displayed doing the dance. Male colleagues made no secret of the fact that they disliked his arrogant ways and his success with the prettiest chorus girls. It was the tradition that top of the bill would 'have first crack of the chorus' and Carlino was nowhere near top billing. Nevertheless every woman in the chorus line and the audience fantasized about him. But the reality, Annalie thought bitterly, was a different story. Admittedly she had felt much the same as everyone else at first but it only took a few performances of the Dance des Apaches to disillusion her. As far as she was concerned, returning home every night bruised and throbbing with pain from top to toe was not conducive to tender romantic feelings, although she still retained a certain amount of admiration for the straight-backed elegance of his physique and his undeniable skill as a dancer. Maurice Rutherford had reminded her of this skill when she'd gone to his office to complain.

'You'd never get another partner like him, my dear.'

'I don't want another partner like him,' Annalie protested. 'That's my point. He's a horrible man. A real sadist. I can't stand him!'

'Now calm down, my dear.' Maurice blinked earnestly at her across his desk. 'Have a dram with me and let's both talk this through.'

'I've said all I've come to say. I don't want to work with Tony Carlino. I'm black and blue every night because of him.'

Maurice fidgeted nervously with his bow tie for a few seconds before pouncing on the whisky decanter at his elbow.

'Do join me, my dear. You'll feel the better for it.'

'No thanks, the only thing that'll make me feel better is if you get me a different partner.'

Maurice poured himself a whisky and downed it before saying, 'The pair of you make such a good team. Everybody says so. That's why I'm getting you so many bookings. Without Tony . . .' He shrugged and spread out his hands.

It had to be admitted that she did respond passionately to him during their performance. The trouble was that he expected her to fall into his arms not just during the dance but after they'd quit the theatre. Of course he was used to getting any woman he fancied and had not made any secret of it, so apart from anything else, irritation at his conceit prevented her from giving in to his romantic overtures. Her rejection of him had proved both a blow to his pride, and a challenge.

Violet, one of the chorus girls, had said, 'I can't believe you don't find Tony attractive. He oozes sex. He just needs to look at me with those smouldering eyes of his and I feel my knees buckling. I wish he'd make passes at me.'

He was sexually attractive, there could be no doubt about that. Sometimes she asked herself why she didn't just give in and enjoy a purely sexual encounter. She wasn't sure if it was pride that held her back, or fear, or simply caution – 'once bitten, twice shy'. And it wasn't just sex she wanted. She was a passionate woman but she was an intensely loving one as well. When she gave herself she needed to give all of herself, and with a man like Carlino this was a very dangerous thing to do.

'Let's celebrate our last night here,' Carlino said now. 'Have supper together. Crack a good bottle of wine.'

'Surely every place will be shut at this time of night. Anyway it's only the last night of the season,' Annalie said, 'it's not as if we're bidding the place goodbye for ever.'

'Why do you feel you must contradict everything I say?' He loosened his scarlet necktie and pulled off the black beret that was part of his costume for the act. His longish hair was oiled and brushed back from his angular face. 'I think we both need to relax, and what better way than over good food and wine?'

The invitation was certainly tempting. She hesitated and he said:

'Look, if it's the dance that's worrying you, we could talk about it. Maybe we could change the routine?' He flashed another smile at her. 'You called me a sadist. At least give me a chance to defend myself.'

They had reached the curving iron stairway that led to the dressing rooms and had to stand aside and wait until a couple of dozen chorus girls clattered down twittering and screeching like a clamour of seagulls. Annalie shivered. Even when it was bright and sunny outside, here, a shadeless electric bulb gave feeble light and no heat. Icy draughts cut at legs and thighs and her fishnet stockings and black satin skirt slashed to mid-thigh gave little protection.

After the chorus girls flew past she descended the stairs, high heels beating a noisy tattoo. She was thinking of the lonely night before her if she didn't accept Carlino's invitation. She didn't know how she was going to face the silent, claustrophobic kitchen in Cumberland Street. The trouble was, after the violent theatre performance and then the excitement of the applause she couldn't settle. Often as not she escaped from the house to walk aimlessly and alone around the Gorbals streets. Already she'd lost touch with the Angels, partly because it was too late after a performance at the theatre to meet any of them for a visit to the cinema, their favourite night out. Because of the early start the Angels had to make in the morning they liked to get into the first house of the picture. At weekends, some of them went to one of the dance halls in town, but after a couple of strenuous performances of the Dance des Apaches – there was always a matinée on a Saturday – Annalie was in neither the mood nor the condition to dance again. There was also the fact that even if she'd managed to get there early enough, she and the Angels didn't seem to have anything in common any more. It wasn't so much that she felt this, as that they made her feel it. They had closed ranks. She was an outsider now, no longer one of their tight-knit community. They were still friendly. They hailed her with cheery greetings if they happened to come across her. Nevertheless, after a few minutes she would detect an awkwardness, a plethora of pauses. They were uncomfortable, impatient to be free of her.

'You'll come then?' Carlino said.

'Oh, all right,' she agreed, immediately regretting her words when she saw the gleam of triumph narrow his eyes.

'See you upstairs in about fifteen minutes.'

He swaggered away to his dressing room and, her emotions in confusion, Annalie entered the room she shared with a couple of female acrobats and a hefty male impersonator. The room was little more than a cupboard, airless and furnace-hot with a faulty radiator, so the door was always left open. Rush stools were jammed between the make-up table and the curtain behind which hung the costumes for all performances. Brown paper covered one part of the table and a tattered and badly stained towel was spread over another. Scattered about were sticks of greasepaint, cosmetic pencils, jars of rouge, powder puffs and boxes of powder. There were also good-luck tokens favoured by the different artistes – a rabbit's foot, a miniature horseshoe, a lucky penny, a lucky scarf. Electric bulbs framed the long mirror and the sweet smell of face powder mixed with the sour stench of the nearby lavatory. The male impersonator sighed with relief as she unbuttoned a tight striped waistcoat.

'They were a rotten lot tonight,' she remarked to Annalie, who had divested herself of high-heeled shoes, skirt, cotton top and neckerchief. She was now seated in front of the mirror with a band of white cloth tied round her hair to protect it as she slapped cold cream on her face.

'They grudged every time they put their hands together.'

Now that Annalie came to think of it the audience had not been quite as enthusiastic as usual, even for the star of the show who was a well-known comedian. He had muttered complaints as soon as he'd reached the wings. But comedians were a sour lot at the best of times.

'Maybe it's all this unemployment that's depressing them.'

'All the more reason to be grateful for the chance of being cheered up.'

The acrobats sighed as if they needed cheering up more than anybody. They drooped with exhaustion although it was difficult to make a true judgement of their appearance with their chalk-white powdered faces and eyes enlarged with mauve and white paint and thick black mascara.

Annalie wiped off the cold cream, fluffed some powder on to her face, applied a touch of lipstick and removed the white hair band. Then over her brassiere and knickers she donned a white silk crepe blouse with a wide yolk of smocking in gorgeous peasant colours and an emerald wool skirt and jacket. The final touch was a brimmed cloche hat in shiny straw over her liquorice-coloured hair. She liked to wear vivid colours and knew they complemented her dark hair and eyes. She picked up a handbag large enough to hold all her belongings except the shoes, which she slipped on again.

'Be seeing you,' she called to the others as she made for the door.

They gave her lethargic waves. One of the acrobats shook her head as if at a loss to understand such energetic brightness. Battering up the iron stairway into the gloom of the fusty-smelling corridor she passed some stage hands enjoying a forbidden fag. Carlino was waiting near the stage door, looking immaculate in his blue serge jacket, white shirt, and flannels that were fashionably much wider than the tight trousers he wore during the act. His eyes, deeply set under a slash of black brows, took in her smart appearance.

'You look gorgeous, darling.'

'Everyone else is going home to fall into bed and I don't blame them.'

'We can go to bed right now if that's what you feel like. Who needs food when there's a feast of love to be enjoyed?'

She flashed him a sarcastic look. 'You know what I mean and don't get any ideas just because I've agreed to have a bite of supper with you. I'm your professional partner, remember. Not one of your temporary paramours.'

He tucked her arm in his as they sauntered down the street then boarded a tram. The gas lamps were lit, their quivering circles of light masking the grey pavements and softening the harsh black lines of the tenements. Soon they were passing shops, some with windows still brightly lit, and streets surprisingly busy with people. Of course it was a Saturday, Glasgow's main night out of the week. The fact that they had been celebrating was obvious by the number of drunk men holding each other up at corners or taking the whole width of the pavement as they staggered along.

The restaurant was a dimly lit room in Sauchiehall Street within walking distance of several large theatres and although it looked crowded the waiter, who obviously knew Carlino, showed them to an empty booth at the far end. They had beef cooked in claret washed down by a robust Burgundy wine followed by a clear sharp-flavoured water ice.

'How can you afford all this on the money we get paid?' Annalie wanted to know.

'Don't you worry your lovely head about that. Did you enjoy the meal? That's the important thing.'

'It was a real treat. What's the food like in the digs you've booked? Nothing like this, I'll bet.'

'Afraid not, darling. It's not easy to get any place, most landladies don't like the hours theatricals keep. I always turn on the charm for them. It means with any luck they'll take a booking next time round. I've got one in nearly every town. None of them are up to hotel standards – to put it mildly – but some aren't too bad. One or two are a bit filthy, so be prepared with the old flea powder. But at least we're sure of a place to go to. Most of the others, the chorus girls for instance, have to hump their cases around the streets, knocking on doors and asking if they take theatricals.'

Being reminded of his charm and his powers of persuasion made her ask, 'Did you really mean what you said about changing the act?'

'Darling, I'm perfectly willing to start rehearsing a gypsy or a Spanish dance routine tomorrow if that's what you want, but I'll have to clear it with the management. After all, they've booked us, and probably billed us by now, as an apache act. We can't just suddenly announce that we've changed our minds. You must see that.'

She did of course.

'But you promise to speak to them and try to arrange it as soon as possible? You'd be really good at it, Tony. I can just see you in a short matador jacket and a Spanish hat. Have you ever tried the castanets? I've an extra pair I can give you.'

She felt really enthusiastic. It would be a pleasure to dance her kind of dance with him. She knew he wouldn't just be good at it. He would be electrifying. 'My mother used to bring me presents from her travels, embroidered shawls and petticoats, coloured stockings, frilly, flouncy, long-trained skirts. We could make a really colourful and dramatic act.'

'I promise I'll do my best to persuade everyone. Meantime have you understood what I've said about the apache?'

She hesitated then gave him an uncertain yes. She supposed she did understand in a way. The dance was meant to be alternately passionate and angry and they had to display these emotions as realistically as possible during the performance. The degree of this realism they could accomplish was the measure of their success.

'You still don't sound convinced.' He lit a cigarette and blew smoke to one side at the same time as giving her a sideways glance. 'You still think I'm a sadist? Yet surely you can see that off stage I'm the mildest, most charming of men.'

She couldn't help laughing. 'You're certainly the most conceited. It's terribly late, time I was home. I've still my packing to do before we leave tomorrow.'

He signalled for the bill.

'You'll have plenty of time tomorrow morning. I won't call for you until about ten.'

The only time she'd been outside of Glasgow was with Adam Monkton, at the secret rendezvous he'd arranged when he'd had to work away from home for a few days at a time. He'd booked her and baby Elizabeth in at the same boarding house or digs as him. Landladies had just accepted them as his wife and child and so she and Adam had shared a double bed and enjoyed nights of love that were still as vivid and precious to her as they had always been.

She sighed and Carlino, taking her arm as they reached the street, said, 'Why so sad?'

'I'm tired,' she shrugged. 'This is Saturday, remember.

I've been jerked about and flung around twice by you today. Maybe it's just that you don't know your own strength, Tony.'

'What I do know is that this is a Saturday to remember. The day when the great Tony Carlino was transformed into a Spanish dancer.' He suddenly let go of her to fling his hands into the air, stiffen his arms, arch his body towards her and begin drumming his heels against the pavement.

'Stop it, you fool,' she laughed and they linked arms again and continued on their way. When they arrived at her close he saw her up the shadowy stairway to her door and there he kissed her hand and said goodnight. She was pleasantly surprised, even secretly, and perversely, disappointed. At the same time she was afraid. Not of the man who had bent his dark head over her hand, but of herself and the depth of her emotional and sexual needs.

CHAPTER 12

'You're not still pining after that man,' Nanny said.

Elizabeth refused to meet her eyes. 'I'm all right.'

'You're anything but all right. I've never seen you look so peaky, and no wonder when you hardly touch any of the good food that's put in front of you.'

It was true what Nanny said. She was anything but all right. Dawson had phoned her several times, once at school and twice at home, and it had been an agony to hear his voice. The last time it had been her father who'd answered the phone and he had put a stop to the calls in no uncertain manner. She thought how ironic it was that he should try to protect her from a married man. Obviously no one had protected her real mother against his advances. Now she was alone with the suspenseful wait for her period. To stop herself from thinking about it, at first she'd kept herself busy working during the day. In the evenings she played with Charlie and delighted him with stories until he fell asleep. Then she vied with Nanny in her speed at knitting. She helped Grandma with her charity sale of work and accompanied Grandfather on his visits to his sick parishioners. She even spent a few spare minutes in the kitchen helping Cook beat the cake for Sunday tea. She was a whirlwind of energy. Then suddenly her frantic animation died. She was empty and exhausted. All she wanted to do was collapse into sleep. While her activity was at its peak, she had been at the same time obsessed by the fear of being pregnant, and every night she'd kept her wild sobbing under the bedclothes so that Nanny wouldn't hear.

Now she felt drugged with despair, too exhausted to

weep. Each night she plunged into sleep almost before her head hit the pillow. She would have slept all day if Nanny hadn't shaken her awake. As it was, she dozed off in the tram on the way to college. It was as much as she could do to keep her eyes open during lectures or teaching observations. Her teaching practice was delivered as if in a dream.

Several times Jessie had remarked on how quiet and faraway she was and she too had asked if Dawson, or the lack of him, was the root of the trouble.

'He's not worth making yourself ill over, Elizabeth. He was obviously just out for a good time – a bit of a kiss and tickle on the side. I bet you're not the first and won't be the last, either. I hope his wife gives him what-for. I bet she knew right away what he'd been up to when you phoned.' She rolled her eyes but somehow still managed to look quite jolly. Elizabeth couldn't help wondering how Jessie would have dealt with such a situation. Probably the danger of pregnancy would never have arisen. Jessie would have been quite capable of blacking the eye of any man who took liberties with her, or if intimacy did take place, Elizabeth could just imagine her doing all sorts of outrageous, courageous things like marching into his home and confronting both him and his wife. At the moment Jessie had acquired a boyfriend, a fellow student smaller than herself with horn-rimmed glasses and a long-nosed, earnest face. He was called Eric McLennan and Jessie said he was potty about her. Sometimes Eric would walk with them from the college to the tram stop, discussing with Jessie the day's lectures. Sometimes he met them at the Govan School and walked Jessie home. To Elizabeth his company was a mixed blessing. In one way she was relieved that she didn't need to talk, or think, or do anything. On the other hand being the extra one in a threesome accentuated the loss she felt in no longer having a partner.

'What you need,' Nanny announced, 'is to get right away from the town. There's nothing to beat good sea air to put the colour back in your cheeks. I've told your mother and she agrees. When does this term at college finish?'

'Thirtieth of this month,' Elizabeth answered lethargically.

'Right, come July we're all going to pack up and take a good holiday. Your mother and father don't want to go too far because they've a busy summer ahead. It's got to be within easy travelling distance for them so I've suggested Irvine or Ayr. I like Ayr myself. There's plenty to do in Ayr. I don't believe in lying about on beaches all day.'

Surely she should know definitely by then, Elizabeth thought. Already she was well past the expected time for her period. She kept trying to clutch at straws by reminding herself that she had never been regular. Once before she'd missed a whole month when she'd been worried about passing her exams at school. Remembering this gave her a few blessed seconds of comfort, but too soon it evaporated and her stomach caved in with fear.

It was decided, eventually, to allow the twins to go to scout camp and only Elizabeth and Jason, Mother, Father, and of course Nanny and Charlie would make the journey to Ayr. They went in Father's car. A holiday house had been rented and Flossie, the nursery maid, Mrs Bishop, the cook, Daisy, the scullery maid, and Sarah, the parlour maid, all went too, travelling by train with most of the luggage.

Before the holiday time came, Elizabeth was in a state of physical collapse. She wished sleep would merge into death, complete oblivion. Sometimes, because Nanny wouldn't allow her to retreat to bed but chased her out to get 'a breath of air to put some life into you', she went out the back gate and across to Queen's Park. Unseeing and unaware of the fragrant creamy white blossom of the magnolia trees, the orange-blossom perfume of the philadelphus or the great banks of multi-coloured rhododendrons, she wandered about as if heavily sedated.

Somehow, with the help of Nanny she organized herself sufficiently to accompany the family to the pleasant seaside town and port of Ayr, situated at the mouth of the River Ayr. It was quite late by the time they'd arrived and settled into the roomy villa on Racecourse Road. Nevertheless, her mother and Jason went out for a walk and to explore around. Elizabeth pleaded a headache and stayed with Nanny and Charlie. She promised Nanny faithfully, however, that she'd get out first thing next day and 'get the good of the air'.

First thing in the morning, long before anyone else except the maids had stirred, Nanny forced Elizabeth to get up. Whipping the bedclothes off the bed she commanded, 'Right, up you get, my girl. Into the bathroom with you and then out for a good brisk walk.'

Elizabeth shivered and drew her knees up against her stomach. She really did have a headache now and pain was gripping at her abdomen, making her feel sick.

'Up!' Nanny repeated. 'I've had enough of this nonsense. I've run your bath.'

It was while she enjoyed the relaxation in the hot water that she discovered her period had started. Later, in a daze with relief, she walked along the deserted beach. The early morning mist was lifting off the Carrick shore and the rising sun was setting fire to the rocks and crags of the island of Arran. The blue expanse of water shimmered under its blaze, silvery at the edges as it lapped in over the golden sands. Gradually happiness got through to Elizabeth. Then her heart beat wildly with the joyous hooves of horses from the racing stables, as the sound of them thudded through the still air. She was filled to overflowing with gratitude. It was as if she'd just been given a reprieve from a death sentence. She had never felt so glad to be alive, to be young, to be free, and to be herself. Her period became heavy and painful but she didn't care, she was so grateful. The gratitude was a kind of excitement and the excitement brought colour to her cheeks.

'That's better,' Nanny remarked with satisfaction when she returned to the house. 'Now eat up your breakfast and no more of this picky nonsense.'

It was the first decent meal she'd been able to eat for weeks and she thoroughly enjoyed a bowl of porridge and cream followed by a salty kipper then toast and Cook's home-made grapefruit marmalade. Nanny couldn't wait to report to Christina and Adam Monkton that it was just as she'd said, all Elizabeth had needed was a holiday and a good breath of fresh air.

On Sunday after a breakfast of Ayrshire bacon, eggs, sausages and fried bread, Jason went fishing, and Adam, Christina, Nanny, Elizabeth and Charlie packed into the car and drove the two miles to the cottage where Robert Burns was born. Nanny in the back seat, dressed as usual in her severe buttoned-up navy coat and navy hat pulled well down, played a phonetic game of I Spy with Charlie. Adam and Christina talked about the renovation of some property that Christina had just bought. Elizabeth, still enmeshed in the extreme throes of gratitude, gazed out of the car window as if hardly able to credit the loveliness of the wide blue expanse of sea, then the green shelter of Rozelle Woods.

When they reached the village of Alloway they visited one of the most famous cottages in the world. It sat under a low thatched roof, its white walls sparkling in the sun, and nearby was the museum.

Elizabeth read Robert Burns's love poems and songs and felt deeply moved, especially by

> Ae fond kiss and then we sever
> Ae fareweel and then for ever . . .

It reawakened her feelings for Jack Dawson and her pain at losing him. Her emotions had gone out of control, and with them her imagination. She remembered what it was like to be held in Dawson's arms. She wanted, longed, ached to be held in them once more. There were times when, trembling at the wickedness of her thoughts, she told herself that she *could* be with him again. All she needed to do was say the word. The chances were he would make a visit to the school in his capacity as HMI. How could she not warm to him, agree to meet him again? She visualized their secret reunion. She experienced the thrill of it.

Safe in the knowledge that she'd had her period she even wished she had been pregnant, that she'd had part of Jack Dawson inside her. She imagined having his baby. She heard him telling her that she had no need to worry, that he would leave his wife and look after her.

For the rest of the holiday, while helping build sandcastles for Charlie or telling him stories, while walking, while going for drives in the car, she secretly dreamed of being with Dawson.

There was only one occasion when she was spurred from her reverie.

They had all been going to the theatre – all that is except Nanny and Charlie. Then suddenly, for no apparent reason the outing was cancelled.

'But why?' Elizabeth asked. 'You've got the tickets and everything.'

Christina lit a cigarette and said coolly, 'We decided that the programme wasn't suitable for you and Jason.'

Jason shrugged. 'Well, the Gaiety's not my taste. I'd rather go to a concert or spend some time fishing. But why not let Elizabeth go if she's so keen?'

Elizabeth's heart warmed to him. He had always tended to be dreamy and distant, but of her three half-brothers he was the one who was most sensitive towards her.

'She's not going and that's that,' Father said.

All Elizabeth's frustrated emotions latched on to the unfairness of this situation. It gave her a more immediate focus for her distress.

'You're always telling me I should grow up. How can I grow up if you keep treating me like a child?'

'Trust us,' Adam said. 'We have your best interests at heart.'

'But what's wrong with the programme?' Elizabeth wanted to know.

'You're just not going, I said.' Adam lifted a newspaper and flicked it open as a barrier between them.

Elizabeth experienced heart-thumping anger. It seemed so unfair. Surely she was at least entitled to an explanation. Next day she studied the variety bill posted outside the theatre. A comedian, burlesque instrumentalists, a female vocalist, mechanical marionettes, apache dancers, sketch artistes, a juggler. She could not imagine what was supposed to be unsuitable in any of these acts unless the comedian was outrageously vulgar. Nanny abhorred vulgarity and could have influenced the decision. But surely the comedian wasn't that bad otherwise he wouldn't be allowed to perform. Anyway, how did Nanny or Mother and Father know, when they hadn't been to the show? Another thing, she was a grown woman now, not a child. She ought to be able to make her own decisions. She had some money and, on a reckless impulse, bought a ticket for the matinée. Feeling more like a criminal than the independent woman she was longing to be, she went into the theatre, glancing furtively around as if afraid somebody might recognize her. Her seat was in the gods – all that she could afford – but she had a good view of the stage. She was wickedly excited now, ready to secretly enjoy herself, determined to prove that forbidden fruits were always sweeter.

CHAPTER 13

It was hot high up in the gods, the seats were hard and seemed tipped uncomfortably forward. Nevertheless Elizabeth enjoyed the show. She couldn't fathom what her parents could find objectionable in it. The comedian's jokes were a bit rude at times, but harmless, surely. The worst the female vocalist produced was the verse:

> Oh Flo, what a change you know,
> When she left the village she was shy
> But alas and alack,
> She came back
> With a naughty little twinkle in her eye.

She came to the conclusion eventually that it must be the apache dancers. She could well imagine Nanny seeing something wicked about them. The act, even the setting, was different from all the others. The stage was darkly lit with the background a painted Parisian street scene. On the stage were a table and chairs, as outside a Parisian café, and a street lamp. The act consisted of two dancers – a man with a lean hard-looking body dressed in tight-fitting trousers, striped tee-shirt, scarlet necktie and black beret. His eyes were deeply set over a strong beak of a nose. The woman had a riot of thick ebony hair and flashing black eyes in a tanned, rivetingly beautiful face. Her body was slim but her breasts were clearly defined under a tee-shirt, and her hips bulged provocatively under a too-tight black satin skirt. The skirt was slit at one side to reveal most of a shapely leg in a black fishnet stocking. Like the man, she too wore a beret and scarlet neckerchief.

Elizabeth had no doubt that Nanny and her parents,

especially her mother, would consider this woman, and the way she was dressed, the height of vulgarity.

They would entirely miss the fact that the dancers were terrific performers. Elizabeth was filled with admiration at how the dance alternated so realistically between passion and anger. One minute they were locked in embrace, the woman's leg wrapped around the man's hip, her back arched until her dark head almost touched the floor. The next minute the man had discarded her, flung her to the ground, where she clung to his leg and was dragged across the stage.

There was a strong sexual element in the act and that, more than anything else, would have offended Nanny, although Elizabeth still couldn't fathom how Nanny or Mother and Father knew if they hadn't seen the act. Unless, of course, they'd seen it on some previous occasion. That had to be the explanation.

She emerged, blinking, from the cool shadows of the theatre, into the bright glare of sunlight. Couples were strolling along arm in arm, the girls in floral cotton dresses that flattered the soft curves of their bodies. Nanny frowned on bright colours and anything that might be construed as attractive and 'a temptation to men'. As a result Elizabeth was wearing a navy double-breasted suit with a white handkerchief-linen blouse and a grey felt hat banded with navy. She did have a few pretty dresses, thanks to Mother's insistence, but so strong was Nanny's influence she felt self-conscious, even vaguely guilty at wearing them.

She decided to have a walk around the town before returning home and perhaps have a cup of tea somewhere. No doubt Mother and Father would be at the races – Ayr was the racing town of Scotland – and Nanny and Charlie, and probably Jason too, would have had their tea by now.

As she walked she took deep breaths of the clean salty air in which seagulls circled and noisily squawked.

She felt depressed and the sight of so many happy holiday couples did nothing to raise her spirits. She felt more alone in the busy High Street than she did sitting by herself in her room. She was suddenly terrified she'd shame herself by weeping, and told herself she was being a fool to miss Dawson. He was at home with his wife where he belonged. She must put him out of her mind. Yet that night in bed she shed copious tears, so acute was her longing, so much did she ache for him.

Even after she'd returned to Glasgow with the family, although outwardly physically fit as a result of long bracing walks and sea air, she still felt heart-sore. Soon it seemed as if they had never been away. Although, because she was not due back at Jordanhill until September, her normal routine had not yet been re-established. Nanny could always supply a piece of sewing or knitting to keep idle hands busy, though it was different of course if Elizabeth was studying. Nanny also insisted that at least one hour every day must be spent at her books. In her blue starched uniform dress she sat opposite Elizabeth at the nursery table busily knitting a pair of socks for one of the boys, or sewing buttons on their shirts. The coal fire, behind its wall of metal fireguard, energetically crackled and sparked. Even in August it could become cool enough for a fire, much to Flossie's chagrin. One of the nursery maid's jobs was to light the fire and keep it going.

Flossie was a small frizzy-haired busty girl with a dramatic turn of mind, much addicted to lurid serial stories in magazines and murder trials in newspapers. There was nothing she enjoyed more than relating to Nanny or Elizabeth the dramatic or gory details of whatever she had been reading. Talking of such things in front of Charlie was strictly forbidden but Elizabeth suspected Nanny quite enjoyed Flossie's bug-eyed stories. Although of course her tight, disapproving mouth would never admit to such a weakness.

Half the time Elizabeth didn't listen. She believed she was beginning to get a grip of her emotions. She had stopped shedding nightly tears into her pillow. She no longer made secret pilgrimages to where she and Dawson used to meet or had been together. Never again, she assured herself, would she sit about in the Regal Cinema choking with emotion at a ridiculously sentimental film. Then, unexpectedly, she bumped into Dawson in Sauchiehall Street.

'Darling.' The word had a sad, slightly accusing ring to it as if he was blaming her for everything that had happened.

'How are you?' Elizabeth enquired.

'I miss you.' He gazed down at her, his eyes deeply questioning.

'Back to work soon,' she began to chatter, 'and before I know it, it'll be my exams. I hope I get a job. They say that too many girls will be left without one. They say it can sometimes take years to get a place.'

'My car's in for a service,' he interrupted, 'so we can't go for a drive, but let's at least find somewhere for a cup of tea and a talk.'

They went into the nearest place which happened to be Daly's. A palm court orchestra was playing – 'Smoke Gets in Your Eyes'.

Elizabeth kept feverishly asking herself what she was doing there. At the same time her brain was registering how dashing her tall companion looked in his grey flannels, navy-blue blazer and neatly tied cravat tucked inside his open-necked shirt.

'I've never stopped thinking about you, Elizabeth. I've ached to be with you, to hold you, to . . .'

'Please . . .'

'I can't help it. Surely you feel the same.'

She couldn't deny it and he put a finger under her chin and tipped her face up, forcing her eyes to meet his.

'We love each other. Surely that can't be wrong? I'm

111

so miserable without you, darling. Please say we can meet again. I'll try once more for a divorce. I'll plead with my wife. I'll humiliate myself, go down on my knees, anything to be free of her.'

Elizabeth's face was pale with worry under the darkness of her fringe. 'That doesn't seem right either. I don't want to be responsible for breaking up your marriage.'

'Darling, I've told you before – my marriage was finished long before I met you. There's nothing between Donna and me any more.'

She gazed at him with anxious eyes. Putting a name to his wife had made her more human, a real person. 'Are you sure? You're not just saying that?'

Gently he lifted her hand from the table and kissed it, making her blush so hotly even her ears tingled.

'Elizabeth, I love you.'

The touch of him brought back the time they'd made love; the intimacy, the rapture, the wickedness of it.

He pressed her fingers between his. 'We must see each other again. Next Wednesday, usual place, usual time? Please say yes.'

She thought afterwards that if he hadn't touched her she might have been able to resist his plea but the contact with his warm skin was too much for her. For the next few days she floundered between excitement generated by erotic dreams and the knowledge that they were about to come true, and furtiveness generated by guilt at deceiving Nanny and Mother and Father. If they only knew, she kept thinking, and trembling.

She was longing to unburden herself to Jessie when they went on Saturday to Crawford's tearoom in Argyle Street. It was one of their favourite meeting places. Jessie revelled in its scarlet and gold decor and sparkling white napkins. 'This is like another world from my place,' she'd say.

Usually they had an afternoon of looking at the

112

shops, then tea at Crawford's, then the pictures. Tonight they were going to see Jean Harlow in what had been advertised as the picture of the year – *Dinner at Eight*. Both girls were looking suitably smart as they always did on those Saturday outings. Elizabeth wore her maroon-coloured suit with its fashionable leg-of-mutton sleeves. A little cloche hat with a turned-back brim trimmed in pink made a soft frame for her short black hair. Jessie was more flamboyant in turquoise, and a trilby with its brim tilted down over one eye.

Elizabeth ordered steamed haddock in white sauce with peas, unconsciously choosing this because it was what Nanny would have approved of. Jessie wolfed into steak pie and chips in between chatting about the clothes and jewellery they had admired but not bought in the various shops they'd been wandering around.

Then suddenly Jessie cried out, 'Oh here, you'll never guess who I saw the other day.'

'Who?'

'That big thin guy you were so potty about.'

'Jack Dawson?' For a moment Elizabeth teetered on the verge of saying that she'd also met him the other day but Jessie rushed on.

'Bold as brass. He even raised his hat and said good evening to me.'

Elizabeth shrugged. 'Well, why not? He must have remembered you from the school. He visited your class, didn't he?'

'I suppose. But it didn't seem right. I felt like murdering the rat.'

Elizabeth laughed. 'I appreciate your loyalty, Jessie, but isn't that going a bit far?'

'Well it was seeing his wife like that. I suppose it must have been his wife. She was hanging on to his arm, and obviously pregnant.'

'Pregnant?' Elizabeth's face sagged with shock.

113

'Not a bad-looking girl. She was wearing one of these new hats with an eye veil. I wonder if we'd suit one of them? Elizabeth, are you still with me? You've gone all glazed-looking. I bet you haven't heard a word I've said.'

Elizabeth's mouth twisted and her voice acquired a bitter edge. 'Oh, I heard you all right.'

CHAPTER 14

Elizabeth was sent to a school in the Townhead district. Townhead with its warren of grim tenements, she discovered, was the most ancient part of Glasgow. It was dominated by the huge black Royal Infirmary in Cathedral Square, which had been opened in 1794 and several times extended. The infirmary even dwarfed the cathedral which was situated to the east of the square.

Sloping up the back of the cathedral and stretching out to the side was the ancient burying ground of the city – the Necropolis.

Elizabeth shuddered. She was very sensitive to atmospheres and the history of the ancient Townhead district fascinated her yet made her feel sad.

The tenements that crowded in and around the area, blackened by soot, were becoming a familiar sight to her, being little different from many she'd already seen in Govan.

One of the first jobs she was given in Townhead was to make out a list of ailments for the school nurse. In the part which stated 'Condition noted' she was instructed to use simple euphemisms like 'head', 'ears', 'eyes', 'nose' or 'general'. 'Head' meant that nits or lice had been detected. 'Ears' could indicate an unpleasant pus similar to that of 'nose'; 'eyes' could mean red, crusted or squint; 'general' meant that the child needed delousing and an all-over scrub.

Before the morning was over Elizabeth found herself scratching frantically at different points of her anatomy and longed to be back home in order to delouse herself and soak in a bath liberally laced with Dettol.

Miss Thornton was the regular teacher of primary

three. A tall, flat-chested woman with salt and pepper hair, she informed Elizabeth with brittle brightness, 'It's part of the job. I have to have a bath every night as soon as I get home. My parents used to complain about me using up all the hot water. Now I'm on my own and it doesn't matter.'

The staff room was even worse than the one in Govan, a depressing hole painted dark brown and smelling of dust. Someone had already boiled the kettle on the gas ring and a chipped enamel teapot was filled with equally dark brown tea.

Elizabeth made a brave attempt to eat her sandwiches and drink a cup of the tarry brew. But it was more than she was capable of to add to the crescendo of chatter about what had happened to everyone during the holidays.

She hadn't got in touch with Dawson to cancel their meeting that evening. If she'd phoned it might have been his wife who answered. Although it would have served him right, she thought bitterly, if she did have a talk with his wife. But what good would that do? What was the use of upsetting a woman she'd never even met? No, the only thing was to stand up Dawson. She took no pleasure in the thought. Despite her bitterness, she still loved him. She could not lightly give up love. So great was her need in fact part of her still believed they would meet again. She could not wrench herself away from living in her imagination.

Back in the classroom after lunch she was dragged from her reverie by the sound of Miss Thornton chastising a particularly neglected-looking little boy in ragged Parish trousers, frayed jersey and dirty bare feet. The harshness of the teacher's voice and the way she was dragging him out of his seat by his ear made Elizabeth wince.

'Dirty, stinky little tyke!' Miss Thornton's voice had almost reached screaming pitch. 'Get out. Get out of

116

this class. Go and fetch the janitor. Ask him to come and clean it up. I've had enough cleaning up after you.'

Elizabeth remembered from the list of names on the register that the child was called Tommy McGilvery. Skinny and grey-faced with scabby, shaven head and big frightened eyes, he looked as if he'd never known anything else but angry voices and rough treatment.

After Miss Thornton had literally flung him from the room the door clattered shut and she turned stiff-faced to Elizabeth.

'I'm so sick of that boy. I'm sick of telling him. Over and over again I've told him all he needs to do is put up his hand and say if he needs to go to the toilet. But does he? No, he does not. He just sits there time after time and makes a stinking mess of the place. As if all the other smells weren't bad enough without the stench of urine.'

Elizabeth could sympathize with Miss Thornton on the subject of smells. The classroom even at the best of times stank to high heaven. Even when the 'spray bath' van came and the children were scrubbed, their filthy clothes had to be put on them again and the heat from their clean bodies seemed to make the stench worse instead of better. It was stomach-turning and a very difficult atmosphere to work in. Elizabeth made a mental note to add 'bladder' to the list for the nurse. She felt sorry for Tommy, indeed for all of the children. Miss Thornton seemed unduly hard on them. Although she soon discovered that the thin-lipped, rigid-backed teacher was very good at the job of teaching and had obviously put a great deal of conscientious thought and preparation into her lessons. But she was a stickler for discipline. She demanded absolute silence and unnatural stillness at all times unless when answering a question or raising a hand for the toilet request of 'Please may I leave the room?'

She noticed Elizabeth cringing when she'd given Tommy McGilvery two of the belt, and explained.

'I know how you feel. I used to feel exactly the same. But you'll learn, as I did, that this is the only language they understand. This is a tough neighbourhood and we've got to be tough as well if we're to survive. And we've got to drum the lessons into them to give them any chance of learning.'

Elizabeth gazed at the children in the gloomy dark brown classroom, imprisoned in row after row behind uncomfortable dark brown desks, and was not convinced.

'They might look harmless enough just now, but give them an inch and they'll take a mile,' Miss Thornton assured her. 'That goes for the mothers as well. Some of them would be up here all day and every day if I let them. They come with complaints. They come with family problems. I do my best with those and you'll have to learn to do the same, but there's a limit to what we are able to do. As I say, it's a matter of survival for us as well as for them. Of course the parents you most want to see you've a devil of a job to get hold of.'

'How do you mean?'

'Tommy McGilvery's mother, for instance. He never has a coat to his back or a pair of boots for his feet even in the dead of winter. She could try to get what he needs from the Parish. I sent note after note asking her to come and see me so that I could advise her, but did she come? Not her. I've done everything I could to get that woman organized, I've even called at her home – and that was a ghastly experience, I can tell you – all to no avail.'

'I wonder why she's like that?' Elizabeth was still affected by her psychology lessons. 'Was she in her turn a neglected child and because of her own lack of love . . .'

'Oh, you can forget all that,' Miss Thornton interrupted. 'There's too much theory taught at Jordanhill. Then they fling us straight into places like this and we haven't a clue. I was the very same. I had to learn the hard way and so will you.' She firmly secured a couple of hairpins that were threatening to escape from the bun at the nape of her neck. Then, after tugging up the high collar of her starched white blouse, she added, 'You can start right now. I've a meeting with the headmaster. I'll leave you in charge of the class.'

Elizabeth didn't feel unduly worried in the face of the incredibly good behaviour of the assembled children. They were like wooden dolls with hardly a blink of the eyelids between them. Even because of this, she felt sorry for them. It wasn't natural, surely, for children to be so still and quiet.

She smiled tentatively at them after Miss Thornton had left.

'We'll have some storytelling and drawing now, shall we?'

She was immediately taken aback by the unexpectedly enthusiastic and protracted yells of 'Ye-e-es'. It took her some considerable effort to make her next words heard above the din. She hadn't realized that the children were only too well aware of the difference between a student and a 'real' teacher.

'I'll need two of you to give out the paper and pencils.'

This was her second mistake. Most of the class, certainly most of the boys in the class, struggled from their desks and literally fought their way down the aisles to reach the front.

It took shouting at the top of her voice and a determined stance in front of the cupboard, arms and legs stretched wide, to put a stop to the turmoil.

'Get back to your seats at once — all of you!'

Once comparative order was restored she chose one of the girls who had remained sitting and Tommy McGilvery to distribute the paper and coloured pencils. Tommy flushed with pleasure at this honour and Elizabeth noticed his hands trembled as he handed each pupil a sheet of paper. At Jordanhill she'd been taught that the type, size and colours of paper or other material for a specific purpose should be chosen by the child. The aim of the teacher should be to help the child to make decisions. Lists of available materials had been given – clay, Plasticine, papier-mâché, cloth, strong wool, cardboard, mosaics of pebbles, beads, buttons, toy-making felt. The Jordanhill list had been endless. Here, however, there was only one size of paper and pencils. There was also a buzz of talk but Elizabeth managed to quell it and draw the class's attention to herself by loudly calling out that she was going to tell them a story about a little boy and girl who went on a visit to the zoo. After the story they'd all draw an animal. She began the story by roaring like a lion, which greatly surprised and intrigued the children. She acted the parts of the little boy and girl characters, and all the animals they met at the zoo, so that the story became a dramatic living experience. The concentration, energy and imagination needed to keep the attention of the class banished all thoughts of Dawson from her mind, and she didn't only capture their attention, she riveted it. Her talent for telling stories, and the practice she'd had with Charlie, stood her in good stead.

It was only after school when she was travelling home that her mind filled with pain once more. It had been raining and the wet heavy air added to her depression of spirits.

In the nursery she ate her evening meal automatically, thankful for Flossie chatting to Nanny and taking up Nanny's attention with hair-raising details about a recent murder case.

'They'll hang her,' Flossie prophesied dramatically, 'as sure as my name's Flossie.'

'Maybe so,' Nanny said, smartly gathering up the plates. 'And maybe she deserves to be punished. But it's unhealthy to gloat over such things. Take these dirty dishes down to the kitchen. Daisy will be waiting for them.'

After Flossie had bustled away downstairs Nanny said, 'If that girl wasn't so good with Charlie and so biddable into the bargain I'd give her her walking ticket.'

Elizabeth's eye was on the nursery clock.

'Are you going out?' Nanny asked.

Elizabeth shook her head.

'Have you any studying to do?'

'I suppose I could . . .'

'Well, either get your books out or get on with that sock I gave you yesterday.'

Elizabeth chose the books, thinking that they would take up her attention, keep her mind safely occupied. But the words remained dead things on the page. Her head was alive with pictures of Dawson getting ready, getting into his car, driving to meet her, leather-gloved hands loosely leaning on the wheel. With mounting pain she saw him arrive at the Regal to stand gazing around, watching for her. The hands of the clock on the nursery wall moved slowly and relentlessly round. Now he would know it was over, once and for all. But at least he had a partner to go back to. She felt bitterly alone in her misery. Her pain created an intense vulnerability to the pain of others and next day in the classroom she could hardly bear it when Miss Thornton strapped Tommy McGilvery yet again. Admittedly he had been very difficult with his sums and kept making the same mistakes over and over again.

Afterwards, Miss Thornton had to go for another meeting with the head – this time with one of the mothers to discuss another problem child. 'What can we do with this one?' Miss Thornton's pale face was flushed with harassment. 'The child's father is in Barlinnie prison and his big brother's in a remand home.'

Elizabeth went to Tommy McGilvery's desk and spent time beside him helping him to master the counting that he had earlier made such constant mistakes with. Miss Thornton had obviously lost patience with him. This was not surprising when there were forty-nine other children in the class needing her attention and a new headmaster, a blond bombshell of a man dashing about all over the place, not only expecting but demanding splendid results from all of them despite the size of classes. Elizabeth had been told at college that there were Day School Regulations covering the maximum number of pupils but this was something else that didn't work out in practice. Tommy had been nervous but the first time he got one of his sums right she gave him a reward of a Boy Blue Liquorice Nougat and an affectionate hug. This made him so pathetically eager to please her she wasn't sure what had been most important to him, the sweet or the gesture of affection. The child visibly trembled with eagerness.

'I think you're a very clever boy, Tommy,' she told him for good measure.

While she had been concentrating on Tommy, the rest of the class had disintegrated into chaos and she was struggling to quell the riot when Miss Thornton returned. Immediately there was silence — Miss Thornton just needed to stare at them. It was a kind of mass hypnosis. Elizabeth wondered if she would ever master the art. She wasn't good at discipline. She had already discovered that. But she felt she had some better teaching ideas than Miss Thornton.

For reading practice Miss Thornton made the pupils read one after the other about one line each round the class until the story was finished. 'That way,' she explained, 'they all get a chance.' She was also a stickler for keeping the place. Keeping the place obviously became more urgent and important to the pupils than what the story meant. Elizabeth believed that reading should be a matter of understanding rather than elocution. She brought pupils out to read to her individually, so that each could read at his or her own level and rate.

Miss Thornton dismissed this method as unworkable. 'It takes far too long.'

'But we were taught at college . . .'

'I told you – you'll learn more here than ever you did at college.'

In actual fact, all she learned at the school was how to fill in the register. It was 'made up' at the end of the quarter when thousands of attendances were supposed to be entered in their proper columns and enormous calculations of averages and percentages had to be struggled with.

It was only too easy to make mistakes and even one mistake could cause total confusion. Many an extra hour she'd spent after school trying to get it all sorted out.

But it wasn't time for making up the register yet and she had arrived at the tram stop comparatively early. Her thoughts had returned, as too often they still did, to Dawson, when she became aware of a warm, sticky hand slipping into hers. Looking down she saw Tommy McGilvery beside her. She controlled the aversion she felt for his scab-encrusted head and smiled at him.

'Hello, Tommy. Are you waiting for a tram too?'

He shook his head.

'Oh, so you've just come to see me off, have you?'

He nodded.

'Well, thank you, Tommy, that's very kind of you.'

His nose was running but she knew it was no use asking him if he had a handkerchief.

'Your nose is running,' she said, struggling with herself as to whether she should desecrate her own dainty lace-edged scrap of cotton. Before she could come to any decision, however, he had wiped the offending nose on the sleeve of his jersey.

'You've got lovely black hair and black eyelashes to match,' he said, gazing up at her with such adoration

123

that she didn't know whether to laugh or cry. She managed a solemn look of gratitude.

'Thank you, Tommy. Oh, here's my tram. See you tomorrow.'

He stood helplessly watching her as the tram bundled away.

Poor wee boy, she thought. For the rest of the journey she could think of no one else. Not even Jack Dawson.

CHAPTER 15

'Louder! Louder!' Miss Thornton commanded.

The class was practising Christmas carols and the loudness was necessary in order to exercise the lungs in the hope that it would stimulate the circulation of the blood. This was urgently necessary owing to the failure of the hot water to circulate in the pipes that snaked round the classroom. The atmosphere was arctic. Breaths issued from mouths like puffs of steam into the icy air.

All the children had been allowed to keep their coats on after they'd been shaken free of snow, and they'd been instructed to stamp along the corridor en route to the class in order to loosen the snow from their boots and shoes. Nevertheless every seat had a puddle underneath it – making Tommy McGilvery, for once, undistinguishable from the rest. Tommy was now the proud possessor of a pair of boots thanks to the Parish, but helped initially by Miss Thornton reporting Mrs McGilvery to the Green Lady, as the local health visitor was known, and threatening also to report her to the cruelty man. She'd done this on a previous occasion, apparently, when bruises and weals had been distinct on Tommy's body. Apparently there was no Mr McGilvery and Mrs McGilvery drank. Sometimes she didn't appear to collect Tommy after school and he had learned to find his own way home, even crossing busy main roads by himself.

After the carol singing and the Christmas project they were engaged in, the children were asked to tell, each in turn, what Santa was bringing them. Some of the answers were obviously figments of fanciful imaginations

125

and wishful thinking but when it came to Tommy's turn he simply announced:

'He disnae come tae oor hoose.'

'He doesn't come to our house,' Miss Thornton automatically corrected.

Afterwards she said to Elizabeth, 'That woman's a disgrace. But what can we do? It's a hard enough job trying to make something of the children.'

They had done their best to make the school Christmas as pleasant as possible. The school funds did not run to a tree, and teachers' salaries were pathetically inadequate. Nevertheless Elizabeth and Miss Thornton had shared the expense of a small fir and candles with which to decorate it. Helped by the children as part of their Christmas project they'd made coloured paper decorations to brighten the bleak walls of the classroom, and Elizabeth had splashed out on a bag of jelly babies for each of the children. All this extravagance meant she had very little left of her wages at the end of the day. She had, after all, presents to buy for the family and Nanny as well. But she didn't mind. The children needed some colour in their lives and some sort of treat at this time of year to make it feel special.

She worried about what would happen to Tommy McGilvery during the Christmas holidays and expressed her concern to Miss Thornton.

'Oh, he'll survive.' Miss Thornton's mouth tightened. 'He's quite a little hard man already. The only way *we'll* survive is to forget about the whole lot of them during the holidays.' She added as a grim afterthought, 'That includes the Head.'

The new headmaster was proving a sore trial. A man of apparently ceaseless and abounding energy, he was constantly exploding into classes for one reason or another, or no reason at all. Primary three, it seemed, was a favourite target. So much so that the frequency of his visits became a subject of gossip in the staff room.

'I think it's you that's the attraction, Miss Monkton,' Miss Carruthers giggled. It went without saying that it couldn't be Miss Thornton who was older than the headmaster, as stiff as a board from head to toe, and had eyes like rapiers. No man would dare to think romantic thoughts about her.

'Nonsense,' Elizabeth protested. 'It's only that he's keen to see how the children are progressing. He's just a very keen sort of person.'

'Keen about you, you mean. He blushes to the roots of that blond hair of his every time he goes near primary three.'

Elizabeth tutted. 'You know perfectly well he has a highly coloured complexion. He's like that all the time.'

Secretly she had begun to wonder about the frequency of his visits herself and more than once she'd caught him gazing at her with blank sheep's eyes. Each time he'd been caught he'd looked quickly away to fix a bright interested gaze on the rows of children, who looked as if they didn't dare breathe.

The idea that the headmaster might have an unprofessional interest in her made Elizabeth feel apprehensive. Indeed she trembled at the thought of being once more plunged into the mental and physical agonies she'd experienced before. A safe routine had been established now. She attended Townhead School and Jordanhill time about. She was interested in the college lectures. She even enjoyed them, despite their length, the hard seats that had to be endured and the sore fingers suffered as a result of writing so many notes in her neat careful hand. She did not enjoy the hockey in the snow or travelling through thick Glasgow fogs in winter, but then nothing was perfect.

Townhead School certainly was not perfect but she'd become absorbed with the children and their needs. The regularity of little daily routines gave her a sense of security and she had come to realize that despite its difficulties, she had chosen the right profession. It was a satisfying thought and she looked forward hopefully to passing her exam and getting a job.

Any ideas about or suggestions of romance complicated things and upset her. She had reverted to her normal shyness. The episode with Jack Dawson, especially the lovemaking, seemed incredible now. She blushed with guilt and acute distress at the mere thought of her shameful behaviour, and she decided she must have a terrible weakness where men were concerned. It was surely something that had to be conscientiously suppressed and guarded against. Every time the headmaster crashed into the room, hitching his black gown over his Fair Isle pullover and brown tweed trousers, she immediately shrank inside herself. She struggled to empty her mind of all thoughts except observation of Miss Thornton's lesson, or teaching a lesson herself.

It wasn't that she particularly disliked the headmaster. Everyone, even Miss Thornton, admired his energy, his enthusiasm, his almost boyish optimism, although not everyone agreed with his methods.

It was some time after the Christmas holiday and not long before she had to leave Townhead School that the headmaster made his first unprofessional move. Elizabeth was walking towards the tram stop in Castle Street when the headmaster's car drew alongside her. His ruddy face creased into a grin.

'I'm going your way. I'll give you a lift.'

Elizabeth didn't know what to say. She wished there was a magic wand that could make her disappear. Getting a tram straight home was no problem. Should she tell him this? Or that she didn't want to trouble him? She couldn't very well say, 'Go away! I don't want anything to do with you.'

Already he had leapt from the car and was holding the door open. 'No problem. Hop in.'

She felt harassed as he grabbed her elbow, levered her inside, then banged shut the door. In a matter of seconds he had thumped down on to the driving seat beside her and they were off.

'So you'll soon be leaving us,' he announced as the car careered along at what felt like a rash and careless speed.

'Yes,' she said, eyeing the road ahead with some trepidation.

'Then it'll be your exams.'

'Yes.'

'Then another school.'

'If I'm lucky enough to get a job.'

'You'll make a good teacher eventually. Just as well you want to teach in primary, though.'

What did he mean 'eventually', she thought with indignation.

'Why?'

'A bit on the timid side for secondary. Liable to make mincemeat of you.'

She stiffened. She suspected he was right. However, she informed him in a polite voice, 'I believe I would be perfectly capable of coping with older children.'

His loud guffaw filled the car. 'That's the spirit!'

As she lowered her eyes she noticed his big hard-looking thighs encased in the coarse brown tweed. She hastily averted her gaze and looked out the side window, wishing she'd been left in peace. She enjoyed the tram journey and the quiet walk along Queen's Drive after she alighted. At school there were such noisy crowds of people all the time.

The headmaster's hands restlessly tapped at the steering wheel. 'What do you do with yourself after school hours?'

'I study.'

'Of course, your exams.' Then after a moment, 'But not all the time, surely?'

She groaned inside. Any minute now he was going to ask her out. Why was this happening to her? Was it because she was the youngest member of staff? Or that she wasn't actually a member of staff like the others? It surely wasn't because of her teaching methods. He obviously didn't think all that much of them. It surely couldn't be because of her looks. There were some other very pleasantly attractive teachers at the school.

'Not all the time, eh?' the headmaster repeated.

'Well, no . . .' Why couldn't she just tell a lie, she asked herself. But lies never came easily or quickly enough to her.

'There's a lecture in the uni next Friday. "Future Methods in Primary Education". Thought you might be interested.'

'Oh yes?' she murmured vaguely.

'Next Friday's your last day isn't it?'

'Yes.'

'Well then.'

She remained silent.

'Pick you up at seven,' he said cheerfully. 'Lecture starts at half past.' He grinned round at her and she gave him a harassed smile in return. She had never been any good at, indeed had never even had the temerity to think of, fighting authority.

At Monkton House he leapt out of the car and had raced round to fling open the door for her before she had time to put her hand on the handle.

'There we are,' he announced, 'delivered safe and sound.'

In helping her out he almost lifted her off her feet. 'Don't forget . . .' He gave her a wave and returned to the driving seat. 'Put next Friday in your diary.' The car shot off, leaving her still standing at the pillared gates of the house.

'Oh dear!' she tutted to herself. She couldn't understand it. Later in her bedroom she examined her reflection in the wardrobe mirror. She couldn't for the life of her see anything that would make any man attracted to her, although Jessie said she must be daft not to.

'I'd give my eye teeth', Jessie said, 'to have your smooth glossy hair instead of this thick mop that insists on standing up on end all the time. And look at how slim you are and what a good pimple-free skin you have. You should be down on your knees thanking your lucky stars.' She'd let out a howl of laughter. 'They say most teachers end up as old maids. I bet you won't! I won't either. Not if I can help it!'

Elizabeth didn't want to end up an old maid. She had vague romantic dreams of being married and having children of her own one day, but in the very far distant future. Meantime she just wanted to get on with her career. When she did dream of romance it was very vague indeed, and always with someone tall and slim and elegant.

The reality of any man, especially such a solid masculine man like the headmaster, making sexual overtures to her was frightening.

Jessie enthused when she heard about the headmaster. 'And he's got a car as well! How lucky can you get? No ordinary teacher can ever afford a car. There's not even many headmasters have one. I'm telling you, you're born under a lucky star.'

'Some lucky star! What about Jack Dawson? He turned out to be married.'

'Och, but I bet it was fun while it lasted. Think of all the times he treated you to the pictures, and for runs in his car. Look on the bright side. There's worse things happen in China.'

Elizabeth wished she could take things as lightly and cheerfully as Jessie. But try as she might she could not look forward to Friday with anything but panic.

To make the day even more upsetting, when Miss

Thornton announced to the class that this was Miss Monkton's last day at the school, she saw tears fill Tommy McGilvery's eyes. It occurred to her then that in all probability she had been the only person in his young life who had ever said a kind word to him. It had been a wrench to leave the place and all the children, but Tommy in particular. Now she just wanted to go quietly home to lick her wounds.

Instead she had to hurry and get ready for the headmaster coming. She put on her soft lavender wool suit and grey chenille beret with the lavender pattern on top that Nanny had crocheted her for Christmas. Grey leather gloves and handbag completed the outfit. She took a quick glance in the mirror. Her eyes were huge, peeking apprehensively out from beneath the ends of her fringe.

The headmaster was loudly ringing the doorbell. Sarah was letting him in.

'Oh dear,' Elizabeth tutted. But she had no option but to go downstairs and face him.

CHAPTER 16

The overture ended with a flurry of cymbals and a final roll of tymps. The musical director turned to face the spotlights and took a bow. Backstage the stage manager flicked the switch that sent the heavy plum house tabs or curtains swirling up. A haze of dust was caught by the spotlights as they panned up and across to where the chorus girls waited tense and silent. Lighting dimmers slid to full up. The band struck the first few bars and the satin front runners shimmered in the reflected footlights as they opened.

Annalie, later joined by Carlino, watched the show from the wings. It was Monday and the first night of a new run, and she liked to be ready early. She was always too restless and keyed up at a time like this to sit waiting in the dressing room listening to the show over the Tannoy. She was not alone in her first-night tensions. Other performers waited in the shadow of the wings, each alone with his nerves and his secret hopes and fears. There was a story of how Beatrice Lillie always stayed in the wings to watch the other turns when she was playing in revue and every night her dresser had to drag her by the ears to her room with barely enough time to change and be back on the stage for her number. Annalie supposed people in the audience would have been surprised to see some of the performers waiting in the wings. One man was smoking a cigarette and attempting to read a newspaper. Another woman, in glittering costume, was knitting a pair of socks. There was also the flurry of dressers tearing costumes off and on performers in between acts.

Annalie always found it hard to reconcile herself to

the difference between the two sides of theatre. On the public side the brightly lit plushly curtained stage, the gilt-adorned chandelier sparkling in the auditorium. On the artistes' side, feebly lit draughty corridors and coldly echoing stairs leading down to sordid airless cells of dressing rooms and filthy lavatories. She felt the same resentment and anger at these conditions as she'd long ago felt for housing conditions in the Gorbals. She'd managed to stir up other women's anger there for a time to such an extent that they'd followed her in protest marches. They'd attacked the factor and prevented evictions. They'd had rent strikes which succeeded in freezing the rents and stopping the unfair increases that no one could afford to pay.

But in the theatre, although everyone agreed in private that conditions were atrocious and many grumbled about them, few were willing to *do* anything. Unemployment was too frightening a spectre. Too many artistes were happy and grateful to get a booking anywhere, at any price and in any conditions. Annalie was well aware of the difficulty in getting bookings. She and Carlino had been luckier than some but they too had their difficulties and 'resting periods'. There had also been problems in trying to change their act to flamenco dancing. They'd had a couple of chances but on both occasions the management had told them that the apache routine had much more appeal for audiences and that was the only one that would be of interest in the future.

She'd even tried to get an engagement as a solo turn, also without success. She'd met Maurice Rutherford for a drink a couple of times. She'd also climbed the stairs to his office more than once.

On each occasion he'd sadly shaken his head. 'Sorry, my dear, I've nothing for you. I've tried and I'll keep trying, but so far no luck.'

The money that any of the artistes were paid was not commensurate with the nervous tension, the insecurities, the energy needed for the job as well as the working conditions backstage. But there was more to the job than the money or the working conditions.

There was the eager thumping of the heart. There was the smell of the naked timber of the set. There was the excitement of listening to the audience before the show started, a sustained sound like the corporate vitality of a mass of insects swelling in intensity by the minute. There was the knowledge that each audience was another peak to conquer. There was the rush of adrenaline. Then the terror and the thrill of being the object of hundreds of pairs of eyes. And finally, the joyous thunder of applause.

The dancers came streaming off now and Janice Smith, The Little Nightingale, stood ready for her turn. She was a pretty dark-haired girl of around twenty, almost the same age as Elizabeth must be now, Annalie thought wistfully. She wondered what she looked like and what she was doing. Hardly a day passed that she did not think of her daughter with pain and longing. Often she'd been tempted to try to find out something about her. Once she'd gone as far as to loiter in Queen's Drive in the hope she might catch a glimpse of her. One Sunday she'd sat on various benches in Queen's Park, hoping she'd see the family having their after-lunch stroll. But she hadn't stayed long after the panicky thought occurred to her that they might see *her*. She had no desire to be noticed by Adam or Christina Monkton, or Elizabeth for that matter. Once she'd caught a glimpse of Christina going into Daly's department store, as elegant as ever in a black cape and black toque with one end hanging down the side of her pale face like a scarf. An expensive-looking pearl choker glistened round her neck. Annalie had been glad that Christina hadn't noticed her then. She had been looking anything but elegant, rushing to rehearsal wearing a shabby Burberry and a pull-on felt hat over her

135

thick curly hair. She certainly wouldn't have wanted Elizabeth to see her. No doubt Elizabeth would be like Christina, elegant and ladylike. Perhaps Elizabeth was married by now. She imagined her in a beautiful villa of her own with a handsome wealthy man to take care of her. This thought gave Annalie strength and comfort and made her all the more certain that she'd done the right thing in giving up all rights to her child.

The Little Nightingale was singing her last song. It gave a deeply evocative picture that reminded the audience of the hard times that were with them just around the corner.

> It's the poor that helps the poor
> When poverty knocks at the door . . .

After The Little Nightingale, on bounced and tumbled the Ravelli Troupe, the kings of the double and treble somersaults.

Watching them Annalie felt Carlino's hand slide over her waist. She knocked it off and glared round at him.

'How many times must I tell you?'

He shrugged. 'I only placed an innocent hand on your waist.'

'Don't make me laugh.'

She'd long since learned not to trust Carlino in anything. Especially she did not trust his mock innocence, the raising of the brows, the wheedling smile. She'd gone out alone with him a couple of times for supper after the show and everything had seemed all right on the surface. But looking back now she realized she'd always felt a glimmer of unease in his company. Then one night he'd tried to make love to her. At first her passionate nature had been aroused but very soon she realized what she might be unleashing. The sadism she'd recognized during the apache dance was now showing itself in the way he grabbed her hair and jerked

136

her head back, in the way his fingers were painfully digging into her flesh, in the way his lips were bruising hers. She'd fought free of him, run into her house and banged the door shut. For a few minutes she'd leaned her back against the door, unable to move she was trembling so much. She hadn't gone out alone with him again, but on tour when they were in the same digs it was difficult to steer clear of him. More than once he'd tried to get into her bedroom and she'd had to move furniture against the door before going to bed, if there wasn't a key.

Over and over again she'd told him and in no uncertain terms that, apart from professionally, she wanted nothing to do with him. Indeed if she could get any solo engagements she would have nothing to do with him professionally either. But he never gave up. He pestered her ceaselessly, brushing against her, touching her. It was more than just a case of wanting sex with her. He was enjoying tormenting her in every way he could. On and off the stage he harassed her, never gave her a minute's peace. Sometimes she felt so desperate to be free of him she contemplated leaving show business altogether. Then she'd see the length of the dole queues and realize that the chances were she wouldn't be able to get another job of any kind anywhere.

If they'd been able to get engagements as flamenco dancers it would have been more bearable. The apache dance routine was so passionate, so intimate and Carlino took advantage of, made the most of, every touch, every body contact. He had come to dominate her life. Even when she did manage to escape from him for a few hours the thought of having to dance with him again continued to torment her.

Sometimes she'd think she was free of him for a few precious hours. She'd be wandering down the main street of a strange town window-shopping and wondering if she could afford to have a bite to eat in a café rather than go back to the digs. Then she'd see Carlino's reflection behind her in the shop window. He'd been following her. She could have killed him. The longing to be free of him obsessed her. But far from leaving her alone, he was insinuating himself more and more into every corner of her life.

It was because of Carlino more than anything that she had stopped trying to find out about Elizabeth. One day someone had bumped into her as they were leaving the theatre and she'd dropped her handbag. The contents had spilled out, including an old photograph of herself and Elizabeth. It had been taken outside the Gorbals paper shop where she'd once worked, and was dated. Carlino had snatched it up before she could stop him.

'Give that to me!' She'd fought to retrieve the photograph but he'd laughed, twisting and turning and holding it out of reach.

'Well, well.' His voice was gleeful. 'So this is your dark secret, darling.'

'Don't be malicious. That's a neighbour's daughter that I sometimes used to look after.'

'Come, come, darling. I'm not blind. That child is your double.'

'You're mad, I'm telling you. She's nothing like me. She hasn't even got my curly hair. Give it back to me at once!'

'It's the eyes, ducky. It's the eyes. She must be about twenty or so now. A stunner, I'll bet, and just ripe for the picking.'

She had gone icy cold with fear. So much so that she couldn't struggle with him for the photo any more. She'd turned away so that he wouldn't see her fear, and busied herself tucking everything else back into her handbag. He'd returned the photo eventually but she'd sensed the gleam of triumph in his eyes without seeing it. She'd known that far from ending this new line of torment he had just begun it.

Since then she'd kept telling herself that she'd nothing to worry about. Carlino couldn't possibly find out about Elizabeth. No way could he learn either where Elizabeth had been when the photo was taken, or where she was now. And even if he did, what could he do? Her fear was stupid and immature and she must be sensible and banish it from her mind. Yet still she felt keenly apprehensive. Often she'd become conscious of Carlino's deeply set eyes under their slash of black brows glittering at her with lascivious glee. There was something different from the usual lustful way he stared at her. His eyes were now telling her that he was thinking lewd thoughts about her daughter. Nonsense! she kept saying to herself. You're letting your imagination run away with you. She was never convinced, however. Fear grew until it turned to hatred. It showed in her eyes as she and Carlino stood together in the wings waiting for their turn to go on.

Each time they were on tour now, she tried to find separate digs from Carlino. For hours she'd lug her suitcase around the town knocking on doors and asking if they took theatricals, all to no effect. The digs were either already booked or they didn't take theatricals. In the latter case the door was usually slammed in her face without as much as a 'sorry'. She was forced to go eventually to the digs that Carlino had booked. Annalie hated sharing digs with him almost as much as dancing with him. It meant passing in the corridor in dressing gowns en route to bathroom or lavatory and suffering his eyes undressing her, sitting at the same table at breakfast and suffering his hand accidentally on purpose brushing against hers as he passed the marmalade, or sitting too close beside her on the settee in the cramped sitting room. And all the time, everywhere there was his needle-eyed stare.

139

Not that she was the only one to be tormented by him. Violet, one of the chorus girls who'd so much admired him, had shared his attention and his flat for a time until she had eventually been tossed out. But not before he had beaten her up on several occasions, although she always denied that he had caused the black eyes and the bruises on her body. She had fallen down the stairs, she said, or walked into a door. After Carlino had thrown her out she'd confessed about the beatings to Annalie, adding tearfully, 'I still love him no matter what he's done.'

'More fool you,' Annalie had said. 'If you want my advice, the quicker you put him out of your mind the better. After all, he's put you out of his.' Then she'd rubbed her fingers through her hair in exasperation. 'I'm sorry if I sound cruel, Violet. It's just, I hate to see you go on suffering like this.'

There had been others as well as Violet, gentle vulnerable girls most of them. They seemed to get younger each time. Recently one girl, a fan, had been barely sixteen. He'd first met her when she'd managed to slip past Bill, the stage-door keeper, to reach Carlino's dressing room and plead for his autograph. He'd made a date to see her afterwards.

Grant Bartholomew and The Great Gavin (Magician Extraordinaire), with whom Carlino shared the dressing room, had been disgusted and warned him that he'd better be careful. They'd even spoken to Annalie about it.

'Carlino might end up in jail because of this one. And serve him right. She's just a child. She's definitely under age.'

Annalie too hoped he would end up in jail, although she was sorry for the girl. But if he was jailed, branded, publicly discredited, found out, it would mean there would be less chance of him ever charming or seducing or causing any harm to Elizabeth.

She rolled eyes at herself in exasperation. She was getting an obsession about Carlino and Elizabeth and there was absolutely no need. They lived in different worlds. She was allowing Carlino to play on her fears, and felt ashamed of her weakness. Normally she was a spunky kind of person, full of cheek and fight and to hell with the consequences.

With a toss of her head and a defiant swagger of hips she left the wings and took her position on the stage ready for the curtain to go up on the fury of the dance.

To hell with him, she thought.

CHAPTER 17

He began to ask, 'When am I going to meet this beautiful daughter of yours then?'

Each time she ignored him, just gave him a disdainful look, but he persisted. Once he said, 'Jealousy, that's your problem, darling. You can't bear me showing the slightest interest in any other woman.'

She laughed without humour. 'What conceit!'

There was no doubt that Carlino had a very high opinion of himself. Even in what he wore he seemed to be shouting to the world, 'Look what an attractive fellow I am.' Sometimes he sported flannels and coloured shirts and blazers with gold buttons and a cap sparkling white against his black hair. Sometimes he boasted a pinstriped suit with natty waistcoat, dashing silk tie or cravat, and a snap-brim fedora.

'You can't pretend with me, darling. You hate it when I indulge in little affairs of the heart.'

'I hate the way you treat women,' she said. 'Your pleasure is in causing them pain, emotionally as well as physically.'

'Darling!' His eyes widened. 'I love women. And you most of all.'

'Well, I have no love for you. Quite the reverse.'

'Ah, but there is a very thin dividing line between love and hate. Especially when accompanied by desire.'

'What desire?' she scoffed.

'You can't fool me, darling. You're a very passionate creature.'

'Not for you.'

He shrugged. 'Who else?'

It was true that there was no man in her life and

had not been for some time. When they weren't touring she tried to spend what little spare time she had between rehearsals and shows with her aging father and with old friends and neighbours in the Gorbals. People like Flo Blair, Mrs Rafferty and Mrs McClusky. The latter had owned the paper shop in which Annalie had once worked for a time. Or at least, the business had been owned by Mr McClusky but he had long since died. After a while Mrs McClusky had sold the shop and retired to her room and kitchen up the close next to the paper shop.

Thinking of Mrs McClusky reminded Annalie that the photograph of her with Elizabeth had been taken by Mrs McClusky outside the shop. The shop had been quite clear in the photo with the street number on the door. Had Carlino noticed that? She knew she was being neurotic but couldn't help imagining Carlino seeking out the shop to ask about her and Elizabeth. The new owners would send him next door to Mrs McClusky who knew everything about what had happened. How Adam Monkton was Elizabeth's father and how Annalie had taken the child to Monkton House. That way Carlino could quite easily find Elizabeth. Annalie struggled to banish the thought, until eventually she decided to do something about it. She went to see Mrs McClusky.

'Come away in, hen,' the old woman greeted Annalie with delight. 'I'm that pleased to see you. It's been a wee while since you've been.' Her ruddy cheeks glowed with pleasure. 'But of course I knew you'd been travelling around. I met your da the other day. He's fairly aging. I thought he looked quite frail. And he was always such a big, strong man.'

She made a pot of tea and put out some iced tea-bread and treacle scones liberally spread with butter.

'I worry about leaving him so often,' Annalie said.

143

'Not that he'll let me do much for him when I'm there. He's very withdrawn nowadays.'

'It must be depressing for you at home now, hen. It can't be the same without your Aunty Murn.'

'I still miss her terribly,' Annalie sighed.

Mrs McClusky chewed at a treacle scone, making the grey hairs sprouting on her upper lip and chin waft about.

'Aye, she was one of the old school, your Aunty Murn.'

'She was a great help to me when I was pregnant and trying to cope with the baby. It was she who found me that single end I had for a while. I was so glad to get away from Mrs Rafferty's.'

'I'm not surprised. Mind you, she's doing much better for herself now. The family help, of course.'

'Getting out of that hellhole she used live in helped more than anything, I bet.'

'I don't know how you stood it down that dunny for as long as you did, hen.'

'I hadn't any choice. Aunty Murn would have let me stay at home but after Daddy threw me out that was it – until Mammy persuaded him to forgive me.'

'Do you never hear from your mammy now?'

'No. She could be dead for all I know. There was no love lost between us after what she did to Elizabeth.'

Annalie hesitated and then said with forced nonchalance, 'Has anyone been asking about me or Elizabeth?'

Mrs McClusky nodded. 'Oh aye.'

'What? Who?'

Annalie's eyes flew wide and she jerked so violently her cup rattled in her saucer and splashed out tea.

Mrs McClusky looked startled. 'What's wrong, hen? Are you thinking it was your mammy? There's no need to worry. Like you, I haven't seen hide nor hair of her for years. No, it was just Mrs Steele and Bella Baxter. And oh, aye – Jeanie Docherty. We often have a wee blether and exchange news about you when we meet in the Co-op or when we're fetching our *Herald*.'

'Oh.' Gradually Annalie relaxed. 'Thank goodness.'

'Mrs Steele's sister was at the theatre in Troon while she was on her holidays. She said you danced great. Here, let me empty your saucer. You gave me quite a turn jumping like that. I don't know why you're needing to bother about your mammy.' She gave a laugh that heaved her fat frame. 'There's no fear of her snatching your lassie away now. Wee Elizabeth can't be that wee any more. She must be − what − twenty?' Her laughter simmered down and she shook her head. 'I was awful fond of that lassie.'

'I still worry about her,' Annalie said.

'I'm sure there's no need, hen. She's well off. I bet she's never wanted for a thing. And give credit where credit's due, that Monkton woman's aye been good to weans.'

'Christina?'

'Aye, she's done a lot for Gorbals weans with her clubs and holiday houses.'

'Yes, I've never had any doubts that I did the right thing by Elizabeth. I felt sure she would always be all right, until recently that is.'

'How do you mean?'

'Well . . .' Annalie laughed in an embarrassed way. 'You'll think I'm just being silly and neurotic, and I expect I am. But you know how I've always been about Elizabeth. I can't help it. Her happiness has always meant everything to me.'

'I know that, hen.'

'Well, you see, this man that I dance with . . .'

'Tony Carlino? Aye, Mrs Steele's sister said he was great as well. But awful rough with you, hen. She said you must be black and blue every night the way he flung you around.'

Annalie felt herself begin to tremble. 'I hate him.'

'Does he really hurt you sore?'

'Yes, but that's not the only reason I feel as I do. He's a terrible womanizer. I mean, he hurts women in other ways as well – not just physically. He's not to be trusted. And recently he saw a photo of me and Elizabeth. Remember that one you took outside the shop not long before I took Elizabeth to Monkton House?'

'Aye, I mind it fine. She looked lovely in that photo. I've got a copy myself and I often look at it. She'll be a lovely-looking young woman now, you can be sure.'

'That's what he thinks. He keeps asking when he's going to meet her. It gives me the creeps. He's such a horrible person, Mrs McClusky.'

There was silence for a minute and then Mrs McClusky said, 'But even if he did decide to look for Elizabeth, hen, even if he did find her, why should she have anything to do with a man like that?'

Annalie's face creased with worry. 'I don't know. As I said, probably I'm just being neurotic and silly. All the same, if you knew him as I do . . . You see, he doesn't look horrible. At least, his looks seem to appeal to a lot of women, or maybe it's the aura of sexuality that the dance gives him. Even out of the theatre he's very flamboyant and theatrical-looking. He wears colourful clothes, snappy hats, a flower in his lapel, that sort of thing.'

'I still don't see, hen . . .'

'He could tell her he knew her real mother. He could stir up all sorts of trouble just for the hell of it.'

'Do you not think you're letting your imagination run away with you a wee bit? You were always a great one for imagining things.'

'I keep trying to tell myself that but I know him, you see.'

'Do you not think he's just trying to torment you by talking about Elizabeth, hen?'

'That would be typical of him, right enough. He enjoys tormenting people.'

'Well, then . . . just ignore him. Don't give him the satisfaction. That's the best way to treat torments, if you ask me.'

'Maybe you're right.'

'And if by any chance he did come around here – but I'm quite sure he wouldn't do any such thing – rest assured I'd give him short shrift.'

Annalie managed a smile. 'Thanks, Mrs McClusky.'

She was glad she made the visit. She felt much the better for it. The acuteness of her anxiety had been soothed. Some of her old bounce returned as she swung along from Mrs McClusky's house to her own close. The old woman was perfectly right. She mustn't let Carlino get her down. He must have been getting a real kick from seeing how worried and anxious she'd been recently. Damn him, she thought. One way or another he'd been a torment to her right from the beginning, because despite his temporary liaisons with other women he'd never stopped making passes at her. She resolved to be free of him. She would go to see Maurice again. She would plead with him to find her a solo spot. She dreaded every performance with Carlino, every tangle of strong emotions as well as the intimate locking of bodies. More and more she felt she could not go on. Every night she had to force herself. She felt trapped. She had never been superstitious like other performers, but now her mind turned to lucky charms to ward off evil. There had been a string of beads Adam Monkton had once given her. Many times long ago she had been happy wearing them. Now she kept them with her all the time. Around her throat or in her pocket, and all the time she fingered them like a rosary. Something had to be done.

CHAPTER 18

Reggie's sister Nance loaned Elizabeth her bike and she and Reggie cycled a lot. Reggie was also a keen rambler. In some ways she quite enjoyed these outings. Nanny said getting out in the fresh air so much was putting colour into her cheeks at last. She'd always been too pale for Nanny's liking.

It was certainly good to get out and around and see a bit of the countryside. But, unlike Reggie, she didn't want to be expending such energy all the time. Reggie Wordsall was as constantly energetic during his leisure hours as he was on duty as a headmaster. She had tentatively suggested that they do something else and he'd cheerfully dragged her off to Edinburgh to listen to a lecture on modern education. This was all very well. She wanted to continue learning as much as she could. Just because she'd passed her exams and left Jordanhill did not mean, as far as she was concerned, that she knew everything there was to know about teaching. But she longed for visits to the cinema and to the theatre. To please her they did go a couple of times but he'd been so fidgety and restless it had spoiled her enjoyment. (He'd been the same at the lecture.) The truth was she didn't really want to go anywhere with him. It wasn't so easy to get out of their regular meetings, however. For one thing he bustled her along at such a rate on his gusts of enthusiasm it was difficult to get the chance to say anything. For another thing, he was basically such a nice man she couldn't bring herself to hurt or disappoint him. He totally enjoyed their outings. She knew this not only by the way he whistled or lustily sang with her trotting breathlessly at his side trying to keep up as he marched along country roads, but also by the bear hugs and kisses he gave her – though kiss seemed too delicate a description for what he subjected her to. The vulgar word 'smacker' was more appropriate, and noisy smackers at that. She really couldn't go on like this. She didn't love him. She suspected that if they went on much longer she wouldn't even like him. She was already having quite severe bouts of irritation. She feared that one day she would be capable of cruelty towards him and that would be most regrettable. He really was a very nice man. He was jolly. (He often made her giggle.) He was honest and kind. (He was always giving his mother and sister noisy smackers as well.) His mother had told her he was the best son in the world. Elizabeth felt the unspoken words were that he'd also make the best husband in the world. But oh, how she longed for somebody different from Reggie. Somebody slim and elegant and artistic and sensitive. Not that Reggie was insensitive. This was proved when she developed a temperature that heralded a sudden bout of flu. He insisted on abandoning their day out on the Campsie Hills and rushed her straight home. He asked Nanny if there was anything he could do and Nanny sent him to the chemist for a tin of kaolin with which to make a poultice for Elizabeth's chest.

'I've always had to be careful with her chest,' she confided, and Reggie willingly and immediately raced off to the chemist. After he'd come back he'd hovered anxiously about, getting in Nanny's way until she had firmly ordered him off the premises.

Elizabeth was quite glad of the flu. At least it gave her a temporary respite from Reggie and a chance to think. To make sure of this she pleaded with Nanny to keep Reggie at bay.

'Even his voice tires me out,' she explained. 'He doesn't mean any harm. It's just the way he is – a terribly energetic man.'

Propped up in her single bed with its white lace-trimmed pillows and bedmat, she felt safe. She could relax and feel content. She loved this room. She gazed in appreciation at the pale wallpaper with its delicate floral print, the pink curtains, the white furniture, the grey rug with its delicate pattern of pink and lavender. A wonderful modernization all over the house had been the introduction of electricity. With the touch of a switch the room could now be bathed in light. There was a bedside lamp within easy reach, which was handy for reading in bed. On the table also sat her teddy bear, legs splayed and arms outstretched. Beside it was propped her rag doll with its blonde pigtails, pretty gingham dress and white lace-edged petticoat and drawers, and a Dutch doll sat on a nearby chair.

Charlie, now a big boy of six and at school, had been moved from Nanny's room to the nursery guest room. He hadn't been at all keen on being on his own at first. Soon, however, he had settled in quite happily with his teddy for company and Elizabeth sitting on a stool beside his bed telling him his favourite stories.

At the moment he was out at the park with Nanny, taking a boat to sail on the pond. William and Daniel were at the swimming baths and Jason was downstairs practising on the piano. The nursery was silent and peaceful.

Elizabeth wondered if the problem with Reggie would resolve itself because the summer holidays were nearly over. He would be going back on duty at Townhead School and she would be starting work in the Hill's Trust School in Govan. She'd always hoped she'd be able to find permanent work in the Gorbals where Mother owned so much property. However, she'd been lucky to get a job at all – lots of girls from Jordanhill hadn't yet been given any school.

But somehow she couldn't feel optimistic. They might not be able to go out during the day but there were always the evenings and weekends. He didn't take a class so he wouldn't have the normal piles of marking to take home. She didn't suppose he even needed to do any preparation work as other teachers did in their so-called spare time. She could always use the preparation of lessons and projects as an excuse. The trouble was, he'd volunteer to help her with her work so that it could be done quickly and allow them to get out and about. She knew him only too well. Nothing daunted him. Nothing was too much trouble.

That evening Jessie arrived with her usual big grin and cheery 'Hallo there!' It was the first time she'd been in the bedroom and she enjoyed a great gust of hilarity at the sight of the teddy and the dolls.

'I might have known you still play with dolls.' Jessie shook her head. 'You look like a doll yourself sitting there.'

'I don't play with them,' Elizabeth protested. 'They're only ornaments. My father brought them from abroad. He'd be offended if I got rid of them.'

The truth was she loved them dearly and even on occasion still cuddled them into bed beside her.

'They're okay,' Jessie conceded. 'I'm just jealous. Are you feeling better? You look great. Pale but interesting, as they say.'

'I'm fine now, thanks. Actually I've quite enjoyed being confined to bed. At least I've escaped Reggie for a wee while.' And she confided the problem of Reggie to Jessie.

'I think you're daft to want rid of him,' Jessie said. 'He's potty about you.'

Elizabeth winced at the 'rid of him' bit. It sounded as if she wanted poor Reggie dead.

'I don't wish him any harm,' she hastened to assure Jessie, 'it's just he's not the one for me. The trouble is, you see, he believes I'm the one for him.'

'He seems such a nice, cheery, kindly man,' Jessie

said. Once she and her current boyfriend, Frank Turner, had gone on a hike with them. Jessie and Frank had been quite at home with back packs and hiking boots, and enjoyed the energetic outing. Elizabeth had stubbornly refused to wear either. She'd carried a basket over her arm and compromised with a pair of flat-heeled school shoes.

'I know he is,' Elizabeth agreed. 'But I'm just not in love with him. It's not fair on him to go on letting him think that . . . that . . . you know . . .'

'You think he's liable to pop the question?'

'One of these days, yes.'

'Oh well, I suppose . . . Seems a shame though.'

'I know. I feel awful. But I can't help it.'

'You that loves security so much. He could give you security. You won't have your precious Nanny for ever. Nor even your mother and father.'

Anxiety showed in Elizabeth's face. The very thought of losing Nanny brought palpitations. She knew her feelings were completely out of proportion but still they kept surfacing from deep inside her like terrifying ghosts. Seeing Elizabeth's eyes widen with anxiety, Jessie laughed.

'For God's sake, Elizabeth, you've got to grow up and stand on your own two feet some time.'

Elizabeth flushed. 'I can stand on my own two feet perfectly well. Nanny's only here now because of Charlie, not because of me. But it's only natural that I'd miss her if she left. I've known her all my life.'

'All right, all right,' Jessie said, 'there's no need to get on your high horse. So what are you going to do about Reggie?'

Elizabeth eyed her friend uncertainly. 'Tell him, I suppose.'

'Best not to shillyshally and beat about the bush,' Jessie advised. 'Give it to him straight – although I can't see you doing it. You're too soft, that's your trouble. You didn't want to go out with him in the first place, did you?'

Miserably Elizabeth shook her head.

'There you are, you see. That's when you should have given him a definite no.'

'You're just making me feel worse.'

'Sorry, pal. But it's the truth, you know it is. You'll have to learn to be more positive and stand up for your rights. You have a right to say no, especially to men.'

Jessie could certainly stand up for herself. Everything about her, from her great frizz of blonde hair, pencilled brows and vivid slash of lipstick, down to her high-heeled, pointed-toe shoes was daring and fearless.

Elizabeth toyed with the idea of writing Reggie a letter, but Jessie immediately shot that one down.

'You couldn't be that cowardly. I don't believe it.'

'I am just wondering if writing would be kinder,' Elizabeth explained with at least a grain of truth.

'No. Facing him, looking him straight in the eye and telling him's the only decent way.'

Elizabeth nodded. 'You're right. Yes, as soon as I'm up and about I'll tell him.'

'Pity,' said Jessie, 'you might go further and fare worse.'

CHAPTER 19

'I'm sorry, Reggie,' Elizabeth said yet again. They were in the car on the way to Monkton House after a day's cycling out to Campsie Glen and then supper at Reggie's, cooked by both Reggie's mother and Nance. It had been rather a heavy meal consisting of heaped plates of beef stew, dough-balls and potatoes, and a pudding of spotted dick. The meal lay like a sack of stones in Elizabeth's stomach and had made it all the more difficult for her to concentrate on what she had planned to say to Reggie. She wanted to break it to him as gently as possible, but hadn't been able to speak to him in private earlier. First of all, the whole of Reggie's cycling club had been with them every minute of the day, swooping through the countryside like a noisy gust of starlings.

Then during supper there had been Mrs Wordsall and Nance, two plump pigeons cooing over them.

It was now or never. So she'd blurted it out in the car. She'd imagined having to argue with Reggie, who'd loudly try to talk her out of her decision, in a good-natured way of course. Reggie was overpowering but not domineering. She'd foreseen that she'd feel awful, she'd been feeling bad enough ever since she'd made up her mind to tell him. What she hadn't reckoned on was the depth of her distress.

The trouble was that Reggie didn't shout and bluster and guffaw and insist she didn't mean it. A second before she'd spoken, his voice had been filling the car with its usual head-splitting volume. She had been amazed that he had heard her soft-spoken words: 'I don't love you, Reggie and I don't want to go out with you again. I'm sorry, but that's how it is.'

He was suddenly silent. His bouncing energy deflated. Even the muscles of his face sagged. Staring helplessly ahead he said nothing. She couldn't bear him being so hurt and sad. Miserably she repeated her apology and when the car reached Monkton House she murmured it again. His hands and forearms rested on the steering wheel as if for support and still he never said anything, never even turned his head to look at her. For a few seconds she was tempted to put her arm comfortingly round his shoulders to tell him she didn't mean it, and everything was all right. Anything to stop his distress, and her anguish at having caused it. She was saved from this rash act by Reggie giving a big sigh and saying:

'I knew it was too good to be true.'

Then from the quiet, vulnerable man of a few minutes before he suddenly did a Jekyll and Hyde transformation to the robust, noisy Reggie she knew and couldn't stand. He bounced from the car, raced round to open her door and heave her out.

'It's been great.' His voice boomed, shattering the still evening air and quiet dignity of Queen's Drive.

'Appreciated your company. You know where to find me if you change your mind. God bless.'

Then with a thump of seat and crash of door he was off.

Elizabeth felt quite harrowed. She stood at the pillared gateway for a minute or two trying to pull herself together before going up the drive and facing Sarah, the maid who usually opened the door. She wasn't allowed a key until she was twenty-one, which was the traditional age for being presented with a door key. That would come in December. Meantime she had to pass the interest and curiosity in Sarah's eyes. Sometimes the maid would say encouragingly, 'I hope you've had a nice evening, miss.'

Elizabeth always just smiled and murmured, 'Very

nice, thank you,' and hastened upstairs. As often as not Nanny would be hovering in the nursery hall in her shabby dressing gown, hawk-faced and suspicious-eyed, plaited hair dangling over one shoulder. Her long nose would jut forward, intent on sniffing out sex. Nanny never trusted her to behave herself when she went out with men. Not that she'd been out with any men except Jack Dawson and Reggie Wordsall. But maybe Nanny had a point. She didn't seem to have behaved in a very creditable manner with either of them.

As she climbed to the top of the house she prayed that Nanny would be asleep. Carefully she opened and shut the heavy door that isolated the nursery quarters like another world from the rest of the house. The nursery hall was in darkness but as she was tiptoeing along it Nanny's bedroom light snapped on.

'Why are you sneaking in without putting the light on?' Nanny propped herself up in bed in her modestly high-necked flannelette nightgown. She peered narrow-eyed across the room. 'What have you been up to, miss?'

Elizabeth blinked in innocent protest. 'Nothing, I just didn't want to disturb you.'

'You know perfectly well I never sleep until you're safely in. You've been up to something. I see it in your face. There's guilt written all over you.'

Elizabeth sighed. 'I told Reggie I didn't want to see him any more.'

Nanny's lips tightened. She shook her head. 'The men you go through!'

She made it sound as if there had been an endless string of them. Elizabeth had a sudden urge to giggle. Head down, she made for her room.

'Goodnight, Nanny.'

The barely suppressed giggle had lightened her spirits and brought a welcome sense of relief. Lying in bed cuddling her dolls she thought: No more painful hikes through prickly heather and nettles. No more pushing myself to exhausting limits on Nance's bike. No more Reggie. She sent a silent cheer up to the ceiling before contentedly settling down to sleep and dreams of her new job.

For the next few days she was busy preparing for work in the Hill's Trust School. Previously when she'd worked in Govan on a temporary basis for teacher practice she hadn't taken much notice of the place. Now, when it was to be her permanent base, perhaps for many years, she set about not only exploring the area, but finding out more about its history. She travelled first of all on the top of a tram and later on foot, fascinated by the sights and sounds along the riverside. Govan was a shipbuilding place and ships were in every stage of development in the various yards along the Govan and Linthouse stretch of river. The noise of the riveting hammer, louder than the machine-gun fire it was often compared with, was a constant and penetrating feature of Govan life. Giant cranes of various shapes reared up from behind high walls to pierce the sky in jagged lines. Big ships were a spectacular sight.

Elizabeth thought the sight was even more stunning at night because they were extravagantly lit and sparkled like moving Christmas trees.

But what she could hardly credit was how noisy and lively Govan was. As well as the deafening din of the riveters there were the ships' sirens, ranging from the high-pitched whistles of tugs and smaller boats to the deep blare of the bigger vessels. And there were all the different works' horns loudly blaring out morning, noon and night to add to the general din of the place.

The school itself was a grey stone building with three different entrances, the main one facing Golspie Street being impressively pillared. It had also a tower rearing up above it containing, she later discovered, the medical room on the first floor and the aging inadequate staff room on the very top. Pigeons nested in the eaves and their throaty noisy rustlings and flappings vied with the chatter of the teachers and the racket of the children in the playground. Or if classes were in, the monotonous chanting of arithmetic tables.

On Elizabeth's first day she hurried excitedly up the narrow stairs to the staff room, took off her coat and donned the new lavender smock she'd made herself, helped by Nanny. She was the first arrival but was followed soon after by Miss Pierce, a thin, angular woman in her late forties with a pasty face and sad, defeated eyes.

Elizabeth smiled expectantly at her. 'Hello, I'm Elizabeth Monkton.'

She was rewarded by a wan smile in return. 'Your first day?'

Eager-eyed, Elizabeth nodded. 'What is it like?'

'At Hill's Trust? I'm Mae Pierce, by the way. And you'd better not sit there. That's Charlotte Birnie's seat.'

Elizabeth hastily rose from the wooden chair and continued the task of changing into her flat-heeled working shoes by hopping about and wobbling from one foot to another.

'The headmaster seemed very nice.'

Mae shrugged. 'He's all right, I suppose. We hardly ever see him. He's more interested in the older children. He often takes the qualifying class. You're primary three, aren't you? Miss Simpson's lot.'

'Is she the one who's just retired?'

'Lucky her. She started just like you. Dedicated her whole life trying to educate seven-year-olds who leave school when they're fourteen and go into the shipyards or domestic service or the dole. She might as well not have bothered for all the good it did either them or her.' Miss Pierce sighed. 'Made her a lonely dried-up old maid. That's what teaching's done for her. That's what it does for all of us. But at least she's away from the soul-destroying grind now.'

Elizabeth's eyes turned anxious. 'An exaggeration, surely.'

Miss Pierce's lip curled. 'Oh, of course, it'll probably be different for you. You're one of the Monkton building people, aren't you? No doubt you'll be able to afford a fruitful social life out of school hours and you've got looks on your side as well. Those who have, always get more,' she ended bitterly.

'I was meaning that teaching surely cannot be truthfully described as a soul-destroying grind. It's not been my experience. Quite the contrary . . .'

The conversation was cut short at that point by a sudden noisy influx of teachers. Elizabeth was thankful to see that at least some of them looked younger and certainly more cheerful than Miss Pierce.

Introductions were chattered out while chairs were squeezed past and coats hung on pegs along one wall, making the room shrink even more.

'Come on.' Miss Jenkins jerked an auburn head at Elizabeth. 'I'll show you to your room, otherwise you're liable to get lost. Whoever planned this place was completely mad. There's just no sense in the layout.'

'That's very kind of you. Thank you very much.'

Elizabeth followed the bobbing red head in great thankfulness. There were two staircases facing different directions, corridors going this way and that for no apparent reason except to confuse, and classes that sometimes led off one another. At least the classrooms were bright and airy, with many unusually large and high windows. But this was still August. Only too soon she would find that although these windows were splendid for letting in light and sunshine, they could also rattle in the winter winds and allow freezing draughts to shiver round the room.

Thirty-five seven-year-olds sat waiting for her. There was silence when she entered and she gazed around at the slightly apprehensive faces then smiled and said, 'Good morning, children.'

'Good morning, miss,' they immediately chorused out.

'Now first of all before we settle down to our lessons, I always have on Monday mornings what I call news time. You tell me your news about what has happened during your weekend.'

This was one of what other teachers had dismissed as her 'fancy ideas'. Many arguments she'd had about it. She felt that children needed to express themselves and this was one good way. The general consensus had been, however, that such an attitude could lead to a dangerous lack of discipline, and learning was bound to suffer. Her cry of 'but it's only for a few minutes once a week' fell on deaf ears. Admittedly there were dangers and Elizabeth handled the procedure with some caution. She had discovered it was prudent to vet most of the news before permitting it to be announced to the class.

Her first day at Hill's Trust School was no exception. After the first few minutes of disbelief at her announcement one little boy in a badly holed Parish jersey started dancing up and down in his seat, excitedly waving his hand. She judged him a likely candidate for censorship.

'What's your name?' she asked.

'Geordie McDougal.'

'Well, come out and whisper your news to me first, Geordie.'

Geordie galloped noisily towards her in big tackety boots.

Elizabeth bent down and he whispered in her ear.

'Ma mammy's got new teeth.'

It seemed innocent enough.

'All right, dear,' she said, indicating the class.

'Ma mammy's got new teeth,' Geordie cried out to

an interested audience. 'And they bite. And my daddy says they bit his bum. And . . .'

'That's enough,' Elizabeth hastily interrupted, managing to add, 'Thank you, Geordie, you may return to your seat now.'

The truth was that news time was always fraught. But the children so much enjoyed imparting their news, and Elizabeth was convinced that it improved their self-confidence to be able to express their life experience. She was determined to continue with this little Monday morning routine as long as she could get away with it.

News time was followed by religious instruction which consisted of a short Bible story and the singing of 'Jesus Wants Me for a Sunbeam', then counting, then playtime. Elizabeth longed for a cup of tea but reckoned she would never find her way up to the tower staff room in time and so went out to the playground and shared playground supervision with Miss Jenkins instead.

After playtime it was spelling and reading and then lunchtime. The children were marched in strict and silent order to the cloakroom where the putting on of jackets or coats was supervised. Then they were instructed to leave the building as quietly as possible.

Classrooms were locked and the janitor roamed eagle-eyed around corridors and playground to make sure no one tried to enter before the appointed time. Elizabeth decided to walk to the park and eat her sandwiches there. She went out the Golspie Street door and had only gone a few yards along the road when she noticed a little green shop with rather nice cakes in the window. She couldn't resist an Empire biscuit to have after her sandwiches and so she went in. A bell tinged announcing her entry and a slim man with horn-rimmed glasses stopped hacking open a sack of sugar and looked round at her.

'Yes?'

'An Empire biscuit, please.'

He smiled as he put the iced and cherry-topped

confection into a bag. He had a nice smile, rather tentative, a bit shy.

'You're new. From across the road, aren't you? Is this your first day?'

She was astonished. 'How on earth did you know?'

'This is the first day after the summer holidays.'

'I mean how did you know I was a teacher?'

He smiled again but avoided her eyes. 'They have a kind of look.'

'Have they? What kind of look?'

He shrugged. 'Difficult to say. But I usually can tell.'

'Oh.' She accepted her change. 'Thank you.'

'I expect I'll be seeing you again.'

'I expect so.'

The bell tinged again and she continued her journey along the street, tremors of anticipation mixing with pangs of unease.

CHAPTER 20

Mrs McClusky was last to leave after the funeral. Annalie wanted to plead with her to stay all night but the old woman was away before she could force the words out. Normally a wildly emotional person, all day she'd been wandering about in a daze. She hadn't even shed a tear. One of the neighbours whispered sympathetically that she was in shock. Admittedly her father had looked frail for a while but to suddenly drop dead like that . . .

'Your daddy was a decent man,' Mrs McClusky reminisced, chewing her false teeth, eyes vague. 'He kept himself to himself. Every day for years he came in for his *Herald* and just a polite nod and a good morning to me. Often though he'd have a wee blether with my man. The last time it was about that Hitler chap in Germany and the way he's persecuting poor folk, socialists like himself, your daddy said. And Jews and gypsies and anyone else he didn't fancy.'

This brought her father back so vividly to Annalie. Politics was the only thing that could occasionally fire him into speech with her. But he'd been in the habit of having many such conversations with his workmates in his local pub. They came to the funeral to pay their respects and told her of the many heated discussions they'd enjoyed with 'old Hugh'. Annalie remembered her father's eyes flashing and his walrus moustache quivering with anger after the German Reichstag went up in flames in February 1933.

'Hitler's blaming the communists,' he'd told her. 'But it's a dirty lie, just an excuse for him to grab all the powers of a dictator. He's persuaded von Hindenburg

163

to sign a decree that suspends all guarantees for personal liberty. That means freedom of speech and the press and the right of assembly. Now he's really cracking down on socialists and Jews and anybody that opposes him.'

When later he read in his newspaper that the Nazis had burned huge piles of books in front of Berlin University, and harassed the unions, he was outraged.

'They've arrested the labour leaders now. They're herding good socialists up and flinging them into concentration camps.'

She would miss her father's big dour figure in the leather-lugged chair by the fire, either moodily puffing at his pipe or immersed in his newspaper. It had always been reassuring to know that every night he was through in the room bed having a read at one of his Left Book Club publications before settling himself to sleep.

After Mrs McClusky left, the tiny two-roomed flat oppressed Annalie with its silence. For a few seconds she felt panicky and frightened. She thought she wouldn't be able to bear it. Struggling to get a grip of herself, she fixed her mind on the fact that her father had been in his seventies and couldn't be expected to live for ever. She would miss him and it was natural to grieve for him. But she wasn't a helpless child left alone in the world. She was a grown woman and had nothing to fear from anyone.

Then into her mind, unbidden, came Carlino. She fought to banish him. He had no place in her thoughts today. There never had been any connection between him and her father. Hugh Gordon had never even met her dance partner. Nevertheless, in losing her father she felt as if a protector had gone. She was more vulnerable to Carlino than she had been before. She went to bed early and prayed for sleep to shut the curtains on her mind. But she lay for hours tossing and turning in the hole-in-the-wall bed in the kitchen, pain-

ful memories unrolling across her mind's eye like a film
that was impossible to ignore. She witnessed the happy
transformation of her father every time Saviana re-
turned. Her mother was the only one who could bring
a sparkle to his eye and make laughter explode up from
his chest. She remembered her mother's bold eyes, her
gypsy earrings and bangles, her flouncing red skirts and
frilly petticoats. No doubt she too would be dead now.
If only they'd never parted with such anger and ill
feeling. But Annalie did not regret snatching Elizabeth
back from her. Elizabeth had a far better life now than
she would ever have had brought up in a gypsy camp.

Thinking of Elizabeth brought the tears at last. She
longed for her own flesh and blood. What a beautiful
child her daughter had been. She saw the soft round
face, the large dark eyes, the ebony fringe of hair, and
her arms ached to hold and kiss her again. Her weeping
loudened unashamedly. It racketed up to the ceiling. She
thrashed about the bed in tragic abandon until at last
she collapsed exhausted into sleep. She dreamt that she
and Elizabeth were together again and Elizabeth was
the baby that she remembered. It was a beautiful dream
at first, then Carlino appeared and kidnapped the child.
After that it somehow got mixed up with the Lindbergh
case in America when Charles Lindbergh's baby had
been kidnapped. The papers had been full of the story.
It had affected Annalie deeply at the time. Now, like
the Lindbergh baby, Elizabeth was found dead.

She woke up crying out and soaked in sweat. Even
after she got up and had a brisk wash-down the horror
of the dream still clung. She wondered fearfully if it
was a kind of premonition. She was, after all, of gypsy
descent and some gypsies were supposed to have
strange powers. After a cup of tea and a slice of bread
and jam she pooh-poohed the idea. Hadn't she found
out long ago that her mother's gypsy fortune-telling was
just a lot of trickery? Elizabeth was fine. Elizabeth had

a wealthy home and everything she could wish for in life. That was all that mattered.

There was some time to spare before she went to rehearsals. Although she and Carlino knew their dance routine off by heart, every stage was different, every theatre's wings were different and so there were still technical rehearsals. The kind of lighting and sound that would be needed had to be planned by technicians. She and Carlino did their routine without being in costume; their movements were blocked and even where they had to stand was carefully planned and noted. Then there was always a dress rehearsal.

Annalie toyed with the idea of going through to the room to sort out her father's clothes ready to give to one of the unemployed men in the street. She knew several who would be glad of them, especially with winter coming on. She couldn't bring herself to set foot in the room, however. It was bad enough being confronted by her father's empty chair. Tomorrow would be soon enough to face the wardrobe. Or even one day next week. She retreated back to the kitchen table and stared bleakly around. The place held so many memories of her Aunty Murn and her brothers as well as her father. All gone.

After a deep determined breath she vowed that as soon as she could, she would redecorate both the kitchen and the room. One of the Rafferty boys would help her. And as soon as she could afford it she'd get new chairs. Her father's leather chair was all cracked and stained, and sagged in the middle. Aunty Murn's rocker was chipped and shabby-looking as well as being old-fashioned. As for the rag rug . . .

A knocking at the door interrupted her reverie. She hurried gratefully to answer it, thinking it was one of the neighbours come to keep her company. But she found Carlino waiting on the doormat. Her face darkened.

'What do you want? You've no right to come to my home.'

'No right to come and offer my condolences?' He raised a brow. 'Why didn't you tell me, darling? How do you think I felt, hearing about my partner's bereavement from a stagehand? Aren't you even going to ask me in?'

He looked and sounded serious enough. Yet she thought she detected a glimmer of something behind his stare. Was it pleasure? Surely not.

Reluctantly she stood aside to allow him to enter, hoping at the same time he could feel the hatred jabbing out at him as he passed her in the shoe box of a lobby and sauntered into the kitchen.

'You could have offered your condolences later at the theatre.'

'Charming,' he said, 'you certainly know how to make a friend welcome, darling.'

'You're no friend of mine.'

He took off his hat and tossed it on to the bed before settling himself down on the sofa.

'So you keep telling me. Although why you should have such an antagonistic attitude I don't know.' His lean, tanned face split into a grin. 'I know I'm not every man's favourite person. But I'm always a hit with the women.'

'I'm not interested in what you are or what you do outside of working hours. My working life and my private life are separate and I'd prefer if you remembered that and didn't come here again.'

'A bit difficult in our line of business, darling. Especially on tour, wouldn't you agree?' With long fingers he selected a cigarette from a silver case. 'Anyway, whether or not you're interested in me, I'm interested in you. I was chatting to some of your neighbours before I came up. A friendly lot standing gossiping at the close mouth.'

Annalie's voice loudened. 'You'd no right. How dare you!'

He lit the cigarette and puffed leisurely at it.

'What a strange creature you are, darling. I was only sympathizing with your plight and so were they. I said how terrible it was for you to lose your father. As if you'd not suffered enough, I said, with not having your daughter to comfort you. They said they were sure it was comfort enough just to know Elizabeth was so well placed with a family as well off as the Monktons. A good life was all you had ever wanted for Elizabeth, they said.' He smiled at Annalie through gently drifting cigarette smoke. 'Monkton's is that building firm with offices in Pollokshaws Road, isn't it? I've seen their boards all over the place. I suppose it was the usual story. The master of the house having his wicked way with the maid. Unusual that he kept the child, though. Interesting. She must be really special.'

Annalie turned her back on him and busied herself washing her hands at the sink so that he would not see them tremble or notice the fear filling her eyes. Through the window she was aware of children happily playing in the yard. Their laughter echoed up as if from a deep well. They seemed miles away.

'You were originally in domestic service, weren't you?' Carlino enquired politely.

'It's none of your business what I was.'

She briskly dried her hands on the towel hanging on a nail behind the cupboard door.

'What did Monkton have that I haven't got, I wonder?'

'Look,' she said, 'I've things to do. I can't get anything organized with you lounging around here. I'm afraid I'll have to ask you to leave.'

He rose from the sofa with catlike grace. 'As I told you, darling, I only came to offer my condolences. Losing your father was a sad blow. But I'm glad you're not alone in the world. It's good to know you have your daughter.'

'I've no contact whatsoever with my daughter. Nor do I want to have any.'

'Do you think that's fair either to yourself or to her?'

'She has her own life and I have mine, and as I've told you already – none of this is any of your business. Now will you please leave?'

He reached for his hat.

'I was only trying to help. See you later.'

After he left, Annalie didn't know what to do next. Her mind was in such black confusion.

CHAPTER 21

'Would you like to come to tea on Sunday with me and my mother?'

Elizabeth could still hardly believe the man in the grocer's shop had uttered the words, far less that she had agreed to go. His name was Alec Harper and because of her own shyness she recognized his. She had got into the habit of going into the shop two or three times a week for biscuits, tea and sugar for the staff room's lunch and tea breaks.

Harper's was a cramped but pleasant shop with warm sweet smells and darkly varnished wood. Rows of little drawers had crystal handles under which was written the name of the contents, like lentils, peas and barley. Honey-coloured sacks of potatoes and sugar bulged on the floor alongside a biscuit rack holding big tin boxes with hinged lids. The marble-topped counter held brass scales and hunks of cheese with black and white price tickets stuck in them. Alongside the cheese was a yellow mound of butter and wooden butter pats. The counter also held a clutter of sweets for children and bars of chocolate. On a shelf at the back were big black tins called Japan tins for different teas. Above them, another shelf displayed glass jars of toffee balls, pan drops, black-striped balls, coconut tablet and Pontefract cakes. The floor was yellow-gold with sawdust.

Sometimes she and Alec Harper exchanged a few words about the weather, or about the children who came into his shop for sweets, or the children she taught in her class. But on the whole he wasn't much of a talker. Once she'd seen a group of children buying sweets and one ragged barefoot boy was hanging back trying to appear unconcerned. Alec asked what he wanted and the boy shrugged and said:

'I'm just looking.'

'Here.' Alec passed a bar of Highland Maid toffee over the counter. 'You can come in after school and sweep my floor to pay for that.'

'Aw thanks, mister.' The boy had torn the paper off and was hungrily sucking the toffee before he'd reached the street.

'That was very kind of you,' Elizabeth remarked when it came her turn to be served.

Alec's eyes behind his glasses were evasive. 'There's too much poverty around here. Even the men in work have very poor wages. It's the children I'm sorry for. They shouldn't have to suffer.'

Her heart warmed to him. 'That's exactly how I feel. I get really upset when I see some of my children come to school with bare feet and no coats. Especially now that the winter's coming in – no wonder there's so much illness.'

She'd met his mother several times in the shop. Mrs Harper was a tall woman with hair scraped back into a tight bun under a crocheted wool tammy. Her coat was long and black and her shoes were large, lumpy and irregular in shape to fit her bunions. Elizabeth felt uncomfortable under the constant fire of her nervous glances.

They'd politely passed the time of day at first. Then Mrs Harper had suddenly asked:

'Monkton's an unusual name. You're not one of the builder Monktons are you?'

Elizabeth nodded, flushing under Mrs Harper's intense scrutiny as if Monkton's Building Company was something to be ashamed of.

'They must be worth a pretty penny.' Mrs Harper addressed her son who looked as uncomfortable and embarrassed as Elizabeth. 'Her grandfather – her

171

paternal one that is – worked his way up from nothing. It just shows what can be done if you work hard and watch the coppers. As I've always said – if you watch the coppers the pounds'll take care of themselves.'

It seemed odd to Elizabeth how Mrs Harper was served by Alec just as if she was any other customer. She paid by carefully counting out silver and coppers from a shabby black purse. Elizabeth had imagined the mother of the owner would be able to help herself for free. Once when Elizabeth was waiting among a crowd of women including Mrs Harper, one of the women had whispered:

'She comes in here to spy on poor Alec. Watches him like a hawk in case he gives any of us a wee bit overweight or lets us have broken biscuits a halfpenny cheaper. She's a right old miser.'

Elizabeth felt sorry for Alec and the way he flushed when some of the women kidded him on and tormented him about his mother when Mrs Harper wasn't there. He never failed to come to her defence.

'Mother's had to count her pennies. She's had a hard life . . .'

'You must be joking, son,' one woman howled with laughter. 'Lizzie Harper's life has been a bed of roses compared to the half of us. She's just a miser, son. Always was and always will be.'

'It's not right to talk about her like that.'

Everyone said what a good loyal son he was.

Alec and his mother lived in the Linthouse part of Govan and Elizabeth took a blue tram to get there when the day of the visit came. Jessie said Linthouse with its red sandstone tenements was known as the Garden of Eden by other Govanites. This was because the tenements there had tiled – or what was known locally as wally – closes. Elizabeth was glad it was a Sunday and the works were shut. On weekdays it was usual for Govan people to say:

'We'd better get home before the works come out.'

Workmen rushed out of the works in such droves you could be knocked down by them. And they messed up the tram seats with dirt and oil from their boiler suits. Today all was Sunday quiet. There was no clatter of workmen's boots on the cobbles. No street hawker trundled his barrow or led his horse along Govan Road. No little boy armed with bucket and shovel pounced on heaps of steaming horse dung to sell to better-off people with gardens or plots. No riveters stuttered with excruciating loudness as they assembled ships' hulls. No clatter and clanging of steel plates being moved about vied with the riveters' racket.

The Harpers lived in Drive Road in a close tiled to shoulder height in bottle green. The staircase walls were painted dark brown to the same level. Above that height, walls and ceiling were whitewashed. Elizabeth had to climb to the top flat past half landings each with a double window looking down on to the back court, with centre panes of plain glass and long narrow stained-glass borders.

Jessie said that Alec must be well off because he had a shop and lived up a posh close in Linthouse beside the park. To Elizabeth however, used for a lifetime to the spacious luxury of a large villa, the draughty close and gloomy stone stairway were extremely depressing. As for the tiny cluttered grocery shop, she suspected it would be a type far beneath Mother's dignity to enter. Even in Elizabeth's estimation neither the close nor the shop were posh.

The brass nameplate, the bell pull, the letter box were all highly polished and glittered like gold in the shadowy landing. The fanlight above the door was in darkness and for a minute Elizabeth wondered if she'd come on the wrong Sunday. The place seemed so dark and quiet and empty. Then, unexpectedly, the door opened and she saw Alec standing in the shadows. He

173

looked like a different person. Normally, in the shop he was in rolled-up shirtsleeves showing hairy arms and with a white linen apron tied round his waist. Now he looked smart but funereal in a dark suit, white shirt and dark tie.

'Good evening,' he greeted her. 'Please come in.'

The hall was pitch-black except for the faint crack of light around a door to her right. Alec indicated towards it.

'Just go right through to the front room.'

A gas mantle over the fireplace puttered feebly. Its misty light didn't reach the corners which lay quietly in shadow. Mrs Harper jerked up from her seat beside the fire.

'Hello, Miss Monkton. My, aren't the nights drawing in. I tried to keep off lighting the gas as long as I could but thought I'd better light it when I saw you coming down the road. I'll draw the curtains now and save the heat.'

Elizabeth was taken aback by the loud burst of strident sound against the shadowy quietness of the room where even the ticking of the grandfather clock sounded muffled. Alec drew another chair nearer the fire.

'Take a seat, Miss Monkton. Mother's just going through to the kitchen to make the tea.'

'Do call me Elizabeth, please. I get enough of Miss Monkton at the school.'

Alec looked slightly uncomfortable but his mother cried out with delight.

'The very same as me! Of course I've always been called Lizzie but you're quite right in keeping it proper. Of course it's to be expected that it would be proper with your background. The kettle's boiling. I won't be a minute.'

The room retreated gratefully into quiet after the trauma of Mrs Harper's voice. In the silence Alec and Elizabeth half smiled at each other. The gas mantle hissed gently above their heads and occasionally the fire gave a sigh as it sank under its dark burden of dross and briquettes. Elizabeth could see, over by the window, a round table covered by a fawn lace cloth and set with gold-edged china decorated with roses, a plate of bread and another of scones and pancakes. A matching milk jug and sugar bowl and a dish of blackcurrant jam also graced the table.

'We usually eat in the kitchen.' Mrs Harper fired words at Elizabeth as soon as she bundled back into the room. 'This is in your honour. We've a big flat here, two good-sized rooms and kitchen and inside toilet, and it takes a lot of lighting and heating. I'm always on at Alec to watch what he's doing. He tends to turn up lights and fling on coal as if we're made of money.'

'Would you like to move over to the table, Elizabeth?' Alec's voice was smooth but Elizabeth detected a tinge of strain. 'I expect you'll be glad of a cup of tea to heat you up.'

'Aye, the days have got longer right enough,' Mrs Harper observed. 'But they'll get colder still. I eke out my coal with dross and briquettes. If you bank it up careful-like, it'll last twice as long. I've to see to it myself of course. If I let that one there' – she pointed to her son – 'put a hand near my fire we'd be in the poorshouse before the year was out.'

'Do you take milk and sugar, Elizabeth?' Alec politely enquired.

'Just milk, thank you.'

Mrs Harper flung a knowing look at her son. 'Think of all the sugar she'll save in a year. It'll mount up to a pretty penny, I'm sure.'

'Mother.' Alec's voice remained even, too even. 'Elizabeth doesn't like sugar, that's all.'

'That's as maybe, but she'll still save a lot of money.'

Elizabeth could see how much Alec was suffering and

she felt sorry for him. With an obvious effort he smiled at her and said:

'Would you like some bread and jam? It's Mother's home-made blackcurrant.'

'Thank you. It looks delicious.'

'We sell jam in the shop.' Mrs Harper finished pouring the tea then tugged a tea cosy over the teapot before sitting down. 'But I wouldn't dream of wasting good money on it. Far cheaper to make my own. I put some carrot in it to save the sugar. What do you think of it?'

'It tastes delicious.'

'Of course with your background you'll never have needed to scrimp and save.'

'Mother,' Alec murmured.

'Your mother'll never have needed to make her own jam. She'll have a skivvy to do it for her. Or a cook. I bet there's even a cook. Am I right or am I not?'

Elizabeth's mouth was full and she couldn't answer.

'Am I right or am I not?' Mrs Harper repeated excitedly.

With a desperate effort Elizabeth gulped down the bread and jam. 'Yes, we do have a cook.'

'There, what did I tell you!' She turned in triumph to Alec. 'A cook and maids and everything that money can buy.' Then back to Elizabeth: 'It says a lot for your mother and father that they've been able to build up such a good business and made such a gold mine out of it. You must be real proud of them.'

Elizabeth smiled uncertainly. She'd never given the building business much thought and she realized now that her lifestyle was something she'd taken completely for granted. Up until the time she'd gone into teaching, in fact, she'd believed without thinking about it that everyone else was as well looked after and as well fed as herself. Even yet it was hard to credit the fact that children in the same city could go barefoot and hungry, could look so neglected. She shuddered to think what their homes must be like if Jessie could call Linthouse and places like this a Garden of Eden. Although the house looked clean and respectable enough. Everything from the orange-brown chenille curtains and orange and brown rug to the high chiffonier looked spotless. The linoleum and furniture gleamed like dark mirrors and even the brass pendulum of the grandfather clock looked as if it too had been vigorously polished.

'The shop barely keeps body and soul together.' Mrs Harper's chest under her black bombazine heaved in a sigh of regret.

'Mother' – Alec gave another of his small smiles – 'the shop does all right. It makes us a decent living. But I'm sure Elizabeth doesn't want to hear all this. Tell us about your job, Elizabeth. Do you enjoy it?'

Elizabeth opened her mouth but Mrs Harper beat her to it.

'A decent living?' she scoffed. 'Is that what you call a decent living? When I've to scrimp and save to put a penny by me. That's the trouble with you. You've the wrong attitude. You don't care. You've never cared about where your next penny's coming from. No wonder I'm a nervous wreck.'

Elizabeth felt so miserably embarrassed she couldn't swallow the mouthful of bread she'd thoughtlessly indulged in. It lay in a glutinous mass in her mouth. Staring down at her cup she wondered if a drink of tea would help.

'Mother,' Alec intoned quietly, 'of course I care. I care about the shop and I care about you.'

Mrs Harper unexpectedly returned her attention to Elizabeth. 'I expect you're the apple of your mother and father's eye. I bet they've lavished everything on you. You wouldn't need to work, but work you did. And good for you, I say.'

'Do you enjoy your job, Elizabeth?' Alec tried again

and Elizabeth opened her mouth only to be once more beaten to it.

'That's beside the point. The point is she had the good sense to know that an extra few pounds never goes wrong and the gumption to buckle down to earn them. If I didn't keep my eye on you, you'd be the ruination of that shop and well you know it.'

Elizabeth had never pitied anyone so much in her life. She wished she could put her arms protectively around Alec as she would have done with one of the children in her class, and try to help and comfort him. He was trying so hard to be patient. But she suspected that underneath that smooth exterior simmered very different emotions. She couldn't stop thinking about him and worrying about him, even after she was back in Monkton House. She went to sleep haunted by his lowered head and evasive eyes.

CHAPTER 22

The fact that neither Mother nor Father liked Alec Harper made Elizabeth more loyal to him than she might otherwise have been. Even Nanny was against the friendship.

'You're keeping company with that man out of sheer perverseness, my girl. You've always had a moody, contrary bit about you.'

'What have you got against him?' Under her black fringe Elizabeth's eyes widened and cooled. 'He's always been perfectly polite to you. And to Mother and Father. It's not fair the way you all go on about him.'

'To think you turned down a nice, considerate, warm-hearted, well-educated man like Reggie Wordsall.'

'I wasn't in love with Reggie.'

Nanny's face strained close. 'Don't tell me you're in love with Alec Harper.'

Elizabeth shrugged. She felt resentful at the way everybody was interfering and trying to run her life and make her do what they wanted.

'What if I was? Nobody goes on like this at Jason or the twins.'

'Nobody needs to go on at them. They have good taste and a sense of their own position in life. Jason is walking out with young Lady Marjorie and the twins have very nice girlfriends who are at present attending Hutcheson Grammar School. The father of one has an architect's firm in town. The other girl's father is a well-known surgeon.'

Elizabeth's cheeks burned with anger. 'So it's nothing but snobbishness. I might have known.'

'Good breeding will out.' Nanny's voice dropped to a mutter. 'Bad breeding too, it seems.'

'What do you mean?' Elizabeth demanded, suddenly anxious. 'Are you hinting at my background? Exactly what do you mean? I've a right to know.'

'I only meant that it's obvious Alec Harper has no good breeding.'

'No, you didn't. You meant me.'

'And there's something strange about his eyes.'

Elizabeth was diverted for the moment. 'I've never noticed anything strange about his eyes.'

'When they're not evading you, they're staring at you blank-like as if they're trying to hide something.'

'I keep telling you, he's shy.'

'There's something wrong with his mother as well.'

'How do you mean? You've never even met her.'

'That's the point. More than once your mother has told you to invite Mrs Harper to tea so that we could all see what kind of family he has. Why haven't you? After all, he's met your family.'

'You're all trying to make too big a thing of it, that's why. Alec and I are only friends. Nothing more.'

This was the truth. At least that she and Alec were just friends. They'd been keeping company for some time now and he still gave her no more than an affectionate peck on the cheek when he bade her goodnight.

'Well I hope you're right. The man's old enough to be your father. I don't know what on earth you see in him.'

Perhaps his age was partly what explained his attraction, Elizabeth decided. And he was so good with his mother. He was steady and sensible and gave Elizabeth a feeling of security. He had a calming influence; it was also good to be able to talk to him about all the happenings, good and bad, at the school and even to some degree about what happened at home. Jason had gone to continue his music studies in Paris. He wrote to Mother, and some snippets of news were occasionally passed on to her. Nevertheless she felt completely estranged from him. He never wrote to her. Not even a postcard. (Twice he'd sent Nanny a postcard. One showed the Palace of Versailles and the other the Arc de Triomphe.) Of course she and Jason had never been all that close. Not that he'd been particularly close to anyone except perhaps Mother. He and Mother had a love of music in common. She was also an accomplished pianist and had admitted that she'd once dreamed of a musical career. Jason was a dreamy character, very much wrapped up in his music.

The twins had always had each other, and now they were working closely with Mother and Father in the business.

Elizabeth didn't feel she belonged in Monkton House. The trouble was not knowing where she did belong. But she didn't go so far as to confide these feelings to Alec. Perhaps one day she would, but so far she had been grateful for his company and his attention and the way he had helped her overcome her shyness by being such a good listener. Sometimes he commented on the film they'd seen. Sometimes he spoke about the children they both knew in the district. Sometimes he told her anecdotes about the people who came into his shop, many of them the mothers of the youngsters who attended her school. Often his comments were tinged with humour that would bring a wry twist to one corner of his mouth.

He had been quiet but polite each time he'd been invited in to Monkton House and he looked very presentable, even studious with his sleek dark hair and heavy horn-rimmed glasses. It was very unfair of Mother and Father and Nanny to be so opposed to him. Mother and Father said it was his age but it was more than that, Elizabeth felt sure. Nanny had indicated a snobbish attitude. Probably that's how Mother and Father felt too. They'd never admit it, of course.

Although Elizabeth suspected that as far as her parents were concerned it was more to do with ambition and business success than breeding. Alec was nearly forty years of age and all he had was one small grocer's shop. If Mother or Father had started with one small shop they'd have had a chain of department stores by now. That's what they were like. But in the building up of their business success they'd delegated the bringing up of their children to Nanny. They had not only spent most of their days attending to business in Glasgow but were often away from home for weeks at a time.

Alec was an entirely different type of person. That was probably why Mother and Father didn't understand him.

Elizabeth wondered if the admiration and affection she felt for Alec was a kind of love. After all, she wasn't very experienced on the subject. She certainly wasn't having the same pangs she'd had for Jack Dawson. There were no heart flutterings, no sexual longings. Only a comfortable, safe kind of feeling.

It was a pity about his mother but she supposed nothing in life was perfect, and, after all, it wasn't his mother she was going out with. She tried, as far as possible, to avoid meeting Mrs Harper – a highly strung, twitchy person impossible to relax with. It was also very hard to bear the way the older woman kept denigrating Alec, plus the fact that her only other topic of conversation was money. Elizabeth didn't know how Alec stood it. It would have been perfectly forgivable in Elizabeth's eyes if he'd throttled his mother. She'd only been in Mrs Harper's company about once a week or sometimes just once a fortnight. Even so she'd often been on the verge of doing something drastic. The fact that Alec was in daily contact with that high unstable voice and desperately searching eyes didn't bear thinking about. It was enough to drive anybody crazy. Some people said he must be a saint not only to put up with it, but remain so quietly patient.

Elizabeth had found one clue to his behaviour. Apparently, according to his mother, he'd once run off to England while his father was still alive – he'd found a job there.

'Left us up here to sink or swim,' Mrs Harper informed Elizabeth with great bitterness and twitching of eyes, 'and he was supposed to be the one who adored Fred Harper. Oh yes, there was nobody like his father. It was always his father he went to. Like two peas in a pod they were. Then he ups and leaves. His father tried to tell me he'd encouraged him to go but I knew it would be the death of him and he knew it too. Fred had always been a weakling of a man. Always ailing with something. He couldn't manage on his own. The shop was losing money like he was throwing it away. He dropped dead behind the counter. On a busy Saturday it was too. I always say to Alec if he hadn't gone and left him it would never have happened.'

Elizabeth could imagine the secret burden of guilt Alec must be labouring under. He never mentioned his father however, and she respected his need to keep his grief to himself. She could never have spoken to anybody outside the family about not belonging to the Monktons, and having a mother who had long ago abandoned her. Some things were too personal, too painful to talk about. She'd even stopped bringing up the subject inside the family. But the longing to learn about her roots and to know her real mother had never diminished. At least Alec's mother tried in her own restless, fussy way to make her welcome in Drive Road. She was always given preferential treatment by having tea in the sitting room, or front room as they called it. The best china and lace table cover were invariably used and Mrs Harper baked scones and pancakes and pressed her to:

'Eat up. I made them specially for you.'

Mrs Harper also did everything to encourage Alec

in his relationship. She not only left them alone in the room after tea but kept nudging Alec about when he'd be seeing Elizabeth again.

'I'll leave you two on your own now. I'll just turn the gas down a bit first. No use having two jets going full blast anyway.' A giggle and a twitching of eyes preceded an announcement that 'it's more romantic to be in the dark.'

In the shadowy half-light Elizabeth and Alec would sit in embarrassed silence for a time just listening to the clock tick-tocking. Eventually Elizabeth would think of something to say and a desultory conversation would follow. It was anything but relaxed or natural and she was always relieved, and she suspected he was too, when it was time for her to go. Politeness forced Elizabeth to call out to Mrs Harper before leaving.

'Goodnight, Mrs Harper. Thank you for the lovely tea.'

Mrs Harper immediately hirpled from the kitchen as if she had been waiting eagerly behind the door.

'We'll see you again soon, I hope. Alec will bring you back soon. Of course I know you won't want to come here every time. He'll want to take you to the pictures next time, won't you, Alec?'

Alec always averted his eyes and muttered something incoherent.

Once they'd made their escape and were well away on their own they relaxed and talked in an easier and friendlier manner. A hint of tension returned when Alec came to asking her out again but she had become used to that and it didn't worry her. She would go quite happily to bed thinking about the film they had planned to see at their next meeting. It gave her something to talk about in the staff room too. A temporary change from the usual school gossip was always welcome. So often the conversation revolved round which mother had called at the school with a problem or complaint, or the headmaster's latest dictum, or the progress or lack of progress of the children. The many and varied trials and tribulations of the teaching profession in general were endlessly raked over.

She didn't see Jessie so often now to talk to. Jessie had got a school in Possilpark and was walking out with a riveter from Stephens' Yard.

'He's a real man,' Jessie proudly informed Elizabeth. 'He's got muscles on him like I don't know what. And he's taller than me. I was getting so fed up, going out with weedy men smaller than myself.'

Elizabeth found big Gordon McGill with his shaved head and broken nose rather frightening, but as long as Jessie was happy and so obviously in love, she was happy for her. And she was pleased that Jessie seemed to like Alec. In fact nobody had ever said a word about him except Nanny and Mother and Father, which just proved that they didn't care whether she was happy or not. All they cared about was material success. Her anger and resentment against them settled over her like a heavy cloud. They didn't believe her relationship with Alec was only friendship. Anyway, what if there was more to it than that? It would serve them right if she and Alec decided to get married. As they themselves had pointed out, marriage was the usual result of walking out regularly. The thought depressed her, however. Alec wasn't exactly the man of her dreams. He wasn't in the slightest romantic. He wasn't even handsome with his rather gaunt face and lean build. He was presentable, in a serious, respectable sort of way, but far from the dashing Lothario of her secret imaginings.

CHAPTER 23

In the spring of 1935 Flo Blair gave a party to celebrate the Silver Jubilee of King George V and Queen Mary. Not that she was a great royalist, or any kind of royalist for that matter. It was simply a case of any excuse for a party. The wireless and the newspapers had been full of the jubilee celebration. Everyone learned of how Queen Mary looked resplendent in white with a necklace of five rows of pearls and brilliant stones, and how on her head sat a toque also in white. The King was in the scarlet uniform of a field marshal.

The whole nation, the newspaper said, was alive with street parties. They must have meant England. Even Flo couldn't imagine enough interest, far less enthusiasm, being drummed up for a Gorbals street party in honour of some rich couple in England. Even if they did happen to be the King and Queen. But any party in Flo's house was different. That was good news.

Flo had been one of Annalie's neighbours when she'd lived with baby Elizabeth in a single end further along Cumberland Street. She had been a good friend, looking after Elizabeth while Annalie was out at work. That was before Annalie had moved to the room and kitchen with bathroom in the part of Cumberland Street known as the posh end because it had tiled closes. She had loved the house and it had been so wonderful having a bathroom. But the rent had been paid for by Adam Monkton and when the relationship ended, she moved out and returned to her original home with her father and Aunty Murn. But Flo and other old neighbours like Mr and Mrs Steele remained friends. Of course with touring about so often now she didn't see as much of them as she used to. The party would be a good way of meeting with everyone and catching up on all the news. It was such a comfort to be with her friends. It gave her temporary release from the constant stress and tension in her life. In between doing her party turn and having a laugh, she sampled Flo's corned beef sandwiches and clouty dumpling, which was as dark and rich as a Christmas pudding. It filled the house to overflowing with the smell of fruit and spices. After enjoying a piece she had a rare chance of a heart-to-heart talk. She was able to confide in Flo and Sadie Steele about the constant torments she went through with Carlino.

'Oh here, is that not terrible,' Flo sympathized. 'We all thought when we saw your act that there must be some sort of trick to it. I mean, that you weren't really getting hurt. Fancy him trying it on as well. Thinks he's God's gift to women, I bet. Could you not find another job, hen?'

'I keep pestering my agent, but so far without any luck. If only it was just a physical thing. I'm hardened to that now. If only it was just him harassing me sexually. I can just about cope with that as well. It's all his hints and sly digs about Elizabeth I can't stand.'

'How? What does he say? He's never met Elizabeth, has he?'

'No, but I'm so afraid that one day, somehow, he will.'

'What does he say?' Mrs Steele wanted to know.

'It doesn't sound very much, I suppose. He just keeps dropping her name. I wonder where Elizabeth is today or what Elizabeth is doing today? That sort of thing.'

'Och, I wouldn't worry, hen,' Flo comforted, 'it's just talk.'

'Sometimes he says he's looking forward to meeting her.'

'Just talk,' Flo repeated, before she was dragged away by her husband, Erchie, to join him in their 'wee turn', which meant singing one of their favourite duets.

Mrs McClusky, who had arrived at the tail end of the conversation, shook her head.

'Are you still worrying about that? I told you before, you'd no need. If he hasn't done anything by now he never will. Anyway what could he do? You'll be making yourself ill with your imaginings. I always say that's what killed my man. He was always worrying and going on about something or other.'

Annalie knew the old woman was right. The trouble was being bound night after night to a man she hated so intensely. The panicky need to escape and the knowledge that she was trapped were driving her mad.

Not long after the party, Carlino arrived on her doorstep again. She tried to shut the door in his face but he was too quick for her. His foot was jamming it and then he was pushing the door wide and he was in. She followed him, trembling with outrage.

'How dare you push your way into my home? What do you think you're doing?'

'Just making a friendly visit, darling.'

'Don't talk rot. You know you're not welcome here.'

'Just wanted a little chat. I thought you'd be interested.'

'Well, I'm not. Now get out!'

'I've seen Elizabeth.'

Annalie's legs gave way and she collapsed on to a chair. Carlino took his time lighting a cigarette, his dark head bent over a silver lighter, a present from a lady admirer. He often received gifts from adoring female fans.

'I happened to be over in Queen's Park,' he said eventually, 'and passing Monkton House, when out came this gorgeous girl.'

'You were hanging about spying on Monkton House,' Annalie cried out. 'How could you? What right, what reason could you possibly have for doing anything so outrageous?'

Carlino's eyes sparkled. 'I followed her.'

'Followed her?' Annalie echoed in horrified disbelief.

'I was curious and so are you, you just won't admit it. She travelled in the tram to Govan and eventually disappeared into the Hill's Trust School. She's a teacher, darling. Very popular with the children. One little chap informed me that Miss Monkton keeps a tin of toffees in her classroom cupboard and shares them around if the children behave themselves.'

'Why are you doing this?' Annalie's voice was anguished. 'Why? What do you think you'll gain by it? Or is it just the pleasure of tormenting me?'

'I told you, I thought you'd be interested.'

'Liar. You know perfectly well that even the mention of her name hurts and torments me.'

'I'm sorry, darling.'

'Lying bastard.'

'Now, now, no need to get nasty.'

'Oh yes there is. There's every need. If I was a man I'd fling you out of here and kick you all the way down the stairs.'

'Quite a little firecracker when you're angry. I love the way your eyes flash like that. You've wonderful eyes, darling. Wild and wonderful.'

'Get out!'

'Is that all the thanks I've to get for finding out about your daughter? Maybe she'll be more generous when she hears about her long-lost mother.'

'What are you getting at?'

'I fancy having a little chat with the dear girl. No, to be honest, darling' – his eyes narrowed as he inhaled cigarette smoke – 'I fancy more than that. She really is very attractive. Not in the same wild, gypsy way as you. No, she's neat, large round eyes and short straight black hair with a fringe that gives her a rather childish appearance. Innocent even. I find innocence irresistibly sexy.'

'Don't you dare go near her again.' Annalie was visibly shaking. 'I gave her up so that she could be safe and well looked after.'

'She seems very well looked after. But you're forgetting. She isn't a child any more.'

'I'll kill you if you go near her again.'

'No, darling, not a child, sweet and innocent as a child perhaps, but with the ripe and inviting body of a woman in her twenties.'

'Keep away from her, I'm warning you!'

'That depends.'

'I'm warning you.' Annalie's voice loudened with hysteria. She hardly knew what she was saying. She felt distraught. Every instinct to protect her child was careering wildly, desperately about looking for a solution. She couldn't, she wouldn't allow anyone to hurt or torment Elizabeth or ruin her life. But all she could do was keep repeating, 'Don't you ever go near her again.'

'Darling, you've no right to tell me what I should or should not do any more than you have any right to interfere in your daughter's life. She's a grown woman. The pity is she might get too set in schoolmarm ways and that would be such a waste. Most teachers end up as dried-up old spinsters.'

'I'm not interfering in her life and you'd better not either. You've interfered with enough women. You're disgusting.'

He laughed. 'You know all the women love me, and your prissy little schoolmarm of a daughter would be no exception if I decided to get to know her better. I don't think she would be nearly such a challenge as you've been, darling. I tell you what, let's have a bet on it. I bet I could have little Elizabeth eating out of my hand in – let's say a couple of weeks. I tell you what – just to make it more exciting, I'll keep you informed of my progress, step by step, word by word, touch by touch . . .'

190

She had to stop him. She couldn't allow all these empty years without her child to go for nothing. Both hands shot out clawlike to scrape her nails wildly down his face, making scarlet lines glistening wetly. He gave a gasp of pain before retaliating with a blow to her chest that snatched her breath away and doubled her over in agony. As he jerked her up, her dress tore apart, revealing the vulnerability of her breasts, but her fury made her recover quickly and she kneed him with all her strength in the groin. Howling with rage he kicked out, giving her such a crippling blow on the leg it buckled under her and she fell, knocking over a chair as she thumped down on to the linoleum. He kicked her again, blows to the stomach and groin that nearly made her lose consciousness. To save herself she clung to his leg in a travesty of the dance. She managed to unbalance him with her grip until he too fell. But he was up again almost as quickly as her and they were struggling violently until a blow to her face made her stagger back. The punch almost blinded her and she dazedly groped at the table for support. It was then her hand made contact with the bread knife and she brought it up and lunged it into Carlino's neck. Horror flung open his mouth and eyes for a second or two. He stood staring at her in disbelief as blood pumped and frothed from him and splattered over her like a scarlet fountain. In matching horror she dropped the knife then tried to catch Carlino as he crumpled down on to the floor. His eyes were still open but the blood had stopped pumping. She stumbled on to the floor with him, shouting his name and trying to revive him but all the time she knew he was dead. She was drenched in his blood. His blood had lashed out, rioted all over the small room, the floor, the table, the walls. She got up and stood whimpering in distress, wondering what to do. The scarlet mess was soaking through her dress and sticking to her skin. In sudden revulsion she tore off all her clothes and ran to the sink to splash herself with cold water and rub herself with the wash-cloth until she was shivering and sobbing with cold as well as horror. She stumbled through to the room and, snatching clothes from the wardrobe and chest of drawers, pulled them on. But they didn't stop her shivering.

She thought maybe it couldn't be true that her kitchen was desecrated by a dead body, and scarlet-stained clothes strewn all over the floor, and the hot smell of blood thickening the air. Any minute now she'd wake up and it would just be one of her nightmares. She'd been having so many nightmares recently. But she didn't wake up. She caught sight of herself in the wardrobe mirror, her face a startling white against her black hair, her shoulders hunched with tension, her hands clutching at each other. The terrible thought occurred to her that she couldn't stand there for ever, safe and silent in her own front room. She would have to go out and face the world and tell them what she'd done. Then the most terrible pain came over her. What if Elizabeth found out? The shame, the scandal, the disgrace would ruin Elizabeth's life far more than any-thing Carlino could have done. She couldn't bear it. Whatever happened Elizabeth must never find out.

In a daze she left the house and went across to knock on her neighbour's door.

'Oh, hello, hen.' Mrs McAuslin's smile of greeting faded at the sight of Annalie's chalk-white face. 'Is something wrong?'

'Tony Carlino's dead.'

'Your dance partner?'

'I didn't mean to do it, Mrs McAuslin.'

'You've done him in?' Mrs McAuslin screeched.

'It was an accident.'

'Holy Mother of God! Wait there till I fetch my shawl, hen. I'll come with you to the police station.'

CHAPTER 24

The first awful thing that happened was Nanny announcing that she was leaving. Mother and Father had decided to send Charlie to Father's old school in Edinburgh where he would be a boarder. This meant he would only be at home at holiday times. Mother said Nanny could stay on if she wished but of course there was really nothing much for her to do any more. As soon as Nanny had put in her resignation and said she'd work a month's notice, Flossie was told by Mother that she too must leave at the end of the month.

Elizabeth could hardly believe it. Charlie being sent away was bad enough. But losing Nanny would be like a death in the house. Nanny had been more of a mother to her than Christina, was the one who had always been there since Elizabeth was a baby. Nanny had been the one who'd nursed her when she'd been ill, who disciplined her and taught her the rules by which to live. Mother had been a visitor, a welcome visitor but a beautiful, elegant stranger. Mother had been someone she'd admired and wanted to please. Someone from whom she'd longed for warmth and recognition but from whom she'd never quite managed to attain these things. Mother could be kind but was always distant. She seemed to have an invisible barrier around her that said 'Do not touch'. Elizabeth had never understood her and, at times, had even been a little afraid of her.

But Elizabeth knew and understood Nanny, and loved her with all her faults.

'Please don't go, Nanny,' she pleaded. 'What'll I do without you?'

'You'll grow up, I suppose. You've been far too dependent on me. It's not healthy to be so clingy to a nursery.'

'But this is my home.'

'There's more to your home than the nursery.'

'But I've never known anything else.'

'Well it's time you learned, my girl.'

Elizabeth wanted to weep broken-heartedly, to cry out that she couldn't bear the separation, but instead she put on her stubborn, moody face and said:

'I don't want you to go.'

'That's as maybe, but I have to go and that's an end to it. There's a new baby due in a month's time at Bearsden Hall and I'm going to be needed there.' Then she added in a kinder tone, 'Bearsden isn't the other end of the world. Maybe we can meet in town some time for a cup of tea and you can tell me how you're getting on.'

'It won't be the same.'

'Nothing stays the same for ever.'

Just then Flossie arrived with the tea tray and Nanny began busying herself with the teapot.

'Here, you'll never guess!' Flossie was bug-eyed with excitement and her plump face framed with frizzy hair burned fiery pink. It was easy to guess that the maid was about to plunge into her favourite subject – murder. 'There's been a horrible bloody murder barely a stone's throw from here. It was in last night's paper but I've only just heard. It was Daisy who told me. She seen it in the paper last night after she'd gone home. Last night was her night off . . .'

'In Queen's Park?' Nanny looked outraged. 'Surely not?'

'Well, not exactly,' Flossie admitted, 'but near enough. In the Gorbals.'

Nanny rolled her eyes. 'A stone's throw indeed.'

'Well, it's south of the river like us.'

'And I'll have none of your swearing, miss,' Nanny said as an afterthought.

'I didn't swear,' Flossie protested indignantly.

'Don't lie to me, girl. You said B.L.O.O.D.Y.'

'But I wasn't using it as a swearword. I meant it was a murder with lots of blood.'

'Pass Miss Elizabeth the bread and butter. You're always the same. It's not healthy to have such an interest in violent crime. If it's not the newspapers it's the wireless.'

'But this is different.' Flossie was nearly jumping with delight. 'I've actually seen them. The killer and the victim. I've actually seen them in the flesh.'

'Nonsense, girl,' Nanny scoffed but Elizabeth's attention was temporarily diverted from her fears of losing Nanny.

'How do you mean? Do you know them?'

'Well, I've seen them on the stage. They were both dancers. They danced an apache dance, I think it was called. Something like that. Anyway they were really marvellous. It was supposed to be in a café in Paris or something like that and they were dressed in striped cotton tops and berets and kind of neckerchief things and her skirt was split right up the side showing the whole of her leg and . . .'

'I've seen them too,' Elizabeth gasped. 'Which one got stabbed?'

Nanny glared at Flossie. 'You're putting us off our tea going on about such things. Just you hold your wicked tongue, girl.'

'But I want to know,' Elizabeth protested. 'I'm interested.'

'Well you shouldn't be. I don't want another word said about this, do you hear?' Elizabeth had never seen Nanny so agitated. 'Not another word.'

Astonished, Elizabeth asked, 'Why are you so upset? Flossie's always going on about murders and you've never bothered before.'

'I've kept telling her it's unhealthy.'

'But you've never got upset. Never in the slightest.'

'I'm not upset, girl. Get on with your tea.'

They ate in silence while Elizabeth tried to puzzle things out. As soon as tea was over she'd go downstairs and read all about the case in Father's paper. Perhaps that would give her a clue to why Nanny had taken such exception to this particular crime.

But downstairs she couldn't find the paper anywhere. This was strange because it was delivered every morning and Father read it as soon as he arrived home. He liked to relax with a glass of whisky and his newspaper every evening before dinner. She asked Sarah if she knew where it was and Sarah said:

'The Master has cancelled delivery of it. He said he was just going to collect it and read it in the office.'

'But why should he suddenly do that?'

'I don't know, miss.'

It was almost as if he didn't want her to see the paper. She felt confused. It must be because of the murder case. No doubt it would be headline news. But surely it was ridiculous. Why should Nanny and Father suddenly be so overprotective? This wasn't the first murder case to be reported in the newspaper, after all. Her puzzlement was beginning to sharpen into anxiety. A flutter started in her stomach along with vague apprehension. As soon as she could she stepped out and bought a paper then went up a close in Pollokshaws Road to search through the pages. There was an article about Germany's massive rearmament programme. Another about the opening of the new Leicester Square tube station which had the largest escalator in the world. One news item told of a motorbike accident, as a result of which T. E. Lawrence – Lawrence of Arabia – was seriously ill. At last she found what she was looking for.

A woman was accused yesterday at Glasgow Sheriff's Court of murdering Anthony Carlino. She is Annalie Gordon (38) of

Cumberland Street, Gorbals. It is alleged that on Wednesday she assaulted Mr Carlino at her home, striking him on the neck with a knife.

No plea or declaration was made and Sheriff John Master remanded her in custody for further enquiries.

Elizabeth read the words over and over again, at the same time remembering the woman on the stage, how wild and sensuous she'd looked with her dark hair and eyes and voluptuous movements. They gave the words in the newspaper a special poignancy. But to anyone who had never seen Annalie Gordon and knew nothing of her, they would surely seem very matter-of-fact and no different from any other such news item. She glanced through the rest of the paper and could see nothing that could warrant any secrecy. She re-read the item about Annalie Gordon, anxiety still needling her. Then gradually memories came wafting across her mind's eye, fragile as veils. The feeling of being cuddled against a woman's soft body, of dark hair swinging close, of dark eyes gazing down at her. From far, far away she heard a husky voice crooning lullabies.

Then suddenly she knew. She knew why Nanny had been upset. She knew why Father hadn't wanted her to see the newspaper. It was some time before she could stop trembling enough to emerge from the close and make her way back to Monkton House. Mother and Father were in, lounging on either side of the fire.

Elizabeth collapsed down on to the settee, the paper still clutched in her hand.

'I've read this,' she said. 'Now I understand why you didn't want me to go to the theatre that time in Ayr and why you've tried to prevent me from reading about this case. Now I understand a lot of things.'

Father hesitated. He looked very prosperous in his dark grey pinstriped suit and gold watch chain looped over the front of his waistcoat. At last he said, 'We've always had your good at heart.'

'I had a right to know.'

'That's a debatable point.'

'I always wanted to know. Always. You should have been honest with me.'

'We've always done our best for you. What could knowing the truth have done for you? It could have ruined your life. It still could if you're not careful.'

'Careful?'

Mother lit a cigarette with a silver cigarette lighter. 'And discreet.'

'Discreet?' Elizabeth echoed.

Mother sighed. 'It must be obvious to you now why we didn't tell you.'

'Right from the beginning I mean.'

'That's what I mean too. She was never the type of person you'd want to associate with.'

Elizabeth had never felt so angry. Anger licked like a flame inside her head and behind her eyes.

'I should have been allowed to be the judge of that. As soon as I can I'm going to see her.'

Mother's glance became icy. 'Don't be ridiculous. She's in prison.'

'I'll go to the prison to see her.'

'You'll do no such thing,' Father snapped.

'You can't stop me.'

'Elizabeth, you can't get involved with this sordid mess. What good would it do either to you or to Annalie Gordon? I'm sure it would be the last thing she'd want.'

Sordid mess? Her father's words echoed sarcastically in Elizabeth's mind. He was a fine one to talk! What did he know about what Annalie Gordon wanted? If he'd done the decent thing and married Annalie, this dreadful business would never have happened. But he, like Jack Dawson, had only been interested in using a woman for his own selfish pleasure.

'You don't know what she wants any more than you've ever known what I wanted.'

'I know she wanted only the best for you. There is no way that she'd want you dragged through the mud with her. Believe me, Elizabeth.'

'Your father's telling the truth,' Mother said. 'I remember Annalie Gordon's exact words when she brought you here. She said . . . "I couldn't make Elizabeth suffer for anything I could or couldn't do. I've always wanted her to have a good life." '

'I have had a good life,' Elizabeth managed. 'And I appreciate all you've done for me. But I think it's now time I faced reality.'

Father said impatiently, 'This *is* your reality. Here with us in this house. Annalie Gordon belongs to another world. You have no part in it.'

'She's my own flesh and blood. There's no way I can just ignore her. Especially in the predicament she's in. They could hang her!'

The awful thought made the heat of anger drain from Elizabeth's face. She felt such an urgency to be with Annalie, she wanted to fly from the room with its stylish decor and aura of every comfort that money could buy and run all the way to Duke Street prison.

Father averted his gaze and began fumbling for his cigar case but Mother remained looking perfectly relaxed and cool.

'If she killed the man, and there doesn't seem any doubt about it, then she will hang. There's nothing you can do to prevent it.'

Elizabeth felt herself crumple helplessly inside. 'How can you sit there and calmly say a thing like that?'

'You spoke about facing reality. That's facing reality.'

'No, you're being cold-blooded and absolutely heartless. But then, you always have been.'

Mother paled and turned her face away and Father shouted, 'Elizabeth, apologize to your mother at once.

199

That's a downright lie and you know it. Christina has been good to you, and far more patient with you than you deserve.'

The acuteness of her horror and distress about Annalie made Elizabeth cry out in reckless abandon, 'And you're perfect as well, I suppose? Don't make me laugh. Why didn't you marry my real mother? She wasn't good enough for you, I suppose. So you took me from her and left her to rot.'

'Now you're being stupid.'

'Oh yes, I've been stupid all right. Stupid not to see what the pair of you have been like all along.'

'You ungrateful little wretch,' Christina said without bothering to look at her.

Elizabeth stumbled to her feet, desperate to escape from the room before she shamed herself with tears.

'There speaks my loving, patient, so-called mother.'

'Come back here at once,' Father shouted after her but she had escaped and was running upstairs to the nursery where Nanny still peacefully sat as if nothing had changed.

CHAPTER 25

'You'd better keep this strictly between us,' Jessie warned.

'Why? She's my mother. My own flesh and blood. I don't care who knows it. Oh Jessie, why won't she see me?' Elizabeth's face crumpled. 'I can't bear it. But I'm not going to give up and I'll be in court when the case comes up whether she wants me there or not.'

'You could ruin your life with this if you're not careful.'

'Oh, not you too,' Elizabeth groaned. 'That's what my father and Christina said.' She'd started referring to Mother as Christina now. Although she often forgot and still called her Mother.

'Well, I don't know, but I suspect your headmaster and the Education Department might not be all that keen to have the daughter of a murderess teaching young children. The parents of the children could object as well. There's no telling how daft people can be at times. Then as soon as it came out, the press would be pestering you at the school. That wouldn't go down well with the powers that be either. Take my advice. Be on the safe side and don't breathe a word to anyone.'

Elizabeth sighed. 'Oh, all right. I wouldn't feel so bad if only she'd agree to see me.'

'Maybe she's too ashamed. Think of it from her point of view. Duke Street prison isn't exactly the best place to welcome anyone, especially a well-brought-up miss from Queen's Park. Anyway, she wanted you to be a lady. That's what your mother said, wasn't it? And ladies aren't supposed to visit dumps like Duke Street prison.'

'Her name's Christina.'

'All right, that's what Christina said. But I think you're daft suddenly calling her Christina after she's been Mother for all these years.'

'She's not my mother.'

'You know fine you're just being daft.' Jessie threw back her blonde head and let out a yell of hilarity. 'I wish to God my ma had given me away to some rich woman. I'd have been only too glad to call her Mother. You don't know when you're well off.'

The awful thing was, she did. She acutely regretted the awful things she'd said to Father and Christina. She knew perfectly well they'd been good to her in their own way. The business took up much of their time but they'd always made sure their children weren't neglected. Christina was cool and distant, it was true, but that was just her nature. She was the same with everyone. In fact Elizabeth felt much more resentful towards her father than towards Christina. Now that Elizabeth knew the identity of her real mother, Nanny's secretiveness evaporated. She spoke quite freely on the subject. She said Beatrice Monkton, Adam's mother, had been mistress of Monkton House then and she had dismissed Annalie on the spot as soon as she'd found out the girl was pregnant. Apparently Father had been up north on a job at the time so perhaps he hadn't found out about the pregnancy right away. All the same, he obviously got to know eventually. In fact, he and Annalie had been lovers for some time after his marriage to Christina.

Nanny said no doubt Annalie Gordon was a great temptation and she reminded Elizabeth that he'd taken full responsibility for his child and brought her up with every care and comfort. This couldn't be denied and she was grateful. She had been saved the suffering and deprivation of so many of the children she saw in her class every day.

Nevertheless the admiration that had been akin to adoration of her father had gone. So had the warmth between them. She grieved for this. She longed for it to return but everything had been spoiled. Perhaps something could be salvaged of their relationship if she did what Father and Christina wanted and gave up all thoughts about having anything to do with her real mother. But she couldn't do that.

She couldn't tell Jessie how she was dreading Nanny's departure either. All her relationships seemed to be disintegrating around her. Jessie, who enjoyed a surfeit of close relationships with such a big family and now with big Gordon McGill, would never be able to understand how desolate she felt at losing Nanny. Especially now, when to all intents and purposes she'd lost Mother and Father as well.

What made matters even worse was that Nanny was leaving during the school summer holidays, which meant that Elizabeth hadn't even her work to fill her days and take up her attention. When the awful day came Elizabeth awoke very early. She was dressed before Nanny, who was usually the first person in the house to be up and getting everyone else organized. She hung around at Nanny's elbow while she finished her packing, wordlessly trying to be as close as possible before it was too late.

'Will you get out of my way,' Nanny burst out in exasperation eventually. 'I can't move for you. You'll be making me forget to pack something.'

They ate breakfast in strained silence. Elizabeth wondered if this meant that Nanny felt as miserable as she did. Yet she looked exactly the same with her hair severely pinned back from her angular face, and crisply smart in her blue uniform dress. The only difference was she hadn't put on a white apron. All her starched bib aprons had been packed away in her suitcase. Flossie had left a couple of days ago. Charlie had gone off to school camp the day before and Mother and Father had said their goodbyes downstairs before driving off to work. They'd had to leave earlier today because they'd to go through to Edinburgh for a special meeting. They'd ordered a taxi for Nanny, however, to take her all the way to Bearsden. It was due any time now.

Nanny donned her brimmed felt hat and jerked it well down over her brow. Then she buttoned her navy coat up to her neck and pulled on her matching leather gloves. She looked very stiff and straight-backed and her eyes had never been harder or sterner. They were saying quite plainly to Elizabeth, 'Don't you dare make a scene. Remember, you're supposed to be a lady.'

Nevertheless Elizabeth's eyes stretched huge and tragic. They began to brim over with tears and her lips violently trembled.

'Behave yourself,' Nanny commanded. 'You don't want the servants or the taxi driver to see you making a silly fuss. I'll be in touch. We'll meet for afternoon tea in Daly's or Copland and Lye's – somewhere nice.'

Elizabeth nodded, not trusting herself to speak. Then before she could say or do anything Nanny had marched away. She hurried after, feeling hysterical with unhappiness. She had never believed in her heart of hearts that Nanny would go. Now she wasn't prepared for the wrench of parting. Their feet drummed the linoleum of the nursery corridor to the door that sealed the nursery world off from the rest of the house. On the other side of the door the sound was silenced by thick carpets. A little knot of servants was waiting at the door to wave Nanny goodbye and before Elizabeth even had time to kiss her she was away in the taxi without as much as a backward glance.

Elizabeth flew swiftly back upstairs. The nursery door banged shut behind her as she ran to the dayroom window, desperately seeking a last sight of the taxi before it disappeared down Queen's Drive. But it had gone. How quiet the nursery was. Everything looked old and dead, the screen with scraps of angels and cherubs stuck on it and varnished over seemed a relic from another age. The rocking horse with stirrups dangling was a ghost. The shelf of wooden toys and drooping teddy bear and golliwog was also from a long-dead era. A panic of depression frightened her. She hurriedly left the room, only to find every room off the nursery corridor just as bleak and lonely. She couldn't even bear her bedroom because off its proximity to Nanny's room and the memories it evoked. She knew she wouldn't be able to sleep alone there tonight. But later when she was given a room downstairs she felt even more alone and desolate.

All through dinner Father and Christina talked business with William and Daniel. She felt so much out of place and that she had so little in common with any of them that she couldn't bear to sit in the drawing room with them for the rest of the evening. She told them she was going out and wandered about in the park for a while. At first she was tempted to take a tram over to Govan to see Jessie. Then she remembered that Jessie was going out with Big Gordon. Of course, even if Jessie had been at home she wouldn't have welcomed finding Elizabeth at her door.

She mentioned this next time she met Jessie.

'Sometimes I think – okay, why not?' Jessie told her. 'Then I remember what you've been used to and I think – no, never!'

'But I don't care what your home's like, Jessie. It's just you I care about.'

'You just think that.' Jessie shook her head. 'You don't know what it's like. You'd be shocked.'

'You're so easy-going about everything else and we get on so well together. I don't understand why you're like this about your home and family.'

'I have my pride the same as you. Not that there's

anything wrong with my family,' she hastened to add. 'They're the salt of the earth. It's just how we have to live. I'm not going to allow anyone to look down their nose at them or be shocked by them.'

Elizabeth felt hurt. 'I thought you knew me better than that. I'm not a snob.'

'I'm glad to hear it,' Jessie laughed. 'Never mind, when I marry Big Gordon and we get a wee place of our own you can come and visit me there. I'll have it all nice and respectable and even fit for the likes of you to see.'

'You're getting married then?' Elizabeth was surprised, and secretly appalled at the thought of Jessie wasting her life on someone so coarse. 'What about teaching? After all the studying and work you've done.'

Jessie shrugged. 'There's worse things happen in China.'

In her lonely desperation, Elizabeth looked forward with longing to seeing Alec Harper. She even looked forward to having tea with Mrs Harper before going to the pictures with Alec. At least Mrs Harper made her welcome and obviously thought the world of her.

'I keep telling Alec', she assured Elizabeth, 'that he's a very lucky man having such a sensible girl and with such a good background. What more could any man want? He should snap you up while he's got the chance, that's what I keep telling him. He's a bit slow at times, Alec is. His father was the very same. I'd to keep prodding him on as well.'

Recently she quite often laughed that high-pitched nervous laugh of hers and a dark red burned up from her neck as she said, 'Hasn't he popped the question yet, Elizabeth?'

And both Alec and Elizabeth would flush and not know where to look.

Or Mrs Harper would say, 'Don't tell me he hasn't

asked you yet?' And she'd turn a face fired with angry blotches to Alec and say, 'I've warned you, you'll lose her yet and it'll be your own stupid fault.'

Then one evening, not very long after Nanny had left, Elizabeth was over visiting Alec and at first Mrs Harper hadn't been in. She'd had to run out to the fish van. When she returned Elizabeth and Alec had been chuckling over a story Elizabeth had been telling about one of the children in her class.

Mrs Harper burst into the room crying out, 'Good, you've asked her at last. I can tell by your happy faces. Congratulations, the pair of you. And about time too. Alec, go and fetch that bottle of sherry in the kitchen cupboard and we'll have a toast.'

'But Mother,' Alec mumbled with embarrassment. 'You don't understand . . .'

'Go on.' Mrs Harper's voice loudened with desperation and her eyes flashed a warning. Alec hesitated, his gaze fixing on his mother with what looked for a moment like hatred. But the look disappeared so quickly Elizabeth decided she must have been mistaken.

'Very well,' he said and went to fetch the bottle.

In a way Elizabeth was quite relieved. Almost happy. She assuaged her guilt about not protesting to Mrs Harper that there had been no proposal by telling herself that she was doing Alec a kindness. She felt pity as well as tenderness for him. He would have been forever tongue-tied on the subject of marriage if he hadn't been helped out. After all, he wanted to settle down with her, otherwise why would he be walking out with her so regularly? They would be all right despite his mother's pathetic trickery. (Mrs Harper knew perfectly well, Elizabeth felt sure, that Alec had not proposed.) They got on fine together. She was fond of him and he was obviously fond of her.

Then, for the first time, she understood something of how Jessie felt. It was a kind of protectiveness. Only

it was the other way around. Elizabeth couldn't bear
to see Alec and Mrs Harper subjected to Mother's and
Father's disapproval or at best their patronizing polite-
ness. There was also the regrettable fact that, in their
eyes at least, she always seemed to be letting them
down. Bringing Alec and Mrs Harper into the family
would be letting Mother and Father down more than
ever before. And so she didn't tell them about her
engagement. She and Alec just quietly went on seeing
each other as before. She'd worry about the wedding
when it came. Meantime, the security of his friendship,
unknown to him, supported her in the dark days before
and during Annalie Gordon's trial.

CHAPTER 26

Duke Street prison was bounded by High Street, Duke Street, Drygate and part of John Knox Street. The area was the oldest in Glasgow and steeped in history.

It contained not only the prison but the pre-Reformation cathedral, the Necropolis, the ancient Provands Lordship and the huge Royal Infirmary, grim and black like the prison itself.

The place depressed Annalie beyond words. From the first moment when she'd seen it from the outside on the day she'd been brought here, its tall black walls and row upon row of small barred windows weighed heavily on her spirits. The section of the prison in which she was incarcerated was made up of four floors which were laid out in hanging galleries or corridors, with a well or open space in the centre. The cells ran on each side of the building. Sometimes there were periods of loud clanging and echoing. At other times there was the silence of the dead. She felt claustrophobic. She had always been a free spirit and the daily routine, the sitting for long periods in a confined space on her own was an agony to her mind, body and spirit. She had to pace about back and forth, round and round in frantic attempts to give herself relief. Elizabeth's letters and pleadings to allow her to visit did nothing to allay the anguish. She longed to see the girl, ached for the comfort of her own flesh and blood, but at the same time felt she would die of shame if Elizabeth saw her in such circumstances.

Elizabeth knowing who she was and the awful thing she'd done was tragic enough. She had only to look at the letters and see the neat measured writing to weep out loud. It was so unlike her own careless dramatic scrawl. It characterized someone careful and correct, someone who was used to order and proper, respectable behaviour. Why should such a person want anything to do with a notorious murderess? Curiosity? Pity? Pride that was almost an anger made Annalie stiffen with resolve, toss her head and assure herself that she neither needed nor wanted anyone's pity. Yet every night she was tormented by nightmares. She would waken up crying out in horror and tearing at her nightclothes, believing they were soaked with blood. And all the time, how she longed to see her daughter. As grey winter crept in through the bars of the small high window of the cell and the days and nights became icy she shivered with cold as well as longing. The letters would not leave her in peace. She always vowed that she would tear up the next one without reading it but she could never bring herself to do this. So she would torment herself with the neat, rounded handwriting and the lists of reasons why they should meet. The last letter said, 'Please don't feel ashamed or embarrassed because of your surroundings. There's no need. All that matters to me, all that I would see, is you. You must be horribly lonely and my heart goes out to you. I long to comfort you. I have a right to comfort you as a daughter should ...' It ended with the simple plea, 'Oh, do please allow me to see you, even if it's just for the one time. You surely cannot go on making me suffer like this. If you have ever loved me you will want us to meet, even for only a few precious minutes.'

'If you have ever loved me ...' The words twisted in Annalie's heart. She had loved her child from the beginning and would love her to the end. But oh, what a terrible end. Her heart quailed at the thought. They would hang her. That was the penalty for murder, and she was guilty. The only thing she felt glad of was that her father and Aunty Murn had not lived to see her shame. If only Elizabeth had never found out. Had Adam or Christina told her, she wondered? But surely they could not have been so foolish, or so cruel.

'If you have ever loved me...' The words kept reaching out to her until she persuaded herself that she was being wickedly selfish in not allowing Elizabeth to visit her. The girl desperately wanted to come. There was as much longing in her letters as in Annalie's heart.

'You surely cannot go on making me suffer like this' the letter said, and the thought of making her child suffer was too much in the end. Annalie agreed to see her on the next visiting day. Immediately she had done so she was filled to overflowing with doubts and fears. Thrashing about in the hard, narrow bed in her cell she tore at her hair in mounting anguish and regret. When the day came she couldn't eat, she was so distracted.

At last she was led into a room with a table in the centre at which sat a young lady in a buttoned-up navy wool coat with a hint of white blouse showing above it. An off-the-face felt hat with a folded-back brim had something of an angel's halo look and suited the girl's sweet, open face. Good leather gloves covered hands that were neatly folded on her lap and a navy leather bag lay on the table in front of her. She rose at the sight of Annalie and Annalie, heart bursting with pride and joy, flew towards her with arms outstretched.

Elizabeth was startled. She hadn't expected Annalie to be as wild and emotional as she'd appeared on the stage. Nor as beautiful. She was strikingly lovely even in the drab prison uniform. When Annalie raced towards her and grabbed her and hugged her and wept loudly and uncontrollably against her, Elizabeth was too shocked to respond immediately. An angry wardress prised Annalie roughly away with a warning that if she didn't sit down and behave herself she'd be taken back to her cell. Annalie wiped her eyes on her sleeve.

'I'm sorry, Elizabeth. I won't pounce on you again, I promise. It's just I was so excited. It's been such a long time. How are you? Are you happy? Do you like your job? Have you a gentleman friend?'

Despite feeling dazed Elizabeth managed to reply to the rapid stream of questions.

'I'm fine. I like my job. I am keeping company with someone.'

'What's he like? Is he nice? What does he look like? What does he do?'

'He's quiet and shy. He's about the same height as me. Well, maybe an inch taller so he's not very tall, but tall enough. He looks a bit thin but it's just the way he's made. He's very fit really. He has dark, straight hair and he wears horn-rimmed glasses which give him a serious, studious look. He has his own business.'

'Wonderful! Wonderful!' Annalie clasped her hands together under her chin in rapturous delight. 'He sounds a very sensitive, well-brought-up young man, and doing so well too. His own business! And you're a teacher. I couldn't have wished for anything better. Oh, it's so wonderful to know that you're making something of your life and you're happy.'

'Never mind about me.' Elizabeth fixed a serious gaze on the flushed emotional face. 'Have you got a good lawyer? Are they treating you all right?'

Annalie's eyes were greedily taking in every inch of Elizabeth. 'I'll be all right so long as you're all right. Oh, I hope you never thought that I gave you away because I didn't love you. You meant everything to me but I thought I was doing the best I could for you at the time. And I was right. I can see I was right. Oh, I'm so glad.'

'I did worry about why you gave me away. But not any more. All I'm concerned about now is you and what's going to happen to you. Do you have a good lawyer?' she anxiously repeated.

Annalie brushed the question aside with a flip of a hand. 'Oh, he's all right I suppose.'

'You suppose? But this is vitally important. Your life could depend on him.'

'Yes, yes, he'll do his best. He's going to make a plea of self-defence. But tell me more about yourself. I want to know everything. Absolutely everything. Did you have lots of lovely toys when you were small? And parties and beautiful friends? Tell me about your room at home. Is it just the way you like it? Have you a wardrobe full of lovely clothes? What kind of food do you enjoy? Does your boyfriend take you to posh restaurants? Oh, you've got a ring, an engagement ring! Oh Elizabeth, it's beautiful. Congratulations!'

Elizabeth had automatically taken off her gloves and folded them beside her handbag. Now she barely glanced down at her hand. She only wore the ring when she was visiting the Harpers. It had belonged to Mrs Harper's mother and Elizabeth had been very touched when she had been presented with it.

'Yes, I like it. But please, tell me you're going to be all right. It was self-defence, wasn't it? You didn't mean to kill him. That's what everyone's saying.'

'I'm so glad you're going to have a good man of your own to look after you.'

'You're not listening to me.'

Annalie shook her head. 'You mustn't think about me. After you walk out of here today you mustn't give me another thought.'

'But that's ridiculous. I couldn't possibly . . .'

'How did you find out about me in the first place?' Annalie interrupted. 'You didn't remember me, did you?'

'I'd seen you on the stage. And for a long time there had been so many things said and not said. So many things done and not done. I just pieced everything together eventually. Now I've found you I'm never going to let you go.'

'You mustn't talk like that or feel like that. It'll only cause you unhappiness. I won't have it. I won't have it, do you hear?'

'Sh . . . sh . . .' Elizabeth hushed her as if she was an overexcited child. It was strange, she was usually the helpless one but now she seemed much more mature, more in charge of the situation than this beautiful wild creature sitting in front of her. 'Calm yourself. We're together now. We're going to be all right.'

'All right? All right?' Annalie gave a hysterical laugh. 'You don't know what you're talking about. They're going to hang me.'

Elizabeth paled and had to struggle with herself not to panic. 'You mustn't say that. The trial hasn't even begun. A jury could set you free. If it was self-defence . . .'

'I won't have it, do you hear?' Annalie repeated. 'Whether they hang me or let me walk out of here it doesn't make a bit of difference as far as you and I are concerned.'

'It'll make all the difference in the world. I don't care what you say. I'm going to leave home and live with you as soon as you get out of here and I'm sure you will get out.'

'Leave home?' Annalie echoed. 'Leave your lovely home? Are you mad? You don't know what you're saying. What would your fiancé think of that?'

'I don't care what he thinks. I don't care what anybody thinks. I'll break off my engagement. From now on you come first in my life. We've so much lost time to make up for.'

Annalie was silent for a long minute, then she said, 'It wasn't lost time for me. I made a career for myself. Before that I was tied to a boring job in a paper shop in the Gorbals because of you.'

'I don't understand.' Elizabeth's voice shrank warily.

'I gave you away so that I could have a life of my own and do what I'd always wanted to do. Be a dancer.'

'But you said . . .'

'Yes, yes, I loved you. It was a wrench giving you up. But I needed my freedom. I wanted to go on the stage and that meant unusual working hours and touring about the country. I wanted a good life for you too, of course, and I knew you'd get that with your father. And Christina promised me she'd treat you like one of her own.'

Elizabeth had lost every vestige of colour. 'You're only saying all this because you think I'd suffer deprivation or what you think would be deprivation if we stayed together now.'

'Elizabeth, believe me. I haven't regretted giving you up. It was no joke being saddled with an illegitimate child and if I get out of here I've no intention of being saddled with an unwanted daughter. I'll want to savour and enjoy my freedom more than ever.'

'Don't, please . . .'

Annalie's gaze flicked restlessly around. 'Well, you would come. It's your own fault. You can't say I didn't warn you. I did everything I could to stop you. Even though I was wild with curiosity.'

'I wouldn't be any trouble.' Elizabeth struggled to hold back her tears. 'I just want to be near you. I belong with you.'

'Don't talk rubbish. You're a stranger to me.' Annalie bounced to her feet with a defiant toss of her head.

'What would my life be like with a prissy schoolmarm stuck to me all the time?' She gave a sudden, wild burst of laughter. 'It doesn't bear thinking about.'

She was away like a sudden storm. The wardress had shut and locked the door before Elizabeth had recovered from her shock. Indeed she didn't think she'd ever recover. Her legs were hardly able to carry her to the tram car that took her home. She felt weak and shaken as if she had been suffering from a long debilitating illness. Alone in her bedroom she wept broken-heartedly. Then from somewhere at last came courage and calmness. She dried her eyes.

The distraught woman in Duke Street prison needed help and whether Annalie wanted it or not she was entitled to comfort and support from her own flesh and blood. Going to the court and being as close as possible to Annalie for the length of the trial was one way of giving her these things. Elizabeth felt determined to go, yet at the same time she dreaded witnessing Annalie's ordeal. It was as if there had never been any separation. The years apart had melted away in the welter of emotion between the two women. Elizabeth was haunted by the picture of Annalie as a wild creature, trapped and panic-stricken, yet somehow clinging to dignity and courage. Her heart ached for her. She feared for her. She felt desperately protective towards her. Every moment of every day she worried for her health, her welfare, her safety.

She had never felt so intensely, urgently emotional about anyone in her life before. Not Jack Dawson. Not Mother or Father. Even Nanny paled into insignificance.

CHAPTER 27

'What next?' Christina rustled the *Glasgow Herald* but remained hidden behind it. 'Non-belief in Nazism has become legal grounds for divorce in Germany.'

'Too bad if you're Jewish as well,' Adam said, lighting a cigar. 'They've not only been deprived of their German citizenship, they've been excluded from employment in public services and had their pension rights taken away. I was speaking to a man in Sloane's the other day. He's come to Scotland with his wife and family and hopes to set up in business here, with the help of some relatives in Glasgow. He says Hitler's making it impossible for Jews over there. They're barred from teaching, journalism, farming, radio, the theatre and films. They're being excluded from law and medicine. Not to mention the ruination of their businesses.'

Christina put down the paper. 'What's he got against the Jews? They're good business people. Surely they would only help the German economy, and Hitler's supposed to be wanting to do everything to build that up.'

'It's not only the Jews he's after. He's a bloody madman. And what worries me is he's declared all men from eighteen to forty-five army reservists. He's building up for a fight, if you ask me.'

'It would fit you better,' Elizabeth interrupted, 'if you would show a bit more concern for troubles nearer home.'

They were sitting round the electric fire in the drawing room, or living room as it was more often referred to now. Adam was reclining in one of the armchairs, cigar smoke drifting out in front of his expensively clad figure in its three-piece crisply tailored navy suit and blue shirt with fashionable white collar. Christina was sitting opposite him, slim and elegant in an afternoon dress of printed silk georgette in peach, blue-grey and black.

They both turned steely, disapproving stares on Elizabeth. Christina said, 'If you are referring to Annalie Gordon, as no doubt you are since you have an absolute obsession with the woman, then I must remind you that her troubles, as you so euphemistically put it, were brought upon her by herself. There's nothing we can do about them.'

'You don't care, do you?' Elizabeth gazed helplessly at the older woman.

'Frankly, no, I don't.'

Adam flicked ash into the ashtray on the small table at his elbow. 'Elizabeth, what good do you think you're doing to anyone or anything going on like this?'

Elizabeth fixed him with huge dark pools of eyes. 'I'm so afraid for her.'

With a sigh Adam went over to the cocktail cabinet and poured a whisky for himself, and a gin and tonic for his wife.

'Do you want a drink, Elizabeth?'

She shook her head.

'I realize', Adam said after returning to his seat, 'what a shock all this has been to you. But the hard fact is Annalie Gordon is a stranger to you. It was a lucky day for you when she brought you here. It's time you faced the fact.'

'I agree,' Christina said. 'What kind of life do you think you would have had with a woman like that, Elizabeth?'

Faced with Elizabeth's wretched silence Adam tried again:

'It's sad that she should end like this. Very sad indeed. But it's true what Christina says. She has brought this on herself, Elizabeth.'

'She was always a troublemaker,' Christina sighed. 'Wild and undisciplined. Remember the rent strikes?' She gave a delicate shudder, half closing her eyes. 'I'll never forget her at the head of that dreadful rabble of women, carrying a live rat.'

Elizabeth's face blanched. 'I don't believe you.'

'It's true,' Adam said. 'She had a live rat in a cage held aloft a pole and she was leading a riotous mob of women. She caused a great deal of trouble for us for a time.'

'And of course you never caused any trouble for her?' Elizabeth protested bitterly.

'No, we didn't,' Christina said. 'And before you come out with your usual boring accusations about your father having his wicked way with her, your father payed dearly for that little indiscretion.'

Elizabeth felt sick. She despised herself for getting into such a destructive conversation. She longed for comfort and support from Mother and Father but her distress about Annalie was so acute she had to take it out on someone.

'In what way?'

Adam cut in. 'In putting up with you for all these years, for a start.'

'Your father didn't mean that,' Christina said.

'You keep making us both say things we don't mean.' Adam took a deep breath. 'Elizabeth, you've always been treated as an accepted and cherished member of the family. You must know that.'

'I was talking about Annalie, not me. It's her I'm concerned about, not myself.'

'What more can I say?' Adam stubbed out his cigar. 'I did all I could for the woman when I knew her. I gave her an allowance. I set her up in a comfortable flat. When her mother kidnapped you I nearly died in the attempt to get you back to her. I did all I could,' he repeated. 'And it was her decision in the end to give you up and go her own way.'

'And she has gone her own way,' Christina said, 'and I will not have you dragging her back into our lives like this, Elizabeth. I'm sure it's not what she'd want you to be doing either. Why not be honest and admit it?'

Elizabeth miserably lowered her eyes and Christina insisted:

'Well, is it?'

'No.' Elizabeth looked up through a mist of tears. 'It'll please you to know that in fact she wants nothing to do with me. I went to see her in prison and it was a most unsuccessful visit, to say the least.'

Adam's face turned rock hard. 'You were specifically forbidden to go near that place.'

'I had to see her.'

'No, you did not have to see her. I'm warning you, Elizabeth, my patience is wearing very thin. You are not to go near that place again or have anything more to do with Annalie Gordon. If you can't put her out of your mind and your life then you'll no longer have any place in our lives. Do I make myself clear?'

She managed to rise with some dignity although she was collapsing with despair inside. 'Oh, perfectly. You'll welcome the excuse to throw me out.'

Adam smacked a palm against his brow. 'You've become bloody impossible, Elizabeth. We'd have to be saints to continue putting up with you.'

'As it happens,' she said, 'you won't need to put up with me for much longer. I'm engaged to be married and I'll be leaving here very soon.'

'Not to Harper?' Adam groaned. 'Spare us that.'

Christina said, 'There's nothing we can do, Adam.'

'Have you no sense at all?' Adam's voice loudened. 'The man's a moron. He can hardly string two words together. He must be about the same age as me and he's only got one piddling little grocer's shop in Govan. One thing's certain. He won't be able to keep you in the style to which you're accustomed.'

Elizabeth was having a hard struggle to hold back the tears. The whole situation had run away from her. She hadn't meant to say anything about getting married. She didn't want to get married.

'I don't care about money,' she said.

'That's because you've never needed to care about it,' Adam shouted. 'Can't you see what you'll be doing to your life, you bloody idiot . . .'

Christina cut in, her voice cool and calm. 'There's no point in getting all worked up, Adam. All you do is risk giving yourself a heart attack.'

Adam sank back into his chair. 'Get out of my sight.'

Elizabeth bumped blindly into chairs and tables as she left the room. Somehow she reached her bedroom, but it was a strange place, nothing like her old familiar retreat in the nursery with its pretty shades of pink and lavender. This was a brown room with brown-painted walls, brown polished boards, a brown and fawn rug, brown and fawn curtains and a sickly cream bedmat. She found the place profoundly depressing despite the wall lights with the new uplighted shades. Further along the corridor were the doors to the boys' rooms and Mother's and Father's room. Elizabeth lay on top of the bed and listened but she could hear no sound other than her own sobbing. She could hardly believe all that had happened. As if she hadn't been wretched enough, she'd piled misery upon misery in some sort of masochistic orgy. She ached to run back downstairs to Mother and Father and plead for their forgiveness but knew everything had gone too far. They were sick of her and she didn't blame them. For a long time she trembled at the thought of being banished from home and especially of being married and having to go and live in Drive Road in Linthouse. Not so much because of Alec but his mother, with her nervous tics and hot flushes, and bunions so painful they made her walk with a strange flat-footed, sometimes hirpling gait in her grotesquely deformed shoes.

Then gradually she brought herself round to thinking that marriage to Alec might not be so bad. After all, they wouldn't need to live with Mrs Harper for long and she wasn't such a bad person when one got to know her. She was more to be pitied, really. Alec would soon find another place, then she would be mistress in her own home with everything to her taste and she and Alec would be on their own and could relax. The more she thought about this line of action the more comforted she became. If Mother and Father attended the ceremony it would be an ordeal, but why should she care about what they thought of Alec or Mrs Harper? Mother and Father would probably make some excuse about being away from home on business and not attend. Or they would just refuse point-blank to have anything do with it.

At least Annalie would be pleased if she got married, Elizabeth thought ruefully. She would write and tell her, and post the letter first thing in the morning. Yes, she would be pleased. Perhaps the fact that her daughter would be safely settled in marriage would make Annalie change her mind about seeing her again and continuing some sort of relationship. Elizabeth felt a little cheered and slightly more hopeful.

CHAPTER 28

Mrs Harper was hysterical with delight. Elizabeth was overwhelmed by the older woman's wild-eyed triumph – Mrs Harper couldn't have been more excited if she'd won the football pools. Elizabeth had been worrying about how best to broach the subject of the wedding date to Alec. She suspected that he was the type who would be quite content to remain engaged for years. She didn't want him to feel she was rushing him or making him comply with anything he didn't feel completely happy about. She hoped, however, that if she explained everything, he'd understand.

She'd planned to talk to him after they'd had tea and Mrs Harper had left them on their own. She'd barely made a tentative beginning, however, when Mrs Harper, who must have been listening at the door, burst into the room. She hadn't even bothered to take off her floral wraparound apron before rushing into the front room, one of the things she was normally fussy about when Elizabeth was visiting. Elizabeth felt harassed by Mrs Harper's reckless attitude: as far as she was concerned they could be married tomorrow. Elizabeth, struggling to quell panic, reminded herself that she wanted to escape from Monkton House as soon as possible. Father had given her no option but to leave. But even if there had not been Father's ultimatum, life had become too painful with Nanny gone and Father and Mother and even the boys treating her like a social outcast.

Father had made another attempt, however, to persuade her – as he put it – to see sense and have nothing more to do with either 'that woman in Duke Street prison or that idiot Harper'. To call Alec an idiot was so insulting and unfair she'd bristled on his behalf.

'You obviously don't know Alec.'

'I don't want to know him and I certainly don't want him as part of my family.'

'He's a good, kind man.'

'I'm a better judge of character than you, Elizabeth. I'm in the business of assessing men's characters. I employ hundreds of them. That man's not only weak, he's not only a loser, there's something shifty about him. I wouldn't trust that ferret with a load of bricks, far less my daughter.'

Elizabeth was hurt to the point of tears on Alec's behalf. 'He feels uncomfortable with you because you're always so rude to him.'

'That's a lie! I admit it's been one hell of an effort but I have managed to be polite.'

'You can't hide the fact that you don't like him.'

'I *don't* like him. I'm not denying that.'

There was silence for a few seconds as both of them fought for control.

'Elizabeth, you're a good-looking girl. You could do better than him. And you're young. You've plenty of time. You've your whole life ahead of you. I thought you enjoyed teaching.'

'I do.'

'You'll have to give up your career.'

This was something she hadn't thought about at first. But she had made enquiries and done some reading on the subject and discovered to her surprise, chagrin and indignation that a marriage bar did in fact exist. Apparently the churches were very concerned about the falling birth rate among the middle and artisan classes, and as women teachers most likely came from these kinds of family, or would marry into them, their example in living the ideal domestic life of housewife and mother was valuable. This had been the basis for the introduction of a marriage bar in September 1915 and nothing had changed since. Indeed one minister, the Reverend Mr McQueen, seemed to have made the 'spinsterization' of the teaching profession his goal in life. Elizabeth was distressed by the unfairness of this prohibition.

Her half-brother Daniel did not make her feel any better by saying: 'You can be sure of one thing, I won't be at the wedding. You're daft enough to have that murderess at it if they let her out. Not the kind of company I care to keep.'

'Oh, they'll never let her out,' William said. 'She'll be buried in Duke Street. There's a place inside the walls . . .'

'That's enough, William,' Adam warned.

Elizabeth struggled for a cool voice to hide her pain. 'I wasn't expecting any of you to be at my wedding. I know what dreadful snobs you all are.'

'Your mother and I will fulfil our obligations and attend the wedding,' Adam said coldly. 'But after that, as far as I'm concerned, you're his problem not ours.'

'No doubt your grandfather would perform the ceremony if you asked him,' Christina said without looking at Elizabeth, as if the whole business was no longer of any interest to her.

Elizabeth's eyes became vague in an effort to appear equally nonchalant. 'Perhaps the registrar's office would be best. With Grandfather's health and all the worry about moving . . .'

Grandfather Gillespie was retiring and moving from the manse next door to a bungalow in Newton Mearns. It was an upheaval that neither he nor Grandmother Gillespie was very fit for at the moment. Anyway Elizabeth had no wish to include them in any family disputes. Up till now they hadn't met Alec, although she suspected that Mother had confided in Grandmother about the opposition to him and how unsuitable he was thought to be.

Christina said, 'Very well. But do try to tell us the date in reasonable time so that we can leave a space in our diaries. You know how busy we always are.'

'Oh, indeed I do.'

'Spare us the self-pity,' Adam snapped. 'Both your mother and I have worked hard to provide you with every luxury. You've obviously never had the slightest appreciation of this fact. It seems you prefer a different lifestyle altogether and completely different types of people from us. But I'll ask you just *once* more, will you give up your obsession with Annalie Gordon and your crazy idea of marrying this middle-aged nonentity?'

It was then resentment of her father turned to hatred hot and sharp and disdainful. She glowered her refusal at him. How dare he forbid her to have anything to do with her natural mother? How dare he criticize a decent man like Alec? Who was he to criticize anyone's character? She could forgive him for marrying Christina but never for taking such cruel advantage of the young Annalie who had worked in his house.

It amazed her how composed Christina was about what she'd referred to as 'that little indiscretion'. She must have felt and must still be feeling much more beneath the glacial calm. It was this elegant composure, this unflappable poise that Elizabeth had always so keenly admired. From as far back as she could remember she had set Christina on a pedestal and lived in the hope of some gracious crumbs of attention being tossed in her direction. She treasured the memory of every kind word that Christina had ever uttered to her. She never tired of analysing each word and each inflection in determined and optimistic attempts to find affection.

She longed to be like Christina – clever, elegant, socially successful, always knowing what she wanted out of life, and getting it. Not the mixed-up person she was, always saying and doing the wrong thing and getting everyone's back up. She had begun to have a sneaking suspicion that she might be more like her real mother, who seemed to have an all too obvious talent for getting herself into trouble. This thought horrified and frightened Elizabeth. She had not the slightest desire to be like the volatile, emotionally unbalanced woman she'd met in Duke Street prison. She comforted herself with the knowledge that in many ways she was exactly the opposite of Annalie. She was a typically conscientious and concerned schoolteacher, her quiet authority softened by affection for the children in her care. She enjoyed her many little routines at school just as she'd felt comforted by the many routines Nanny had imposed in the nursery. Admittedly there were times when she had clashed (in a tentative or at worst stubborn way) with some teachers over teaching methods. They accused her of being far too lax and having too many silly or fancy ideas. But on the whole she tried to keep an even keel, to please everybody, to be friends with everybody and fit in with the accepted norms.

She couldn't imagine Annalie being a routine kind of person. In one way she felt towards Annalie as she would to one of her most wayward schoolchildren. She worried about her, felt protective towards her, was terribly saddened by her present situation and full of fear and apprehension for her future. It was strange to think that she'd known and admired and loved Mother for as far back as she could remember yet after only one meeting with Annalie her feelings for her were far more powerfully disturbing and acute than they'd ever been for Christina.

She'd meant to tell Alec about Annalie and how since she'd met her and become so attached to her (it was almost as if she was imprisoned along with her) everything had become impossibly fraught and difficult at home. She'd meant to work up gradually to her reasons for wanting to set the marriage date as soon as possible.

But, as usual, she'd gone about things the wrong way. She'd started by saying, 'I was wondering, Alec, what you'd think about setting the date for our wedding quite soon. The reason I'm making this suggestion . . .'

She hadn't got any further. Mrs Harper had exploded into the room, beaky face under big crocheted beret afire and quivering like an excited turkey cock.

'He thinks it's a great idea, don't you Alec? What's the point in putting it off? That's what I keep telling him. He's not getting any younger and neither am I. I want to see him settled before I'm put beneath the clay. I'm sure your mother feels the same about you. A wonderful woman, your mother. There's nobody I admire more. And your father of course. They've got to the top of the tree and no mistake. I keep telling him. Take an example from Elizabeth's mother and father and you'll not go wrong. Alec, don't just sit there like an accident looking for somewhere to happen. Go and fetch my bottle of sherry.' It was then she remembered her apron and tugged it off to reveal the shapeless black dress she always wore livened up with different accessories – modesty fronts in cream or white linen, imitation lace collars and cuffs, or net jabots.

After they'd drunk a celebration sherry Mrs Harper's face came up in fiery blotches and she announced that she had a brilliant idea. Why not make it a Christmas wedding? That way the shop needn't be shut any more than was absolutely necessary over the Christmas and New Year period and therefore very little, if any, money would be lost.

'But, but . . . Christmas is only a few weeks away,' Elizabeth stammered. 'I wasn't thinking . . . I didn't mean . . . We couldn't anyway . . . Could we? They surely wouldn't allow us so soon . . . Isn't there a legal waiting time or something?' She felt confused and more than a little frightened. It had all been just words before. Now everything was turning into reality.

228

'Special licence.' Mrs Harper's eyes had a mad look and a nerve was jerking visibly in her cheek. 'Why not, eh? No reason in the world why not. No, there'll be no problem there. Especially you coming from such a well-known, influential family.'

'Oh, no.' Elizabeth shook her head. 'There's no need for that.'

'You can stay here of course until you get yourself organized. I've no doubt your mother and father will see you well placed soon enough.'

'I really don't think . . .'

'You can't tell me they're short of a bob or two.'

'It's not that. You don't understand . . .'

'Mother,' Alec murmured. 'Will you please calm down and allow Elizabeth and me to get a word in edgeways?'

'What's there to say? You do think you should get married, don't you?'

There was only the merest hesitation before he said, 'Yes. But I think it's up to Elizabeth and me to discuss the details.'

'Alec.' Elizabeth gazed worriedly over at him. 'I don't mean to rush you or anything. I just wanted to discuss the possibility . . .'

'I know him,' Mrs Harper interrupted. 'He always needs somebody to give him a push. You did quite right, Elizabeth. He would have been content to go on for donkey's years the way things were. I would have been under the clay and you drawing your old-age pension and still just engaged if you'd left it to him. I take it your mother's seeing to some sort of reception?'

'I think they mentioned having a meal somewhere. Just the two of them and us. But, to be honest Mrs Harper, it would be better if they weren't there. You see . . .'

'Nonsense! I know it has to be a quiet affair in the circumstances. There wouldn't be time to organize a big do, but of course your mother and father will have to be there. There's only Alec and me on our side so what could be quieter? Oh, I'm really looking forward to meeting Mr and Mrs Monkton. Funny we haven't met before. Of course, they're such busy people. So well-thought-of and so well heeled. They must be two of the wealthiest folk in Glasgow.'

'Oh no. I'm sure they're not . . .'

'You're far too modest, that's your trouble, Elizabeth. Fancy you out working too and never any need. Good for you, I say. Every extra penny helps.'

Elizabeth gave up. The idea of her not needing to work was too ridiculous for words. Even if Mother and Father had been as wealthy as Mrs Harper imagined, they still would never have entertained the idea of anyone in the family being idle. And such a thought was as much anathema to Elizabeth as it would have been to them. Nor had she ever thought of work in terms of money. She doubted if money had ever been Mother's and Father's main incentive either. They were both ambitious. No doubt they both liked the power that money gave them but basically they were just obsessed by and addicted to work, as an alcoholic is obsessed by and addicted to alcohol. Elizabeth felt sorry for Mrs Harper with her silly and wrong ideas and her hysterical happiness at the wedding. She and Alec shook their heads at the older woman's excitement and just continued their calm, friendly relationship, both preferring to discuss the latest film at the local Lyceum rather than their wedding. Anyway, Elizabeth had other even more urgent things on her mind. Annalie's trial was now due and she was distracted by worry about that.

She did say to Alec on one of the few occasions they were alone before the wedding, that Mother and Father didn't approve of the match. Alec had told her not to worry. He knew they didn't like him but they'd come round in time. It was understandable that they should be concerned about who their only daughter was marrying. He wasn't worried, he assured her and, giving one of his rare, shy smiles he repeated, 'They'll come round in time.'

'But you don't understand, there's more to it than that. I have to tell you, Alec . . .'

'Sh . . . sh.' He placed a gentle finger against her lips, silencing her. 'Try not to cause any more trouble.'

This had both surprised and irritated her. If anyone was causing trouble it was his mother with all her rushing around and continuous interfering. Not to mention the embarrassment of her never-ending boasting to all and sundry. From the moment they'd got engaged Mrs Harper haunted the shop, supposedly to help Alec behind the counter, head well covered with her outsized crocheted tammy, tongue waggling increasingly until there wasn't a customer who didn't know her son was getting married to the daughter of the Monktons of Monkton's Building Company. Now she sent the news of the Christmas wedding flying round like wildfire. Several times in the shop Elizabeth had to suffer jokes about hasty weddings and shotgun affairs. She stopped going and begged a supply of tea, milk and sugar from Cook instead. Cook hadn't been too keen at first. She was in the habit of keeping a conscientious check on all her supplies and was as careful with them as if their cost was coming out of her own pocket. But she'd shrugged and said, 'Oh well, for all the time . . .'

It made Elizabeth realize with a flutter of panic that indeed she didn't have much time left in Monkton House. She wished Nanny was there. She wanted to run upstairs to the nursery and hide her face in Nanny's apron. But Nanny was immersed in another world now, with other concerns and interests. At the same time Elizabeth quite looked forward to all the fuss being over, when she and Alec could find a place of their own. At times she even played games in her mind about how she'd furnish her new home and look after it and cook nice meals. Although in fact she had no idea how to cook. It was one of the things she would have to learn. Meantime, there were more urgent things to take up her attention.

She phoned the school and told them she had a dose of flu and would have to stay in bed for a few days. Instead, as soon as she'd phoned, she made her way to Jail Square and the High Court in the Justiciary Buildings where the trial of Annalie Gordon was being held.

CHAPTER 29

Jail Square was at the foot of the Saltmarket and the
first building on the right was the red-brick mortuary.
Rearing up next to it was the much more imposing
High Court of Justiciary and both buildings faced on to
the wide flat expanse of Glasgow Green and the lofty
Nelson's Monument. Public hangings used to take place
in front of the Justiciary and a common Glasgow insult
was 'You'll die facing the monument'. Despite being
cosily dressed in her fur-trimmed hat, leather gloves and
cashmere coat with its neat fur collar, Elizabeth shivered
at the thought of someone being put to death on the
very spot she was walking over. She hurried past a row
of constables standing on the pavement in front of the
court, their suspicious eyes fixed on the people gathering
about the gate of the green. Some were unemployed
men, hands deep into the pockets of their shabby suits.
White artificial silk scarves were crossed beneath chins
and tucked into waistcoats. Knots of women, some in
shawls, some in cheap coats shiny with age, whispered
together and kept glancing hopefully over at the court
building. Elizabeth felt revolted by such morbid curios-
ity. No doubt it was the same emotion that had brought
people in their thousands to watch public hangings.
Aware of the curiosity now aimed at her as she hurried
up the steps and between the double row of giant Doric
columns, she flushed with embarrassment.

She found herself in a white and black marble hall
and stopped, unexpectedly awestruck and uncertain.
Clerks and journalists, lawyers in wigs and gowns,
bustled about. Some stood talking together, even laugh-
ing. There were policemen too and as she stood gazing

233

helplessly around one of the constables approached her and asked if she was a witness.

She shook her head. 'I just want to know where the Annalie Gordon case is being held.'

'The North Court.' The policeman pointed towards a door in one of the corridors leading off the hall.

'Thank you.'

Another policeman gestured her to be silent as she approached and she found that there was a second door within the door indicated. After pushing her way through both as quietly as possible she found herself in a sombre courtroom made dark by wooden panelling on walls and benches. The judge's bench, elevated above everything else, boasted rich carving. High on the wall behind was a splash of vivid colour, the coat of arms bearing a lion and a unicorn rearing up towards each other on either side of a shield.

At a horseshoe-shaped table below the judge's bench lawyers in white wigs and black gowns were sifting through papers. Directly facing the bench and filling Elizabeth with apprehension, the wooden dock awaited the prisoner. Stretching on either side of it and behind it the rows of benches were already filling up. Elizabeth was unable to sit as near to the dock as she'd hoped and she glanced around, wondering how many of the public on the benches were friends of Annalie, people who cared about her, and how many just people with a ghoulish interest in murder. She decided the woman sitting next to her with a checked shawl clutched round her bony shoulders came into the latter category. An air of eager excitement was widening her eyes and making her restless. She nudged Elizabeth and whispered:

'Look hen, there's the Lord Provost. I bet that gold chain's worth a fortune.' She pointed over to the left of the lawyers' table to where a man was settling himself on one of the leather-covered benches. 'Too bad they don't give us padded seats. These are bloody hard.'

Elizabeth tried to quell the woman with one of Mother's cool disdainful stares, but failed.

'Are the jury's seats the same as his? Can you see, hen? Oh look, there's the Chief Constable sitting beside the Provost now. Isn't he a picture in that uniform? I always say, you've got to give credit where credit's due . . .'

'Hush!' Elizabeth reverted to her more natural schoolteacher's expression. 'If you don't be quiet you'll be put out.'

This worked like magic. The woman immediately subsided with a guilty apologetic look pinching her hollow cheeks.

Suddenly a loud fanfare of trumpets echoed through the court followed by a call of 'Court' which brought everyone to their feet. Then a procession filed in headed by the macer carrying the mace. Lord Dunvegan, the bewigged judge in rich white and scarlet gown, stared dourly at the macer's back. Each white silk panel of the judge's gown was emblazoned with a scarlet cross and Elizabeth wondered if this had some religious significance. There certainly must be some religious note in the proceedings because following the judge came the Minister of the cathedral dressed in lace and silk gown and doctor's hood. After him came court officials. The macer ceremoniously hung the mace on the wall behind the bench and beneath the coat of arms before retreating.

As soon as the judge sat down, everyone else sat except the Minister, who stood on the judge's left and raised a hand and solemn voice in prayer:

'Lord, we pray for the health and strength of the Royal Family, and for His Majesty's Government and justice for all who come here.'

Elizabeth was not listening. Sitting stiffly on the edge of her seat clutching her handbag on her lap, she gave her whole attention to the prisoner, who had been brought up from somewhere underneath the court to stand in the dock between two heftily built and grim-faced policeman. In comparison with their solid girth, Annalie seemed physically frail, yet the look of wildness was still there. She held herself very straight with head high, and within her eyes was a mixture of defiance and panic. Her beauty and vulnerability nearly made Elizabeth moan out loud with the tragedy of it all. She longed to snatch Annalie away and hide her from the curious, ghoulish eyes of the public and the apparent indifference of the representatives of the law. She wanted to protect her from harm and humiliation.

The clerk of the court rose and said, 'Call the Diet His Majesty's Advocate against Annalie Gordon.'

Annalie's lawyer got to his feet, cleared his throat and with a tug of his gown announced, 'I appear, my Lord, for the accused, who adheres to her plea of not guilty and also to her special defence of self-defence.'

A jury of fifteen was then empanelled.

Elizabeth was somewhat reassured to see that Mr Ramsay, Annalie's lawyer, was a giant of a man with an intimidating eye. He looked more than capable of defending his client and crushing anyone who had the temerity to oppose him in his task.

The clerk of the court was reading out the indictment: 'Annalie Gordon, prisoner in the Prison of Glasgow, is indicted at the instance of the Right Honourable George Whittaker, His Majesty's Advocate, and the charge against her is that on 12th May in a house in Cumberland Street, Gorbals, Glasgow she did assault Anthony Carlino, and did stab him in the neck with a knife or other instrument and did murder him.'

The clerk then said to the jury who were all standing, 'Do you fifteen swear by Almighty God that you will well and truly try the accused and give a true verdict according to the evidence?'

'I do,' they replied and then sat down.

The special defence was then read which said that on the occasion labelled the accused was acting in

236

self-defence, she having been assaulted by the said Anthony Carlino.

The first witness for the prosecution was called by the prosecution and the judge, according to the custom in Scotland, administered the oath. Lord Dunvegan stood to tower above the court and with hand raised sternly addressed the witness:

'Hold up your right hand and repeat after me. *I swear by Almighty God . . .*'

The witness raised her hand and took the oath.

The Advocate Depute scraped back his chair and stood gazing down over his spectacles at a sheaf of papers on the table before asking, 'What is your name?'

'Frances Peterson.'

'And your address?'

'Sixteen Parnie Street, Knightswood.'

'What age are you?'

'Twenty-four.'

'And you are a chorus girl by profession?'

'Yes.'

'Did you know the deceased, Anthony Carlino?'

'Yes.'

'What was the nature of your relationship?'

'We loved each other. We were planning to get married.'

The judge suddenly boomed out, 'Keep your voice up so that the jury can hear you.'

The witness cleared her throat. 'We were planning to get married.'

The Advocate Depute shuffled some papers on the table. 'Did you know Annalie Gordon?'

'She was Tony's dancing partner.'

'Could you be more specific? Did you meet her sometimes, or often, or what?'

'I was sometimes on the same bill as her. She was very possessive. More than once she threatened to kill him. We had to be very careful not to arouse her jealousy.'

Elizabeth became more and more agitated as the questions and answers built up a picture of Annalie as someone far more liable to murder from passion and premeditation than self-defence. Nor did it ease her anxiety to observe that the witness was an attractive woman and likely to impress the jury not only with her slender figure and long shapely legs but also with her apparently guileless sincerity.

Eventually Mr Ramsay rose to cross-examine.

'You say that Annalie Gordon was very possessive with Mr Carlino.'

'Yes.'

'What makes you say that?'

The witness hesitated, eyes bewildered. 'I . . . I don't understand.'

Mr Ramsay's voice acquired a note of impatience. 'Why do you believe that Annalie Gordon was very possessive towards your lover?'

Miss Peterson flushed. 'He told me she was.'

'He told you.' Mr Ramsay's tone gave ridicule to the words. 'I see.'

'He told you about her jealousy too, did he?'

'He wouldn't lie to me.'

'Did he tell you about his other lovers?'

'Tony was faithful to me.'

'I put it to you, Miss Peterson, that Mr Carlino was a womanizer who had a lover in nearly every chorus line in the country, not to mention those among his adoring fans.'

'That's not true.'

'In due course if we hear evidence to the contrary what would you say?'

'I don't know.'

'I suggest to you, Miss Peterson, that far from Annalie Gordon being possessive and vying for Carlino's attention she was probably the only woman who consistently refused his advances.'

The witness fumbled for a handkerchief. 'You obviously haven't seen the passionate way she danced with him.'

'Ah, the dance! Yes, I don't think anyone could dispute the fact that Annalie Gordon was a very talented professional entertainer. But, I put it to you, Miss Peterson, that it's not how she behaved or what she did during her professional hours that is under question. Mr Carlino visited Miss Gordon several times at her home. Were you aware of this?'

'No.'

'She did not seek him out before or after working hours. Yet he did go there. Indeed he was killed there.'

'I know he was killed there.'

'That's correct, Miss Peterson. He came to her. Why do you think he did this?'

'I don't know. Probably to discuss dance routines.'

'To discuss a dance routine is surely not just a matter of words. It means testing the words by putting the routine into practice, does it not?'

'Yes.'

'I suggest to you that Mr Carlino and Miss Gordon always practised their routines in the theatre and not in Miss Gordon's tiny tenement flat where there was barely enough room to squeeze past the furniture. I further suggest that it is much more likely that Mr Carlino's reason for visiting Miss Gordon is exactly as she says – to pester her and to make a nuisance of himself with his sexual advances.'

'No!'

Miss Peterson became even more distressed when later she was asked if she attended the mortuary on a certain date and there identified to Mr John Bentley, pathologist, the body of Anthony Carlino.

Another witness was sworn in. This time it was a stagehand who had heard Annalie threaten to kill Carlino after one of their dance routines. The man was obviously telling the truth but Ramsay tried to establish how stressful the dance routine was and how easy it would be for anyone to make such a statement in the heat of the minute without meaning it. Indeed how common this statement actually was. Something that he reiterated when a Troon landlady took the oath and told of how she witnessed Annalie and Carlino quarrelling and immediately afterwards Annalie had remarked, 'So help me, one of these days, I'll kill that man.'

Elizabeth agreed wholeheartedly with Mr Ramsay that it was the kind of thing that many people say without meaning it. She had heard the mothers of some of her pupils say in quite a cheerful tone about their husbands, 'One of these days I'll swing for that useless layabout.'

Still, in Annalie's desperate situation the threat to kill sounded ominous and damning.

Elizabeth left for the lunch break with an anxious heart. She had no appetite and for a time wandered blindly about the streets unaware of the grey blanket of fog muffling down over the city. Even the tram cars slid along like ghosts and buses lost their colour and disappeared over bridges as if the River Clyde underneath had sucked them into its cold, dark waters.

Eventually the icy air pierced through her consciousness and she went into a café, ordered a cup of tea and forced herself to eat a digestive biscuit. The hot liquid rallied her and gave her enough energy to return to the busy thoroughfare of Argyle Street and along to Glasgow Cross where the High Street, the Gallowgate, London Road and the Saltmarket met. She shuddered at the thought of the Gallowgate. In the days even further back than the public hangings in front of the High Court the street called the Gallowgate must have been the way to the gallows. She turned down Saltmarket, hurrying, almost running now in her anxiety to get back to Annalie.

CHAPTER 30

There was no doubt that Annalie had killed Carlino but the fact that they had quarrelled frequently and on several occasions Annalie had threatened to kill him made Elizabeth fear that the prosecution would make nonsense of Annalie's plea of self-defence. They certainly made much of the fact that she had, as they put it, 'calmly washed and changed her clothes after the murder'.

Elizabeth tried to will Annalie to look round and see her so that she could in some way convey her love and support. But Annalie never turned her head in the direction of the public benches. Occasionally her gaze lowered on to her lap and her shoulders sagged a little as if becoming fatigued. She did not look up as Mrs McAuslin told under questioning of how Annalie had admitted to her she'd killed Tony Carlino.

'Would you tell the court Annalie Gordon's exact words?' the Advocate Depute persisted.

'Tony Carlino's dead. I've killed him.'

Afterwards the police gave evidence of Annalie's confession in custody. Elizabeth's heart sank lower and lower. But she struggled to keep up a positive outward appearance of hope and optimism for Annalie's sake. Only once, at the end of the day's proceedings, did Annalie's eyes meet Elizabeth's. Annalie was being led back down to the cells and it was such a fleeting moment that nothing was communicated except distress.

Elizabeth was relieved to find the house empty except for the servants when she arrived home. She had no wish for Mother and Father to see what a state she was in and to throw bitter 'I told you sos' at her.

'No good will come of you going to that trial,' Mother had warned.

Thinking of Christina, Elizabeth felt torn. One part of her longed for the old status quo, for Mother and Father safe on their pedestals, for the serenity of the nursery with Nanny looking after her and baby Charlie, for Jason, Daniel and William being boys again, quarrelling with her over nothing more serious than a game of Monopoly. Where had that world gone?

She wandered into the living room, flung off her coat and hat and had just collapsed into one of the deep armchairs when Sarah knocked on the door and asked if it was too late to serve tea.

'No, just go ahead, Sarah.'

In a few minutes the black-frocked, frilly-aproned maid had returned with the trolley on which sat a silver tea service, delicate china and a three-tier cake stand. Elizabeth's stomach tightened and not even the daintiness of the crustless sandwiches, the home-made scones or the crisp sugared fingers of shortbread could tempt her to eat. But she was grateful for the piping hot tea. At least it managed to calm the shivering partly caused by the bitter December wind and partly by her fear and distress.

She remembered that Mother and Father had gone to a business conference in London and wouldn't be back for a couple of days. She should be glad of the release from an atmosphere of icy disapproval, she told herself, yet she felt lonely and bereft.

When Sarah returned to remove the tea things Elizabeth asked:

'Are my brothers going to be in for dinner?'

'No, miss. Are you feeling all right, miss? You haven't eaten anything.'

'Just cold. It's bitter outside.'

'Forgive me, miss, but I still think it would have been better to have kept the coal fire. I know these electric things are fashionable now but a coal fire was much warmer.'

'A lot more work though.'

'Oh, nobody minded that, I'm sure. Will that be all, miss?'

Elizabeth had a sudden impulse to confide in the maid, to pour out all her worries and fears as she would have done to Nanny. With great difficulty she controlled the madness, helped by the knowledge of how such a breach of the proprieties would horrify Mother and probably Sarah as well.

'Yes thank you, Sarah,' she said politely, 'that will be all.'

Before leaving however, Sarah drew the curtains, shutting out the evening darkness. The curtains made a hissing sound. The tea trolley rattled away. The door shut. Elizabeth was abandoned to the muffled silence. She became aware of the monotonous whispering of the clock on the mantelshelf. And with awareness came panic. Suddenly in her imagination she was in Duke Street prison beside Annalie Gordon, with death hovering like a spectre at her elbow. She fought to calm herself.

This was her testing time. She must cope with this crisis without Nanny, without Mother and Father. Without even Alec. Time enough when they were married to depend on his comfort, help and support. First she must prove herself. She must cope on her own.

The next morning Elizabeth left the villa and was immediately enveloped in the thick mist that hung low over frosted spikes of trees and the glittering iced pavements of Queen's Drive. Lights were faint and fluffy and gave an eerie look to the place. Elizabeth tugged her fur collar further up round her ears and made her way with careful steps towards Pollokshaws Road where she would catch her tram into town.

Crossing the busy road was a nightmare of black ice and ghosts of trams, motorcars and horse traffic, the horses' breath puffing out in moist grey clouds. Yet the road was strangely quiet as if everything had been wrapped in cotton wool. It seemed to Elizabeth that the morning had an ominous feel about it and she was filled with dread at having to face another day in court.

Lamps wavered feebly over the city and inside the Justiciary Building.

Elizabeth felt sorry for the policemen outside, rubbing their hands and stamping their feet in their fight against the cold. Although inside the court it was little better, with fragments of mist insinuating themselves around the lamps and hazing and chilling the air. Annalie looked white and pinched with cold and somehow more pathetic than the day before. The depressing atmosphere didn't seem to have any effect on the first crown witness, however.

'I'm a paperboy, sir.' Billy Brown, a chirpy, freckle-face lad, looked intent on enjoying his share of the limelight.

'And am I right in saying that you were delivering papers in Cumberland Street on the day of the murder?'

'I was, sir. Up the close where he was knifed. I passed the door.'

'What door?'

'The door of her house.'

'You are pointing at the accused, seated in the dock?'

'That's right.'

'Do you pass that door every day delivering your papers?'

'Yes, sir.'

'Was there anything you remember about that particular day?'

'Yes. As I was passing her door I heard bangs and thumps and I heard a woman scream.'

'Did you take any kind of action as a result of what you heard?'

'No,' Billy scoffed. 'I often hear women getting a belting on my rounds. Didn't think anything of it at the time.'

In the defence came a string of witnesses including the doctor who had examined Annalie in police custody. It was established that she had suffered a vicious physical attack. There was facial bruising, bruises on the breasts, the legs and most severe bruising on the abdomen where she had obviously been kicked several times. But as far as Elizabeth could make out, the defence case seemed to rest mainly on Carlino's womanizing and his constant sexual persecution of Annalie – because persecution was what it had amounted to, several of Annalie's friends and neighbours claimed. Annalie Gordon, Ramsay said in his closing address to the jury, began by fearing rape and then, as she tried to fight Carlino off and the attack upon her increased in brutality, she feared for her life. In a desperate attempt to save herself, to defend herself, she'd grabbed the nearest weapon that came to her hand and stabbed Carlino with it. It was by a most unfortunate chance, a chance in a million one might say, that her single blow found Carlino's jugular artery. It had been in a state of absolute horror, not calmness, that she had flung off her bloodstained clothing and got rid of Carlino's blood from her person. When she had arrived on a neighbour's doorstep to tell of what had happened, she was in a state of collapse.

The judge in his summing-up seemed impartial, nevertheless Elizabeth see-sawed with uncertainty about what effect or influence he might have on the jury. The knowledge that Annalie's life hung in the balance had never been so agonizing. She watched the jury anxiously as the judge's solemn voice echoed throughout the court.

'Members of the jury, it is now my duty to sum up this case for your consideration, and to give you guidelines in law which must govern your consideration of the evidence you have heard, and offer you such assistance in your consideration of the evidence as you may find of value in considering and determining your verdict.' The judge continued to define the legal nature of the charge and of the 'special defence' but Elizabeth, oblivious of the judge, tried to will, by the strength and desperation of her stare, each of the jurors to think 'Not guilty'. Over and over again she fought and prayed with all her strength to transfer these two words from her mind to theirs. But the jurors were not looking towards the public benches. Most of them were gazing intently up at the judge. A few of them were staring down at the pencil or notes they were holding but at the same time they had a concentrated listening attitude.

She did not hear the judge's oration to the jury as he explained to them what was their function in considering the evidence and returning their verdict.

'It is for you to weigh the evidence, assess the credibility and accuracy of the witnesses, decide whose evidence you accept and decide on your judging of the evidence to what conclusion you will arrive, always bearing in mind that it is for the Crown to prove its case beyond reasonable doubt and that there is no such burden on the defence.'

Annalie could not bear to look at the jury. Her gaze flickered from the judge to the Lord Provost, to the Chief Constable, to the bewigged and black-gowned lawyers and back to the judge again.

She was afraid. At first, after her arrest and imprisonment, her main distress and worry had been about Elizabeth becoming involved, and the girl's life being tainted by the scandal. It had been a bad mistake allowing her to visit the prison. No matter what happened she would never meet her again. She could feel nothing but gratitude and relief that neighbours and friends had listened to her pleas to guard her secret and never mention her worries about Elizabeth and the harm Carlino might do her, not to the press and especially not when giving evidence in court. Even though Mrs McClusky and Flo said it might help her case, might even save her life.

'I'd rather die', she fervently assured them, 'than drag Elizabeth into all this.'

Her friends, however, were only persuaded to keep their mouths shut about Elizabeth when Annalie pointed out that instead of helping her case it might well have the very opposite effect.

But today as she was led from the cells underneath the court and along the sallow-tiled and mortuary-type corridor, she trembled. She didn't want to die.

'You will not forget', the judge was saying now, 'that you and I are only ministers of the law. You will now retire and consider your verdict and when you have reached your conclusion, let me know.'

She managed to turn with some dignity to descend back down into the cold and gloomy corridor. But such was her distress she didn't even notice if Elizabeth was still in the public benches. Fear and suspense gripped her by the throat and sucked away all strength.

The policemen had to support her on the way back to the cell.

It seemed a lifetime had passed with agonizing slowness as she sat waiting but it was only about twenty minutes before the policemen were given the signal that the jury had reached a verdict.

Back in the dock Annalie made a supreme effort to stand unaided and with dignity.

The clerk of the court asked, 'Members of the jury, what is your verdict?'

The foreman of the jury replied, 'Not guilty.'

A gasp of relief came from the public benches but Annalie remained stiff with suspense, not believing.

'Do you find unanimously or by a majority?'

'Unanimously.'

The clerk recorded the verdict, read it out to the jury for their approval and then the judge said to the accused, 'In the light of the jury's verdict you are discharged and free to go.'

Still in a daze Annalie allowed herself to be led downstairs again where, miracle of miracles, she was given her coat and told that she was free to go. She left by a side door and was met by Flo and Erchie Blair and Mr and Mrs Reid, who physically protected her from the desperate crush of newspapermen who were shouting and pushing and jostling around her. There were other people too, a vast crowd it seemed of wildly curious men and women. But just before her friends managed to pull her into the safety of a taxicab, she caught sight of Elizabeth's flushed, excited face.

Annalie felt saddened. That genteel figure in the expensive fur-trimmed hat and coat had no place in the life of Annalie Gordon from the Gorbals. If she had never been sure of anything before, she was sure of that now.

CHAPTER 31

Elizabeth had been so obsessed with the trial and now with her efforts to contact Annalie that she'd barely given her impending marriage a thought. She had made her usual weekly visit to Linthouse and was vaguely aware of taking some part in the discussion about the wedding arrangements with Mrs Harper and at home with Mother.

In the end Grandfather Gillespie, on hearing that she was getting married, insisted, despite the harassment of his house removal and his frail health, that he would perform the ceremony. This meant having it at home and both Grandfather and Grandmother Gillespie staying for the wedding meal. A lunch had been suggested at first so that Grandfather Gillespie wouldn't become too tired. Mrs Harper had, however, become agitated when she'd heard of this. It meant, she explained to Elizabeth, that Alec would have to shut the shop for the whole day. That would mean losing more money than they could afford. High tea was decided on as a suitable compromise.

Mother and Father had squashed the first idea of being married on Christmas Day. Elizabeth didn't reveal to them that Mrs Harper had suggested this because the shop always closed on Christmas Day anyway. For their part Mother and Father did not reveal to Elizabeth that they had no desire to have her wedding spoiling their Christmas celebration. Elizabeth was quite sure, however, this was what they felt. Friday 20 December was eventually decided upon and by that time she had passed her twenty-second birthday, which was on 6 December. There was no party because of the wedding being so close and anyway Mother and Father were away on their travels that day. This had happened on so many birthdays, at least since she'd grown up, that she'd become used to these absences. There had always been a pang of disappointment but she'd soon got over it. There was always Nanny to share the cake and the pleasure of opening presents. This time Elizabeth felt Mother and Father had purposely deserted her and even the fact that Nanny remembered and sent a card failed to assuage the hurt.

Mrs Harper had kindly baked a cake and they enjoyed a very nice tea after which Alec took them to the theatre. Mrs Harper was thrilled at the treat and shuffled around getting ready as fast as her bunions would allow. She donned her best black coat which was unfashionably long, almost down to her ankles, and instead of her usual crocheted tammy to hide her few wisps of grey hair, she wore an equally dated high-crowned cloche hat. The hat, also in black, was decorated with a cream and coffee petersham ribbon that nicely matched, she said, the cameo brooch which she proudly pinned to her lapel.

'That brooch belonged to my mother and her mother before her,' she told Elizabeth as they set out, on either side of Alec and arm in arm with him, 'and once I'm under the clay it'll be yours.' She gave the brooch a pat. 'It's worth a pretty penny, this brooch. It would cost a fortune to buy one like this nowadays. And those beads I gave you are worth something too. My mother was always proud of those jets.'

'I'm not surprised,' Elizabeth agreed. 'They're lovely. I'm so pleased with them.'

Her hand went automatically to her neck where, earlier, Alec had fastened the jet beads. Their dark glitter looked really effective against the turquoise wool dress she was wearing. Alec had given her earrings to match, each earring consisting of a small jet bead dangling on a tiny silver chain. She was very pleased with them too. Mother and Father had given her a cheque. They must have left it with Sarah with instructions to place it on her plate at breakfast on the morning of her birthday because that was where she found it.

She was grateful to Mrs Harper and Alec for making her birthday so pleasant. Without them it would have been a very lonely and unhappy affair, made all the more miserable by thoughts of losing contact with Annalie again. Her work during the day kept her mind occupied. It was the evenings that she dreaded.

They went to the Alhambra in Waterloo Street and enjoyed the pantomime that was showing there.

Mrs Harper told how she and her husband had been at the opening of the Alhambra twenty-five years ago in 1910 to celebrate their wedding anniversary.

'The seats cost three shillings for the orchestra stalls. That was a lot of money in those days. I nearly died when I found out. We could have got a perfectly good tip-up cushioned seat in the amphitheatre for ninepence or a gallery seat for sixpence.'

'It must have been a really glamorous occasion,' Elizabeth said.

'Oh yes. There were carriages lined up all round. And everybody was saying what a lovely building it was.'

'Who was on the programme? Did you keep it? I'd love to see it.'

'I should think I did! Paying those prices! I'll show it to you next time you come.'

Alec wanted to buy ice cream in the interval but Mrs Harper wouldn't hear of 'such a wicked waste of money'.

'We've brought sweets from the shop. Surely that's enough for the pair of you.'

Elizabeth assured her that she was perfectly happy with the liquorice caramels.

'Not a good-selling line,' Mrs Harper explained, 'so you don't need to feel guilty about eating them.'

A few days later when Mother and Father returned she told them of the pleasant evening she'd had and how kind Alec and his mother had been.

'If it hadn't been for them' — she couldn't resist allowing her resentment to show — 'I would have had a pretty poor birthday.'

'Well,' Father remarked, 'it won't be long now until you'll be free of your wicked, neglectful mother and father and be for ever joined to the kind and attentive Harpers.'

'And your *real* mother no doubt,' Christina added with equal sarcasm. But there was a note of bitterness in her voice too.

'You haven't asked her to the wedding, have you?' Father asked in sudden horror. 'You couldn't be that insensitive and stupid.'

'Don't worry,' Elizabeth said stiffly, 'Annalie won't be at the ceremony.'

The truth was that despite her efforts she still hadn't been able to find Annalie. Jessie had warned her that the Gorbals wasn't a place to wander about in the dark, so she hadn't gone after school hours. But during more than one lunchtime and during the day at weekends she'd walked through the caverns of tenement-lined streets asking people if they knew Annalie Gordon and where she lived. The people she spoke to just shook their heads, although they must have known of her because of all the publicity of the trial. Elizabeth got the feeling they just didn't want to tell her. She sensed people closing ranks against a stranger. Whatever the reason, she'd found no leads at all. Nor had she had any reply to the last letter she'd written to Annalie while she was still in custody. She had not given up hope, however. One day she would find her.

Meanwhile, before she had time to concentrate any proper attention on it, the wedding date was upon her. So much had been happening and in such a short time that all Elizabeth could feel was a wish to get it over with as quickly as possible. The atmosphere at home had become so cold and unwelcoming she would be glad to get away. She also felt sorry for Mrs Harper and Alec. Especially for Mrs Harper. At least Alec knew what it could be like in Monkton House and would be prepared, although even he looked pale, tense and nervous. But poor Mrs Harper was in terrible confusion. Even the day before the wedding when Elizabeth had called in to see her after school she was in a state of nerves bordering on collapse. Elizabeth had promised to view what amounted to a dress rehearsal. Mrs Harper had originally planned to wear her best dress.

'Not a thing wrong with it,' she'd informed Elizabeth several times. 'Cost a pretty penny in its day, that dress did. Feel that material. The best that money could buy. That and my good amber beads, good enough for any occasion, don't you think?'

Elizabeth assured her, at least a dozen times, that indeed the dress, the beads, even the cloche hat would be perfectly all right.

'There's no need to worry, Mrs Harper. After all, it's only to be a quiet occasion at home with my parents and grandparents. I'm just wearing a suit.'

She'd bought the suit with the allowance Father had always paid into her bank account and for the first time the realization hit her that once she was married not only her wage as a schoolteacher would stop, but her allowance too.

'I know,' Mrs Harper wailed, 'but they're all such important moneyed people. And it's such a big posh house.'

'You don't know what the house is like. You've never been there.'

'I know Queen's Drive all right. My Aunty Bella used to live in Pollokshaws Road and me and Alec used to visit her. Remember Aunty Bella, Alec? We used to go for walks through the park and all around there. Remember, Alec?'

She was blotchy-faced and sweating. Scanty strands of hair clung wetly to her scalp. Her eyes were popping with anxiety and a nerve twitched almost continuously at one side of her face.

'Your dress and beads are lovely. Please don't worry,' Elizabeth soothed. But at the last minute Mrs Harper had gone completely over the top and bought a whole new outfit. Everything except a coat. Even a new hat, brimmed felt in maroon that cocked to one side. On a young woman it might have been quite pretty and fashionable. On Mrs Harper it just gave her a drunken look.

Elizabeth thought the original 'best dress', which had been made by a conscientious dressmaker, was much better in quality and fit than the cheaper-looking ready-made that Mrs Harper had rashly purchased for the occasion. The dress was a plum-coloured artificial silk. The colour clashed horribly with Mrs Harper's patchy-red face, and the material, as well as looking cheap, was far too cold for such bitter December weather. Elizabeth had been much more practical and chosen for herself a warm suit that she could wear right through the winter and even during the spring. It was a Madeleine de Roche model in dark grey with astrakhan used for revers, epaulettes and narrow edging at the wrists.

'You look very nice,' she told Mrs Harper. 'But I'm worried about your shoes.'

'What's wrong with them?' Mrs Harper shrieked. 'I payed a pretty penny for them. Far more than I could afford.'

'There's nothing wrong with them,' Elizabeth hastened to assure her, 'I'm just thinking of the agony you'll be in. You suffer terribly with your feet at the best of times.'

'I know, I know.' Mrs Harper trembled near to tears.

'But my other shoes were such terrible-looking things. I was afraid they'd laugh at me.'

'Laugh at you?' Elizabeth echoed in horror. 'Of course they won't laugh at you. They wouldn't dream of doing such a thing.'

She felt quite certain that Mother and Father, Grandmother and Grandfather were far too well bred to commit such a breach of good manners. What they would say after Mrs Harper had left was another matter.

'Mrs Harper.' Elizabeth gentled her voice. 'Please believe me, no one is going to notice your shoes. The only way anyone is going to notice is if you're hobbling about in obvious agony. That way you'll draw attention to them and then you'll have to explain about your bunions. Take my advice and be comfortable. Wear your other shoes.'

Eventually she had been persuaded but it had been most harassing and she'd barely got away in time to meet Jessie and some of her school colleagues and friends for a meal.

After a few drinks in a private room in the Central Hotel before having their meal, they expressed their sympathy at the prospect of Elizabeth having 'that old harridan', as they called Mrs Harper, for a mother-in-law.

'She's not so bad once you get to know her,' Elizabeth protested.

'We know her,' Jessie said, 'she's been in the shop often enough, kidding on she's a customer – or even worse, trying to serve behind the counter. It's all to spy on poor Alec and see that he doesn't waste a farthing or do anybody a good turn. She's so mean . . .'

'It's maybe just a sign of insecurity,' Elizabeth said. 'She's terribly highly strung. But all things considered, I get on very well with her.'

'I still wouldn't like to be in your shoes.' Miss Smithers shook her head then hastily added, 'Not that there's anything wrong with Alec, of course.'

'And he's the one I'm marrying,' Elizabeth agreed.

Jessie gave one of her hearty laughs and raised her glass in Elizabeth's direction.

'And the best of luck to you. Old Alec's not my type, but everyone to her own taste.'

'I thought you liked him.'

'I do. He's a very nice, mild-mannered, quiet-spoken man. I just happen to prefer them big and rough and tough. My Gordon is a right bastard but I'm crazy about him.'

The women round the table tittered in an ashamed, embarrassed kind of way. All except Miss Smithers who said:

'I hope you never use bad language in front of the children, Jessie.'

Jessie roared with laughter. 'Don't be daft.'

Elizabeth sighed. 'I'll miss the children.'

'Yes,' Miss Smithers agreed. 'Marriage is a big step to take. I have never felt the urge to make such a drastic change in my lifestyle.'

They all smiled politely, well aware that Miss Smithers had never been given the chance. Although there were teachers they knew who, for the sake of the children, had purposely dedicated a lifetime to teaching.

Elizabeth wondered, had things worked out differently, if she might have been one of those dedicated women. A sadness settled over her. She felt deeply depressed.

'Cheer up!' Jessie gave one of her roars of hilarity. 'You're going to be married, not buried!'

'Maybe you shouldn't drink gin, dear,' Miss Smithers said kindly. 'Don't worry. Everything's going to be all right. Tomorrow's your lovely day, the happiest day of your life.'

CHAPTER 32

'How do you do?' Mother had never looked cooler or more distant as she offered a limp hand to Mrs Harper. Nor had she ever looked so beautiful. The draped Schiaparelli dress in beige wool seemed to accentuate not only her elegance but her untouchability.

'Pleased to meet you.' For a horrible moment Elizabeth thought Mrs Harper was going to curtsey but her machine-gun chatter was just as embarrassing. 'Isn't it funny we've never met before? I mean with my boy and your girl being so pally. Of course with you being away a lot. Alec's in business too. Of course you'll know that. Nothing like yours of course, Mr Monkton. Oh yes, pleased to meet you, Mr Monkton. We make peanuts compared with the likes of you, but it's a living and I try to be careful and save a penny or two. Oh, so you're Elizabeth's granny and grandpa. Pleased to meet you too I'm sure. Funny you doing the ceremony Mr Monkton, or is it Reverend? It makes it real unusual having a relative . . .'

'Gillespie,' Elizabeth corrected in as firm and at the same time as soothing a tone as she could manage. 'My grandfather is the Reverend Gillespie. Grandfather and Grandmother Gillespie are my mother's parents.'

'Right.' Mrs Harper looked as if she was feverishly trying to concentrate. 'Right.'

The maid had divested her of hat, coat and gloves and she now looked strangely naked and vulnerable in her ill-cut cheap-looking dress with its low neckline drawing attention to her loose lizard skin. Thin straws of hair were unable to cover a scalp that looked milky white and delicate compared with her face and neck.

Alec was much more presentable in his dark suit, immaculate white shirt and highly polished shoes. And he was as silent as his mother was garrulous. He never said hello to Mother and Father and only gave a slight inclination of his head when introduced to the grandparents. Elizabeth felt keenly for him. He was as embarrassed by Mrs Harper as she was. Probably more so. Even without looking at his pale, stiff face, Elizabeth could sense the agony he was suffering. Impulsively she linked her arm through his.

'Shouldn't we get on with the ceremony right away?'

'That's right, dear,' Grandmother Gillespie said. 'Then we can all have a nice cup of tea and go home.'

Mrs Gillespie peered anxiously across at the bewhiskered figure of her husband slumping in the chair opposite. 'Are you going to be all right, William?'

'Of course, my dear. Of course.' The Reverend Gillespie heaved his body from the chair and tugged at the flowing black clerical gown he wore over his grey suit. Elizabeth thought he needn't have been so formal. Just his suit and dog collar would have been perfectly all right for the occasion but Grandfather had always believed in stinting nothing when it came to what he regarded as his Christian duty.

'Shall we allow the servants in now, dear?' Mrs Gillespie addressed Christina. 'You know how keen they are and you did promise.'

'Yes, Mother.' Christina rang the bell to summon the parlour maid, the chambermaid, the kitchen maid and the cook, who entered and stood in a tight little knot near the door.

It reminded Elizabeth of the custom in her grandfather's house of holding morning and evening prayers, which the staff always attended.

The Reverend Gillespie gave a little stagger that brought his wife hurrying towards him, only to be stopped in her tracks by his raised hand. He had once been a heavily built man but grief at the tragic loss of his only son and his subsequent ill health had made his flesh gradually shrink away.

'Dearly beloved brethren' – the words were almost a sigh, a mere shadow of the organ-like tones in which he had so often delivered them in the past. They elicited from Mrs Harper a high-pitched travesty of a laugh which was only quelled by one of Elizabeth's unblinking accusatory stares. She'd perfected this look as part of her gentle repertoire for disciplining children.

'We are gathered here together in the sight of God,' the minister continued sadly, 'to knit these parties together in holy matrimony which was instituted and authorized by God himself . . .'

Elizabeth had taken off the jacket of her suit. She was wearing a cashmere sweater, and the little strand of pearls Jessie had given her for her birthday lay very prettily against its lavender colour. It matched her pearl studs and her hair was tucked back behind her ears to show the studs to full advantage. The shop assistant who'd sold her the sweater said the colour accentuated the unusual flecks in her eyes and looked wonderful with her black hair. She'd had her hair trimmed for the occasion. Her fringe grew very quickly and she'd acquired the habit of peering up and through its glossy ends. Today, however, it sat above her eyebrows in a neat, straight line.

'Do you, Elizabeth Gordon Monkton,' the minister was intoning, 'take this man, Alec Harper, to be your lawful wedded husband . . .'

It had been a shock when she'd recently been given her birth certificate by Father and found that on it she was recorded as Elizabeth Gordon, not Monkton. Her father had explained that according to Scottish law you can be known by any name you choose. It had not been necessary even to change it by deed poll.

'I do,' she said.

Alec's voice had been equally quiet but firm. It occurred to Elizabeth that he too was caught in a very unhappy and stressful home situation and no doubt would be glad to get out of it. They both knew that theirs wasn't a wildly passionate, or even a very romantic relationship, but it was comfortable and trustworthy. They respected each other. They were good friends and companions.

The sadness of the night before had evaporated. The butterflies of this morning had settled down. She felt quite calm and pleased with herself as Alec slid the wedding ring on to her finger. There was still the strain and embarrassment of Mrs Harper, of course, but she felt reasonably confident that she could keep the older woman's hysteria within bounds. They would all survive the ordeal of the high tea and soon be safely on their way home. It was strange how she no longer thought of Monkton House as home. It had become such a cold, unloving and unwelcoming place. There was nothing for her here any more. She didn't belong.

As it turned out the meal was not such an ordeal after all. It was not enjoyable because Mother and Father hardly addressed one word to Alec and ignored Mrs Harper altogether, concentrating intently on Grandfather Gillespie. What saved the situation from complete disaster was Grandmother sitting next to Mrs Harper and engaging her in conversation. Grandmother had years of experience in dealing with 'problem parishioners' and 'sensitive situations'. All her married life she had, with an expression of earnest pursuit, busied herself continuously with charities, church social occasions and other Christian duties, not the least of which was dealing with the bereaved. It was her sympathetic, respectful and patient manner, usually reserved for them, that she was using now. It seemed to have intimidated Mrs Harper who only transgressed from time to time with one of her inane bursts of laughter. But she managed to clear her plate of fresh haddock in a light, creamy mustard sauce and do justice to Cook's scones, pancakes and crumpets, not to mention her attack on the three-tiered cake stand from which she greedily sampled a cake with apples in it, a piece of prune cake and a cream sponge.

Eventually polite goodbyes were said. Elizabeth's belongings had been packed and delivered to Linthouse the previous day. So she had just to don her astrakhan-trimmed jacket, her neat little hat and leather gloves, then pick up her handbag and she was ready to go. It was then, unexpectedly, the sadness returned and with it panic. Suddenly, as if she'd never known it before – everything was *real*. She was really married. Mother and Father and the boys had no longer any time for her. There was no longer any place for her in their home. This was really goodbye. Of course Mother and Father mouthed a polite invitation but it was to the Harpers in general, not Elizabeth in particular and it was obvious that they didn't mean it.

'You must visit us again,' they murmured as they shook hands with Alec and Mrs Harper. To Elizabeth they gave a cool peck on the cheek.

Mrs Harper, however, had not noticed anything wrong.

'What a wonderful couple,' she enthused. 'Especially your mother. Now that's breeding for you. It's not surprising of course with such a gem of a Christian woman for a mother, and being brought up in a manse. That dress must have cost her a pretty penny. Your mother, I mean, although your granny looked really well off as well. I know good garnets when I see them. But that dress your mother had on, I bet you anything it was a Paris model.' She stopped for breath and took in big enjoyable gulps of air. 'Oh and that house! Did you ever see anything like it, Alec? Of course, you'd been there before. You don't get all that modern style for nothing. Some of those ornaments were worth a fortune. Oh, there's money in that house all right.'

'You enjoyed the wedding then?' Elizabeth asked, not meaning to be sarcastic and no sarcasm was taken.

'What a day!' Mrs Harper's face was peppered with blotches, her eyes alight with rapture. 'Wait till I tell everybody. And it was different and special having your grandpa do the honours. A real old gentleman. Did you see that watch chain and fob he was wearing? That must have cost a pretty penny. Of course it would probably be a family heirloom, handed down by his father and his father before him. Poor soul, he must have lost a lot of weight though. You could see after he took off his gown, his clothes were just hanging on him. Good clothes though. Top-quality worsted . . .' She rattled on continuously on the way to the tram.

She'd been horrified at Elizabeth's idea of taking a taxicab.

'Why waste good money when there's plenty of trams and buses to take us?' She chattered non-stop on the tram, then along Drive Road and up the stairs to the house. Every now and again Elizabeth smiled at Alec as if to say, 'Let the poor old soul enjoy herself. She's not doing anybody any harm,' and Alec gave one of his small vague smiles and looked away.

The house was tiny and cluttered after the spacious villa in Queen's Park. It was dark, too, even after Mrs Harper lit the gas mantle. Elizabeth felt strange here now. A shyness came over her, and a childishness. She stood helplessly in the middle of the front room until Alec said:

'You'd better come through to the bedroom and hang up your jacket. We've half an hour yet before we need to leave for the theatre.'

They were going to the half-past-eight show at the Kings. Just her and Alec. She had originally been looking forward to it but after the gamut of emotions she'd gone through all day, she was exhausted to the point of depression.

She trailed obediently after Alec.

'I didn't unpack your case or anything,' he said. 'Do you want to do that just now or leave it till after?'

'I'll have plenty of time tomorrow. I'm too tired just now. I'll just take out what I need for tonight.' The sight of her nightclothes made a pulse flutter in her neck. She didn't want Alec to share the sight of flesh-coloured satin. The thought of any kind of intimacy with him suddenly dismayed her.

'Right. There's plenty of room in the wardrobe and there's two or three drawers empty in the chest of drawers.'

'They look big enough anyway,' Elizabeth said. The furniture was huge and old-fashioned, dwarfing and dominating the room. The bed was recessed into the wall and was so high Elizabeth couldn't imagine how she'd ever get into it. The thought of being in it with Alec was appalling. She had an almost overwhelming urge to run away. Rust-coloured plush curtains hung either side of the bed, matching those at the windows, and a fawn valance hid whatever was kept underneath. As well as the giant wardrobe and sideboard the room held a black leather armchair, two spar-backed chairs and a small table on top of which sat a large jug and basin. A what-not crammed with miniature ornaments was jammed in a corner and photographs filled the room to overflowing. There were also sepia photographs, large and small, crowding the walls.

'Take off your jacket then.'

She nodded, unbuttoning it with trembling fingers and draping it over the back of a chair. 'For all the time,' she murmured by way of explanation for not putting it away in the wardrobe.

Mrs Harper shouted from the kitchen, 'Do you want a cup of tea before you go? I've a pot here ready.'

'We're just coming, Mother,' Alec called back. 'She's a great one for her tea,' he said in a quieter voice.

Elizabeth found herself gazing at him through a haze of tears. 'Oh Alec, do you think we've done the right thing?'

He gave a high-pitched laugh that was horribly like his mother's, only smaller and quieter.

'Too late to worry about that now.'

CHAPTER 33

Alec had gone to the shop. He had flung a look of distaste at Elizabeth before he left, saying, 'I hope you're not going to lie there all day.'

Nervously she plucked at the blankets that protected her against the icy cold of the room. Although all the fires at Monkton House had been converted to electricity and were not as pervadingly or as cheerfully warm as the original coal, they quickly took the chill off the air. Betty, the new chambermaid, had always come into her bedroom first thing in the morning and switched on the fire. She also brought a cup of tea. By the time Elizabeth was ready to leave her bed in Monkton House to get dressed, the room was cosy.

After Alec had gone, Mrs Harper called through, 'There's a cup of tea left in the pot when you're ready.'

'I'll be through in a few minutes,' she called back.

There was something so normal about a cup of tea. Once she managed to get up and go through to the front room – or should it be the kitchen now – she would feel all right. Strange to think though, she'd never been in the kitchen. Until now she'd always been the honoured guest, served in the best room with the best china and specially baked scones and cakes.

Her mind fastened on the comfort and normality of the tea, dodging any thoughts of what had happened the night before.

Stiffening herself in preparation against the cold she flung aside the blankets and leapt from the bed. The shock of the icy linoleum on her bare feet made her gasp and quickly find her slippers. She reached for her dressing gown, meaning to go straight through to the kitchen for the warmth of the tea. Instinct stopped her halfway towards the door. Mrs Harper was an endlessly energetic woman despite her bad feet and the chances were she would take a poor view of Alec's wife lounging around at this time of day in a state of undress.

Rapidly she flung on her clothes, all the time violently shivering. Even her wool dress wasn't able to warm her and she had to search for a cardigan to pull on top of it. She longed for a hot bath but knew only a wash-down was possible. She had gone through this ordeal the previous evening with cold water and had no wish to repeat it so soon. Mrs Harper had been shocked at the mere idea of her 'wasting kettles of hot water' after, on her own admission, having had a hot bath at Monkton House the night before.

'She's no idea about anything,' Alec had said. 'She's been pampered all her life.'

In the dark lobby she found the toilet and groped her way in. One postage stamp of glass high up on the wall that looked on to the landing was the only source of light. But the gaslight on the landing was too weak and set too low down to shine in. Even during the day only a dim greyness hovered at ceiling level. The rest of the tiny box of a place remained in darkness. Elizabeth had been disgusted to find that there wasn't even a basin at which she could wash her hands. What there was in abundance was the reek of tobacco. Mrs Harper wouldn't allow Alec to smoke his pipe anywhere else except in the toilet.

'I can't do with smoke getting into curtains and cushions and bedclothes,' she explained. 'Or into food in the kitchen.'

Her ban was understandable in a way because Alec smoked thick black tobacco which was the most vile, strong-smelling stuff. The strength of it in the toilet nearly suffocated Elizabeth and made her feel sick. She groped her way along the lobby again until she reached the kitchen door. After her visit to the toilet her longing for a bath had increased but she thought it prudent not to mention the subject so soon. When she'd said the night before that she was in the habit of having a bath every day Mrs Harper had nearly taken hysterics.

'Every day? Fancy! Do you hear that, Alec?'

'I told you,' Alec said with a smile that made Elizabeth feel afraid.

'It's well seen your folks are well off, Elizabeth,' Mrs Harper rattled on. 'Alec has his in the zinc bath on a Sunday morning because that's the day he doesn't need to go into the shop. I have mine on a Friday. I keep the bath under the kitchen bed.'

'Can you imagine her using our zinc bath?' Alec said.

'Through here,' Mrs Harper now called, and when Elizabeth tentatively eased open the door and gazed round it Mrs Harper twitched with embarrassment and said, 'I suppose now that you're one of the family you'll have to eat through here. We only use the front room for special occasions. We stay through here most of the time. I know it's not much but no doubt you'll be getting your own place soon and it'll be better.'

'This is fine.' Elizabeth allowed her eyes to roam around. 'Very nice.' At best the room was clean, she thought, but even the cupboards in Monkton House were more spacious than Mrs Harper's kitchen.

Mrs Harper had obviously been up for ages. The recessed bed was smoothed over with a multi-coloured patchwork quilt, snuff-coloured bedcurtains had been pulled halfway over and the matching valance hung with tidy precision. The fire was lit and banked up with coal briquettes and dross, and the range had been vigorously black-leaded and the steel edgings attacked with emery paper until they reflected like mirrors. On the high black mantelshelf sat a wooden biscuit barrel, an egg-timer, an alarm clock, two brass candlesticks with candles, a box of Swan Vestas and two china dogs.

'I've added fresh water to the teapot,' Mrs Harper said. Then in a desperate hilarity, 'Sit down, sit down. These kitchens are all much the same but we're lucky we've got an inside toilet. Most houses haven't.'

Mrs Harper poured out a cup of weak-looking tea that nevertheless had a stewed taste. Elizabeth drank it gratefully.

'I've made some toast,' Mrs Harper said, 'and that's some of my home-made marmalade. Just help yourself.'

'Thank you.' Elizabeth reminded herself as she ate, and Mrs Harper busied herself at the sink peeling potatoes, that she had no servants now and the quicker she learned to do housework herself, the better. This had been brought to her attention by Alec's attitude. In the past he had never commented on how Nanny fussed over her, or the fact that neither she nor Christina ever did any housework. Nor had he said anything when, more recently, she had spoken tentatively of one day having a home of her own to run. Now however, she could guess what his averted eyes and secret smiles had meant.

'Mrs Harper, I'm afraid I'm very ignorant about housewifery duties. With your help, however, I'm hoping to learn. At least I have been a working girl of sorts.'

'A working girl,' Mrs Harper echoed as if savouring a clever joke.

'Just tell me what to do around the house. I must do my share.'

'We all learn soon enough when we have to. You won't need to, though.'

'Why not?'

'Once you have your own place you'll have somebody to do it for you.'

'Will I?' She was surprised. She hadn't expected Alec

268

to provide anyone to help her in the house. She tried to draw comfort from the thought.

'But you must let me help you while I'm here. I can't just sit around letting you do everything.'

'I'm used to it.' Mrs Harper laughed apologetically. 'I'd rather you got out from under my feet. Away and have a wander round the shops in the town or assist your mother until it's time for your dinner. I don't have much in the middle of the day when other folks have their dinner. Alec has a piece in the shop or a pie and we have our dinner when he comes home at night. We couldn't afford to shut the shop in the middle of the day. If you're here in the middle of the day you could have the same as me. I usually just have bread and jam.'

'That would do me too,' Elizabeth said. 'But I think perhaps I'll have something out today.'

'You're not thinking of throwing good money away in a restaurant, surely?' Mrs Harper looked genuinely alarmed.

'No, no,' Elizabeth hastened to assure her, although in fact she did intend to do just that.

Mrs Harper's expression changed to pleasurable excitement. 'Oh, your mother's. Fine, fine. You can tell her you're getting on fine and I hope we'll all be able to get together again soon. Tell her I fairly enjoyed my visit yesterday.'

For a brief moment Elizabeth was tempted to explain everything to Mrs Harper. Then she realized she didn't feel up to it. She didn't feel at all well. And she was dreadfully worried. She had more on her mind than to launch into a long involved story about her origins, her estrangement from Mother and Father, finding her real mother, the recent traumas of the trial, and now the task of renewing her search for Annalie.

These things did still urgently occupy her mind and it would be a good chance and a way of passing the long day if she tried yet again to find some clue to Annalie's whereabouts. But as well as her worry and concern about being reunited with Annalie, other anxieties were crowding in to torment her, anxieties about Alec, although Annalie, when she came to think about it, might be the very one to help with these new worries. She couldn't imagine talking to anyone else about them. Mrs Harper was out of the question. So was Mother. She shrank with horror at the mere thought of talking to Mother about anything so personal. Even with Jessie it would be too shameful and embarrassing. But Annalie, who had suffered at the hands of men, might understand and be able to advise her.

She returned to the bedroom and gazed at her coats and hats in the wardrobe. Although it was such a big piece of furniture, she had discovered that there was not as much room as she'd thought for her clothes because Alec and Mrs Harper also kept their clothes in it. It became embarrassingly obvious, too, that Elizabeth had rather a lot of clothes, which made the older woman's garments look pathetically cheap and shabby. She decided on a navy cashmere coat which fitted her like a soft skin, and a navy pull-on hat not unlike Nanny's. She smoothed on her gloves. No lady ever stepped over a threshold without wearing gloves, Nanny used to say.

'I'm away, Mrs Harper,' she called from the gloom of the lobby.

'Alec's back about half seven.' Mrs Harper came through, wiping her hands on her apron. 'Fancy, and most shops open till eight or nine. I keep telling him he's losing a pretty penny. He worries me to death sometimes.'

'I think it's quite sensible of him to finish when he does,' Elizabeth said. 'It's a long enough day for him.'

'The only sensible thing he's ever done is marry you.'

Elizabeth was touched, and on an impulse she

reached up and kissed Mrs Harper's cheek. Her mother-in-law flushed, avoided her eyes and gave a little giggle of embarrassment. But Elizabeth thought she seemed pleased.

'I'll see you later.'

Out on the landing she began to wonder if Mrs Harper expected her to stay away until Alec came home. It was a daunting thought. She couldn't even look forward to Alec's return. Her marriage had scarcely begun yet already she felt estranged from him. All at once she didn't know where to go. She suddenly realized how much she missed the Hill's Trust School. Standing on the draughty landing, it hit her with terrible clarity and pain that she could no longer be with the children. To her horror her face crumpled and she began helplessly weeping like a child herself.

CHAPTER 34

'I told Maurice I had a good mind to turn it down,'
Annalie said. 'When I was desperate to get away from
Tony and get a solo spot he told me there was no
chance. Now he gets me a solo turn no bother.'

'You've got to eat, hen,' Flo said.

'I know but it's awful to think it's because of all the
notoriety of the death and the trial. Good publicity, he
said. It'll pull them in, and it has. It makes me feel
awful. And it's strange, although I'm dancing on my
own I often feel Tony's still there. Sometimes I wake up
in the middle of the night, sweating and shaking because
I think we've been dancing together. I know it's just my
imagination, it's only a dream. But it's so vivid. I can
even smell that pomade he used on his hair.'

'You'll get over it in time, hen. You've been through
a lot. I don't know how you've survived it all so well.'

Flo refilled their cups with a dark brew from the
brown delft teapot. 'Help yourself to another soda
scone, hen.' Tuesdays and Thursdays were Flo's scone
days. On Fridays she made her cakes.

'And not one wrinkle on your face either.'

Annalie laughed. 'You're needing new specs, Flo.'

'Not a bit of it.' Flo's sallow, leathery skin was deeply
lined. She'd always been too busy looking after her big
family to pay any attention to herself. Now they were
all married and living in their own houses. Hardly a
day passed, however, that one or several of them
didn't drop in to see her and Erchie. She would have
been perfectly content except that Erchie, who had been
wounded in 1917, had recently become a prophet of
doom and kept saying that by the looks of things there

was going to be another war. When he wasn't talking about Germany and Italy he was regaling her with the horrors of lynch mobs in America. Erchie's leg pained him and made him irritable and bad-tempered. Flo was thankful he'd folk like Hitler, Mussolini and the Ku Klux Klan to pick on. Rather them than her. Although she suspected the pain in his leg was as much caused by old age and rheumatics as his war wound. It meant he couldn't get out and around as often as he'd like and that was why he sat for hours devouring the *Herald* or the weekly *Forward* and complaining bitterly about what was going on in the world. All the same he did manage to hobble along to the library most days to see the rest of the newspapers. A couple of times a week he struggled to reach the pub. That's where he was now.

'I can't go on dancing for ever, though. I'm thirty-eight. Can you imagine a forty-year-old flamenco dancer drawing the crowds? The publicity about the trial will have been forgotten by then.'

'Listen, hen –' Flo pointed a half-eaten scone at Annalie '– I've seen pictures of real Spanish dancers. Our Ella had a schoolbook about Spain and some of them women were no chickens by the looks of them.'

'But still . . .'

'It's not like you to give up so easy. You've always been such a rare wee fighter.'

'Oh, I'm not giving up. I'm only saying I won't go on dancing for ever. I could maybe switch to acting. Now as an actress I could go on for ever. I can just see myself playing doddering old ladies.'

'Here, I could do that now, hen.' Flo chuckled. 'But you're still enjoying the dancing?'

'This new company's quite good and it was interesting being on tour in England. We travelled on a Sunday just the same but we met all the different theatre companies at Crewe. The train took the scenery and props and it was great being able to have a gossip with everybody.'

'I was thinking maybe you felt it lonely travelling about so much.'

'No. We've a lot of laughs. Except with the comedians. They're a sour lot.'

'Here was me thinking they would be real cheery company.'

'Anything but.'

'So you're not thinking of leaving the stage when you give up the dancing?'

'Jobs aren't that easy to come by. Anyway, it's my life now. I've got used to it.'

She'd got used to the elderly stage doormen. The long passages with their ceiling-high spaghetti of pipes, the cement stairs, the bare brick walls, the heavy swing doors that led into the stage had become the background to her life. The heat under the lights and the great shadowy bowl of the auditorium sent her pulse racing. There was also the camaraderie with the other performers, all of them talented and special in their own way. There was the colourful panoply of conjurers, whistlers, harmonica players, roller skaters, speciality bands, big bands too. They created a different, far more vivid and exciting life than she'd once known sorting rags in the coffin works or serving behind the counter of the paper shop. Even her original job as maid in Monkton House paled into monotonous drudgery compared with her life on the boards. Not that it was easy. Quite the reverse, in fact. Nor was it as glamorous as many people who did not work in the theatre tried to make out. Dress rehearsals could start at eleven o'clock in the morning and go on indefinitely, often late into the night. Performances could be exhausting, especially in theatres which were all glitter out front but worse than slums backstage. There were many things about theatrical life that were anything but admirable.

But for all its faults and difficulties, she loved the life. She didn't go around saying so. She could enjoy a grumble as often as the rest. She seldom admitted to herself how she really felt. But the theatre was in her blood. Even the travelling about and having to suffer some appalling digs was better than the boring, comfortable routine of living at home all the time.

'Have you heard anything of Elizabeth since the trial?'

'The prison forwarded on a couple of letters. They were behind the door when I got back.'

'I think it's been her that was asking around.'

Annalie's eyes flew wide with anxiety but before she could voice her fears, Flo added soothingly:

'Don't worry, hen, nobody would say a word. There was newspaper folk at first and we all gave them short shrift. They got fed up eventually. I haven't seen any around for a while.'

'Thank goodness for that.'

'Are you sure you're doing the right thing about your lassie, hen?'

'Flo, I've told you before. There's no place in my life for her, and there's no place for me in her life. She's married now and comfortably settled. Think of the can of worms the press would open up if they found me reunited with a long-lost daughter. Imagine what it would do to her.' She violently shook her head. 'No, it doesn't bear thinking about.'

'All right, all right, hen. I just wondered.'

Annalie hated it when anyone brought up Elizabeth's name. She tried so hard not to think about her although never a day passed without her losing the battle. Mostly by worrying about the danger of Elizabeth tracking her down and confronting her again. It had been all right while on tour, especially in England, but she had a Glasgow booking coming up and her name would be on the billboards. Not in big letters at the top of the

275

bill, but there for all to see nevertheless. It was of some comfort to know, however, that addresses were never given out and stage doormen were very conscientious in protecting performers from unwelcome visitors. Anyway, the chances were that Elizabeth, now living in the suburbs and with a husband to attend to, would never see the bills stuck up outside the theatre.

She hoped and prayed that would be the case. There had been enough worry and trauma in her life to last her to the end of her days. Now she was as happy as she could be with her unsettled gypsy kind of life. It had given her a much better understanding of her mother and the way Saviana could never settle down for more than a few weeks at a time. She had come to the conclusion that at heart she must be a travelling person like her mother. The room and kitchen flat that her Aunty Murn had once been so proud of and kept so spic and span no longer interested her. Since her father died she seldom used the front room. At least the kitchen was cosy. But all too soon she'd itch to get away from the place. Since her father and Aunty Murn had gone there was no longer any anchor for her. The house was only a pigeonhole of sad memories, especially of her young brothers who had been killed in the war. She wasn't one to sit and brood about the past if she could help it. It was true what Flo had said – she was a fighter.

'I'll wrap up a scone or two, hen,' Flo was saying now. 'They'd maybe do your tea tomorrow. Do you take a piece to your work?'

'Yes, especially during rehearsals. There's never time to go out for anything.'

'I wonder you need to rehearse. You're that good at it.'

Annalie smiled. 'That's why I'm good at it. It's the hours and hours of practice that makes perfect, Flo.'

'Och well, every man to his own trade, I suppose.

It's funny how Elizabeth turned out so different from you. A respectable schoolteacher, of all things.'

'Oh thanks.'

'Och, you know what I mean, hen. No offence.'

Annalie rose and stretched nonchalantly, making her scarlet blouse tighten over her breasts.

'None taken. It's time I went home. You'd think I'd nothing to do. My house is like a tip. God, how I hate housework.'

'You never used to, hen. I mind when . . .' Flo stopped herself, afraid she was going to put her foot in it again.

'When I had my nice room and kitchen and bathroom and Adam Monkton used to come and see me?' Annalie finished for her.

'You used to have that place like a new pin. You were that proud of it. Especially the bathroom. Do you remember?'

'Of course I do. I would have done anything to please that man. In fact I did. Anything and everything.'

'He might have let you keep that place on.'

'I suppose he would have, but I couldn't afford the rent and couldn't let him go on paying it.' She shrugged. 'It was good while it lasted. But it's a long time ago.'

'Maybe you'll fall for somebody else yet,' Flo ventured, 'you're a fine-looking woman and I bet there's still plenty of loving left in you.'

'I wouldn't be a bit surprised, Flo.' Annalie winked at her, picked up the parcel of scones and, hips swaying provocatively, sauntered from the room.

CHAPTER 35

Elizabeth sat on the top of the tram as it rocked its way into town. Gazing from the window she caught fleeting glimpses of Fairfield Shipyard on one side and Elderpark and the pond on the other. Then the conglomeration of buildings closed in Govan Cross railway goods station, Harland and Wolfe's shipyard platers' shed, other workshops, and the dry dock where ships were repaired. After that the road was bordered on the dockside by a high brick wall over which a forest of masts and funnels could be seen even from street level.

She found the high walls, the masts, the sheds, and the grim tenements crowding so close to them, claustrophobic and depressing. She heard the sound of bells and saw the fire engine, its solid tyre wheels giving the crew, sitting back to back and open to the elements, a rough and noisy ride on the cobbled road. It crushed her spirits even lower. It reminded her of the children and how the sight of the fire engine always excited them. Their most treasured ambition was to be the fire officer who sat beside the driver and clanged the bell by pulling a lanyard attached to the bottom of the clapper violently back and forth.

She had come to look on her teaching experience as the happiest of her life and never a day passed but she longed to return to it. She had a role to play as a teacher. She had respect. As Alec's wife she felt she had neither. His mother insisted on doing everything in the house despite Elizabeth's protests. She even complained to Alec, but he did nothing nor said a word to support her. He could make sneering remarks about his mother under his breath in the privacy of their bedroom; in front of his mother however, or in any public situation, he was the soul of discretion.

He had no such scruples as far as his wife was concerned. He often spoke about her in the shop. He'd sigh and tell customers in a good-natured but long-suffering tone, 'Her nanny forgot to teach her a few things. She doesn't even know how to boil water for a cup of tea.' Or 'If my mother wasn't there to make my dinner, I'd starve.' Or 'She tried to iron one of my shirts yesterday and now I've got a scorched tail. I'm beginning to think I ought to have asked her to bring her nanny with her.'

Elizabeth tried to laugh with the rest, but she was hurt by his disloyalty. She avoided going into the shop now. She was too distressed by the gulf Alec was creating between her and everyone else, including himself. Every day she longed to be back at teaching again. She missed it so.

She suspected Jessie did too although she was too proud to admit it. Jessie's wedding to Gordon McGill had been a real shotgun affair, as Jessie was already well on the way with the baby before the knot was tied. She had remained cheerfully loyal to him despite the fact that several black eyes and other injuries made it obvious that he was abusing her. Elizabeth had tried to sympathize and bring up the subject of husbands and their abusing behaviour, not only because of concern for Jessie, but desperation about herself. Jessie, however, brushed aside all attempts at such conversation with a loud guffaw of a laugh and remarks like:

'Gordon thinks he's Benny Lynch when he's had a few drams on a Saturday night. But I give as good as I get. There's worse things happen in China.'

She could just imagine Jessie's big fists lashing out and probably flooring Gordon if he was drunk enough to be unsteady on his feet. But it was a terrible way to live, despite the fact that, according to Jessie, during the week when he was sober nobody could ask for a better man than her Gordon.

It was strange that now she and Jessie were both married and had known each other for such a long time, they were less close than they'd been at the beginning, even though they were on equal visiting terms. She visited Jessie nearly every week in her room and kitchen in Langlands Road and Jessie visited her most weeks too. Now since Jessie was heavily pregnant she didn't get out so much because of the stairs and the problem with her blood pressure. It was because of Jessie that Elizabeth was having one of her few visits into town. She was determined to get something special for Jessie's baby. In one way she felt sorry for her friend, whose pride had taken some painful blows since her marriage. In another way she envied her. She longed for a baby and every time she saw Jessie, the pain of her longing was intensified. She sometimes thought, however, it would be so much better for both Jessie and herself if they could conceive without needing to depend on a man.

Recently a drunken McGill had arrived at Linthouse and threatened to attack Elizabeth because, he claimed, he'd had enough of a toffee-nosed bitch like her putting fancy ideas into his wife's head. Elizabeth didn't know what he was raving about. As far as she was aware she'd never put any fancy ideas into Jessie's head. She could only guess that Jessie was trying to keep up a decent and civilized standard of living, struggling to get nice things for her house, trying to make Gordon behave himself.

She would never forget or forgive Alec for the way he handled the situation. He had sided with Gordon, agreed with every insult he'd made against her. More than that, he'd sighed, shook his head and suggested by his general self-pitying manner that he had to put up with a great deal, being married to her. Even worse, he'd betrayed a confidence and told of how she wasn't even a true-blue Monkton. She was just somebody from the Gorbals the Monktons had taken in out of pity. This had so intrigued Gordon that it almost sobered him up. He couldn't wait to get back to tell Jessie the truth about 'her precious pal'.

Alec had insisted afterwards that everything he'd said to Gordon was for her sake. 'It got rid of him, didn't it? What else could I do?' he asked. 'He's about double the size of me.'

But she had seen that he was not only enjoying his self-pity, he was getting pleasure out of hurting her.

The scene had other repercussions because it was the first time Mrs Harper had heard about her not being a true-blue Monkton. Previously, Mrs Harper had worked herself up into a terrible state about 'dropping her mother and father'. Why wasn't she going to visit them, Mrs Harper wanted to know. Why hadn't Alec and Mrs Harper been invited to Monkton House again? They were family now. Why didn't she invite her mother and father to Linthouse? Was she ashamed of her husband and mother-in-law? Why hadn't her mother and father seen about providing her and Alec with a house? They were in the building trade, and they'd promised.

It was no use Elizabeth protesting that nobody had promised anything and, after all, they had given her and Alec a very generous cheque as a wedding present. Anyway, they didn't have any property in Govan or Linthouse.

She had tried, without success, to explain that her mother and father travelled so much on business that it was difficult to catch them at home. It had also been a waste of time trying to persuade Mrs Harper that Mother and Father had no inclination for socializing. Mrs Harper had seen an item in the gossip column of a newspaper that Mr and Mrs Monkton had been two of the guests at a dinner given by the Lord Provost.

Elizabeth had gone to visit Mother and Father once

since her marriage and she vowed to herself that she would never go again. William, Daniel, Mother and Father spoke mostly to each other, only forcing themselves to address the occasional polite remark or enquiry to her. Politeness was mixed with a kind of supercilious pity that made it all the worse for Elizabeth to take. When Mother had asked, 'Are you happy?' she'd answered, 'Of course', in the same supercilious manner. It had been a strained, unhappy experience for all of them and she was sure they were as glad as she was when it was over.

'You've fallen out with them,' Mrs Harper wailed. 'They'll cut you off without a penny if you're not careful.'

Eventually Elizabeth confided in Alec that Christina wasn't her real mother and that the truth was her father had got a maid into trouble. She was the result, and Christina had taken her in and brought her up. She had meant to tell the whole truth but she'd seen the gleam of pleasure in Alec's eyes and had drawn back in instinctive caution. More and more she was feeling a need to protect herself against Alec and the need had never been stronger than on that occasion. He wasn't like Gordon McGill. He never beat her but there were many other methods of ill-treatment so subtle it would have been difficult to explain them to anyone without seeming foolish.

Nevertheless she felt certain that Alec found pleasure in anything he thought hurt or humiliated her. To protect herself and to deny him this pleasure, she had been forced to shrink further and further into a deep core of secrecy within herself. It had been a terrible mistake, she realized now, to tell him about her origins. She could only feel grateful that she'd managed to stop in time from revealing Annalie's identity or mentioning anything about the killing. She didn't know what Alec might do or say about it if she had told him. She just felt instinctively that she must hug the secret close inside herself for Annalie's sake as well as her own.

She longed to confide in somebody about the most intimate side of her marriage, however, and there had been times she was so desperate she'd nearly blurted out an appeal for help to Mrs Harper. Again she managed to contain herself. Mrs Harper would only have taken hysterics. Or worse. Sometimes Elizabeth thought Mrs Harper was a likely candidate for a stroke. It had been bad enough when she'd discovered that Christina was no blood relation. Elizabeth had felt seriously concerned for Mrs Harper, she'd looked so ill. Her face and neck, even her arms had fired up with sweaty blotches, and nerves twitched rapidly in eyes, cheeks and mouth. High-pitched little gasps of laughter teetered near to moans and she kept pleating and re-pleating the dishtowel she'd been holding.

The tram was now crossing the River Clyde at King George V Bridge and Elizabeth could see plenty of movement down on the left with boats and steamers that shuttled holidaymakers to and from Glasgow and the Clyde resorts of Rothesay and Dunoon. To the right her view was blocked by the massive railway bridge and the forest of girders of its underside. Once across the river she left the tram in Oswald Street opposite Wilson's Zoo and made her way towards Argyle Street until she reached the imposing building of Lewis's Polytechnic. There she finally decided on a cot for Jessie's baby. She'd discovered that not many local parents were able to afford such a luxury. Most babies slept in sideboard drawers or in bed recesses beside parents. Jessie would be proud of the cot, she felt sure. She spent her last penny on the gift, knowing that she was being over-extravagant as well as over-generous but eager to please and be of some practical help to her friend. At the same time she nursed a tentative hope that the gift would act as a kind of bribe to elicit help for herself.

Jessie flushed with pleasure when the cot was delivered. She walked round and round it, sometimes caressing its wooden spars with red work-coarsened hands, sometimes admiring how smoothly its drop-side worked.

'This looks big enough to do the wee one until it's at least two or three. It's really great. Thanks, Elizabeth.'

'What'll you do about a pram?' Elizabeth asked worriedly. She knew that Jessie wouldn't want to be a 'shawlie' like so many women in the district. When Elizabeth suggested this Jessie just laughed and said:

'There's nothing to be ashamed of in wearing a shawl. My mother carried all of us in her plaid and she said it was as cosy as a bug in a rug. When I was working I saved up and bought her a coat but she says it's nowhere near as warm.'

Despite Jessie's spirited defence of the shawl, Elizabeth saw the tremor of wounded pride in her friend's eyes.

'I never said there was anything to be ashamed of. I was only thinking how much more convenient a pram would be. Maybe you'll be able to pick up a second-hand one somewhere.'

Jessie shrugged. 'Maybe. Could you go a cup of tea?'

'Yes please.'

'The kettle's boiling.'

Elizabeth watched Jessie lift the black iron kettle from the hob and fill the teapot. The range, indeed the whole kitchen, was identical to Mrs Harper's kitchen. High above the wooden dresser, opposite the fireplace and stretching about the whole length of that wall, was a wooden shelf. On the shelf was displayed the gold-edged tea set decorated with roses Elizabeth had given Jessie for a wedding present. Mrs Harper's shelf boasted a blue and white dinner service including two large and lidded soup tureens.

Treading in the measured balanced way of pregnant women, Jessie barged purposefully about the kitchen, squeezing with difficulty past chairs and into the press to fetch cups, a jug of milk and a plate of home-made pancakes.

'There's jam on the table. Help yourself. I'm getting a right dab hand at pancakes.' She gave a whoop of laughter as she poured out the tea. 'But they're not what I take notions for. I was enjoying a bit of coal yesterday, would you believe?'

Elizabeth made a face. 'You could poison yourself.'

'No fear. It would take a damn sight more than that to get rid of me. Strong as a horse, Gordon says.'

'Oh, I don't know.' Elizabeth worriedly nibbled at her lip. 'Just because you're big made . . .'

Jessie laughed again. 'I'm big now, all right. A bloomin' elephant has nothing on me. When it happens to you I bet you'll still look neat and dainty. Any luck yet, by the way?'

It was her chance. The opening she needed.

'Just between you and me I'm terribly worried, Jessie.'

Jessie thumped down on to a chair and tried to make herself comfortable. Then she took a swig of tea before asking, 'Well? Spill the beans . . .'

'It's Alec. And, and . . .' Miserably she flushed and lowered her eyes. 'You know.'

'Sex you mean?'

'I suppose so.'

'What do you mean – you suppose so? Either it is or it isn't.'

Elizabeth was so ashamed she felt sick. Yet something had to be done. 'I wanted to ask you. Are there different ways of doing it?'

Jessie spluttered some tea out with hilarity. 'Of course there are. Is that all that's been making you look as if you've got all the troubles of the world on your shoulders? You're damned lucky if Alec's been treating you to a bit of variety.'

'But . . . I thought . . . I mean I can't see how I could

285

ever have children. And I . . . I mean, what's the point of life without children?'

'Why can't you have a family? Is he using something?'

'No . . .' Elizabeth's cheeks were bright crimson now and tiny beads of sweat were beginning to trickle down from under her fringe and remain glistening in the dark hair of her brows.

There was a silence for a few seconds during which Jessie's expression became incredulous.

'Buggery you mean?'

Suddenly Elizabeth burst into tears. Jessie tried to heave herself forward to comfort her, but failed. Instead she said:

'You can soon put a stop to that.'

'How?'

'Tell him it's illegal. Threaten to tell the police.'

It was Elizabeth's turn to look incredulous. 'Is it?'

'He could get flung into jail.'

Elizabeth wasn't convinced, but she wondered if the threat of exposure might be enough. It could be no more than a threat because she couldn't imagine herself going through the agony of speaking of such a thing to any stranger. She suspected however that it was important to Alec to keep in with people and create an image of being a respectable, kindly and generous person, always a good son, and now a good husband.

She had come to believe that the need for approval was the only thing they had in common. She could imagine the fear of exposure might well make him stop. But it was such an embarrassment to broach the subject. She dreaded it.

'I'll try talking to him again.' She mopped at her eyes with an unsteady hand.

'I should think so too.' Jessie was indignant. 'Fancy him being such a dirty old devil. I'd threaten to cut it off if I were you!'

CHAPTER 36

'Aim at the audience,' Hector Bellamy said. 'And project for all you are worth.'

'You really think I could do it?'

'What?' His rich dramatic actor's voice boomed out. 'You are a natural. Do you not know, are you not aware that you act during the dance?'

'I suppose I do.'

They were sitting in the dining room of Mrs Tunniecliffe's digs in the capital city of Edinburgh, struggling through one of the landlady's jam roly-poly puddings. It was a small room cramped by a half-dozen wax-cloth-covered tables, a large sideboard and innumerable plants that looked as if they were intent on shutting out any last glimmer of light. Annalie had noticed Mrs Tunniecliffe was in the habit of emptying the teapots into the plant pots, something that seemed to agree with the greenery and perhaps explained its depressing profusion.

'I've been thinking of changing course for a while now but I hadn't mentioned it to Maurice – Maurice Rutherford, my agent. I don't know what he'll say.'

'Do not pay one whit of attention to what that gentleman says. I am telling you, you are a natural.'

'God, this pudding's purgatory.' Annalie tossed her spoon down on to the tomato-coloured wax cloth.

'And if I may say so, you have fantastic sex appeal,' Hector continued.

Annalie grinned at him. 'You think I should give some producer the eye?'

'I know you, my dear. You would be more likely to give him a punch in the eye.'

'You've only known me for a few weeks.'

'That's time enough.'

Annalie raised her head in a proud, warning gesture. 'Time enough to hear what happened to my dancing partner, you mean?'

'My dear, I can assure you it has nothing to do with that. I never knew the man but I have heard he was a cad if ever there was one and deserved all he got.'

'I wasn't dishing out justice or punishment or anything else. It was an accident. I didn't mean to kill him.'

'I believe you. There is no need to be so touchy.'

'Anyway —' Annalie relaxed again '— there are so many out-of-work actors, what chance would I have?'

'I will have a word with Dave Lawson, our producer. We will be needing somebody to replace Mamie Allerton soon. She has got herself pregnant and keeps rushing off stage during rehearsals to throw up.'

'I think I know Mamie. She's married to Johnny Spender, isn't she?'

'Yes. Allerton is her stage name. If you ask me she will be glad when Dave gives her the push. She is really under the weather, poor sod. She fainted a couple of times. The doctor thinks it is blood pressure. I will not be surprised if she beats Dave to it.'

Mrs Tunniecliffe appeared then with two cups of chocolate-coloured tea slopping over into their delft saucers.

'Here you are, lovies, the cup that cheers.'

She was a woman who couldn't abide — to use her words — corsets or anything tight and as a result she moved like a giant jelly in bell tents of dresses and enormous smocks. It was said by her long-suffering theatrical tenants (mercifully temporary) that she was too big to fit in a bath and so never had one. This accounted for the stench of perspiration and other sour and equally unpleasant odours that hung around her.

The only thing anyone could find in her favour was the fact that she never laid down rules about noise, or hours of coming in, or mealtimes, or anything at all. The story went that once when someone came looking for digs and asked (as a joke) if there was anywhere to keep his crocodile, she'd replied, 'Sleep with it if you like, son. As long as you pay for the room it's all the same to me.' She was also obliging at washing shirts covered in greasepaint for an extra shilling or two. And she'd been known to sit up half the night applying hot poultices to an acrobat's strained muscles so that he wouldn't lose his pay.

After Mrs Tunniecliffe wobbled off Annalie automatically waved a hand about in front of her face to waft away the smell.

'There'll be plenty come looking for the job though, and more experienced than me.'

'Listen, my dear. Dave has seen you on stage. He thinks you are terrific.'

Annalie began to feel quite cheered. Hector always had this effect on her. They'd hit it off from the moment they'd met. Not in a sexual way. Hector was still grieving for his wife who'd died of cancer after twenty years of happy marriage. Not that he went around with a long face. He put on a brave front and spoke only of what a great girl his Sally had been and how well they'd got on together and what a talented actress she had been.

'Her last words to me were "Be happy", and that's what I try to be. Life must go on,' he told Annalie although she detected a shaft of sadness in his eyes that belied his cheerful tone.

She admired him enormously, for his talent as an actor, for his calm self-confidence and his way of putting over a positive view of everything and making her feel better. They had become friends and had shared the same digs in Edinburgh since she had been dancing at the Edinburgh Empire and he was acting in the Theatre Royal.

'What's the new play called?'

'*Epitaph for a Hard Man*. I will try to get you a copy of the script and you can read up the part. I used to be a boy scout. Be prepared, I have always thought, was damned good advice.'

'I'll have a try,' Annalie said. 'No harm in trying.'

'You might even enjoy it.' He raised his cup. 'Here's to your new career.'

She laughed. 'Talk about jumping the gun!' But she raised her cup too and felt as if she was toasting not only a new career but a new life.

'You do me the world of good, Hector, do you know that?'

'You have cheered me up as well.'

'Me? How?'

'Just by listening, mostly. It is strange how people avoid you if you have had a bereavement. Maybe it's embarrassment. Anyway, they do not want to talk about it and they do not want you to talk about it. They all knew Sally. But it was as if she had never existed the way they just dropped all mention of her. They still never talk about her in front of me. It is very strange. I will have to walk off that meal. Do you fancy coming with me?'

'I'd better. I'll never be able to dance tonight if I don't. I'll go and get my coat.'

He was waiting for her in the lobby when she returned, a big portly man in a wide-brimmed black hat cocked to one side at a jaunty angle. His loose-fitting black coat had wide cape sleeves and looked very dramatic. Nobody could have mistaken him for anything but a thespian.

The turnpike stairs were always in semi-darkness during the day and a woman with a shawl over her head had quietly shuffled past them before they realized she was there. Annalie was not of a nervous disposition, but some of the other girls who lodged up the close

290

were terrified to come back on their own late at night. After the show a few of them always arranged to return together or one of the male performers or a boyfriend escorted them safely through the dungeon-like close and up the stairs.

In this part of Edinburgh called the Old Town the closes and narrow wynds all had this dark, gloomy characteristic. Light filtered faintly between the grey buildings and even on a bright summer's day you only had to turn off the High Street or the Cannongate to see people disappearing into entries of impenetrable darkness.

Today was a beautiful spring day, although chilly. Annalie took Hector's arm as they walked along the cobbled High Street. He squeezed her arm affectionately against the side of his chest but didn't say anything for a while. Eventually he smiled down at her.

'By hook or by crook I am going to get you into our company.'

'It would be great,' Annalie said. 'Far better than being on my own.'

'We do a new play each week, with two performances per evening. It is hard work. But you are used to that. The important thing is usually the length of the play. We have to finish, come what may, at seven thirty to give time for the first house to get out and the second house to get in.'

'Sounds pretty hectic.'

'It is. But things can be worse than that. Sometimes they save money on the typing of parts so we get actor's parts instead of the whole script and there's just five lead-in words from the previous speaker and he is not always named. Believe me, this often leads to some hilarious mix-ups.'

'My God, I hope it's not like that just now. I mean, are you getting the whole script while you're at the Royal?'

He gave one of his deep throaty laughs. 'Do not worry, my dear. The money is good in Edinburgh. We have been playing to full houses so far. And there are still two weeks to go.'

'My agent wants to book me for a summer season in Rothesay. I've to let him know by this weekend.'

'I will speak to Dave tonight.'

'Thanks, Hector. You're a good friend.'

She looked up at his face, shadowed from the sunshine by the broad hat. He had been a handsome man in his youth but his skin had coarsened a little, his jaw had become broader and heavier and lines creased the sides of his eyes and mouth. His brows jutted dramatically over fine dark eyes however, and his wide mouth revealed strong white teeth. He no longer was given romantic hero parts but excelled as husbands and fathers, family friends and occasionally a roué or a villain. Just at that moment, while she gazed up at him, a change came over Annalie's feelings. She wasn't sure if it was triggered off by gratitude or affection but suddenly she found him physically attractive as well. Previously she'd seen him with clear calm eyes as a middle-aged man with thick, wiry hair going grey, and a straight-backed, portly body. Now, suddenly, he acquired a chemistry that sizzled down from his eyes into hers and from there winged like hot darts through her nervous system. She wondered if he felt the same. He never mentioned it and they both looked away and walked for some time in silence. Eventually Annalie blurted out:

'How long has it been since your wife died?'

'Six months.'

'It's a long time to be without love.'

'Too long,' he said.

'I know how you feel.' They walked in silent companionship again until she confided, 'Sometimes I've so much loving in me I ache with it.'

'My dear,' he said.

'I've never been afraid of the truth.' She boldly met his eyes again. 'Nor of loving either. Once I've made up my mind. You said life must go on. You said you wanted to be happy. Could you be happy with me?'

Suddenly he grinned down at her. 'Is this a proposal?'

'Of course not.'

'You wish us to be lovers then?'

'Don't you fancy me?'

'What a question.'

He stopped walking, turned her towards him, and in the middle of the busy High Street he kissed her.

Happiness and excitement raced through her veins.

He shook an admonitory finger at her.

'It is a good job it was not a proposal of marriage. If there are going to be any proposals I will make them. Be warned, I have no intention of allowing you or anyone else to steal my lines.'

CHAPTER 37

She had to stop him telling dirty jokes. At first she had been too horrified to say anything. It wasn't only that they were filthy and unfunny. They were all of the type that degraded women. Especially women's bodies and not only live bodies, even dead bodies were made the butt of his sick humour. He always told them in bed just before, during, or after making love to her, if his bestial activities could be called love. She had stopped that too. It had been quite simple. She had just told him she'd read somewhere it was illegal.

He didn't touch her again. She tried to make herself look as attractive as possible. She tried to be loving and affectionate in the hope, because she so desperately wanted children, of persuading him to make love to her properly. Nothing worked. Eventually she'd burst out in desperation, 'Alec, I want a family. Surely you do as well. You've always seemed fond of children. Think of having a son of your own . . .' He had tried to make love to her then but it had been a terrible experience. He had been impotent. She understood his humiliation and tried to reassure him and say it didn't matter. There was no hurry. Perhaps next time. But there never was a next time. His bitterness knew no bounds. He blamed her. It was all her fault, he said, and sometimes she wondered if it was.

It was a barren existence and often even her longing for the friendship and affection she'd had with him before their marriage was so great she would reach out to him in a desperate effort to find any sort of closeness or understanding. She would say kind, sometimes flattering, things to him in an effort to boost his self-confidence. She would act in a childish ignorant sort of way, so that he could laugh at her and feel superior. He enjoyed that. It made him come to life and look happy and it would seem for a time that they were friends again. They would have an evening at the local cinema and he would chat to her about his customers and tell her how the children were getting on and what teacher had popped in to buy tea and biscuits for their break. Sometimes they lay in bed chatting and holding hands. She would make all sorts of excuses for him, his mother didn't make his life easy the way she criticized him and never gave him any credit for anything. Now that Mrs Harper had given up hope of the Monktons being a bottomless pit of financial support she kept sabotaging any idea of Alec having a house of his own. The shop too was in Mrs Harper's name and she acquired the habit of saying:

'That shop can't keep two rents going. It's hard enough to pay rent and gas and coal and dear knows what else for one place.' Her laugh racketed around. 'You'll bankrupt us if you take on any more expense. Don't forget you've a wife to feed now.'

Alec maintained his smooth patience with his mother, but there were occasions, and they were becoming more frequent, when he vented his frustration and bitterness on Elizabeth. He never raised his hand or his voice, but sometimes his tone contained such quiet venom that her heart was alarmed, or his eyes would glow with hatred and there would be sickening disgust in his voice. The last time she had tackled him about going to the factor to see about a place of their own his face had contorted into ugliness and he'd spat out 'Shut up!' with such hatred she was shocked into silence. But because of the other times when they could be normal and friendly together she kept persuading herself that everything would be different if they could just get away from the strain of living with Mrs Harper.

Her mother-in-law continued to treat her with an embarrassed deference and kept her at arm's length, although underneath the deference was a resentment, an aura of having been cheated. Often Elizabeth would come into the kitchen to find Mrs Harper talking in furtive undertones to Alec. She'd stop immediately she saw Elizabeth and turn away to scrub at the sink board or attack with a duster the already gleaming brass tap. She seldom allowed Elizabeth to help with the housework and once had said with a bitterness that her laughter did little to disguise:

'You? You wouldn't know where to start!'

When Elizabeth did insist on doing something – clean the bedroom she and Alec shared, for instance – Mrs Harper would burst into a hysteria of laughter.

'A fine carry-on in my own house. And not even the dusters washed. I'll give it a proper going-over tomorrow. What an awful waste of soap and wax polish. All that money . . .'

Elizabeth even became self-conscious about the food she ate, feeling all the time that Mrs Harper's eye was on every crumb she put into her mouth and that she was bitterly calculating what it cost. It made her eat greedily when she visited Jessie. Eventually she looked forward to Jessie's pancakes or girdle scones, generously spread with butter and jam, as much as, if not more than, she looked forward to Jessie herself. She was glad of the more relaxed and cheerful atmosphere in Jessie's house too, even though the sight and the touch of Jessie's baby gave her such bitter-sweet pain and increased her longing a thousandfold for a child of her own. Since the birth of Jessie's little boy the Langlands Road house had become cluttered, untidy and dusty.

'What use is a duster in here?' Jessie contentedly fed baby Johnny from her large milky breast. 'The coalman just comes and heaves more coal in and dirties the place all over again. Have another scone, hen. I like to see folk enjoying their food.'

She'd taken yet another scone and tilted more tea down her throat and picked up every crumb from her lap and eaten it.

'Are you still hoping to get a house?' Jessie queried on the occasion of Elizabeth's last visit.

'Yes. Why?'

'There's one going in the next close. A nice wee room and kitchen. The lavvy's out on the stairs but I suppose anything would be better than living with that old harridan.'

'Oh, Jessie! And so near to you too. Wouldn't it be wonderful?'

'Away and see the factor then. Why not?'

In her eager excitement Elizabeth had forgotten why not. Her feet had flown down Jessie's stairs and on to the first tram that came to take her into town and the factor's office. There she was told the rent of the house, which seemed to her hardly anything at all. And wonder of wonders, joy of joys, it could be hers. Or, to be more precise – Alec's. All that was needed was his signature on the missive. Unable to wait until he came home she'd gone to the shop to tell him but the shop was packed with customers and when she'd crushed through them and announced she wanted to talk to him he'd said in a perfectly even tone, 'We'll talk when I get home.' But she could sense the undercurrent of stress that warned her not to press him further. Later, when she had more time to think she decided it would be better to wait until he'd enjoyed his supper, then relaxed with his usual pipe in the toilet before broaching the subject. She was so happy and excited, however, it took all her willpower to keep quiet and wait. Meanwhile she planned what she'd say and how she'd say it. She decided it would be prudent to cajole and flatter and adopt the silly little girl persona that was his favourite. It began to worry her that she had taken the initiative in going to see about the house. He never took the initiative in anything but an illusion had always to be maintained that he had.

At long last he emerged from the toilet and Mrs Harper went in to flip her apron about in violent efforts to dispel the fug and also to hang on the nail beside the lavatory pan more of the squares of newspaper she'd cut and laced through with a piece of string.

'Alec, you'll never guess what's happened.' Elizabeth spoke rapidly to take advantage of Mrs Harper's absence from the kitchen. She'd meant first of all to relate some imaginary and stupid thing she'd done in order to put him in a good mood. But there wasn't time.

'You've discovered you're actually related to the Royal Family and they've invited you to visit Buckingham Palace.'

He had a penchant for sarcasm and always delivered it with a sneering twist to his mouth and a contemptuous glance.

'There's a wee room and kitchen become vacant up the close next to Jessie's. Oh, Alec, wouldn't it be lovely for you to be boss in your own home and have everything just as you want it? I'd keep it nice for you and have nice suppers waiting for you and you could furnish it whatever way you fancied. I'd be perfectly happy as long as you were happy.'

'You're still in never-never land.' He too spoke rapidly and in a low voice, almost a whisper. 'Where do you think I'd get the money to pay a bloody rent, far less for bloody furniture? I get pocket money from her. Bloody pocket money.'

Tears of disappointment welled up in Elizabeth's eyes. 'But surely . . .'

'No buts about it. She's got everything tied up tighter than a badger's arse. This house and the shop'll be mine when she snuffs it. You'll just have to suffer the same as me. You'll just have to play the waiting game the same as me.'

Elizabeth was appalled. Not just because of his attitude but by the thought of being imprisoned for years in such a soulless place. Her spirits sagged under the weight of such a prospect.

'I don't know what you see in that stinking stuff.' Mrs Harper came shuffling breathlessly back. 'You can't tell me you get any pleasure out of it. And when I think of what it costs . . .'

Elizabeth went through to the bedroom. The front room was never used unless for visitors, and even then they had to be judged as being worth the expense of using the gas and the coal for the extra fire. This had never happened since her marriage. Jessie had been the only visitor and Mrs Harper had nearly had hysterics at Elizabeth's suggestion that she should be entertained in the front room. There had been much agitating about and furtive whisperings with Alec. The gas mantle had disappeared from the room and so did the screwed-up papers and sticks with which the room fire was usually set ready to be lit.

Even when the better weather came and neither fire nor light was needed other difficulties and discouragements appeared. Dust sheets were put over the furniture as if the place had died.

'To protect it against the sun and any wear and tear,' Mrs Harper explained. 'I'd never be able to replace any of that good stuff if anything happened to it. Even if I could afford it you'd never be able to get good stuff like that nowadays. They don't make things like that nowadays. It costs a fortune for a lot of rubbish. Everything in that room belonged to my mother and some of it to her mother before her and it's still as good as new because it's hardly ever been used. It's so well taken care of.'

The dust sheets gave the room such a grim and

ghostly atmosphere that even the limited pleasure Elizabeth had gazing out of the front-room window at Elder Park was spoiled. When Jessie came she was just taken into the kitchen. Not that Jessie minded, except she and Elizabeth couldn't get a proper talk on their own. And as Elizabeth said and Jessie agreed:

'It's impossible to relax with Mrs Harper around. She's always shuffling about so quickly yet so painfully. On the few occasions when she does sit down she's continuously on the go with something – knitting, darning, polishing brasses. Even her habit of wearing that big crocheted tammy in the house puts me on edge. It's as if she's always hurrying to go out somewhere. But of course she never does. She wears that thing either to hide her lack of hair on top or to keep her head warm. She's so mean with the coal.'

'She goes out sometimes. Or at least she used to,' Jessie reminded her. 'To spy on Alec. She was always hanging about either behind or in front of the counter in that shop.'

'She only goes out now when I'm out. When I'm in she keeps her eye on me all the time. Even when I try to hide myself away in the bedroom she's always popping her head round the door, laughing that inane laugh of hers and making some excuse about getting something out of the wardrobe or wanting to flick a duster around the place.'

'She's probably checking to make sure you haven't lit the gas or the fire or something,' Jessie said. 'I don't know how you stand it. Think of the difference it would be to your life if you had a wee place of your own. The pair of you might be able to start a family then.'

Elizabeth sighed with pleasure at the thought. 'Oh, it would be so wonderful if we could, Jessie. And I can't tell you what a relief it would be to get away on our own. I'm sure Alec would be different then. He's not that bad, really. I mean he does have lots of good points. If he was just given half a chance . . .'

Now the chance of the room and kitchen in the next close to Jessie had gone. Elizabeth felt heartbroken. Hope guttered low. It came over her like one of Mrs Harper's dust sheets that even after Mrs Harper died Alec would want to stay on here. He would see no reason for moving house. On the contrary, having waited so long for this place he would treasure it as a victory, a reward for his years of patience and endurance. Something to savour.

The bedroom window, like the kitchen, looked down on to the long narrow back courts of the tenements. The back courts within the tenement block were separated by iron railings topped by sharp spikes. Often Elizabeth's hand would fly to her mouth as she watched children clamber up and on to roofs of wash houses and middens, or in the local slang, the midgies. The children would jump from one to the other and risk impaling themselves on the spikes.

Staring down at the back court Elizabeth was reminded of the first week of her marriage when she'd been awakened by a terrible racket. She'd got up and looked out the bedroom window and discovered the noise was being caused by the men of the cleansing department who, she decided, must have the most horrible job in the country. They wore lights attached to their hats like miners, string tied round their trouser legs and large baskets slung over their shoulders. One man had climbed into the midden and was shovelling the rubbish into the baskets before each man heaved one on to his back. By the light of the lamps she could see grey ash running through the baskets and on to the men.

Standing in the icy darkness of the room with Alec snoring in the bed behind her and this scene like something from hell being enacted below, she had the unreal feeling of being suspended on another planet.

Or it was all a dream. For a hopeful second or two she thought she might suddenly wake up in the nursery and everything would be clean and safe. Then she felt the pain of Alec's invasion of her body and knew she would never be clean again.

Even now with the sun glinting against the windows, and the back court echoing merrily with children's voices, she felt destroyed.

'Do you fancy a walk?' Alec asked, coming into the room. 'You look a bit pasty-faced. You probably don't get enough fresh air and exercise.'

She blew her nose and cleared her throat. 'Yes, all right. It's such a lovely night. It's a shame to stay indoors.'

Often they went for a walk on a Sunday during the day. Alec liked to go to a small field opposite the 'fifty pitches' where cattle grazed. He was fond of animals and told her with much bitterness in his voice that he'd always wanted to own a dog but his mother refused to have any animal near the house. They would stand at the edge of the field and watch the larks rising straight up from the long grass, silent at first. Then they began to sing while fluttering their wings in short quick bursts. Higher and higher and quite slowly they rose until they were tiny dots in the blue sky.

That evening she and Alec walked through the dusty sunshine of the streets, side by side, not speaking. It occurred to her that Alec was probably just as unhappy as she was. The thought filled her with pity and with a sigh she linked her arm through his.

CHAPTER 38

The stage manager put the finishing touches to the props and Annalie was reminded of the home in Cumberland Street she'd once been so proud of. Except that there were more ornaments displayed on the set. That was because the ornaments were important to the plot.

'Now let me remind you again. It's Thursday,' Sam Kline, the director, was saying. 'And like every Thursday for the past five years ex-con Charlie McGhee gets ready for his daughter Nan's visit. Although alone in Nan's eyes, McGhee still shares his days with his dead wife Cathy, an ethereal presence who visits the old place and romantically dreams over the china shepherdess.' He tapped his pencil thoughtfully against his teeth for a few seconds and then called over to the stage manager, 'Tommy, better give it more prominence. The mantelpiece is too high. How about the sideboard? Yes, that's at easier eye level. Right, where were we? Yes, Charlie and Cathy's gestures bear witness to a past harmony which Nan is just too blind to perceive. Resentful and bitter, she repudiates her father and with the shadow of a home for the aged looming large over him, she forces the old man to reveal a secret which will shatter her life . . . and his.'

The play was a one-act three-parter, one of three plays that were being offered as the evening's entertainment. Hector was Charlie McGhee, Annalie was the dead wife Cathy, and a young actress called Sandra Remington was Nan. Annalie would much rather have played Nan because she was a fiery emotional character, and she would have enjoyed letting it rip, but Sandra had already been promised the part before

Annalie joined the company. The gentle, subdued and soft-spoken Cathy was quite a challenge to Annalie's volatile nature but with Sam and Hector's patience and persistent coaching she managed a reasonable performance eventually.

'You have done very well, considering,' Hector said.

'Considering what?'

'Considering that you are a sexy, hip-swinging gypsy-type beauty. My dear, it was priceless the way you said the "Charlie is my darling" line at first.' He chuckled, remembering.

'All right, all right. You all had your laugh at the time.'

'Well, my dear, the way you said it had all sorts of erotic and passionate implications. "Charlie is my darling, my darling, my darling . . ." ' he mimicked her husky and sultry expression. 'It was supposed to be sung, too.'

'No, it wasn't. It said in the script softly singing *or speaking*.'

'I know, my love. I am just teasing.'

'Anyway, I got it right eventually.'

'I know. And the make-up. It was wonderful! For you to have transformed yourself so successfully into someone "faded and of indeterminate age" was a real tour de force.'

She had been nervous about everything but especially the make-up. She'd never before used make-up sticks to transform her appearance, only to highlight it. The first dress rehearsal was scheduled to begin at eleven o'clock in the morning but she'd arrived in the dressing room at ten, long before any of the other female actors had arrived. The cleaner had just finished work and hovered in the doorway drying her hands on her sackcloth apron, eager for a chat. But Annalie wasn't in the mood to listen to the latest news about Mrs McPherson's daughter who was expecting twins and who recently had become so constipated that, as Mrs McPherson said, 'It would take a bomb to move her.'

After being forced to speak to Annalie's back or through the long, garishly lit mirror Mrs McPherson gave up after a few minutes and went huffily away. Only then did Annalie get down to the serious business of aging herself and changing her character. Tongue held between teeth she plotted the contours of her face with areas of colour. Craning over the bench to get closer to the mirror she drew fine outlines beneath each eye and down the sides of her mouth. Satisfied at last, she pulled the faded mousey wig over her rich black curls. The transformation was quite startling, except that her dark violet-flecked eyes still tossed out their usual proud challenge. With a concentrated effort she struggled to tone herself down inside, to try and *think* like a gentle, faded, ethereal-type woman.

The director was impressed but her nerves did not decrease. Her palms were hot and sticky with sweat as she faced the huge, shadowy cavern of the auditorium. But the dress rehearsal had gone well and she'd been so exultant afterwards she'd whirled Hector into a mad dance with her until they'd both collapsed laughing into chairs.

On the night the play opened her nerves came back a hundredfold. Hector's assurance that all actors felt the same every time, no matter how experienced, failed to calm her. All day she ran through a gamut of emotions – melancholy, fear, panic. She could see, when she arrived at the theatre, that everyone looked as nervous as she felt, but it did nothing to comfort her either. Sandra Remington looked naked with fright. Hector was puffing anxiously at a cigarette but he winked at her and said, 'Break a leg.'

Epitaph for a Hard Man was the second play on the programme and so they had the extra strain of having to wait through the whole of the first play, which they listened to with only wandering attention over the Tannoy. Then the journey from the dressing room along passageways, up flights of stairs smelling of disinfectant, through heavy swing doors, legs in danger of giving way at any moment. On to the stage, smelling the raw new timber of the set as pungent as her fear, waiting for the curtain to rise, Hector, alone with his own emotions, unaware of her. Then suddenly Hector wasn't Hector any more. He was Charlie McGhee and he was looking at her and saying, 'You still here?'

Later, in the wings, Annalie said to a sweaty Hector, 'The applause isn't bad.' She felt as if she'd taken a terrible risk and was astonished at having survived it.

'Come, my dears.' Hector took her hand and Sandra's and pulled them back on stage for their curtain call.

Afterwards the dressing room was cheerful and re-laxed as if it had never been anything else. Annalie laughed at herself in the mirror and laughed at Sandra doing a little jig around the small room. A wonderful new world had opened up before her. She saw herself acting a whole repertoire of great roles and becoming as famous as Sarah Bernhardt or Marlene Dietrich.

Above their heads the third and last short play of the evening was booming out from the loudspeaker. There was no escaping from what was happening on stage anywhere in the theatre. But soon Annalie's make-up was off and she'd changed into her slim-fitting dress of black, white and green wool with the bright green belt and buttons. She had a three-quarter-length coat to match and a cheeky black hat with a green feather.

'How did it sound?' Mabel, Frances and Jean, the other females in the company, came noisily into the room.

'Marvellous,' Sandra said, moving along to allow the girls more room at the mirror.

'Great,' Annalie agreed. 'The whole thing seemed to go really well.'

Cream was hastily slapped on and wiped off faces. Costumes were hung on hangers while each play and each performance was excitedly, happily picked over.

'You're not going?' Jean cried out to Annalie, seeing her perch her hat on top of her curls.

'Yes, why?'

'There's a party on-stage. You can't just go home to bed while the adrenaline's still pumping like mad.'

Just then Hector put his head round the door. 'There's a party on-stage, my loves, and free drinks are being provided.'

Annalie laughed. 'All right, I'm coming.'

He kissed her in the corridor and she responded with passion, clinging round his neck, pressing her softness against his hardness.

'What did I tell you?' he said, linking arms with her. 'You were brilliant.'

'A slight exaggeration. If anyone was brilliant it was you, Hector.'

They knew they were both exaggerating but they didn't care. They had given of their best and it had been successful in the only way that mattered. They had enjoyed personal recognition and been awarded the comfort of applause. They were walking on air, floating, restless.

Stripped of its bright glare of lights the stage was now just a draughty corridor. Everyone was loudly chatting, unashamedly seeking praise and gladly tossing compliments at one another. But Dave Lawson seemed to mean it when he said to Annalie, 'Congratulations, darling. You were really good. Really.' But Annalie's attention kept straying to Hector. Each time one of the other women laughed up at him or kissed him in congratulation or took his arm in a friendly gesture, she burned with jealousy. Eventually she managed to pull him away and once outside they hastened back to the digs through the darkness. A cold wind tugged at their coats and Annalie had to keep one hand on her hat in case it was whipped away from her. A smirr of rain wavered lamps in the blurred distance and now Annalie's most urgent thoughts were how to reach the shelter of Mrs Tunniecliffe's flat as quickly as possible. Once there Hector followed her to her room and locked the door before putting some pennies in the meter for the gas fire. It was a rusted contraption with a broken mantle and small for the high-ceilinged, football-pitch proportions of the room. Usually several chorus girls shared the three double beds but Annalie's roommates, Sandra, Jean, Frances and Mabel, had been invited to another party after the on-stage one. Annalie and Hector sat in front of the feeble flicker of warmth for a few minutes, rubbing their hands energetically together. Then Hector took her hands in his and kissed deep into their palms. They undressed each other quickly, expertly, Hector making Annalie giggle at one point by saying:

'Thank God we have found a better way of keeping warm than that useless peep of a fire.'

Afterwards they lay between the pink flannelette sheets of one of the beds and chatted companionably. Eventually, reluctantly, Annalie said:

'You'd better go, love. Unless you're planning to share with the rest of the girls.'

'I would not mind, my dear. I am fit enough to take all of them on.'

'Don't you dare!' Annalie punched him and he retaliated by struggling with her and tickling her until she choked out, 'For God's sake behave yourself, Hector. Mrs Tunniecliffe'll hear us.'

'She would not care a damn, my love. As long as we pay up she will be perfectly happy. The only thing she minds is wasted space.'

'A room empty, you mean? I would have thought digs were too scarce for that.'

'No, with dwarfs. She is not the only one who grudges the poor sods a full-sized bed. Do you know Lenny Bakford?'

'Often plays the Pavilion?'

'He told me one landlady always makes him sleep in a vegetable box at the foot of another artiste's bed.'

Annalie rolled her eyes. 'As if he hadn't enough to put up with.'

'I have thought of a better way to save space, my dear.'

'Who for?'

'You and me.'

'I'm not with you.'

'Yes you are. Only I want you to be with me all the time, for the rest of our lives. We could share the one double bed wherever we go. We might even get a cheaper rate for a married couple.'

'Hector.' She laughed gently at him. 'It's not a very romantic proposal, it it?'

He turned towards her. 'I often joke when I want to be terribly serious. It's a failing of mine.'

'No, it's not. It's just another thing about you that I love.'

His eyes glowed and shimmered moistly at her through the darkness. They hadn't bothered with the gas mantle and only the flicker of the fire lit the room.

'Darling, I do love you and I would be so proud and happy if you would agree to be my wife.'

'Yes, yes, yes.' She kissed him after each word.

'Wonderful, wonderful,' he enthused, hugging her in such a fierce, bearlike embrace she became breathless.

'No, darling,' she managed.

'I want to make love to you over and over again.'

'That's what I want too but the girls are bound to be back any minute.'

He gave a deep sigh of resignation and released her. Propping her head up on her linked hands she lovingly

309

watched him dress. At the door he blew her a kiss and made his exit. Hector never simply left a room.

After he'd slipped away to his own room, or at least the one he shared with the male members of the company, Annalie lay wide-eyed, joyously savouring all that had happened that day, swinging backwards from the proposal of marriage to the success of the play. She found herself still in the grip of the excitement of her lines. The last thing she remembered before drifting into a dream-filled, love-blessed. sleep was singing to herself:

'Charlie is my darling, my darling, my darling . . .'

CHAPTER 39

'She seems to have disappeared off the face of the earth.' Elizabeth gazed sadly at Jessie. 'Any time I'm in town now I look at the variety bills but there's never any dancer called Annalie Gordon.'

'She's probably moved to England. You couldn't blame her for wanting to start a new life where nobody knows her, away from all that awful publicity.'

'I suppose not.'

'You've never given up, then? I thought maybe after all this time . . .'

'She was so beautiful.'

'Are you all right?'

Elizabeth nodded absently and Jessie peered closer.

'You've lost weight and you haven't a scrap of colour in your face. Is that dirty bugger trying it on again?'

'No, no. It's not that. It's just . . . oh, I don't know, everything's so negative. There's no joy, no happiness, not even any laughter in life any more. Christmas for instance. I never had such a dreary time in my life. You had what sounded like a bright, cheerful and happy time, Jessie, with all your family and Gordon's family and their children and your Johnny, and all that food you told me about.' She added wistfully, 'It was awful, just the three of us and Mrs Harper complaining about the extra cost of the fruit for the Christmas pudding.'

'I'm surprised she had one at all.'

'It's their custom to have the Christmas meal in the front room. It's the only time it's ever used and honestly it would have been far better and cheerier in the kitchen. She grudged everything so much. The room gas

311

was kept low and the fire was practically non-existent except for some feeble wisps of black smoke. It was a real misery. Sometimes I feel like turning the gas on and not lighting it, just lying down in front of it . . .'

'Here, stop that silly talk.' Jessie gave a shout that wakened Johnny but he just lay in his cot, eyes wide and hazy. He was a wonderfully placid child. 'There's worse things happen in China. You need cheering up, so you do. How about you and Alec and Gordon and me having a night out somewhere? Maybe for a meal or drink or to the pictures?' She gave a whoop of laughter. 'Or all three?'

'What about Johnny?'

'Och, my mother or one of my sisters'll look after him. He'll be all right. What do you say?'

'I'll have to ask Alec.'

'To hell with asking, tell him.'

Elizabeth smiled her acquiescence. There were some things Jessie would not understand and so were no use talking about. If there was one thing Alec couldn't bear it was being organized. It was almost as bad as her 'trying to be a clever dick' or 'trying to pretend you've got brains'. These sneering accusations could arise from the most unexpected and innocent source. Recently she'd remarked that Mrs Wallis Simpson must have a strong character to have influenced King Edward so much that he had chosen to give up the throne for her. She had been reading quite a bit on the subject and knew about Mrs Simpson's background and the names of her previous two husbands. She had also read about how Edward and Mrs Simpson met and was quite enjoying relating all this to Alec. She had little else to do but look forward to a chat with him when he came home from work. She had thought at first that his sneering and disparaging sideways glances were because he hated any strong or clever woman. She had thought Mrs Simpson was his target. She'd since come to the conclusion that it had nothing to do with Mrs Simpson. He was only on the lookout for the slightest sign of any strength or cleverness in his wife, obviously taking any such imagined manifestation, no matter how slight, as an insult or some sort of threat to his manhood.

In retaliation he would nag and sneer at her and diminish her. The way she ate was 'furtive and greedy'. The way she dressed was aimed at 'being toffee-nosed with all the neighbours . . . showing them what a right little posh lady you are. Too good for them by far.' But of course he knew that in fact she was 'only a dirty little bastard'. Or he'd ridicule a hat she wore. Or mimic and exaggerate her neat little movements in putting on or taking off her gloves, or smoothing down her skirt or peering up through her fringe. She didn't walk, she 'minced along'. And, above all, she knew nothing.

If Mrs Harper was around when Alec said anything derogatory, although he seldom spoke to her in front of his mother, Mrs Harper would give one of her nervous bursts of laughter and Elizabeth could never be sure if the older woman was embarrassed or triumphant.

Alec's bitter deprecation of her had become so insidious that she had begun to believe his picture of her. There were times when she was so depressed she really thought she was ugly and stupid and couldn't do anything without him telling her or explaining how to do it. At other times she was keenly aware of watching every word in case it would sound to him too knowledgeable or intelligent. For the sake of peace, and freedom from harassment, she trained herself to speak in only the simplest of terms with the vocabulary of little more than the primary children she used to teach. She was careful not to be caught reading any books except the lightest and most foolish of romantic stories. But any book could be suspect.

'All right for some,' he'd say, 'who've nothing better to do.'

313

(His mother boasted that she'd never read a book in her life.)

'While you were learning to be such a clever dick,' he'd say, 'I was slaving away in that shop.'

He'd left school at fourteen and gone straight into the shop. He'd even missed the war. His father's poor health and the fact that he was needed to help in the business had given him an exemption.

She worried for hours about Jessie's suggestion of a night out. Not about the suggestion itself, but of the way to broach the subject to Alec. She decided the safest thing to do was put him in a good mood first. One way to do that was to make him laugh at some silly thing she had done, or was supposed to have done.

'You'll never guess the daft thing I did today,' she began, widening her eyes and fluttering her eyelashes.

'What?' He brightened unexpectedly, a smile hovering in readiness at his mouth.

'You know how this was my day for going to Jessie's? Well, I must have been dreaming or something because I went up the wrong close. Even went all the way up the stairs and knocked on the left-hand door. That's the position of Jessie's door in the next close. I nearly died when this strange woman came to the door. I felt such a fool.'

He was eager-eyed now and grinning. 'I keep telling you you're a fool.'

'I know. Jessie laughed when I told her. She said she doesn't know how you put up with me. What with you having to slave away in that shop all the time as well. Gordon says what you need is a night out so that you can relax and enjoy yourself for a change.' She averted her gaze from him and willed herself to appear very casual. 'He suggested having a night out, the four of us. But I don't fancy it.'

'Why not?' Alec's voice turned suspicious. 'Is Gordon too common for you? Is that it? It's high time you gave

314

up these snobby ideas of yours. You keep forgetting that you're not Lady Monkton and never have been.'

'No, it's not that,' Elizabeth hastily interrupted before he reached the bastard bit. 'I just thought you'd be too tired after you came home from work to be bothered with company.'

'You said you didn't fancy it.'

'I was only worried about you. If you think it's all right, that's different. You know best how you feel.'

And so it was arranged. They went to town in more ways than one, as Jessie said. They had a slap-up meal and not just one but two bottles of wine in Ferrari's. Jessie got tipsy. Her wild fuzz of hair stuck out and stood up, and her big face glistened with perspiration and became more vividly pink by the minute. Elizabeth took a fit of the giggles and felt she had never enjoyed herself so much in years. In fact everyone was having a whale of a time. They thoroughly enjoyed the asparagus spears rolled in smoked salmon garnished with cream and lemon, followed by cock-a-leekie soup, then Aberdeen Angus beef cooked in Burgundy. She couldn't imagine how Alec was able to afford it all but had no intention of spoiling the treat by asking him. The men took to competing with each other in tall tales about the idiocies of their wives – or as often as not in Gordon's case, Jessie's brass neck – and it was so good to see Alec relaxed and happy. He was always under such a strain at home. It was not because of love and concern for his mother that he was restrained and patient. He was struggling to make sure that he would inherit the shop. Tonight he was so different. It gave her hope again that if only they could get away on their own they could still have a chance of happiness. Alec had said that if he wasn't careful his mother could leave everything to his cousin Benny in Australia, who'd never done a hand's turn for her. His eyes had smouldered with hatred and resentment and every muscle in his body looked tense.

Gordon had progressed to the stage of insisting it was time for the hard stuff and he signalled to the waiter with even more than his usual aggressive self-confidence. It was then that Elizabeth caught Alec looking at Gordon in a strange way. The look only lasted a few seconds before he lowered his eyes. But she'd seen the gleam of something that haunted her for the rest of the evening. She tried to fathom it out, put a name to it. She felt it vitally important that she should, because it seemed for those few seconds a shutter had been lifted and had revealed the real Alec hidden underneath. Drink hazed her mind and she still giggled and chattered with Jessie and thought how huge Jessie was becoming. She had always been a tall, big-boned girl, but since the birth of Johnny, she'd started putting on flesh. She tried to control her girth with stiff-boned corsets, but they just seemed to accentuate her massive solidity and especially the way her breasts bulged up in her blouse like white mountains with a deep pink cleavage in between. Nor did the corsets do anything to hide her muscly arms, and thighs so hefty she couldn't cross her legs.

But all the time through the happy haze of alcohol and the affectionate observations of Jessie, that brief look in Alec's eyes waited, burned, at the back of Elizabeth's mind, concentrated her senses.

There had been such intense admiration, such wild pleasure in it. But more than that, there had been lust. Or had she imagined it? A few seconds seen through a drunken stupor. Yet its hard bright gleam wouldn't go away.

It was late when they left Ferrari's and they sang in the tram all the way home. Or at least until Jessie and Gordon left them. Then she and Alec fell silent except to giggle as they swayed and staggered up the tenement stairs and Alec fumbled with his keys and had to make several efforts before securing the key in the keyhole, shushing one another, suppressing their giggles and managing to reach their bedroom without Mrs Harper hearing.

'That was a lovely meal,' Elizabeth whispered as they undressed. 'I really enjoyed it.'

'It cost a bomb though,' Alec whispered back. 'Mother would have had a fit if she'd seen the bill.'

'You enjoyed it too though, didn't you?'

They were undressing in the dark so she couldn't see his face except by the wan grey moonbeams that were filtering in and making the cramped room, with its giant furniture, look ghost-like. His face seemed ghost-like too, a sickly grey colour, and eyeless after he removed his glasses. Only dark shadows of sockets were left. But she detected a hint of a smile as he nodded.

'Do you mind if I go to the toilet first?' she whispered. 'You take such a long time.'

'All right. But don't go falling over anything and waking her. And don't pull the plug.'

She hitched her pyjama trousers up in case she tripped over them and began feeling her way with excruciating care along the wall until she reached the toilet. There she urinated with equal care and as slowly as possible before feeling her way back and slipping into bed. She felt dizzy when she lay down and closed her eyes but she took deep, determined breaths and soon the room stopped revolving. By the time Alec returned she was drifting into uneasy sleep. Until, suddenly, she felt him mount her and invade her body and cause her such pain that she bled and cried out in anguish and pleaded with him to stop.

'Shut up.' His voice was low and fierce. Yet there was an automatic abstracted air about it.

Afterwards he fell asleep almost immediately he'd rolled clear of her. She heard his deep, catarrhal snoring as she crept out of bed and by some miracle reached the toilet again. There, in the stinking darkness, she sank on to her knees, retching and vomiting into the lavatory pan. Until it seemed everything inside her, including her heart and soul, had been torn away and she knew that she was beyond help. Beyond even a place where Nanny would ever reach her. She had no one but herself and the fear and hatred that had taken root inside her.

CHAPTER 40

Elizabeth had hoped and prayed she'd feel better by the spring. The cold winds and rain of January, February and March were notoriously bad for colds and aches and pains. She had taken several colds and Alec had complained, 'You're always sniffling these days.'

Mrs Harper was more sympathetic about the rheumatism. She erupted with her usual bout of laughter at the spectacle of Elizabeth walking with stiff apprehension because of the pain in her knees or nursing aching elbows or trying to stretch the rheumatic nodules out of her back. But she also confessed to experiencing similar pains herself. It was something they now had in common. It gave them something to talk about. Often Mrs Harper would sound dismissive and unsympathetic. She'd say:

'I just have to get on with it. Work has to be done, I can't afford to be ill.'

At other times she'd confide that steeping her feet in Epsom salts and very hot water helped ease them. She'd fill a basin with the mixture and allow Elizabeth to try it. Elizabeth was profuse in her thanks and the relief, especially of the heat, was intense. The house was always so gloomy and cold. It was an exquisite treat to dip a cup in the water and pour it over her knees and legs and hands and arms. Sometimes she wondered if the tight little knots with which she was riddled could be caused by tension. Especially the tightness in the back of her neck, which could spread its vice-like grip right over her head until even her eyes ached. What made her suspect tension was that she always felt worse when Alec was in. Sometimes it seemed she just needed to look at him to get a headache or cramp in her muscles or an acid digestion.

Alec said, 'You're getting acid right enough, acid-tongued as well.'

This was because sometimes she couldn't bring herself to act the silly little woman, diminishing herself to make him feel big. More and more she was tempted to vie with him in caustic sarcastic remarks. Sometimes she succumbed to the temptation but always regretted it. She did not enjoy being cruel. To hurt anyone made her feel guilty and upset. It made the acid churn and burn all the worse inside her.

Mrs Harper confessed that she was a martyr to her stomach and the secret was bicarbonate of soda. When it made Elizabeth vomit in the kitchen sink Mrs Harper hirpled rapidly away through to the room, making high-pitched panicky sounds.

The hint of a headache began as Elizabeth watched Alec get dressed. All his movements at that time in the morning were leisurely, methodical and careful. He brushed his thinning hair with slow even strokes, preening himself, knees slightly bent as if the mirror wasn't high enough. He smoothed pomade on with flat palms until his head was sleek. He polished his glasses for an excruciatingly long time. She noticed how sunken and lizard-like his eyes had become. He seemed to be shrinking all over. Or was it that when she'd known him and admired him at first she'd just imagined he was taller and more broad-shouldered? There was no longer anything about him she admired. Even his soft voice she now despised as a sign of weakness or hypocrisy. It made her feel bitter and depressed when people she met in Linthouse or Govan continued to speak well of Alec and even say, 'You're a lucky lassie. Marriage is such a lottery, isn't it? Such a nice chap.'

Even Jessie, who thought nothing of calling him a dirty old bugger on occasions, was big-hearted enough not to hold this against him. She could quite easily accept that he had other likeable qualities.

Elizabeth struggled with herself to try to be fair. He could be kind. If she didn't feel well he would bring her a cup of tea in bed before going to work. He could, in fact, make quite a fuss of her, providing that she made sure that when she was unwell she was both helpless and grateful. She had to be profuse in her thanks and her flattering remarks about how good he was and how she didn't know what she'd do without him. She had also to make sure that she wasn't confined to bed for more than two or three days. That was her ration. After that his attitude changed. She could never be sure if he became bored with her or afraid that she was taking advantage of him. The morning cup of tea would still be delivered but with an ungracious 'Here' and tea slopping over into the saucer. He would say things like 'You're getting a right hypochondriac', or 'I've had the flu and God knows all what else but I've never once taken a day off my work', or 'Everybody gets aches and pains but they don't make such a big deal of it', or 'You don't know how lucky you are. If you had ten kids and a man who beat you, you'd know all about it.'

She'd feel guilty then and get up even if she had a temperature. She knew there were many women in Govan and other working-class areas who were indeed much worse off than her. She tried to feel lucky. She saw herself as a terrible nuisance with her delicate health. Although 'delicate' was a word she had to be careful not to use. Only once she'd said to Alec:

'I just seem to have this delicate constitution.'

For some reason the word had angered him.

'You're not delicate,' he sneered. 'Who do you thing you are – Lady Muck?'

She began to see herself as a hypochondriac and felt too guilty and ashamed even to mention how she felt to Jessie. Then she began to suffer from bouts of insomnia.

Especially during the summer nights when the air in the bedroom was stuffy and the heat from Alec's body in the double bed burned her like a fire. She could smell his tobacco, and his sweat, and his old-man odour which reminded her of death. She would cringe as far away as possible, gagging with distaste. Sometimes she'd feel guilty and ashamed at disliking him so much and in such personal ways. She'd feel sorry for him, sorry for them both. Their marriage had been a mistake, that was all. And she couldn't really blame Alec for the marriage because he had been more or less railroaded into it. Then she'd despise him again.

She began to take note of how he looked compared with Big Gordon. They made a foursome with Jessie and Gordon quite regularly, about once a fortnight as a rule. Sometimes they went to the pictures. Sometimes they went for a drink. Sometimes during the summer they just had a walk in the park. Alec seemed so puny and insignificant compared with Gordon. So small, so thin, so indecisive and with such a little snicker of a laugh. He was never the one to say what they'd do or where they'd go. It was always Gordon. Not that she thought all that much of Gordon either. He was loud-mouthed and muscle-bound and he drank himself stupid every weekend. He hadn't just a foghorn of a voice. There were times when he could be foul-mouthed. When he forgot himself and started 'fucking' this and 'fucking' that it was Jessie who always stopped him.

'Here you,' she'd cry out. 'You're not in the yards now. Watch your language!'

Alec never spoke up. Elizabeth despised him for that: 'All you needed to say,' she told him after the first time it happened, 'was "Not in front of the girls, Gordon" – something like that.'

'Aw, shut up,' he snarled at her in reply.

Jessie was pregnant again and Elizabeth could imagine this happening every year, as it had happened every year to Jessie's mother before her. Gradually the fortnightly meetings became monthly meetings. She didn't visit Jessie so often because Jessie's mother or Gordon's mother or Jessie's sisters or Gordon's sisters were always there. Sometimes it was several months before she and Jessie managed to get together and when they did they didn't seem to have anything in common any more. Jessie was completely taken up with her babies and her sisters' babies and her sisters-in-law's babies and talked about nothing else. Elizabeth felt miserably out of place, self-consciously childless among such a healthy fertile breed of women.

A few times during the summer Alec and Mrs Harper and Elizabeth went on a Sunday outing. This was instead of going on holiday. The shop was never shut during the week. Not even during Fair Fortnight, the traditional Glasgow holiday. The Sunday outings were accompanied by a terrific fuss. Mrs Harper was up at the crack of dawn preparing flasks of tea and sandwiches. No matter how early Elizabeth got up in order to help, it was never early enough.

'I'd rather you just kept out of the way,' Mrs Harper would say, with much twitching of eyelids. 'I know what I'm doing in my own kitchen.'

Eventually they'd set off, Alec carrying the shopping basket with the flasks and sandwiches thinly spread with mince left over from the previous day's dinner, or just margarine and jam. Since discovering that Elizabeth wasn't going to be any financial advantage Mrs Harper's economy – as she called it – had become more acute. Elizabeth often thought how much better it was for Alec in the shop all day. He could have the gas lit when he wanted. He even had a paraffin heater. And no doubt he ate as much as he liked from the stock. The last thing Elizabeth wanted, or even imagined she could bear, was being with Alec in the shop or anywhere else all day and every day. But she became so cold and hungry and miserable in the house that she suggested going to work in the shop. Unfortunately, in her desperation she went the wrong way about it.

'I'd be perfectly capable, you know. It would just be a matter of finding where everything is kept. There would be no problem with counting up or giving change. Arithmetic was one of my best subjects at college.'

He turned to his mother. 'Listen to the college girl. Thinks she can teach me a thing or two. A right clever dick.'

Mrs Harper gave a whinny of laughter and shuffled jerkily away to the toilet.

'I don't think anything of the kind,' Elizabeth protested. 'All I meant was . . .'

' "It would just be a matter of finding where everything is kept . . ." ' he mimicked. 'So you think there's nothing to it, eh? I just sit on my backside all day and twiddle my thumbs. I'm too stupid to do anything else, of course. You're the capable one.'

She had given up eventually, secretly cursing herself for not being careful and taking a more diplomatic line.

Sometimes on their Sunday outings they'd take a tram out to Rouken Glen or a bus to Campsie Glen. They'd have their picnic lunch and then Mrs Harper would sit and rest her bunions while Elizabeth and Alec went for a walk. Late in the summer for a special treat they'd gone for a sail down the Clyde in a paddle steamer. They sat on the long slatted seats, Mrs Harper with her maroon and yellow striped tammy pulled well down over her ears against the breeze. Alec wore his flat cap with the skip low down over his brow. He owned a soft felt hat but he kept that for wearing in town on an evening outing. He had worn it when he'd visited Monkton House when he and Elizabeth had been walking out together before their marriage, and looked quite presentable in it. A flat cap made him look smaller and older. Both Mrs Harper and Alec were very excited about the sail down the Clyde. Spots of colour hovered high on their cheekbones and Alec kept getting up and swaggering about the deck, hands jingling coins in his pockets. Elizabeth thought the intensity of their excitement was pathetic. She had gone every year of her childhood and young adulthood on such a sail and spent not a day at Rothesay or Dunoon or any other holiday resort, but two weeks or quite often a month.

Once Mrs Harper arrived at Rothesay she wasted no time in taking off her misshapen shoes and woollen stockings and paddling in the water. After a few squeals caused by the cold she assured Elizabeth that it 'did wonders' for her feet.

Too soon winter came round again. Bitter winds whistled up the close and stairs and under the doors. It made the windows rattle and the fire puff smoke into the kitchen. The gas was kept as low as possible. Elizabeth took to wearing woollen gloves in the house and a scarf tied round her head. Then, just before Christmas, Alec took pneumonia. Mrs Harper was hysterical at the idea of the shop having to shut, especially at that time of year.

'There's no need for the shop to lose all that money,' Elizabeth assured her. 'If you look after Alec I'll go and work in the shop.'

The idea didn't calm Mrs Harper, only added to her hysterical confusion. However, the next day Elizabeth gratefully escaped from the house with the keys of the shop in her handbag. She had left Alec in bed shivering and sweating and delirious. She felt guilty and wished she could have been a good wife and bathed him and tended to him in whatever way was necessary. So great was her dislike and distaste, however, she could't bear to look at him far less touch him. For the first time she thanked God for Mrs Harper. Mrs Harper would surely look after Alec.

She dreaded going back that evening and having not only to see him but to share a bed with him.

After her day's work in the shop, which, as she'd predicted, she'd managed perfectly well, she couldn't think to go back to the house. She walked along the banks of the river for a while, staring at the glittering black water, her collar turned up against the stinging wet air. Eventually, reluctantly she turned towards Linthouse, her feet ringing like a chant upon the pavement. All the time she had been struggling with a terrible thought, trying to banish it from her mind. But it was still there shaming her as she tapped on Mrs Harper's door.

God forgive me, she thought. I hope he's dead.

CHAPTER 41

Annalie had been aware for some time of the general build-up of apprehension and unease. In her own immediate world, however, everything was exciting, interesting and full of promise. She and Hector were happily married and lots of new work opportunities had opened up for them. She had read articles in newspapers about what was going on in the world in general and was shocked by them, of course. It was difficult not to feel horror and indignation at newspaper pictures of laughing, cheering Berliners enjoying the results of a night of anti-Jewish attacks when Jewish property had been destroyed and looted and synagogues burned down. Fashionably dressed Berliners had clapped and screamed with laughter and held up their babies to watch Jews being beaten senseless by youths with lead piping. Non-Nazi parents had their children taken away from them and made wards of the state. Hitler said, 'In future every child will grow up knowing only Nazi values.' A pogrom known as 'the great spring cleaning' was being carried out in Austria. Jews were being excluded from their professions. Jewish judges were dismissed. Jewish artists were banned and Vienna would no longer hear Richard Tauber nor see a Max Reinhardt production. That came too close to home for comfort. The persecution of entertainers gave Annalie, for the first time, the key to the urgent reality of what was going on in the world.

She and Hector and the other actors, usually over meals in digs, began to discuss the situation. Hector thought there was going to be war despite Mr Chamberlain's Anglo-Italian agreement and his assurance that 'The clouds of mistrust and suspicion have been cleared away.' The deal he'd made was fiercely attacked by Labour as 'a sell-out to Fascism' and Hector agreed with this.

Annalie remembered the 1914–18 war. There had been the shortages of food and the women taking over all sorts of jobs that had been done by men before. She remembered the streets awash with the black clothes of women in mourning. There had been streets in Glasgow where every man had been wiped out, every woman had lost a husband, son or father. Unmeasurable bitterness and anger raged after that conflict, which was supposed to be the war to end all wars. Too many men had come home to no jobs and the miseries of poverty and homelessness. Surely it wasn't going to happen all over again? Yet, already there was a new law that made gas-mask drill compulsory for all schoolchildren. She'd seen pictures of them with the ugly, obscene-looking masks covering their faces.

But still, part of her couldn't believe it. Life went on and there seemed much optimism in the opening of the Empire Exhibition in Bellahouston Park. She and Hector had enjoyed the celebrations and had caught a glimpse of the King and Queen. Bagpipes had skirled and flags had flapped and it seemed that not only had everybody in Glasgow come to crowd into the park to enjoy themselves, but everybody in Scotland.

She was enjoying her career too. To make a completely fresh start she'd chosen a new name. For several years now she'd been Annalie Saviana. Saviana had been her mother's name and Hector thought it had a good theatrical ring to it.

'It also suits your gypsy looks,' he told her.

She regarded herself as an experienced actress now and had worked her way through many good parts. She had been given excellent reviews for her performances in *Major Barbara, Oedipus Rex, Hamlet, The Seagull* and *A Doll's House*. She preferred serious or passionate parts to the majority of plays that were currently popular, especially in London. They dealt mostly with middle-class life and were written with snobbish condescension and smart humour about superficial people having weekend escapades in country houses.

The mounting danger and seriousness of the world situation in 1938, and then 1939, wasn't in the least mirrored in the bright musicals that people were queuing up for. There was Ivor Novello's *The Dancing Years*; Binnie Hale and Bea Lillie and the debonair Jack Buchanan were smiling and singing and sparkling in *Me and My Girl*.

Everybody was doing the Lambeth Walk and singing the daft song 'Yes, We Have No Bananas', and Annalie could understand the gay abandon in a way. Either people couldn't believe the worst was going to happen, or, believing it, they were enjoying themselves while they had the chance. Cinemas as well as theatres were doing a roaring trade and when Annalie and Hector tried to catch a matinée they had to wait in long queues. Nevertheless, they had enjoyed Deanna Durbin in *First Love*, and been enchanted with Shirley Temple singing 'The Good Ship Lollipop'. Annalie had been passionately aroused by Clark Gable and longed to have been his Scarlett O'Hara. Hector pretended to be unimpressed by the charms of Greta Garbo and Betty Grable. They both wept unashamedly at *Goodbye Mr Chips* and agreed afterwards that Robert Donat and Greer Garson had done a marvellous job.

But then events began to move with startling swiftness. Crisis followed crisis. A big newspaper headline said: 'Don't Panic, Dig'. Everywhere shelters and trenches were appearing. Barrage balloons floated high in the air. Crocodile lines of city children were led to railway stations, and journeys into country areas totally strange to them. There had been cries of 'Shame!' when the British government recognized General Franco and Opposition shouts of 'Hail Chamberlain' and 'Now the Vultures', but their motion of censure was defeated by 344 votes to 137. Hector pointed out that Mr Clement Attlee was unusually ferocious in his attack on Mr Chamberlain.

'And quite right too,' Hector said indignantly. 'Mr Chamberlain is the one, do not forget, who said he had come back from Germany with honour and peace in our time. Even Hitler's nephew, William Hitler, is saying his uncle is "a menace".'

Annalie shrugged. 'He's safe in New York, of course. I don't suppose he'd dare criticize him if he was in Germany.'

On 3 September 1939 war was declared.

Annalie and Hector were touring in England at the time. Theatres immediately shut down and, not knowing what else to do, they made their way home to Glasgow. They waited as usual at Crewe station along with dozens of other performers. Crewe station was like a huge cast-iron cathedral and notoriously cold. Wind howled through it and chorus girls huddled together on parcel trollies but were cheerful enough to wave to friends on the opposite platform. As usual artistes gathered in the middle of the platform to exchange gossip, only this time it was about war. So heated, so dramatic, so apprehensive were these exchanges that Hector and Annalie were surprised that Glasgow looked normal when they arrived at Central station. Everybody seemed to be calmly going about their business as usual.

'My God,' Annalie groaned when they reached the room and kitchen in Cumberland Street. 'I'd almost forgotten how cramped and dreary this place looks. Do you think we could decorate it between us? Splash some bright colours around?'

'My dear girl –' Hector tossed his hat and cape-coat on to the kitchen sofa with a grand dramatic gesture

'— can you see me, Hector Bellamy, actor extraordinaire, climbing up ladders to paint and wallpaper kitchen walls?'

Annalie kicked off her shoes, peeled off her coat and flopped into a chair. 'No, not really. But you must admit, the place is depressing.'

'We shall employ a painter and decorator. Every man to his own trade, my dear.'

'We'd better wait and see if we get any work before we decide to lay out extra money.'

'I believe the closing of the theatres is a temporary measure. Merely panic reaction. That will quickly pass. The British people will not allow Adolf Hitler or anyone else to con them into hiding in their homes and denying themselves the pleasure of their great establishments of art and entertainment.'

Annalie clapped her hands. 'Hear, hear!'

Nevertheless the house had a depressing effect on her. It seemed full of sad ghosts. It was too late and they were too tired to light a fire and so, shivering, they undressed while the kettle boiled on the gas ring on the range.

'Will there be air raids, do you think?' she asked Hector.

'It looks as if they are expected, my dear, judging by the shelters and barrage balloons and the way they are painting windows black.'

'And people will get killed.'

'Have a cup of tea, my love. The cup that cheers, as Mrs Tunniecliffe always assures us.'

'I couldn't bear it if anything happened to you.'

Hector drew himself up to his full six feet but his dignity was somewhat diminished by the fact he was in his shirt-tails.

'No harm is going to come to Hector Bellamy.' He shook a fist towards the ceiling. 'I defy any stupid Hun to try.'

'Oh darling.' Annalie ran towards him and clung round his neck. 'Please don't tempt fate.'

He gave her a noisy kiss. 'And no harm is going to come to you either. You, my angel, are going to continue going from success to success. You are going to go from strength to strength, receiving all the adoration and applause that you so richly deserve.'

She made the tea and sat nursing her cup between her palms, wrapped in her scarlet dressing gown and with her black hair tumbling about her shoulders and looking ten years younger than her forty-two years. But her eyes strained with anxiety. Hector's words had disturbed rather than cheered. It occurred to her that if anything did happen to her he might find out about her past and, to say the least, feel hurt that she had not fully confided in him. He knew about Carlino and the murder trial, but she had never confessed to him about Adam Monkton and Elizabeth. She had thought it was in the past, nothing to do with her new life with Hector. However, overtired and apprehensive, she was full of doubts.

Hector finished his tea with a flourish as if it had been champagne and said, 'Come, my love. You will see things differently in the bright light of day. Tomorrow we will have a meal in the best restaurant in Glasgow and to hell with the expense. We shall celebrate our happy union.'

'Hector, we have always been honest with one another.'

'Always, my love.'

'I never lied to you. But I have kept something back from my past.'

'There is no need, my dear . . .' Hector began and raised a hand in an effort to stop her.

'No, I'd rather you knew now while I've a chance to explain.'

'Darling, you have no need,' he repeated. 'You are

overtired and understandably frightened by all the preparation for war.'

'Yes, that's true, but I'm as ready as you to put on a brave face and thumb my nose at the Germans. I've never been one to give in to my fears.'

'Well then . . .'

'I still think I ought to tell you everything about myself. After all, you have told me everything about your past. I feel I've known you since you were a little boy.'

'And I feel I have known you from your childhood in this very house. I feel that I know your wonderful Aunty Murn and your dear moustachioed father with his strong socialist views. And your colourful gypsy mother disappearing and reappearing only to disappear again.'

'I was just a young girl when I went to work in a big house in Queen's Park.'

'Yes, I know that too.'

Annalie raised her head in a proud defiant gesture. 'The son of the house, Adam Monkton, seduced me.'

'My dear.' Hector came towards her and pulled her up into his arms.

'I had a child.' Annalie remained stiff and determined. 'His mother threw me out when she discovered I was pregnant. Adam was up north on a job for a while and she told him some story about me having emigrated. When he did discover what had happened he financially supported me and the child for a time. But he married another woman.' Her voice acquired a tinge of sarcasm. 'Somebody in his own class.'

'You poor darling,' Hector soothed. 'Where is the child now?'

'You're not angry?'

'Only at the man who could so misuse you.'

'Elizabeth, she's called. I thought it best to allow her to be brought up by Adam and his wife. They had so much to give her, and I had nothing.'

'You had love for your child, I am sure.'

'It was my love for her that made me give her up. I met her some years ago, Hector. It was awful. I mean meeting in such circumstances. It was while I was in prison.'

'Darling, I am so sorry. You must have suffered terribly. I wish I had been by your side to comfort and support you.'

'She was so beautiful,' Annalie said wistfully. 'And clever. She was a schoolteacher. She's married now to a successful businessman. I'm so glad that everything turned out well for her.'

CHAPTER 42

One good thing had come of Alec being ill. It had been an excuse to stop sleeping with him. That first night she'd come home from working in the shop she'd said to Mrs Harper, 'I'm such a restless sleeper, Mrs Harper, I would just disturb him. I'll make up a bed for myself on the settee.'

She'd slept there ever since, clinging to any excuse after Alec got better. 'I'm so restless and I get up during the night so often to go to the toilet.' (Although in fact she never ventured to the toilet more than once and not even that if she could avoid it.) She told Alec, 'It's a shame to disturb you when you've to work so hard every day. You deserve a decent rest, Alec.'

He'd made a great complaint of it to Jessie and Gordon. 'I can't sleep with her. She's never at peace for a minute. I couldn't stand it any longer. Especially the way she kept trotting through to the toilet. She's obviously got a weak bladder as well as a weak head. I had to turf her out. If I'm not able to work she doesn't eat.'

While he had been ill he had been furious at her managing to run the shop. The fury had bulged from his wild eyes and burned in his unshaven, feverish cheeks. It had been the strength of that anger, that hatred that had pulled him through. He had clung to life with obsessive determination so that he could make her suffer for being competent. As soon as he was up he returned to the shop. He refused to listen to the pleas of both mother and wife that he was not yet fit. Shrunken in body, sunken-cheeked and hollow-eyed, he shuffled back to the shop like a tremulous old man. He refused to allow Elizabeth to accompany or help him.

335

Pity from customers was showered on him. They gossiped about what a shame and a disgrace it was that he had to come out to work so soon, as if he had been hounded out by both wife and mother. Elizabeth knew he did nothing to discourage this view. He had settled into the role of martyr.

Every day she'd worked in the shop she'd secreted something back to the bedroom and hidden it in her underwear drawer. It was a big deep drawer with plenty of room at the back for a secret hoard of biscuits and bars of chocolate. They were a great comfort to her once she had been confined to the house again with its icy draughts and Mrs Harper's obsessive economizing with food. Unfortunately the hoard did not last for ever. She and Mrs Harper began exchanging symptoms again. Mrs Harper showed her how to unravel an old jersey and knit up a scarf, a pixie hood and a pair of ankle socks with the old wool. Elizabeth wore the socks over her stockings and the pixie hat on her head all day during the winter in her efforts to ward off the cold.

She tried to cling to thoughts of her time working in the shop. It helped her sagging self-confidence to remember that she had been able to do it. Nevertheless she was becoming conditioned to believing that she was useless, not only as a wife but as a human being. Even the time in the shop became like a dream until she couldn't believe it had happened.

'You ran the shop?' Alec would scoff. 'Don't kid yourself. You couldn't run a menagerie. The only thing you managed to do in that shop was chase customers away.'

'You! Run the shop? Don't make me laugh. Nobody could stand your toffee-nosed, snobby ways.'

'You! Run the shop? I don't know what you're raving about. You've never done anything for me. You're useless. Even your mother didn't want anything to do with you and your stepmother avoids you like the plague. You make a mess of everything. You're a failure with a capital F.'

It was useless to argue with him. She had discovered that it only made things a thousand times worse for herself. He pounced with elation on her words as a welcome chance to attack her with all the more vigour. He seemed to enjoy the opportunity. It was as if he kept trying to goad her into arguing with him. He wanted her to set herself up so that he could knock her down. She had come to the conclusion, in fact, that he was hell-bent on destroying her. She didn't see Jessie any more. She didn't even want to. She felt too ashamed. She'd had no new clothes since her marriage and everything she had was shabby. She cut her hair herself after Alec had cut it too short and made her look ridiculous. But it wasn't her appearance that made her ashamed, although it was bad enough. It was the fact that she couldn't take Jessie or the children a present, not even a sweet. If she needed any money for anything she had to go through a terrible charade of wheedling and flattering and pandering to persuade Alec to part with a few shillings. Then she had to suffer his grand gestures, his lording over her. He would stand, rocking on the balls of his feet, hand jingling coins in his pocket, and lecture her about how it was time she learned that she wasn't living the life of Riley at Monkton House any more. If she desperately needed something, like sanitary towels, she worried all day about how she would get the money for them. She would wander about the house twisting at her hands, shoulders hunched, bracing herself for the ordeal that could last all evening, simpering, flattering, wheedling, sitting on his knee and acting like a weak and foolish child. She did everything she could to avoid the humiliating experience. She tore up old petticoats and used strips of the material as sanitary towels. She stopped using make-up. She washed her hair with coarse carbolic soap in the kitchen instead of a shampoo. She spent hours darning stockings, mending clothes and polishing down-at-heel shoes. She felt she was fighting a losing battle for survival and it wasn't just for herself as a person. She was gradually losing a grip on life itself. She kept thinking: He's killing me. And nobody will ever know.

There was nothing she could do about it. She kept trying. But more and more she was becoming exhausted by her inward confusions.

The build-up of war news and then the declaration of war barely touched her. She felt no apprehension or fear. For a brief spell in fact it brought a ray of hope. Maybe Alec would be called up and sent away from Glasgow. But she soon discovered he was too old. The only thing the coming of war did was to make Alec even more bad-tempered because now he had ration books and coupons to cope with and all sorts of new forms to fill up. He started nagging at Elizabeth as if everything, including the war, was all her fault. His nagging, complaining voice whined on at her continuously, to the occasional accompaniment of bursts of inane laughter from his mother. Or Mrs Harper would hirple away to the toilet or to peer out the window of the front room.

It was a terrible tragedy when blackout curtains had to be bought. Mrs Harper wrung her hands and shuffled abut, blotchy-faced and twitching as she searched the house for something that could be used as blackout curtains to save the expense of buying them. But nothing could be found.

'We've got perfectly good blinds,' she kept crying out. 'What's wrong with our perfectly good blinds?'

Every window in the street had the same blinds of beige-coloured thick paper or fabric and anyone working at their kitchen sink was silhouetted against the blind, the shadow of every domestic movement perfectly visible from the street – a woman preparing vegetables or washing dishes, a man stropping an open razor and shaving with it, a woman scrubbing clothes against a washboard. Seeing these shadows Elizabeth was always reminded of the popular song:

> Just a song at twilight
> When the lights are low
> As the flickering shadows
> Softly come and go . . .

'The blinds aren't dark enough, I suppose,' she told Mrs Harper.

'What would you know about anything?' Alec chipped in. 'You certainly don't know what all the material is going to cost.'

'Yards and yards and yards of it!' Mrs Harper's voice screeched up to the verge of hysteria. 'It'll cost a fortune. It'll be the death of me. This'll put me under the clay.'

'Of course,' Alec told Elizabeth, 'it's well seen you've never needed to worry about money. First you landed an easy life with the Monktons and now you've got me for a meal ticket. You don't know how lucky you are.'

'Well I should do by now,' Elizabeth said, forgetting herself. 'You've told me often enough.'

It was a mistake of course and she immediately regretted it. It opened the floodgates for a torrent of abuse that she felt far from able to cope with. All she could do eventually was turn from the kitchen, hands over her ears, and lock herself in the toilet. The dark hole of Calcutta, she'd once called it to Jessie. She remained there in the darkness, her back leaning against the door, with Alec's voice jabbing continuously through at her until he lost interest and returned to the kitchen to listen to the latest news on the wireless.

He could buy a wireless no problem, Elizabeth thought bitterly. Of course his excuse was he'd bought it for her as a big favour for which she was meant to be eternally grateful. She daren't touch it however, and never was given the opportunity to listen to any programme of her choice. Even during the day when he was out at work Mrs Harper would become so agitated if Elizabeth attempted to switch the wireless on, probably because of the expense once a battery needed recharging, she just ignored it eventually. The wireless was his and she didn't want anything to do with it. To prove her point when he switched it on in the evening she went through to the front room and sat gazing out of the window.

He always came through and tried to bully her back into the kitchen but it was always verbally. He never attempted to physically force her. She'd sit in silence, hands on lap, eyes fixed on the branches of the trees in the park shaking and wrestling in the wind. She'd ignore Alec's voice and contain the turmoil inside her until eventually he would return to the kitchen in disgust. She would be left alone, stiff with cold and tension in the silent room, its dust sheets making ghosts of the furniture, especially in the winter when the room was in darkness. The gas lamps in the street cast dim yellow light down on to the pavement. They could not reach up to pierce the darkness of the second-floor windows.

Alec accused her of being stubborn, stupid, mad and childish, and threatened to have her certified. This threat brought ripples of fear. Yet she sometimes thought that even being incarcerated in an asylum would be better than here. At least she would not be under the same roof as Alec and his mother – although she believed that Mrs Harper was her own worst enemy and she could feel pity for her. Yet the older woman was very hard to bear at times and made life for both of them such a misery every day. She talked about money so much and the lack of it and the cost of everything that often Elizabeth was on the verge of screaming at her. She was sure there was no need for any of them to lead such a miserable, wretched life with no material comforts whatsoever. She see-sawed between admiration

340

of Alec's stoicism in putting up with his mother's behaviour, and contempt at his fear of offending her.

When rationing of food started in January 1940 it made no difference to them. The ration of four ounces of butter a week, twelve ounces of sugar, four ounces of bacon was more than Mrs Harper had ever allowed for their weekly consumption. What did make all the difference in the world in Elizabeth's life was an article in a newspaper that indicated that there would be such a shortage of teachers there would no longer be any discrimination against married women being employed – 'at least until the period of pressure is past'.

Elizabeth was so exultant, so excited she had to stretch out on the bedroom settee for a few minutes in an effort to calm herself down. It was no use. Her heart was thumping and seemed to be shaking not only the settee but the very floor. She got up and paced about, struggling to organize her chaotic thoughts. She tried to tell herself that both Mrs Harper and Alec would be glad of the extra money she'd be able to earn – she could contribute something for her keep. All the time though she knew that Alec would be outraged that she would even consider going out to work. He would take it as an insult to his manhood, to his capacity to support a wife. All sorts of apprehensions came to undermine her brief surge of happiness. *Could* Alec stop her? Could he spoil her chances of an interview? Could he in some devious way influence the people at the Education Department to believe she was no longer a fit person to be in charge of children? *Was* she, in fact, now a capable enough person to hold down any kind of job? Was she even physically fit? Teaching was difficult, taxing and exhausting. Nowadays, even a walk round the park left her breathless and sometimes her headaches made her so confused she was hardly capable of remembering her own name.

She wept with worry.

341

By the time Alec had come home from work she had decided not to tell him anything until she'd had an interview and been offered a job. If she was not successful then she need never say anything. This would circumvent or at least delay the nagging, and all the difficulties he would no doubt put in her way. She spent a great deal of time pressing her clothes and trying to make herself presentable when she did eventually set out for an interview. Then came the momentous, joyful, incredible news that she'd got a job. She was to start the following Monday at St Rollox School in the district of Garngad.

She wept again, but this time with relief. Then tension began to build up again as the time for Alec's return from work drew near. She was in the bedroom sitting stiffly on the settee when he arrived. The first thing he always did was take off his flat cap and hang it on the hook behind the door. Then he hung his jacket over the back of a chair. The jacket was made of the same thin, cheap material as his baggy trousers. He only had one suit, which was kept in the wardrobe for special occasions. He wore a loose fawn-coloured well-darned woollen cardigan underneath his jacket and his shirt collar had been turned by Mrs Harper to hide the worn bits. Usually Elizabeth felt some anxiety about the thinness of Alec's clothes in such cold weather. She had in fact argued with him on occasions that he should be able to afford decent warm clothing. She'd seen how good the takings were in the shop.

'My *mother's* shop,' Alec reminded her, but she wasn't convinced. He had this martyr streak about him that made her suspicious. However, she had voiced her anxiety to Mrs Harper.

'It upsets me to see him like that, Mrs Harper. Sometimes he looks quite blue with the cold when he comes in. We don't want him to catch pneumonia again, do we?'

As a result Mrs Harper had unpicked an old pair of her woollen stockings and knitted him a scarf to wear crossed over his chest.

Tonight, however, Elizabeth gazed at his ill-clad person without seeing him. She had rehearsed for hours innumerable ways of breaking the news about the job. She had approached the subject from all sorts of devious and diplomatic angles in her imagination but when the time came she suddenly burst out:

'I've got a job.'

'A job?' he echoed incredulously. 'What are you raving about now?'

'There's a shortage of teachers because of the war and they're taking married teachers back.'

'You couldn't hold down a job.'

'I'm starting on Monday.'

'Forget it.'

'I'm starting on Monday.'

'You're not starting anywhere. Your place is here as my wife. You're not even any use at that job. But that's the job you've taken on for better or for worse for the rest of your life. It's me that gets the worst of it, of course. But that doesn't change . . .'

'I'm starting on Monday.'

'Will you stop saying that? You're like a brainless parrot. You couldn't teach a dog to bark.'

Suddenly Mrs Harper's voice, ragged-edged with laughter, called from the lobby, 'I've dished the dinner.'

'I could pay for my keep,' Elizabeth said.

'Aw, shut up!'

She followed him through to the kitchen, hating his skinny back.

The same words kept on repeating and repeating in her mind like a benediction:

I'm starting on Monday. I'm starting on Monday . . .

CHAPTER 43

Garngad was a congested area of tenements that Elizabeth had traced on a map in Elderpark Library. It was, she discovered, off Castle Street just north of that ancient district she'd become so familiar with when she'd worked at the Townhead School. It seemed, looking at the map, that the Garngad tenements and school were hemmed in by railways, railway works, foundries, chemical works, gas works, sulphur and copper works, steel works, a cleansing depot, an asylum, a sawmill and the Monkland Canal. She would have liked to have gone on the Saturday or Sunday to explore the place and be sure of finding her way to the school, but she didn't have the money for the tram fare. She didn't know how she was going to get there on the Monday and worried herself sick about this. She knew there was no use in asking Alec. Pride prevented her from turning up at Jessie's and begging for money, especially when it had been so long since she'd seen Jessie. In desperation she eventually asked Mrs Harper. The old woman gave a squeal of shocked surprise which quickly disintegrated into an embarrassed confusion.

'I'll pay it back,' Elizabeth assured her. 'With interest if you like. I'm going to get a good wage. I'll be able to pay something towards my food as well. We'll all be so much better off. But I've got to get there in the first place. There and back every day until I'm paid my wages. It would be a sin to lose the chance of all that extra money,' she added, seeing Mrs Harper hesitate, blotchy-skinned and sweating.

Eventually, painfully, almost weeping, Mrs Harper counted out the required money to cover the tram fares.

Elizabeth was so relieved she flung her arms around Mrs Harper's neck and kissed her. This sent her mother-in-law into such a paroxysm of tearful hilarity she had to hirple away and shut herself in the toilet until she calmed down.

On the Monday morning Elizabeth wakened early but Alec beat her to it and wakened earlier. He got to the toilet first. She dressed while he was there but as she was going through to the kitchen to wash her face he scuttled out shouting, 'I've to get washed first. I've my work to go to. You just keep out of my way.' He was like a tortoise in slow motion at the sink, first shaving with excruciating care, then splashing his face over and over again with water while she suffered agonies of anxiety about being late. At last she got the use of the sink. Then after washing she sat at the table but couldn't swallow her bread and marmalade. The fury and hatred burning towards her from her husband's stare was so strong it had a voodoo effect. She couldn't even bring herself to lift her cup of tea to her lips. She tried, but her hand shook too violently. Eventually she went through to the bedroom where she pulled on her coat and hat, lifted her handbag and the little parcel that contained her pink smocked overall and two slices of bread and jam, and escaped from the house.

St Rollox School was in Garngad Road. The rough cobbled road started at Castle Street and stretched right through Garngad and on to the chemical works, where it became Provanmill. Elizabeth was a bit early and had to wander around the streets for a time. She had never seen such a crush of grim tenements and so many public houses. There was a pub at every corner and quite a variety of small shops along the road. The shops looked crushed under several storeys of tenement houses and black crumbling walls badly in need of repointing and repair. There were butchers' shops with men in striped aprons. There were paper shops and fancy goods shops, and a superior Seafood and Scotch Farm Produce Shop advertising Aberdeen boneless at five-pence and fresh fillets at sixpence. In greengrocers and dairies the windows were cluttered with adverts for Fry's chocolate, Lyons Tea, Virginia Gold and Black Cat. A dusty tobacconist's window was full of dummy cartons. Already women, heads bedecked with steel curlers, were leaning from open windows, arms folded, bosoms overflowing windowsills. They watched her with interest and one called down, 'Are you lost hen?' Another voice yelled, 'Where are you making for, hen?'

Elizabeth just gave them a shy smile and quickened her steps back towards the school. It looked very old, older even than the jungle of tenements all around it, but it dominated them. Even from the outside it had the forbidding authority of a prison. The stairs and corridors echoed with marching feet as children, their playground noise silenced, moved in neat order to cloakrooms and classrooms.

Elizabeth found herself in charge of primary three, which was made up of seven-year-olds. Miss Fielding, who usually took this class, had slipped on a wet pavement and broken her hip, making a serious staff shortage even more acute. She found the allotted class-room along the white-tiled corridor and stood behind her high desk to gaze at the rows of children. They sat still and apprehensive at dark desks in a 'gallery' ar-rangement. The children's eyes were wide and vulner-able as they waited helplessly for whatever fate she was about to mete out to them. Most of them were dressed in Parish clothes, coarse navy-blue jumpers, gym slips or thick scratchy trousers, top hose and clumpy shoes. Some had shaved heads that reminded her of wee Tommy at Townhead School. Most had pale under-nourished faces and skinny bodies. Elizabeth felt such a surge of tenderness for them all that she could have burst into tears. But the control and the demeanour necessary in the classroom, and which had always stood teachers in good stead, came to her aid. It was something that distanced teachers from children and parents alike because of the feeling of respect: it engendered respect for them as individuals, for the knowledge they possessed and for the authority they wielded. It was these same qualities of demeanour and control, Elizabeth thought sadly, that were not regarded as assets in marriage. She had also come to the conclusion that men preferred to marry women with lesser qualifications and education than themselves so that they never felt intellectually threatened.

She took the register and tried to familiarize herself with the names of every one of the fifty pupils. The register was most important because it was collected every week by the Education Department and checked for absentees and truants. If any absentee was suspected (or even without being suspected), the school-board officer would call at the child's home and have to be furnished with a good reason why the child had not been attending school. Elizabeth never enjoyed the job, especially at the end of each week when various calculations of attendances and non-attendances had to be made. At this stage, however, when everyone was new, it helped her to learn who all the children were.

After the register was religious instruction and Elizabeth decided on the most familiar story of baby Jesus being born in a manger, with particular reference to the animals. She had long since found that young children empathized more with baby animals than human babies. Then she tried to explain about the approach of Easter being a time of rebirth, again with reference to baby animals. The children listened with apparent fascination (although she noticed one little girl's eyes beginning to droop as if at any moment she was going to nod off to sleep).

A search in the classroom cupboard unearthed slates,

chalks, pencils, sticks and Plasticine. Elizabeth chose the Plasticine and called on Isa (the sleepy one) Cathcart, Martha Beveridge, Duncan McGowan and Walter Sloan to distribute it around the class. The night before she'd carefully prepared a lesson on life in prehistoric times. She riveted their attention by telling the story of a little boy and girl just like them trying first of all to find shelter in a prehistoric Glasgow where there were no houses or any buildings at all.

She had planned to encourage the children to ask questions and take part in a discussion on the subject, and make models of trees or caves or whatever kind of shelter they could imagine. But nobody spoke up and Plasticine trees and caves and windshield huts were only made on her suggestion and with her helping each individual child.

She had looked in the desk in front of her to see if there were any sweets she could use for bribery, rewards or encouragement but she found only the Bible and a black leather strap. She wondered if the over-zealous use of the strap, or over-frequent threats of it, had cowed the children. Because cowed they certainly were, and so deadly serious the room was hung with corporate misery. Elizabeth realized that much patient work had to be done before she could gain their trust, and resolved to dedicate herself to this task with every ounce of patience and love that was in her.

She had made all sorts of plans to teach them arithmetic, writing, poetry and reading. She carried out these plans to varying degrees during the day in interesting and original ways, often by vivid storytelling in which she involved the children in little imaginary dramas. She struggled to open up new worlds to them. She was excited with little successes, a half smile lighting up a too serious face, a flicker of interest or understanding, a look of pride when she complimented a child on a good effort or a job well done. As a result she could hardly wait to tell someone, to share her pleasure and sense of achievement.

Mrs Harper was sweeping the stairs when she arrived home, her woollen tammy pulled well down over her ears and her eyes twitching. A baggy woollen cardigan drooped over her apron to protect her against the icy draughts that were whistling up from the close.

It didn't seem the right moment to launch excitedly into how much she'd enjoyed her day and how happy and fulfilled she felt. After Mrs Harper finished the stairs and came in and shut the door Elizabeth said:

'I've made a pot of tea. It'll heat us both up. Sit down for a minute. I'm dying to tell you how I got on.'

'That Murphy woman!' Mrs Harper was flushed and shaking with anger. 'Her and her lot make a pigsty of this close. She's far too many children, that's the trouble. It's not decent. If I had my way I'd send them all packing back to Ireland. My door was all sticky with their dirty hands and the stairs were a disgrace. One of the boys, that horrible wee creature with the squint in his eye, spilled sherbet powder all over them. And it's wicked the tricks they play on an old woman.' She gave a broken whinny of a laugh. 'I've warned them, I'll get the police next time and it'll be the birch for the lot of them.'

Elizabeth suddenly felt tired and depressed. It occurred to her that her mother-in-law wouldn't appreciate, at this moment at least, any rapturous talk about children. She drank her tea in silence. Eventually she said:

'I think I'll be fainting with hunger before Alec comes in. I've only had a couple of slices of bread all day. Is that soup you've got on the hob?'

Mrs Harper clattered to her feet in agitation. She fussed over to the hob, peering into the pot, stirring its contents, muttering to herself as if trying to calculate exactly how many plates of soup it contained and if it would be possible, and if she could bear the pains of parting with an extra one.

'Just a small plateful,' Elizabeth said. 'A few spoonfuls to keep me going until suppertime.'

'This has to do tomorrow as well.' Mrs Harper's voice was tearful. 'I'm frightened we'll be short.' She gazed round at Elizabeth in desperate appeal. 'There's a bit of bread left from the weekend. You could have that with a scrape of marge.'

'Oh, all right,' Elizabeth sighed.

'It's the rationing, you see.' Mrs Harper's relief was immense. 'It's that tight. You wouldn't believe it.'

Elizabeth didn't. Especially when she considered the fact that they were in the privileged position of owning a grocer's shop. However, she accepted the stale bread and margarine with good grace. It was an unwritten law that no one, except Mrs Harper, went into the kitchen cupboard, or put a hand near a pot, or touched the bread tin. Mrs Harper rewarded Elizabeth by topping up her cup of tea with some hot water from the kettle. Then she launched into another grievance about the Murphy children and what wicked stirrers of trouble they were, not only in their close but in the whole area. After she'd finished her tea Elizabeth thought about preparing her lessons for the next day while Mrs Harper busied herself at the sink peeling potatoes. Elizabeth worked at the kitchen table because the bedroom was so icy it made her fingers stiffen up until writing was impossible. Also, the gloom weighed heavy on the mind until it too ground to a halt. It was oppressive enough in the kitchen. She knew instinctively that she should finish any preparatory work and get all signs of it well out of the way before Alec appeared. Yet when the time for his arrival drew near some of her excitement and happiness returned and she longed to share it with him. On seeing his pale, sour face, however, she tempered her joy and shrank back into the comparative safety of self-deprecation.

'I was too early after all this morning,' she told him

while they ate their soup. 'I had to wander about the streets like a lost soul.'

'Trust you,' Alec said.

'The school's a bit like a hospital inside, at least the corridors. You know, all spotless and white-tiled.'

'An asylum. That's where you should have been.'

'It turned out quite nice though,' she ventured. 'And I think I got on well with the children.'

'You would. You've a mental age of five yourself. It's all you're fit for. Trying to act big in front of a crowd of kids.'

'I think I can help them.'

'Help them?' Alec jeered. 'You couldn't help your granny to cross a road without getting her killed.'

'The headmaster seemed pleased with me.'

'It's well seen there's a war on. It would take nothing less than a war to force them to put up with the likes of you.'

Mrs Harper gave a cackle of laughter. 'It's a terrible business, this war. I was just saying to Elizabeth earlier on about the rations. Now they're talking about air raids and us so near to the docks.'

'It's just a lot of talk,' Alec said. 'We'll soon have Hitler on the run.'

Certainly the popular songs on the radio like 'Run, Rabbit, Run' and 'We're Going to Hang Out the Washing on the Siegfried Line' seemed to endorse this sentiment. Nothing frightening had happened in Glasgow despite brick baffle walls being built in front of close mouths, supposedly to stop blast during air raids. This made the closes all the more Stygian, especially now that, by order, all close lights had to be dimmed. The only thing the baffle walls had done so far was to cause terrible black eyes. People were always bumping into them in the blackout. Also to counteract blast, the windows of all the shops and most of the houses were taped with strips of brown paper. Mrs Harper refused to countenance the extravagance of buying the sticky tape.

'They should supply it if they're so keen on us having it,' she complained. 'I told that air-raid warden. "You surely think I'm made of money," I said. ' (She had never recovered from the trauma of having to spend so much on blackout curtains.)

One man in the street who had a car fitted it with two thicknesses of newspaper inside its lights, leaving only a small aperture for a feeble beam. He also painted the bumpers white, as all other car owners did, giving them an eerie appearance. The air-raid wardens were extremely zealous about any kind of lights, and were always yelling, 'Put out that light!' It seemed to Elizabeth rather pointless, at least during 1939, while the glow from Dixon's Blazes, the huge ironworks at Polmadie, still lit up the sky.

Posters had appeared everywhere and said things like 'Be Like Dad, Keep Mum', 'Walls Have Ears' and 'Careless Talk Costs Lives'.

Buses, trams and trains were darkened and the names of stations and destinations obliterated. This made travelling anywhere a terrible strain and very confusing.

But nothing worse than that had happened.

She didn't say any more to Alec about the school. She had developed a headache like a tight iron cap. Anyway, Alec was listening to Alvar Liddell tell of Roosevelt's special peace envoy, Sumner Welles, meeting Hitler and Ribbentrop. The news also contained an item about how MPs in London had attacked the policy of giving Palestinian land to Jews but a censure motion was defeated. Another piece of news was that Himmler had ordered the construction of a concentration camp at Auschwitz near Krakow in Poland.

In London a woman had been fined £75 for buying sugar for 140 weeks' rations; she had taken it home in a Rolls-Royce.

Meat rationing had begun.

Mrs Harper whinnied 'What next?' as if it was the ultimate tragedy, although in fact she bought very little meat and always the cheapest scrag ends, pigs' trotters and tripe.

Elizabeth thought of the suffocating blackness outside and felt, sitting at the table listening to the feeble puttering of the gaslight, that the darkness was gradually seeping into the house.

CHAPTER 44

'I loved Gracie Fields.' Annalie's eyes sparkled with enthusiasm as she walked along, arm in arm with Hector behind the young army lieutenant who had been put in charge of them and the rest of the company of entertainers who were struggling behind. The vehicle in which they had been travelling had run out of petrol and they were now tramping through the French countryside trying to keep up their spirits and courage. 'Anyone could talk to her anywhere.'

'Yes,' Hector agreed. 'I deemed it an honour to accompany her . . .'

'And so exciting. What incredible energy she had.'

They had been on an ENSA tour and met up with Gracie Fields who had also been giving a show to the troops. ENSA, short for Entertainments Service Association, had been set up under the auspices of the NAAFI (which provided canteens for the forces) for the 'voluntary mobilization of all branches of the profession for the provision of entertainment of the armed forces and munition works of a country at war'. Although, because of the large number of amateurs who had volunteered, the abbreviation had become more commonly known to stand for Every Night Something Awful.

Both Hector and Annalie had more than once squirmed and suffered with the audience on hearing some of the awful turns. However, they appreciated that to organize thousands of shows not only in Britain but around the world was not an easy task. There had to be some failures. It amazed them that ENSA, despite being the butt of so many jokes, was such a resounding success and had the support of so many experienced performers. Various plays, light and serious, also went the rounds of camps at home, at action stations abroad, military hospitals, even in air-raid shelters and on the London underground. What the forces most wanted to see (especially overseas) was girls, and Hector had been in one show that had a disastrous start. It had been called *Ralph Reader and the Ten Blokes*. A mistake had been made in the posters, which read *Ralph Reader and the Ten Blondes*.

There was a huge audience who soon began to yell, 'Where are the women?' They were riotous to say the least.

It wasn't easy for women performers either. When Annalie arrived at one army camp for a show, a sergeant had come out in his shirtsleeves and announced, 'The dressing room's in here.'

'Where do the men dress?' Annalie asked.

'In here.'

'Where do the ladies dress?' she wanted to know.

'In here.'

'But we can't dress in the same room.'

'Why not?' the sergeant asked. 'Had a bleeding row?'

The new garrison theatres had no heating backstage. One show Annalie had been in was about a ship stranded in the tropics. This meant the cast wearing very light clothing and supposedly being overcome by the heat of the blazing sun. Annalie would never forget being blue with cold. When she wasn't speaking she had to keep her mouth clamped shut to stop her teeth from chattering. There was all the waiting in draughty railway stations or getting lost while travelling across country with the props in an ancient van. Dancing or acting on rickety makeshift stages was very difficult, as was dashing across freezing fields of mud, all dolled up in her finery, to reach the theatre. It had certainly not been an easy task to give any kind of performance in a Nissen hut with no heating of any kind in the middle of the coldest December in living memory. But at least she and Hector kept together.

'War or no war, I'm not letting a handsome man like you out of my sight,' she told him – half joking, wholly earnest. Chorus girls, actresses or fans knew better than to give Hector even one flirtatious glance. Annalie would pounce like a tiger. So far her attacks had only been verbal but her wild, flashing eyes warned any potential competitor that she was capable of much more.

She found all the wartime problems exhilarating, the challenge of it all, the excitement, the never knowing where one was going to be next. They had been entertaining in Belgium before beating a hasty retreat to France. In France they were forced to make a run for it. They had actually been in the middle of a show as the first enemy tank rolled up the street. They had stopped the show abruptly and had managed, along with the others, to make an escape. Despite being exhausted to the point of collapse and much hampered and held back by fleeing refugees, they had now reached a town called Dunkirk. They were trying to keep going, egged on by the lieutenant, until they could be put on a ship for home.

Dunkirk was a terrible shock and seemed to unnerve the lieutenant as much as the rest, but he covered his feelings by becoming more aggressive and shouting at them to keep together and 'Put a spurt on, for God's sake!' The town had once been much the same as any other seaside town. Hector, who could speak fluent French, had once played here in a summer show. It had the usual hotels and souvenir shops, promenade and three- or four-storey terraced boarding houses. Now, as Annalie and Hector and a straggle of other performers plus the stage manager, a carpenter and an electrician followed the lieutenant as best they could,

356

broken glass ground under their feet. Annalie saw a toy shop with its front blown away and crowds of wax dolls with pink cheeks and glassy eyes staring out. She saw dead men, women and children, littered around like pathetic heaps of rags. Soldiers too, weighed down and bulky with equipment, long coats, rifles and tin helmets, as if they had sunk exhausted into death.

The place stank of death and smoke and stale beer and putrid horse flesh and rank tobacco, cordite, garlic and rancid oil. Doris Severn, the youngest of the actresses, began to moan and cry. Nobody paid any attention to her. Other, more urgent noises were battering at their eardrums. An abandoned ambulance's jammed klaxon vied with the terrified screaming of French cavalry horses wheeling and panicking as the guns thundered; and all the time there was a steady chopping and crunching as millions of pounds' worth of equipment was destroyed. Yet despite the madness of those sounds and the racket of the guns Annalie heard sobbing from one of the buildings. She ran in, ignoring the lieutenant's furious yell:

'Keep together and follow me, I said.'

She found a child, a girl of about three, cowering in a corner.

'Don't be afraid.' Annalie picked her up and nursed her cheek against the child's wet cheek. 'You're safe now, darling. I won't let anyone hurt you.'

'Put that kid down.' The lieutenant had come after her and, harassed beyond endurance, he glared venomously at Annalie. 'We've enough on our plates trying to organize the army and idiots like you lot. We can't cope with French citizens as well.'

'I can't leave her here,' Annalie protested. The child's puny arms were clinging with desperate defiance round her neck and Annalie kissed her reassuringly. 'I just can't.'

'You haven't seen the beaches yet,' the lieutenant

bawled in exasperation. 'It'll be the survival of the fittest down there. She'll be a hell of a lot safer here.'

Despite her fatigue Annalie's eyes flashed anger back at him. 'She hasn't a chance if we leave her on her own, and you know it. She's staying with me. Even if that means I never move from here.'

It was like having to part with Elizabeth all over again. Only given this second chance she wasn't going to let it happen.

Hector came stumbling over the rubble towards her followed by the others, including the now hysterical Doris.

'My love, what is wrong?' Hector reached her, arms dramatically outstretched.

The lieutenant groaned. 'My God, I'll be glad when I'm back in charge of a crowd of squaddies. Anything rather than a shower like you lot. Any minute now the Germans are going to be on top of us. Get the hell out of here. All of you!'

Still clutching the baby, Annalie hurried back on to the street and, running now, the whole troupe kept close to the heels of the young officer.

If the backstreets of Dunkirk had been a shock, the beaches completely stunned them with horror. Oil refineries, warehouses, quays were a holocaust of fire. Smoke belched upwards and sideways, giant beanstalks spreading into black clouds that extinguished the sun. Dive bombers whirled and wheeled and swooped and screamed and fire exploded and water shot high white mountain peaks into the air. In the middle of the inferno many ships, large and small, a motley armada, jostled for space in a fiery sea.

The sky darkened and became heavy with Stukas. The planes screamed with eerie, piercing whistles that von Richthofen had specially invented to splinter nerves and scatter panic. The Stukas fell from the air, swooping, diving so low to drop their bombs that the pilots' faces could be clearly seen before the planes rapidly swerved, dipped and shot upwards again.

'Oh, Hector.' Annalie fought for control. 'God help us.'

The child had begun to cry again, loudly, hysterically.

'My darling, I hate to say this, but the lieutenant was right.'

'About the child? I don't care. At least with us she's got some chance.'

Tina Smythe, a tall, willowy actress, usually perfectly made up and smoothly coiffured, but now like the rest of them dirty-faced and straggly-haired, said, 'What chance? What chance have any of us got of getting out of this hellhole?'

'Wade in,' the lieutenant shouted. 'Don't just stand there. Try to make for one of the small boats.'

But thousands of soldiers were trying to reach the boats. Dead men and live men were bobbing about cheek by jowl in the water. The live men were being weighed down and drowned by heavy clothing and equipment. While on the beaches, under aeroplanes endlessly diving like vultures, a vast multitude of battle-fatigued, shell-shocked men were milling and wandering about. Parties of sailors each with an officer in charge were taking over sections of the beaches, organizing the troops in groups of fifty, leading them to the water's edge and checking them for arms. Apparently the last order from the Admiralty had been: 'Mind you bring the guns back.'

'Follow me.' The officer was already wading into the water. 'See that motor launch coming? It's towing an empty whaler. Try your damnedest to get on to it. It's your only chance.'

'Here, give the child to me.' Hector tried to make himself heard above the racket as they struggled into the water. 'I'll be more able to hang on to her than you.'

But the child clung to Annalie's neck with monumental

strength and they didn't have time to stop and struggle with her.

Like shoals of piranhas, troops were swamping the whaler and the young officer was fighting through them pulling, punching, jerking them aside while yelling back at his floundering charges, 'Come on, you bloody bunch of ninnies. Get on the bloody thing.'

The boat rocked with frantic, clawing hands while another officer on board bawled himself hoarse and nobody paid a blind bit of notice. Annalie couldn't see for spraying water but she fought her way towards the boat, willing herself with all her strength not to fall. In the confusion she felt Hector's strong hands grab her and heave her up and she scrabbled for a hold on the boat with hands and feet and then she was in, and wildly shouting and reaching and trying to grab Hector. Then, miracle of miracles, he was in the boat beside her, his arms encircling her and the child. And all three wept loudly and thankfully together. Not that they were out of danger. German dive bombers were snarling from the sky and ships were cracking like nuts and sinking within seconds. Annalie and Hector fervently prayed for survival all the way to the old destroyer to which the whaler belonged. Then there was the struggle up the side of the ship and Hector had to prise the child off her because she was unable safely to tackle the unstable rope ladder while carrying the little girl. At last they were on board. The ship was already packed to overflowing with soldiers, and sitting low in the water. It began to manoeuvre its precarious way through the crush and conglomeration of other vessels while the bombs still rained down.

'God, let me get out of here. Please God, let us get safely home.'

Hector and Annalie sat huddled close together on the deck, soaking wet and shivering, glad to be alive but still praying. Annalie spotted some other members of the ENSA company and was glad and prayed for them too.

Then the ship had a direct hit. It seemed too cruel. For a second as she hit the water again, Annalie couldn't believe it. She choked and struggled to the surface and tried to see Hector among the myriad of tragic disembodied faces. But he was gone. And the child was gone. For a second she was engulfed in panic. But for no more than a second before her natural fighting instincts came to her aid.

God damn it, she would survive.

She began swimming strongly towards helping hands stretching out from all the little boats bobbing dangerously close to one another in a crowded, red-smeared sea.

And Hector and the child would survive. She *willed* them to survive as she fought her way with passionate determination through wall after wall of khaki bodies.

CHAPTER 45

Miss McLeish said, 'That's what Garngad's known as. The Good and the Bad. And as you'll have found out by now, Mrs Harper, there's plenty of the bad.'

'Oh, the good too,' Elizabeth protested. 'I've some very caring mothers and it says a lot for them when you consider the awful conditions they live in.'

'I've yet to come across them, Mrs Harper.' Miss McLeish had a habit of jerking her shoulders back towards her rigid spine and keeping her head held high. She was an exceptionally tall woman who belted wrong-doers with much ferocity and was feared by every child in the school. 'I rather suspect you look at life in general, and here particularly, through rose-coloured spectacles.'

'No, I don't think so,' Elizabeth said defiantly. 'There are some really wonderful children too. In fact they've all got something to commend them.'

'Really!' Miss McLeish gave a sarcastic laugh. 'Now I understand why you have a very low discipline level, Mrs Harper. They take advantage of the slightest weakness, you know. The trouble is that the teacher following you has the double trouble of disciplining the little monsters all over again. Not to mention the constant distraction for the teacher and children in the classroom adjoining yours.'

'Most of my children have passed their tests. They are successfully absorbing what they are taught and I'm pleased and proud to say that they are happy in the process. That's what matters to me. Even more than exams. That children should be interested and happy.'

'I've met your sort before.' Miss McLeish twitched

her shoulders. 'You're a weak cog in an efficient machine. And believe me, this is no place for weakness. Don't ask me to come to your aid if you are attacked.'

Elizabeth nearly laughed in her face. The idea of one of the children attacking her was ludicrous. Unless, of course, Miss McLeish meant the parents. To be honest she wasn't at all sure abut some of them. She said nothing about this however and Miss McLeish continued:

'I can safely walk through this area in the dark late at night. Nobody would dare lay a finger on me. Could you say the same?'

Elizabeth gave a noncommittal shrug. She did not, it had to be admitted, fancy the idea of walking alone through the black tunnels of streets of the Good and the Bad.

'I know them all.' Miss McLeish's thin thread of a mouth tightened. 'And they know that I know them and can point a finger at them to the police.'

Elizabeth caught Miss Roddie's eye and the latter sent a glance heavenwards. Miss Roddie could use the belt when she deemed it necessary, and taught by strict rote. She was fair with the children however, and gave credit where credit was due. She had none of Miss McLeish's cruel, sadistic streak. Miss McLeish went looking for trouble and couldn't hide a triumphant gleam when she found it.

They were in the staff room, talking against the playground noise racketing outside. It was their lunch break but they had also been trying to catch up with the vast amount of paperwork the Government Education Scheme required. There had been forms for parents to fill in and questionnaires that entailed teacher guidance. Letters of instruction had also to be sent to parents. There had been a great deal of paperwork with one thing and another in connection with the evacuation. And they'd done it all before in 1939. That on top of all the exam work at this time of year had put a heavy burden on teachers. There were also the playground rehearsals for pupils intending to take part in the evacuation in case of emergency. They were divided into groups of twenty-eight and each group allocated to a teacher. Names of each group had to be written out.

There was fire drill as well and now air-raid practice, which meant getting to the playground shelters in as rapid and orderly a manner as possible. It was just as well that many children were going to be away in places like Comrie, St Fillans and Lochearnhead. The shelters could not have protected the full school roll.

Elizabeth was glad that she was always home before Alec because then she could complete as much work as possible before he arrived. As well as the extra work there was always the normal preparation of lessons and the marking of children's work to do.

She was particularly keen at the moment to teach the children about the history of their city. And she always used the story form to stimulate their imaginations and give them a sense of belonging. She involved them in active work too. When she told them a story about Glasgow when it was a little village on the Molendinar burn, the children drew pictures and made models of their forebears fishing for trout, and of the clay and wattle huts in which they lived. Elizabeth watched with pleasure as history became real to them, a living, continuous process. They spoke up and became excited when they came to the 12th century and learned that a market cross had been set up where four streets met: High Street, Gallowgate, Trongate and the Saltmarket. The children *knew* these streets and cried out the news to her that they'd been there, at that very cross. They *knew* the Tolbooth that had been built for the payment of duty on the merchandise brought into the burgh.

They loved the poem she taught them and sang it out loudly and with gusto.

> Oh, Glasgow was a bonny town
> When William Lion wore a crown,
> And Glasgow Fair was thronged and gay
> Upon a July holiday . . .

The school was to remain open during July and
August of 1940 and so there would be no holiday.
Everything was in a turmoil because of the war and it
was extremely difficult to keep any normal and sane
kind of background against which the children could
learn their lessons, but feel secure. The trouble was
that nobody felt secure any more. The Germans had
swept through Western Europe and no matter how
much the press reported Dunkirk as a kind of victory,
calling it Operation Dynamo and telling of crowds
waving Union Jacks and shouting, 'Well done, boys', it
was still a frightening defeat. It was grimly accepted
that a bloody battle on British soil might well be the
next phase of the war. Although some confidence had
been restored with Winston Churchill taking over from
Neville Chamberlain.

Labour had refused to serve under anyone except
Churchill and once Churchill had taken over, the
Labour leader Clement Attlee became deputy Prime
Minister. Elizabeth listened to the news on the wireless
now with as much avid interest as Alec but for different
reasons. Alec had maps he spread out on the kitchen
table and could follow every move of every battle. She
often suspected that he had acquired a secret admira-
tion for the Germans. A hint of pride as well as
excitement seemed to quiver in his voice as he traced
the growing extent of the German Blitzkrieg. Although
after reading in one newspaper that the King was prac-
tising revolver-shooting in the grounds of Buckingham
Palace and had said he would, if need be, die there
fighting, Alec claimed that every responsible citizen
should be supplied with a gun, meaning himself. The
thought of Alec with a gun was strangely unsettling.

She prayed it would never happen. But in these insecure and unsettling times anything was possible.

She struggled with her class every day (now primary four, the eight-year-olds) and tried to keep that part she had of their lives as interesting, as happy and as stable as possible. This was not easy because another aspect of the war was affecting the children. Many of their mothers were now out at work. Some worked shifts on the trams and buses. Others worked in munition factories. There were some nurseries for babies and children up to five, but there seemed to be nothing for schoolchildren. As a result many in her class were having to go home to empty houses. There was nobody to look after them until their mothers returned from work. Not all were lucky enough to have a granny nearby. Anyway, even some of the grannies were holding down jobs. Only the other day Elizabeth had taken Isa Cathcart home after school because the little girl had been sick in the classroom and looked as if she had a temperature. No one had answered the door and the child had clung to her hand and leaned helplessly against her. Elizabeth longed to be able to bathe the little girl, give her a hot drink, tuck her up in a clean and comfortable bed and sit with her to reassure her until she felt better.

But standing in the cold, draughty close at the unwelcoming door she knew this was only a dream, one of her many desperate longings that had not the smallest chance of ever becoming reality. She might have had a chance to look after the children's welfare on a more full-time basis. She had wanted to go with the little ones who were being evacuated, but priority had been given to unmarried teachers. It was just another reason why Elizabeth envied those who enjoyed the single state. It didn't surprise her in the least that the marriage bar had never worked as a controlling mechanism ensuring a turnover of women leaving to marry and allowing newly qualified teachers to enter the profession. It gave women the choice of career or marriage and, against the expectations of a patriarchal society, most women teachers chose to stay single and pursue their careers. The word 'sacrifice' kept being used in government circulars. And women were praised for their 'self-denial' in answering the country's call 'with all it's sacrificial opportunities and responsibilities'. The truth was that most married women were glad to escape from the prison of their homes, and single teachers simply preferred their career to marriage. This was because of the opportunity of leading a more full and interesting life than the drudgery of the kitchen sink. Marriage meant motherhood, which was life-threatening in a physical sense. Maternal mortality had gone up between 1918 and the 1930s and was still steadily rising.

There were mothers in poorer districts who literally starved themselves to feed their children and had no access to free doctors. Elizabeth wasn't surprised that these mothers chose to go out to work.

She wondered if what was needed was a much better supply of nursery accommodation with well-trained staff to care for the children. And not just for the pre-school age. Surely something was urgently needed to help the schoolchildren.

She had taken eight-year-old Isa back to the school, laid her on the settee in the staff room and covered her with her coat while she tried to trace the child's mother. The father was a soldier and nobody knew where he was. It had taken many hours to find Mrs Cathcart and during that time Elizabeth had done her best to nurse Isa. Mrs Cathcart had panicked on returning home from work and from collecting her twin toddlers from the nursery.

'I'd left the key under the mat,' she explained to Elizabeth. 'Isa knew that. I couldn't think where the hell she could be. I've been running about the Good and the Bad like a headless chicken.' She turned to yell in harassment at Isa, 'What the bloody hell do you thing you're playing at? You were supposed to keep the fire going.'

'She hasn't been well, Mrs Cathcart,' Elizabeth said. 'I'd get her straight home to bed if I were you. She really needs to see a doctor.'

'See you,' Mrs Cathcart addressed her daughter again, 'you're just one thing after another. How am I supposed to keep up with all this expense?'

Alec was furious with Elizabeth for arriving back so late to Linthouse. He nagged at her continuously until she escaped to bed on the settee. And even then she got no respite until he fell into a disgruntled sleep.

'It's just as well my mother's here. Otherwise I'd have come home to no dinner. A right poor do of a wife you make. You can't even be in when I come home. It's your place to be here seeing to me, not strangers away at the other end of town. A fat lot they care about you . . .'

She could have said, 'The children care.' But she knew it would only have aroused his derision and encouraged him to nag all the more.

She would never forget when she had once taught in the 'baby class' and had formed a relationship with her pupils. She had mentioned one day that it was her birthday and the children had begun to vie with each other about the presents they were going to buy her. She knew that not one of them had any money to buy her anything, nor would have known how to even if they had. But the loving generosity was real enough.

'Please miss, I'm going to buy you a big box of chocolates for your birthday.'

'Please miss, I'm going to buy you a diamond ring.'

'Please miss, I'm going to buy you a big motorcar.'

'Please miss, I'm going to buy you a big house and I'm going to come and live with you in it.'

She would always remember their breathless joy and excitement and the wistful longing in their eyes.

She was careful not to show any favouritism but one little boy in her present class, James Lockie, tugged more than most at her heart. She had discovered that his mother was dead and his father was an alcoholic. James, who was not yet nine, had to run the house, do the shopping and cooking and see to his sister and brother of six and seven years of age.

James had been having difficulty with his arithmetic and was in danger of failing his test. He just seemed to have no understanding of the subject – until she had hit on the idea of illustrating it in a different way.

'James, if you went to MacAuley the grocer with half a crown and you bought half a dozen eggs at sixpence, half a pound of bacon at threepence and a plain loaf at twopence, what would the messages come to?'

'Elevenpence,' he answered immediately.

'That's right. And what would you have left of your half-crown?'

He concentrated for only a second or two before snapping out, 'One and sevenpence.'

'Exactly. Now you have just proved to me that far from being the dunce at arithmetic that you told me you were, in actual fact you are a very clever boy indeed.'

They had tried other similar sums, all with prompt and total success. James understood and had been so overjoyed at his understanding he'd skipped back to his seat and everybody had laughed and clapped their hands. This had brought Miss McLeish's furiously disapproving head round the glass and wood partition that divided the classrooms, and a roar of, 'Quiet! If I hear another disgraceful outburst like that I shall report the lot of you to the headmaster.'

The giant Mr Hunter was feared by all the pupils but Elizabeth had found him to be a basically kind and conscientious man. His bark was definitely worse than his bite. He certainly had a very powerful voice and that, coupled with his size, his bushy beard and eyebrows and his dark flashing eyes could be most disconcerting, especially to young children.

He liked to boast that he ran 'a tight ship' and was always bursting into classes to test the pupils on one subject or another. He had regular meetings and discussions with teachers too and Elizabeth had been grateful at the patience he'd shown when she'd tried to explain and defend her teaching ideas. He hadn't necessarily agreed with all she'd said, but at least he'd shown interest.

She had in fact been getting into quite a satisfactory routine despite all the extra work and wartime difficulties when the first air-raid siren went and she had to organize the children as quickly and as calmly as possible into the air-raid shelter.

Secretly she felt frightened, not for herself but for them. She looked at their innocent, trusting faces and wondered at the stupidity of men who could wage war and risk hurting children.

'It's all right,' she assured them firmly. 'Just keep close to me and you'll be all right.'

Once inside the shelter she defied any protocol of silent order or discipline and encouraged the children to sing at the tops of their voices. She led them in song and in a competition of who could sing the loudest. The resulting hilarity infuriated Miss McLeish who said she didn't know what the world was coming to. But the noise inside the shelter had drowned out the fearsome noises outside and eventually the children were able to skip away home, happy in their innocence.

CHAPTER 46

GOERING' STRIKES AT PROVINCIAL CITIES the headline said.

Something very odd happened in London on a certain night this month. For the first time in almost two months the air-raid sirens were not sounded . . . On the next night matters became clearer. The German bombers were attacking cities and towns in the provinces . . . The Germans are now making a major effort to knock out British industry . . . The new tactics began with a blitz on Coventry when 600 tons of high explosives and thousands of incendiaries were dropped. Birmingham, Sheffield, Manchester and Glasgow were next . . .

Mrs Harper was beside herself. She couldn't sit still during an air raid. Even if it went on all night she had to be up and about and doing something. She was in perpetual motion, shuffling about wringing her hands, moving, laughing and prophesying doom. Or she polished the grate or scrubbed the floor. Once she even scrubbed both outside and inside of the coal bunker. Most people went down to the bottom flat lobby which was deemed to be the safest place. There was a brick shelter in the back yard but it was a dark, cold, smelly place much frequented by cats. Sitting on pillows or cushions on the floor of Mrs Hennessy's lobby was bright and warm and cheerful. While children slept or tried to sleep on mattresses, the grown-ups had a sing-song. Mrs Harper refused to accept the Hennessys' invitation to join them.

'The Murphy crowd'll be there,' she wailed. 'And the Hennessys are just as bad. The place'll be worse than a tip, and all those filthy children running around tormenting everybody . . .'

'The children will be lying down trying to sleep,' Elizabeth tried to soothe her. 'Nobody's going to torment you.'

'They expect me to bring tea and sugar and food. You'd think I was made of money. They think because we've got a shop we can get as much of everything as we fancy. They've no idea, those Irish. They're thriftless and feckless and a menace to decent folk trying to live within their means and put a penny by...'

'They've been born and brought up in Glasgow the same as you or me,' Elizabeth protested, but it was no use.

'They're not going to get any of my tea or sugar,' Mrs Harper repeated.

It was true that everybody was expected to bring a contribution to the endless cups of tea that would be consumed during the long night. Elizabeth found it hard to believe that Mrs Harper would risk her life just because she was too mean to part with a few spoonfuls of tea and sugar. More likely the poor woman realized she just wouldn't have been able to sit in peace in the Hennessys' lobby. Elizabeth went down, taking with her a packet of custard cream biscuits Thomasina Conroy's mother had presented her with at the school.

'That's for being such a wee gem,' Mrs Conroy had said. 'My wee Thomasina thinks the sun shines out of your arse.'

Alec had thanked the Hennessys for their kind invitation but told them he couldn't leave his mother.

This caused murmurs after he'd gone back upstairs of 'Isn't he the saint of a man, the way he puts up with that miserable old miser?'

Elizabeth felt guilty about not joining Alec and his mother, and began to feel even more so as the raid grew worse. The racket was earsplitting. It became like the painful din of giant fireworks exploding and vibrating in the echo chamber of her head.

'Nothing to worry about,' everyone kept assuring each other. 'It's only our own guns.'

No doubt it would be the big guns on the ships and the guns on the docks, and all the ack-ack guns firing from the street. Elizabeth tried not to be engulfed or confused by the appalling din, the low thrum of planes sounding too heavy for the roof to hold, the sharp crack-crack so near it violently rattled the Hennessy windows, the distant crump-crump of bombs.

They all tried to sing loudly, defiantly:

I belong to Glasgow!
Dear old Glasgow Town,
But there's something the matter with Glasgow for
It's going round and round!
I'm only a common old working chap, as anyone here
   can see,
But when I get a couple of drinks on a Saturday,
Glasgow belongs to me!

They sang it several times and with great gusto as if thumbing their noses at the Luftwaffe. They belted it out, their broad voices energetically bouncing and swagging with typical Glasgow panache.

Eventually the song screeched to an end in a howling bedlam of laughter, above and outside of which Elizabeth distinguished a fast piercing whistle.

Then the building collapsed.

For a few minutes the protesting roar of the tenement took possession of Elizabeth's brain. She was deafened, blinded, knocked off balance. She found herself on her hands and knees wandering around in circles like a bewildered animal. The air parched and thickened with plaster dust. Her eyes stung. She began to cough.

'My weans,' Mrs Murphy was shouting. 'Where's my weans?'

There were other sounds filtering through the blackness. Moans, and muffled bursts of screaming punctuated by brief disbelieving silences. There were sifting, sighing sounds, and creaking, splintering noises. The old building groaned as it disintegrated with as much anguish as the people who were part of it.

'The weans, the weans.' Mrs Hennessy's disembodied, anguished voice had joined Mrs Murphy's. 'Theresa, hen. Frances, Tommy.'

'Please God,' Mrs Murphy was repeating. 'Please God, please God.'

Elizabeth heard one child whimpering and crawled towards the sound until her groping hands found a small warm body. She guessed it was Theresa, Mrs Hennessy's youngest.

'Theresa?'

The child clung to her and Elizabeth shouted, 'Mrs Hennessy. I've got Theresa.'

Gradually other voices made themselves heard. Somebody, it sounded like old Mr Rankin from the top flat, called out, 'We'll be okay. They'll soon dig us out. Just keep calm.'

Most people were calm but it was the quiet bewilderment that shock brings. Elizabeth crouched in the dark with the child in her arms, feeling stunned. It was only much later after rescuers' hands pulled her into the light and led her away to a first-aid depot that her mind awakened with panicking life. She found herself surrounded by strangers, some distributing cups of tea, others dazedly accepting them. Occasionally she spotted a familiar face. She tugged at the arm of one of the helpers.

'I'm from number six Drive Road. My husband and my mother-in-law were upstairs. I've got to find them.'

'Drink your tea, hen,' the man said kindly.

'Do you know how many survived? Have they all been brought here?'

'There were quite a few, I think, but we can't be certain yet. There's a lot been taken to hospital. It was worse at Yarrow's yard. A shelter there got a direct hit from a parachute mine.' He shook his head. 'A terrible business.'

Elizabeth forced herself to drink the hot, sweet tea and felt the better for it. But when she was making for the door a woman in Red Cross uniform stopped her.

'We're taking folks to a rest centre, dear. You're from number six Drive Road aren't you?'

'Yes, but . . .'

'There's no use going back there. If you just hang on until we get everybody organized.'

'But it's my husband and mother-in-law. I went downstairs to Mrs Hennessy's but my husband couldn't go without his mother. She wouldn't leave the house, you see.' Tears filled Elizabeth's eyes. 'I should have stayed with them.'

'No, no, dear. It wouldn't have made a bit of difference. The chances are they'll be fine, you'll see. The stories I could tell you. I know a young couple who left their house on the top flat to go along to friends near the Southern General Hospital. The friends lived on the bottom flat. It turned out that tenement got a direct hit and the couple and their friends were killed. Whereas their own building was still standing and their next-door neighbours who'd stayed in the top flat hadn't a scratch on them.'

'But if they're all right, where are they?' Elizabeth gazed anxiously around. 'I can't see them here.'

'Now don't worry, dear. There's other first-aid posts. Or they might have been taken to the hospital. Would you like me to ring around for you?'

'Oh would you?' Elizabeth said gratefully. 'I feel so worried.'

'I can't promise to find out anything. It's early days and everything's a bit hectic and confused. But I'll try.' She brought out a notebook and pen. 'Give me their names.'

'Mr Alec Harper and Mrs Lizzie Harper.'

'And they're from six Drive Road?'

'Yes.'

'You just take a seat over there. I'll do my best and get back to you as soon as I can.'

Another cup of tea was pushed into her hands as she sat waiting. She drank it automatically, tears still filling up and overflowing from her eyes. She kept thinking: Poor Mrs Harper, her house and all her treasured possessions, all gone. Poor Alec, the house and all it contained that he's suffered so much for and waited so patiently for, all gone.

She wondered about the shop. She remembered how, on the way to the first-aid depot, she'd seen fires and heard the wail of fire engines. Six Drive Road hadn't been the only place in Govan to be hit. She fervently prayed, for Alec's sake, that the shop had been spared. Over and over again she prayed that Alec and his mother had been spared.

At long last the Red Cross woman returned.

'You're in luck, dear. Your family's safe. They've both been admitted to the Southern General.'

'Thank God!' Elizabeth rose. 'I'll go right away.'

'Are you sure you're all right?'

'I'm perfectly all right. Thank you for your help.'

She was hurrying along the street before it occurred to her that she'd forgotten to ask what kind of state Alec and Mrs Harper were in. She fought to get a grip of herself and face whatever she had to with courage. Once in the hospital she was directed to the ward where she'd see Alec. His eyes, deep-set in black sockets, were closed. His unshaven cheeks were sunken. Someone had taken out his false teeth, or they'd got broken. He looked a frail old man.

She sat down beside the bed, touched his hand and whispered, 'Alec.'

His eyes opened and eased round towards her. 'You're all right?'

'Yes, I'm all right. How are you?'

'I wondered if you'd got out. I asked but nobody could tell me.'

'How are you?' she repeated.

'Don't ask me. Ask the doctor. What about the shop?'

'I don't know. I came straight here.' She hesitated then added, 'You know your mother's here. As a patient I mean.'

'Yes.' His voice weakened and his eyes closed again. 'Do me a favour. Find out about the shop.'

'I will. Right away. Don't worry.' She bent over and kissed his prickly, loose-skinned cheek, ashamed of her revulsion and determined to overcome it. 'I'll be back as soon as I find out.'

But before going to find out she hurried to the other ward to see Mrs Harper, although the nurse had warned her that the older woman was sedated and might not be able to talk.

'It's me, Mrs Harper.' She spoke close to her mother-in-law's face. 'Elizabeth.'

Mrs Harper's lips struggled to form words.

'What? I can't hear you.' Elizabeth bent closer.

'Two soup tureens,' she thought she made out.

'Two soup tureens?'

Mrs Harper's head slightly moved, indicating the affirmative. 'The high shelf.'

'Yes.'

'Above the bunker.'

'Yes, I know. Where you kept your dinner service.'

'Two soup tureens.'

'Yes. I know the ones. But please don't worry about anything like that just now, Mrs Harper. Just you get well and strong again.'

Mrs Harper was desperately struggling. Every muscle in her face was twitching and she was fighting to raise herself.

'My savings. All my money. Hundred pound notes. In the two soup tureens.'

CHAPTER 47

Hector had gone round to Mrs Rafferty's to have a private word about Annalie. Mrs Rafferty, he knew, was one of Annalie's oldest friends. It had been Mrs Rafferty who had taken Annalie in and given her shelter when her father had thrown her out – pregnant and little more than a child herself. She had been frightened and had nowhere to go. Hector had a great respect and affection for Mrs Rafferty for having been so kind and compassionate to his wife and was forever trying to repay her with little kindnesses like giving her free tickets for a show. Or presenting her with autographed photographs of stars. And he delighted as well as embarrassed her by always kissing her hand. Mrs Rafferty was a small plump woman who should have worn corsets but obviously didn't. Her body was like a pile of loose cushions that wobbled in all directions when she walked or laughed. Her hair was scant and had long since faded into grey but the pale blue of her eyes could quickly deepen with compassion and concern.

Annalie had told him of the terrible place where she and Mrs Rafferty had lived, down a dunny in Commercial Road. A windowless one-roomed hovel it had been, under stables and, not surprisingly, infested with rats. He shuddered to think of what his love must have suffered and vowed that he would always try his utmost to make sure she would never suffer again. He had felt so helpless to protect her against the onslaught in France. Now, safely back in their own home town, he determined to do his best to promote her happiness and peace of mind. He was seriously worried about her and hoped that Mrs Rafferty would be able to help or influence Annalie in some way.

She now lived in a close down the other end of Cumberland Street in a bottom flat of two rooms and kitchen. Her family were all either married or in the forces and she often laughed and reminded Annalie of how so many of them had somehow managed to squeeze into the one room in Commercial Road.

'And now here I am on my own rattling about in this big house like a pea in a drum.'

It took him a little time to find the close because already winter darkness was enveloping the town, although it was still only afternoon. The baffle walls were a nuisance. One had to walk cautiously, hands outstretched like a blind man in the hope of avoiding collision with them. He found the right place eventually and entered the dimly lit cavern of a close. It smelled of cats and felt cold and damp. And like most tenement closes in the area it was shored up with rough, undressed timber. The idea was to save lives in the event of the building getting a direct hit. Inside, Mrs Rafferty's kitchen was bright and cheerful, if somewhat untidy. Blackout curtains, she maintained, were quite a good idea because they kept out draughts and made the place extra cosy. Immediately he came in she poked the fire into a bright blaze and sat the kettle on the gas ring at the side of it, an innovation of which she was unendingly pleased and proud.

'Such a handy wee thing,' she said again. 'Heats the kettle in no time. Take off your coat, son. Make yourself at home. Annalie said she'd call in on her way back from the town but I don't think she'll be for a while yet.'

'I know,' he said, divesting himself of his voluminous coat and wide-brimmed hat. 'Actually I want to be away before Annalie arrives. She is just coming to show you her purchases and enjoy her usual tête-à-tête. She does not know that I intended paying you a visit too. And I would rather she did not.'

Mrs Rafferty looked puzzled. 'Why not, son? Annalie wouldn't mind you coming along.'

'I wanted a private word, Mrs Rafferty, but I have no wish to risk upsetting Annalie by divulging the extent of my concern for her.'

Mrs Rafferty's eyes widened in alarm. 'She's not ill, is she?'

'Not physically,' Hector said. 'But she has never been the same since Dunkirk.'

'Och well, it's not surprising. Fancy! After managing to get to a boat and then it being blown up. It's enough to go for anybody.'

'It was not that.' Hector shook his head. 'It was losing the baby.'

Tears sprang to Mrs Rafferty's eyes. 'Aye, that poor wean. I lost my man and one of my laddies as well. A great wee laddie he was. Always used to run messages for me. That willing he was. When he was called up to the war he worried about leaving me. I hope he's with his da.' She rubbed her eyes with the back of her sleeve. 'He'll be all right if he's with his da. He's still a wee laddie to me, you see. Always will be.'

'But he was your own flesh and blood. The little French girl was a stranger to Annalie and it's so long ago now. Over a year. Somehow, she associates the girl with losing her own daughter. It is as if she has gone through that loss all over again.'

Mrs Rafferty's plump face twisted in sympathy as she made the tea. 'I mind it fine. It was terrible for the poor soul. My heart went out to her, so it did.'

'Now she has a burden of guilt as well.'

'About the wee French wean, you mean? Och, isn't that just like Annalie? She was always that kind-hearted, so she was. But what happened to the French wean wasn't her fault. She wasn't even holding the wee soul at the time, was she?'

'No. I had her. She was in my arms.' He sighed. 'I remember the blinding explosion and the feeling of her being torn from me. Then I must have lost consciousness. The next thing I remember was being in the water and then hauled aboard a whaler.'

'Och, it's a terrible sad business. Mind you, Annalie seems all right to me. Well, maybe a wee bit stiff even when she laughs. She doesn't seem so able to relax as she used to. I just thought she was overworking. All this travelling about the pair of you do. And even when you're here you're hard at it all the time.'

'She used to thrive on travelling.' Hector sighed again. 'It made her happy and elated. She loved it, and her work, with all the passion that was in her.'

'Oh, surely she still loves her work,' Mrs Rafferty protested. 'One of my neighbours, Mrs Donaldson, works in munitions and she told me the last show of yours she saw was great. She thought Annalie was really marvellous. She put her whole heart and soul into it, Mrs Donaldson said.'

'Yes, she still does that, but somehow in a different way. There is a kind of desperation . . . And afterwards there has always to be somewhere else and something else. More shows, parties, anything and everything to keep her busy. She keeps on pushing herself but there is no joy behind anything she does any more.'

'I'm awful sorry, Hector. I wish there was something I could do to help. I'd do anything for that lassie. Kindness itself she was to me.'

'It might help if you had a talk with her.'

'Anything you say, son. When she comes back from the shops I'll try my best.'

He rose. 'She will probably deny that anything is wrong. She will probably insist that she is perfectly all right. That is what she always does with me. But I know she is not all right.'

'Don't worry, son. I'll try my best,' Mrs Rafferty repeated. 'We've had many a heart-to-heart in the old days, Annalie and me.'

Hector made his way back to the Cumberland Street room. He retained his proud bearing and his head with its luxurious mane of white hair was held as high as usual. But there was a vague look about his fine dark eyes.

Maybe I am wrong about Annalie, he thought. Everyone else seems to believe she is doing splendidly. Overworking perhaps. But are not we all? A little stressed. But is it not a stressful time?

So much had been happening even in this one year. Hitler's deputy, Rudolf Hess, had bailed out over the outskirts of Glasgow. The Germans had invaded Russia. The British army had entered Benghazi. The Royal Navy had sunk the battleship *Bismarck*. The aircraft carrier *Ark Royal* had been torpedoed. The Japanese had attacked Pearl Harbor. Britain and America had declared war on Japan. America had declared war on Germany and Italy.

There seemed no end to the conflict. He had a sudden overwhelming longing for prewar, peaceful days. Days and nights when one could perform on stage without sudden interruptions and the announcement: 'Ladies and gentlemen, an air raid is in progress. If you wish to leave the theatre please do so now as quickly and quietly as possible.'

Few people, if any, did leave and after a minute or two the play would continue from where it had left off.

Sometimes, however, it became impossible because of the noise outside and so they would abandon the performance and lead the audience in a sing-song. He had a strong baritone voice which was much appreciated. Annalie had always joined in with great energy and enthusiasm with both singing and dancing, much to the delight of the audience.

The head of ENSA – Basil Dean – had said, 'Whenever needed we shall send you entertainment and if the work is interrupted from the skies, we will carry our songs with you below ground.'

And they had done that too. They had even, with the staff of theatres, trained as fire-fighters in their spare time and taken their turn at roof-spotting while raids were in progress during the night. Or at times during the day when they weren't doing a show. Fire-watching duties were of the utmost importance and one theatre they'd played in owed its survival to a stage carpenter who smothered incendiary bombs on the roof while a show was in progress. He pounced on two fire bombs and got them both out within three minutes.

There could be no denying that frequent air raids were stressful. And the fact that somebody always had to sleep in the theatre at night didn't help.

Once he had been taking his turn and a bomb had torn a hole in one of the exterior walls, cascading tons of debris on to the floor of the stage. Fortunately the stage had previously been reinforced and it carried the whole load. He and the other four men sleeping underneath crawled out with nothing worse than a headache as rescue workers feverishly searched for them in the wreckage.

No one had been more feverish than Annalie. Word had got around like wildfire that the theatre had been hit and she came running like a wild thing, long hair flying in the wind. He was safely out and dusting himself down when she rushed at him and clung, sobbing hysterically. It had taken him hours to calm her down. Even then she was still in a highly charged state of nerves and tension. She had taken to smoking and on that occasion smoked one cigarette after another. She had also got a little drunk.

He prayed that Mrs Rafferty would be able to get through to her and help her, but he doubted it. Sitting in darkness at the front-room window, the blackout curtains undrawn, he tried to watch for her brisk, defiant figure down on the dimly lit street. The sirens began to wail and he at once became keenly anxious for her safety. He could hear the drone of planes and yellow searchlights began criss-crossing and sweeping backwards and forwards over the navy sky. He got up hurriedly, knocking over his chair and stumbling in the dark to reach the outside door. His heart was banging like a drum in his chest. Forgetting his coat and hat he groped his way as fast as he could down the tenement stairs. Outside now, he cursed himself for not bringing a torch. Twice as he tried to hurry along he crashed into a baffle wall. He felt a wet trickle on his skin as if his face was bleeding. His head and body throbbed with pain. Once or twice he thought a hurrying shadow looming towards him in the dark was Annalie and he called her name. But the shadow passed and there was no reply. Then it came to him and frightened him that he had forgotten which was Mrs Rafferty's close. In such darkness it would have been difficult enough to find even if he had known where it was. But he did not know where it was.

His heart leapt in his chest and began banging even louder. He could hear it above the noise of the guns and the bombs. Then the banging turned into pain. It caught at his breath and made him lean up against a tenement wall for support.

I am having a heart attack, he thought, concentrating on himself and his fight for breath. I must keep calm. I must keep calm and rest. Cautiously he slid down the wall until he was squatting on the pavement. I must keep calm. I must keep calm for Annalie's sake.

CHAPTER 48

The Board of Trade had given special facilities to
theatre people to help them buy stage costumes without
having to use their normal clothes ration. The extra
sixty-six coupons had proved a godsend. It was no joke
at the best of times trying to balance a frock at seven
coupons against a nightdress at six against corsets at
three. Or in Annalie's case, a suspender belt. Her body
had admittedly put on a bit of flesh since her twenties
and thirties, but it was still firm and shapely and did
not need corseting.

Hector had persuaded her to go out and treat herself
to something new to wear in the hope, she supposed,
of cheering her up. She knew he was worried about
her. She tried her best to hide her distress to spare his
feelings, but he knew her too well. He did not, however,
know about shopping. Nowadays shopping mostly
meant standing in queues, anything but a cheering
prospect. Food especially was difficult to track down
even if one had sufficient coupons. The shelves of the
local Co-op grocers were anxiously scanned and in the
waiting lines the conversation dwelt on whether it was
rhubarb and ginger jam this week, or was it plum, or
did it matter anyway? Rumour had it that any jam
there was had been made entirely from turnip and
apples with a dash of spurious flavouring. Eagle eyes
were ready to spot any sleight of hand or favouritism
by shop assistants. On the whole they were not a
popular breed, with their constant and unnecessary cry
of 'Do you not know there's a war on?' Most people
tried to keep in with them, tried to be polite to them,
but there were many murmurs behind shopkeepers'
backs of 'Bloody wee Hitler!'

Feelings of revenge ran high and many a person vowed, 'Just wait till the war's over. I'll give him' – or her – 'short shrift.'

Annalie was glad when she and Hector were on tour and she could avoid shopping, at least for food. They just gave their ration books to the landlady. There was still the search for things like make-up or ideas for substituting when no make-up could be found. She and other actresses had been, on occasion, driven to use beetroot juice for lipstick, soot for eye make-up, and gravy browning painted on the skin as a substitute for silk stockings. Seams were added to each leg with a pencil.

Despite Hector's pleas that she should treat herself to something nice to wear, Annalie felt no enthusiasm. Eventually she found quite a pretty nightdress and a pair of French knickers. She bought them more for the sake of pleasing Hector than for herself. She also saw a smart suit that she believed would look splendid on Hector. It needed twenty-six clothing coupons. There was a nice raincoat too at sixteen coupons. Hector was the one who needed new clothes. He was far too good to her. Love for him melted the brittleness that she had learned to hold around her like a shield. He had been so patient with her since their terrible experience in France. It was over a year ago yet she'd still not recovered from the trauma, not deep down. At first she'd suffered terrible nightmares and woke up sweating and screaming in Hector's arms and with Hector's rich voice assuring her, 'You are perfectly safe, my darling. You are here with me.' It was always the little girl she had been dreaming about. It was the baby arms she felt trustingly around her. It was her own voice she heard. 'Don't be afraid. You're safe now, darling. I won't let anybody hurt you.'

She knew that she was not personally responsible for the explosion that had torn the little girl away in pain, in terror and in death. But nothing could assuage the terrible feeling that she had betrayed a trust.

Thinking of that little girl had made her think of Elizabeth. Not that she had ever stopped thinking of her daughter. Elizabeth was always, if not at the forefront of her mind, forever waiting in the background. Now, however, she thought about Elizabeth in a different way. She remembered her as a trusting child. She went through agonies imagining how that child must have felt awakening one morning to find herself with strangers in a strange place. She would not understand why her mother had disappeared, had deserted her. Annalie now examined and re-examined and questioned her reasons for giving the child away.

Had it really been for the child's own good? That was what she'd once believed. Straining her mind back she tried to remember every detail of that time. The crisis which triggered the decision was when she'd put an ultimatum to Adam Monkton. Or was the trigger when Christina Monkton had come to see her? 'He just lusts after you,' she had said, in that cold calm way of hers. 'He'll never leave me for you. Why don't you ask him?'

Annalie had been equally convinced that he would, so certain had she been of his love. The next time Adam came to see her she made love with him deeply, sweetly, passionately, with all her heart and soul, all the love that was in her.

They were in the front room and as usual she had used some of her precious coal to light the fire. She had cleaned and polished the room very thoroughly before he arrived and made up the bed with her special, crisp white linen sheets. The room had always been her pride and joy, her bower of love, her sanctum. She sat down beside the fire and gazed across at him.

'I love you,' she said.

'And I love you, darling.'

She shook her head. 'Please don't lie to me any more, Adam.'

'Lie to you?' He got up immediately and began pulling on his clothes. 'Annalie, what's wrong? Why are you talking like this?'

'I'm frightened,' she said.

'Darling.' He came across and gathered her into his arms. 'What's happened? Why are you frightened? What are you frightened of?'

She looked straight into his eyes. 'Adam,' she said, 'do you love me enough to leave your wife and live permanently with me?'

'I'm sorry, Annalie,' he said. 'But really, I can't do that. But it doesn't mean I don't love you.'

'Just that you love your wife more.'

'I didn't say that. I admire and respect my wife, but it's you I love. I loved you from the beginning and I'll love you till the end.'

'But not enough to give up your wife and live with me instead.'

'It's not as simple as that. Life never is.'

She had seen the position with terrible, painful clarity. She saw the successful businessman with the perfect partner in the woman who shared his business interests. A woman of his own level of intelligence, of his own area of experience, of his own class. A woman who could effortlessly grace his home and entertain his business and social acquaintances. A woman who could be an advantage to him in every way.

A gypsy girl from the Gorbals had no place in that world.

As usual, before leaving, he went through to the kitchen to kiss Elizabeth goodbye. She was sound asleep and looking as beautiful as ever.

Annalie watched him bend over her and kiss her tenderly on the cheek. It was then, seeing the love in his eyes as he looked down at his daughter, she realized what she could do for her, or so she believed then.

After he left she leaned her brow against the door. She stood like that, unable to move, for a few minutes. Eventually she went through to the front room and stood staring out of the window, down at the gaslit Cumberland Street below.

That was the day and the hour she had decided to give Elizabeth away.

Sitting on the darkened tram on her way to Mrs Rafferty, she recalled every moment, every word, as if a film had been unrolling before her eyes. But much more difficult was to probe into the real reasons for her decision, and to try to judge whether or not she had been totally honest with herself at the time. It was suddenly terribly important that she knew.

She had thought that she was acting only for Elizabeth's good. She had believed she had no choice but to finish her relationship with Adam and try to survive on her own. This meant, as far as she could see at the time, abject poverty. It meant Elizabeth, if she kept her, joining the waifs playing in back yards, often flooded with sewage from lavatories unrepaired and neglected by uncaring factors. It meant risking her joining the children taken away by the dreaded fever van and never returning. Elizabeth could grow up like May Rafferty who, like Mrs Rafferty, had sold her body when she was desperate for money.

Annalie remembered thinking all of these things. She'd thought how different Queen's Park was from the Gorbals, how different Adam and Christina's big villa was from at best the room and kitchen in some ancient tenement that she might be able to provide for Elizabeth.

She had haunted Queen's Drive for days, watching the house, watching Christina and Adam together. Once at a safe distance, she'd followed them into the park. That day their son Jason had been with them, and a smart, uniformed nanny. It was a different world, a safe, comfortable, prosperous world. That's what she'd wanted for Elizabeth. Or so she'd told herself.

Eventually she'd waited in the dark doorway of Monkton House for Christina returning from her office. Adam had been down south and not due back for several days.

Christina had been startled at first but quickly recovered her composure. 'What are you doing here? What do you want?'

'I need to talk to you,' Annalie said.

Christina hesitated, but only for a moment, before saying, 'Very well.'

Once inside she led her into the morning room and indicated a seat.

'Thank you,' Annalie said politely and perched on the edge of a chair by the fire. Looking back she saw herself in a cheap-looking coat and a straw boater with ribbons hanging down the back. A ridiculous outfit for a winter's evening. She could see by the window that it had begun to snow. White flakes were swirling wildly about in a mad dance against the blackness, but there was luxurious warmth and comfort inside. The gas lamp bathed the room in amber light and the fire burning brightly helped to chase away the shadows.

The room was elegantly furnished in quiet good taste. The curtains, not yet drawn, were in soft blue velvet. The carpet was of the same shade and the sofa and easy chairs were covered with a delicate floral chintz picking out the same subdued shade of blue. There was a white bust of Mozart, but no other ornamentation. The room had a calm, uncluttered look.

Christina said, 'You wanted to talk to me?'

Annalie took a deep breath. 'Firstly I wanted to make sure of something. Would you, for any reason, be willing to give Adam up?'

'No, never,' Christina said without hesitation. 'Nothing in the world would persuade me to do that.'

'That's what I thought you'd say.'

Christina raised an eyebrow. 'Well?'

Annalie took another deep breath. 'We can't go on like this,' she said. 'I've thought it all out. What would be for the best, the best for Elizabeth. I've been hearing some good things that you've been doing recently. Things you're doing for children.'

There had been the property Christina owned in the Gorbals that she'd had converted into a gymnasium, and the farm turned holiday home outside of Glasgow.

'Elizabeth?' Christina echoed.

'My baby. Adam's daughter. I don't want her brought up in the Gorbals. I don't think Adam wants that to happen either.'

'I see,' Christina said. Then she lit a cigarette and smoked thoughtfully, silently, for a minute or two. 'You want to do a deal with me?' she asked eventually.

Annalie thought: How typical! Only the woman of property that she was could have thought in terms of 'a deal'.

Remembering that night, picking over every detail, remembering the moment she'd handed the child over, her own flesh and blood, she was amazed and horrified. How could she have done it?

She was no longer convinced of the truth of her original reason. There had been another option. She could have continued as Adam's lover. He would have provided for both her and the child. She had been too proud to be only the mistress. She had wanted all, or nothing at all.

She felt like howling to the moon, there was such mad regret and pain inside her and a blackness that deepened with the dark Gorbals night.

CHAPTER 49

A few lines of a song by Burns came into her head:

> ... Had we never loved sae blindly,
> Never met – or never parted,
> We had ne'er been brokenhearted ...

And yet, if she had never parted from Adam she might never have met Hector, her dearest love.

She did not regret knowing Adam, or loving him. It was just a different chapter of her life. She felt blessed that she had been given the opportunity to love a man so deeply and completely twice in her life. She had loved and lost and now she loved again. Once more with all the passion that was in her, and with total commitment. She loved everything about Hector, his proud dramatic bearing, his rich voice that could reach every corner of an auditorium, or soften for her alone when he wished her the traditional good luck before every performance, 'Break a leg.' She loved his mane of hair now startlingly white, his eyes that could burn with such fierce anger or frightening evil on-stage, but off-stage he was the mildest and most loving of men. Strong yet gentle, firm yet tender, manly yet with an old-world romanticism that she found most touching. He remembered anniversaries. One red rose given with a flourish, a compliment, a kiss on the hand could make her feel like a queen. He made a special event of shared morning cups of tea in bed, or evening buttered toast in front of a gleaming fire. In an age when chivalry seemed dead, he never failed to give a lady a seat. He opened doors. He stood when a lady entered the room. He had a wonderful range of bows: a short dipping of the head; a gentle lowering forward of head and shoulders; a bending with polite elegance over a lady's hand; or a dramatic sweeping bow in which arms and hands were used to full effect.

Even when he'd been ill there was a dignity about him and a concern for any trouble or upset he might be causing. They had been touring the Middle East when Hector had gone down with dysentery in some godforsaken place with only the crudest medical facilities. She had gladly nursed him back to health, passionately grateful to have been with him and able to answer to his every need and comfort.

'How can you love me?' he had exclaimed. 'After seeing me in such a dreadful condition. I never meant you to have to do such revolting tasks for me.'

'Revolting?' she cried out in astonishment. 'Nothing about you could ever be revolting to me. I love you.'

As far as she was concerned that said it all. Being married, belonging together in every way, working together, travelling together, living together made them doubly close. Yet he was never possessive. He respected her space, her right to have time on her own. Not that she wanted to be separated from him for even one minute. It was he who had insisted she have an afternoon 'just browsing about the shops', then a cup of tea and women's talk with Mrs Rafferty on her way home. There was nothing he liked better than thinking up ways for her pleasure and enjoyment.

She looked forward to telling him about the suit and to persuading him to go back to the department store with her next day to try it on. The raincoat would be no use. It wasn't his style. He preferred the flourish of a big black umbrella which he held aloft with great dignity and panache. She hesitated in Cumberland Street, tempted to turn left in the direction of her own close and not bother going to Mrs Rafferty's. But she knew her friend would be waiting for her, eager to hear about her shopping expedition and to see what she'd managed to get. Mrs

Rafferty never complained but Annalie knew she missed having her family around her. She enjoyed company and would be disappointed if she didn't turn up. Annalie went along to the right, her feet feeling their way carefully through the shroud of darkness. Not for the first time she had a sudden longing for the war to be over, for all the lights to be on again. She knew she wasn't the only one to feel her spirits flagging as the war dragged on and deprivation piled on deprivation. Many things were trivial in comparison to what servicemen were enduring. Nevertheless they were adding up, becoming depressing, stamina-sapping and psychologically damaging. The blackout certainly didn't help.

'Hello, hen,' Mrs Rafferty greeted her warmly. 'Come away in. I've the kettle on the boil. Did you get anything nice? I see you've a parcel so you must've got something.'

'Yes, I'll show you in a minute.' She winked. 'Hector'll love it.'

'Oh, frilly knickers is it?'

Annalie flung off her coat and hat and warmed her hands at the fire for a few seconds before opening her parcel.

'Near enough. French knickers.'

'Is that these wide-legged ones?'

'What do you think?' Annalie flicked them out of their wrapping and held them against herself. 'Do they make me seem irresistible?'

Mrs Rafferty laughed. 'Hector would think you were that even in khaki bloomers. But they are lovely, hen. What a bit of luck finding them.'

'And a nightdress as well. A pretty shade, isn't it? More peach than pink.'

'You did well, hen. I wish I could fit into the likes of that. It's a barrage balloon I need.' She laughed again, making her soft flesh wobble. 'Sit down and drink your tea. This has been your lucky day, eh?'

'Uh-huh.'

394

'You don't look too happy though.'

'Don't I?' Annalie's eyes widened. 'What makes you say that?'

'I've known you a long time. I delivered your wean, remember. What a wee pet she was. I was there when you got her and it was me you came back to after you gave her away.'

Annalie lit up a cigarette and inhaled deeply. 'It was a terrible thing, wasn't it? I did a terrible thing.'

'It was nothing of the kind. What do you think you're blethering about? You wanted her to have a good life and be brought up to be a lady and so she has.'

'I keep tormenting myself that maybe I did the wrong thing.'

'You did what you thought was best at the time, hen. What was best for the wean. I remember the state you were in. Oh, I was that sorry for you, so I was. You loved that wean, Annalie, and it broke your heart to part with her. And remember, hen, you were only a wee lassie yourself.'

'But was it best for her?'

'Annalie, the wean got everything. You gave that wean a chance in a million.'

'Materially, yes. But I've come to realize that that's not everything. Love's the most important, the most precious thing, Mrs Rafferty. You know that as well as I do. I wonder how much love Elizabeth's had? The thought torments me. Christina Monkton's such a cold fish. Always was. Elizabeth would have had no love from her. I doubt if even her own children were shown any affection.'

'Och, hen, try and be sensible. You're lassie's a grown woman now and you said yourself how lovely she looked and how well she was doing. And she's got a husband to love her and look after her now. Why are you tormenting yourself like this? There's just no sense in it. You're getting yourself all worked up for nothing.'

Tears had begun to flow freely down Annalie's cheeks but she kept dragging at her cigarette and trying to ignore them.

'She belonged with me.'

'She belonged with her father as well, don't forget. You mustn't be so hard on yourself.'

'No, she belonged with me. I did a terrible thing.'

'No you did not, hen. Now just you stop saying that. You're overworked and overstrained. You've been through an awful lot and it's taking its toll on you. But you must try to put such things out of your mind. For Hector's sake if not for your own. You're doing nobody any good letting your imagination run away with you like this.'

Annalie nodded. 'You're quite right. It's not fair to worry Hector. Oh God, there's the sirens again. Are we never going to get a peaceful night?'

'It might not last long, hen. I quite enjoy it.'

'Enjoy an air raid?' Annalie couldn't help laughing as she wiped away her tears. 'You must be joking.'

'Och, you know what I mean. Not the actual air raid, but all the neighbours from upstairs come down to my lobby and we have a sing-song. It's such cheery company.'

'I'd better go.'

'The wardens will just chase you into the nearest shelter and you know what they're like. The shelters, I mean. Right dismal holes. You'd be far happier in my lobby.'

'It's Hector. He'll worry about me.'

'He knows you're here, hen. He wouldn't want you stravaging about the streets being hit by shrapnel or shouted at by wardens. If you put a foot out of this house before the all-clear goes, I'll worry about you. You know Mrs MacKay from Errol Street? Her man got hit by shrapnel on his way home from work. Killed him on the spot. Poor Mrs MacKay's in an awful state. Oh, there's my door, hen. That'll be the crowd from upstairs.'

She hurried happily away and in a few minutes the

long narrow lobby was packed and noisy with voices and laughter.

They sat on the floor, buttock to buttock, backs supported by walls and legs entangled. Mr Briggs from the top flat had brought his accordion and played a selection of popular tunes. Soon everybody was lustily singing, 'You are my sunshine, my only sunshine . . .' and 'I yi, yi, yi, yi, I like you very much . . .' and 'Bless 'em all, bless 'em all, the long and the short and the tall . . .'

At first Annalie joined in. But she felt restless and ill at ease, until she couldn't bear it any longer. She struggled to her feet.

'I'll have to go. I have to be with Hector. I can't bear the thought of him being on his own and worried about me.'

Mrs Rafferty shook her head. 'You're an awful pair, so you are.'

Somebody else piped up, 'You can't go out just now. There's a raid on.'

'I can't help it.' Annalie was becoming more and more agitated. 'My place is with my husband.' She clambered over all the outstretched legs and reached the door.

'Here, wait a minute, hen,' Mrs Rafferty called. 'Your coat. I'll fetch it from the kitchen. Och, is this not terrible,' she wailed when she came back and passed the coat along to Annalie. 'You could be blown up with a bomb. You're an awful lassie, so you are.'

Annalie hesitated at the close mouth, not because she was afraid, but because she was trying to peer beyond either side of the baffle wall to see if there were any wardens about. Despite the sweeping flash of searchlights and the glow of fires in the near distance, probably the dock area, she could see no sign of any human figure. It was as if she were alone in a nightmare world. She plunged into the darkness of Cumberland Street, the intermittent sweep of searchlights brightening her way. Thankfully she reached her close and ran up the stairs, fumbling for her key and not immediately finding it, so battering an impatient fist on the door. She could hear the silence inside. Unable to believe Hector wasn't there she thumped the door with both fists and called his name. Still no reply. Trembling with apprehension now, she found her key and managed to get it into the lock. The house was in darkness. Not taking time to find the matches and light the gas, she stumbled between the kitchen and the room, still calling out for him. He was not in the house. She couldn't think where he could be. She returned to the landing with panic clawing up inside her. She battered at the other two doors. There was no reply from them either. Then it occurred to her that everybody would be either in one of the bottom-flat lobbies or in the shelter in the back yard. She flew downstairs and rattled the letter box of both flats until one of the doors opened and she had a glimpse of a crowd sitting on the lobby floor.

'Is Hector here?' she asked Mrs Rennie who opened the door.

'No, hen. Do you want to come in?'

'Have you seen him at all?'

'Just this morning. I met him in the paper shop when he was getting your *Herald*. I haven't set eyes on him since then.'

'Where can he be?' Annalie was distraught and speaking more to herself than Mrs Rennie.

'When did you last see him, hen?'

'This afternoon. He was in the house when I left.'

'Och, he can't be far away. I wouldn't worry.'

'Where can he be?' Annalie repeated, wild-eyed now.

'He'll be sheltering somewhere. He'll be fine,' Mrs Rennie soothed. 'There's no need for you to get yourself into such a state. Where are you going? Annalie!' Mrs Rennie called after Annalie's disappearing figure.

'I'll try Mrs Steele's,' she called back.

Hector and Mrs Steele were former neighbours of Annalie's. She hardly knew how she got to their close, or how she managed to race up the stairs. He was not there either. Nor was he at the Dochertys', nor the Pattersons', nor the Taylors', nor the Kerrachers'.

Flo Blair forced her to sit down and have a cup of tea and while she was drinking it the all-clear went.

'There you are,' Flo said. 'He'll be all right now. He'll be making his way back to the house. By the time you finish drinking that and get back to your own place, he'll be there too. If he isn't, you'd better wait there for him, or the pair of you will likely keep criss-crossing each other all night.'

'Maybe I should have waited before,' Annalie groaned. 'Instead of haring about the place like a mad thing. That's what's happened. We've kept missing each other.'

Flo laughed. 'You've always been the same, hen. Never any half measures with you. You always rushed pell-mell into things. And I'll tell you another thing, hen, you've always made big dramas of everything. Life's never dull when you're around. You're in the right trade.'

Annalie began to feel a bit better. Flo was right. She did tend to go over the top at the slightest thing. She made big scenes of the most mundane events. Now that she came to think of it, so did Hector. She half laughed.

'Oh dear, poor old Hector. I bet he's been haring about the place like a mad thing as well.'

'Aye, you're a right pair,' Flo said. 'Have one of my home-made soda scones.'

'No, thanks all the same, Flo, but I'd better get back.'

'Well, I'll put a couple in a bag and you and Hector can enjoy them later on.'

'Thanks. I'll probably see you tomorrow.'

Flo accompanied her to the door. 'Just take it easy, hen. Cheerio now. Tell Hector I was asking for him.'

'I will.'

Annalie went down the stairs clutching the bag of scones and longing for her husband more than she had ever longed for him before.

CHAPTER 50

Alec and Elizabeth went straight back to the shop after
Mrs Harper's funeral. There had been no funeral tea.
Just a brief service in the local church, then to the
cemetery to stand shivering by the graveside with a few
of Alec's loyal customers while his mother was lowered
into the ground.

'I still think', Elizabeth said as Alec unlocked the
shop, 'we should have had a funeral tea.'

'Where?' Alec said. 'In the back shop? There's barely
enough room for the pair of us in there.'

'No. In a restaurant.'

'That's all I needed. I've lost everything. My house,
all my belongings and every penny my mother put by.
When I think of how she scrimped and saved . . .' For
a moment he was lost for words. Then he managed,
'All gone.'

'I know. I'm sorry. It was just . . . well, it was good
of people to come on such a miserable cold day. It
would have been nice to offer them a cup of tea to
heat them up.'

'They'll get tea when they go home. Just put the
kettle on. I'm bloody cold, never mind them.'

The back shop consisted of two rooms. The toilet was
out in the close. The room leading directly off the front
shop was about the same size as the kitchen at Linthouse
had been, only it had no set-in-the-wall bed, no fireplace
and no coal bunker. It did have a sink under a barred
window and Alec had been forced to purchase a gas
cooker from the barras market. He had also made a
table that hinged up from the wall beside the sink, and
two stools. An old army kist (also found at the barras),

kept in the other smaller room, served to hold Elizabeth's clothes and belongings. A couple of hangers and hooks at the back of the door held Alec's things.

The smaller room also had a barred window looking out to a dismal back yard where drains often overflowed and stank to high heaven. Alec had built double bunks and she claimed the top one. In both rooms, which had previously been used exclusively for stock, there were still heaped cardboard boxes full of tins of Heinz beans, jars of meat paste, Lyle's golden syrup, Creamola custard powder, pipe cleaners, and Woodbine and Players cigarettes ('Coffin nails' Alec called the Woodbines).

The only method of heating in the whole shop was one portable paraffin stove. The only lighting in the back was by one gas mantle in the kitchen room. The smaller room, used as a bedroom, had no form of lighting. They undressed with the door open to allow a dim flicker through from the kitchen. Then Alec would pad through in his bare feet to turn off the gas. He had stubbed his toes so many times in the dark while returning to the bedroom, he had eventually been forced to use a candle stuck in a cracked cup.

Elizabeth had begun to fear that he was becoming as mean as his mother. With excruciating care he weighed out their weekly rations and watched her like a hawk in case she filched any extra butter, tea or sugar. Every item, down to a broken biscuit, had to be paid for. He kept his cash in a locked metal cash box until he made his weekly journey to the bank. It was during this time that Elizabeth enjoyed a hasty gorge of Rich Tea biscuits and coconut tablet.

'Have you been touching anything?' he'd query suspiciously every time he returned. He peered and poked around the stock as if he had every item counted. She always feared that he had, and her anxiety never failed to give her acute indigestion.

But she wasn't quite as soft and helpless as she used to be. Admittedly she'd become his unpaid servant in the shop, not serving customers, but cleaning the floor and shelves, restocking shelves, weighing out rations in the evening and on Sundays, while Alec counted coupons and did his books. All this was as well as keeping the travesty of a kitchen and bedroom clean, and cooking meals. Not to mention doing her preparatory work for the school. Alec had changed his tune about wanting her to give up her job. They needed all the money they could get, he explained. He was outraged when she refused to hand over all her wages.

'You're my wife. What's yours is mine.'

'I work hard for my money,' she told him. 'It's not yours. It's mine.'

'You work hard?' he scoffed. 'You wouldn't know a hard day's work if it stared you in the face. I'm the one who works like a slave. I'm the one who puts food in your mouth and clothes on your back.'

'No you don't. I pay for my keep.'

'You pay for your keep?' His face twisted derisively. 'You haven't a clue about money. I've kept you from the day I married you and I'll always fulfil my responsibilities. Everything I do is for you. Who else have I got now?'

He tried every way to force her to give him all her salary. He succeeded in making her feel selfish and guilty, mean and cruel, stupid and irresponsible. But she put her head down and stubbornly held on to her money (except for the sum she'd decided to allot for her keep). She put the rest in the bank. It wasn't much after she'd paid for her tram fares, a few personal things she needed and sweets for the children in her class. But it was better than nothing. It was blessed independence. Or at least it gave her a secret illusion of independence. It was what helped her to survive in an increasingly difficult and stressful situation. She tried to keep reminding herself that there were folks a lot worse off living in the Good and the Bad. There were whole families living in single-end one-room flats in which they had to eat, sleep, dress and generally struggle to survive. Garngad was a highly industrialized place in which even the air people breathed threatened their survival. Some days it was difficult to breathe at all for the fumes of sulphur from the chemical works. It was so strong at times even people's faces became yellow with it. Most houses had no inside toilet and many houses hadn't even water inside. A shared tap outside was quite common.

But none of this made Elizabeth feel any happier or more content with her lot. Indeed there were times when she would be trying to cook a meal among the clutter of cardboard boxes (it was totally impossible after a grocery delivery), tripping over, bumping into things, unable to find a place to put things, and she'd just sink down among it all and burst into tears. Alec had tried to comfort her and then, to her horror, he too had burst into tears.

'When I think of that palace of a house in Drive Road,' he sobbed, 'and it could have been mine. It *should* have been mine.'

She had found strength then to comfort him.

'Never mind. We'll manage. And one day we'll get another house. A better house than the one in Drive Road.'

It was then the idea came to her of asking Christina or Adam Monkton for help. Surely they could give them a house to rent. They had no property in Govan as far as she knew, but anything in any district would be better than what they had for living conditions now. They weren't living at all. They were barely existing. Yet, could she swallow her pride and go cap in hand to the Monktons? The more she thought of it the more impossible it seemed. She cringed at the mere idea.

Never once had they made any effort to see her or, as far as she knew, made any enquiries about her welfare. She could have been killed in the bombing for all they cared. She struggled with her pride for Alec's sake but still she couldn't bring herself to do it. She had made her bed and she would lie in it. She would take one day at a time and somehow she would manage.

Eventually it occurred to Alec to seek help from the Monktons. That she should seek help from them, that is. Perhaps he'd been thinking about it all along but, like her, had been struggling with his pride. When she refused it gave him a focus for all his problems. It gave him somebody to blame. In other words, it was all her fault.

'We don't need to live like this,' he complained. 'Your parents own half of Glasgow . . .'

'That's a gross exaggeration, Alec . . .'

'And all you need to do is ask them for a house and they'd give it to us. But you're so stubborn . . .'

'Even if I did ask them, there's no guarantee that they'd have a place vacant, or that they'd let it to me.'

'Of course they would. You know they would. You're being stupid as well as stubborn.'

'Not so long ago you were talking as if they weren't my parents at all. I was the bastard they'd washed their hands of. They didn't want anything to do with me, remember?'

'They took you in and brought you up. They're decent folk. They wouldn't see us stuck. All you need to do is tell them how we're placed. All you need to do is ask them.'

'If you think so much of them,' she said in sudden bitterness, 'you ask them!'

He was furious. He shook with anger and distress.

'Trust you to let me down. You're no use. You've never been any use as a wife or as anything else. I could work myself into the ground in this shop and you wouldn't care. You wouldn't care if I dropped dead tomorrow. All you care about is yourself . . .'

She hadn't said any more. As he raved on she tried to concentrate on other things in other places. She thought of the children and how their lives were being disrupted by the war. Not only by their mothers being out at work, but by the air raids and the worry, apprehension and lost sleep they caused. The class register had become even more difficult to fill in with any accuracy. Children were absent for all sorts of reasons that were often difficult to keep track of. Sometimes mothers just took children away or sent them to relations in the country without any warning. Often other children trailed in late. Or they nodded off to sleep in the class. Teaching had become more of a challenge than ever and the responsibilities of the teacher more varied and far-reaching.

At one point the military had taken over the school and Elizabeth had to teach children in their own homes. She had taught a group in a single-end where the father, a miner on night shift, had been snoring in one of the two hole-in-the-wall beds. Another group of children had gathered in a front room where the mother of the house had elected herself as the sole administrator of discipline and punishment.

'Here you, you wee midden,' she would shout with an accompanying belt across the ear. 'Pay attention to the teacher.' Or 'See you, you stupid wee ass!' she'd yell, delivering a punch in the back that knocked the child off his chair. 'Answer the teacher. Don't just sit there like a gormless wee nyaff!'

Elizabeth had to use all the tact and firmness at her disposal to remove the offending mother from the room. She had become very good at wielding her own method of discipline, her own kind of quiet authority. Her particular talent was for diffusing angry situations and squalls of potential or actual violence. Only the

405

other day a drunken and angry mother had stormed
into the school intent on splattering Miss Pringle against
the wall. Miss Pringle was the young teacher in the
next class to Elizabeth and she'd made the mistake of
sitting Tina McFarlane next to Alice Crawford. The
McFarlanes and the Crawfords were well-known feud-
ing families. Unfortunately Miss Pringle, fresh from
Jordanhill, had been unaware of the social niceties of
the area.

Mrs McFarlane had bawled her threats so loudly and
with such fury that Elizabeth had gone immediately to
the rescue.

'What seems to be the trouble, Mrs McFarlane?'
she'd asked mildly, smilingly while an ashen-faced Miss
Pringle took refuge behind her desk.

'That Crawford bitch dunted my Tina.'

'Dunted?' Elizabeth looked politely puzzled. 'I'm
afraid I don't know what you mean.' She did, in fact,
know exactly what the word meant but the tactic was
to stop Mrs McFarlane in her tracks and make her
think of another word or another way of explaining
herself. This tended to be off-putting and not conducive
to anger. Sometimes Elizabeth kindly suggested a com-
plaint should be put in writing – which gave even more
food for thought.

She could be strict with the children although she
never used the belt. An unblinking, reproving or re-
proachful stare usually sufficed. Occasionally, in some
of the recent very difficult circumstances she'd been
known to shout in anger. But she never allowed the
offending child to leave at the end of the day still feeling
estranged from her. She would give him or her a sweet
and a swift hug and tell them she was looking forward
to seeing them tomorrow.

The most wonderful compliment she'd ever had as a
teacher was told to her by the mother of Jimmy Brown.
Apparently there had been problems with Jimmy's

sleeping in the past when he'd been in Miss McLeish's class. He had been having nightmares about going to school. Sometimes he woke up in the middle of the night to check again that he'd not forgotten to put his jotter in his schoolbag because Miss McLeish shouted at him if he forgot anything. Now that he was in Elizabeth's class he skipped to school no bother.

'And I asked him,' Mrs Brown said, ' "Does Mrs Harper never shout at you then?"

'"Och yes," Jimmy said. "But she loves me." '

Elizabeth treasured the words. It was true. She did love the children and she loved her job. She tried to love Alec so that their life could be more bearable together. But in this she was only too well aware that she failed. Not only was she a failure as a wife, she was wicked as a person. She denied Alec's words: 'You wouldn't care if I dropped dead tomorrow.' She denied them to herself as well as to him. But in her guilty heart of hearts she knew they were true.

CHAPTER 51

Elizabeth had done her very best with Gerald McGinty but the child was definitely retarded and needed to go to a special school.

'It's no use,' she sadly confessed to the headmaster. 'I can't do anything with him. Perhaps if I could afford to give him more time and attention. But as it is he's just holding up the other pupils.'

'Oh, Lord,' Mr Hunter groaned and energetically scratched his beard. 'This is the kind of situation I don't need at the moment.'

'Telling the parents, you mean? I'll speak to them if you like.'

'You've a brave heart. Or is it innocence that speaks? Have you dealt with this situation before? Do you realize what it means to announce to parents that their own flesh and blood isn't, as they see it, as good as the next person, not good enough in fact to be kept on at the school? They regard it as a personal insult. An affront. More than that. A downright malicious lie. They do not believe it, Mrs Harper. Not one single bit of it.'

'Oh, dear,' Elizabeth sighed.

'And they are angry. No, that is too much of an understatement, Mrs Harper. They seek satisfaction. They threaten. They vow vengeance, Mrs Harper.'

'Oh, dear. But the fact remains, Mr Hunter, Gerald is far below normal intelligence.'

'Mrs Harper, the boy is as thick as two planks. I'm not disputing the fact. He'll have to go to a special school. I'll send a message asking both parents to call and see me tomorrow. Unfortunately the father is available as well. He works in munitions, I believe. Or is he in the chemical works? Anyway, I'll send for them.'

'Well, if there's nothing else I can do,' Elizabeth said, rising.

'Indeed there is, Mrs Harper. You can be here tomorrow to support me. You can back me up, Mrs Harper. Divided we fall, united we stand.'

'Very well, Mr Hunter.'

An angry confrontation at work was the last thing she needed at the moment. It might, she feared, prove the last straw. There had been so many angry and bitter confrontations at home. If the squalid cramped back quarters of a shop could be called home. She could not regard it as such. It felt, for her, only a temporary stopgap, a testing of endurance until something better came along. At the same time she knew that nothing just came along. There had been a time in her life (incredible to think of it now) when she never questioned where anything came from . . . A luxurious roof over her head was never even noticed. A comfortable bed was naturally there. Food appeared in front of her when expected. Clothes were provided as the need, or even just the fancy, arose. Money, in the form of her allowance, kept topping up her bank account. Light and warmth were taken for granted, always there at the flick of a switch.

Not any more. Oh, the misery to waken every morning to scale down from the creaky, loose-jointed bunk bed (Alec had done his best but was really not much use as a joiner) on to the cold, bare wood floor. Then to feel one's way in the dark between boxes and other debris to reach the equally cluttered kitchen. There she had to face the ordeal of washing in icy water at the sink. Dressing and bracing herself to go outside to the draughty close was nothing to look forward to. Reaching the toilet and sitting there shivering in the fousty blackness was no pleasure either. Then there was the next ordeal to face of preparing breakfast. And all the time to the accompaniment of Alec's whining, complaining voice. She knew he felt as miserable as she did, probably more so, but it didn't make her situation any more bearable. Sometimes he nearly drove her demented by nagging on so much about how they could be living in the lap of luxury if it wasn't for her. (She hadn't quite managed to work out the logic behind this.) She would develop such headaches, such suppressed anger and frustration would build up inside her, she would fear that she, like Mrs Harper, would take a fatal stroke. He's going to be the death of me, she'd think, as she'd so often thought before. One day I'll drop dead. He'll be a widower. He'll weep crocodile tears. Everyone will be sorry for him, and he'll be happy. She felt threatened, apprehensive, far more fearful of her husband than of the German bombers which still came to plague them. Yet he was, to all appearances, such a quiet, delicate little man. Who would believe her? When she was safely away from the shop and Alec, when she was in the comparative normality of the school, she could regard her situation and her feelings with a certain degree of objectivity. She could see herself slipping deeper and deeper into neurosis as a result of stress. She could see Alec doing the very same thing. She would resolve to be patient and understanding. She would try even harder to please him, to help him, to reach some sort of closeness between them. Then she would return to the shop. She would see him serving the customers with that shy half smile of his. And she would hate him. She would feel guilty at hating him. She would hate herself. The ever-descending spiral of destruction would begin again. She would see hatred in his eyes when he looked at her in private. (He never nagged or glowered when customers were there.) She would feel threatened, apprehensive, secretly fearful. More and more she was

410

feeling self-defensive. But there was no way in which she could defend herself. To lose her temper and argue with him only made things worse. An outburst of temper, a lack of control on her part left her distressed and defeated. Her defeat made him elated, triumphant. Then he'd become solicitous. He'd lead her to a chair. He'd make her a cup of tea. He'd look as if he'd had a shot of adrenaline. He was happy.

He was becoming worse than his mother. He watched and questioned and grudged every farthing she spent. There had been a fearful row about a pair of slippers she'd bought. It had been an unnecessary luxury and reckless expenditure as far as he was concerned. She was hellbent on ruining him even further, he accused. He watched what she ate with resentful, accusing eyes. There was an almost manic look about him at times.

It was becoming too much for her. That night they had a terrible row. Alec nagged at her, sneered at her, belittled her, baited her, until something suddenly snapped in her head and she screamed in hysteria. No words came. Just screams.

He led her to a chair, made her a cup of tea, tucked a blanket around her knees and put a solicitous palm to her forehead. She withdrew into caution. Polite and apologetic, she took the blame for the row, explaining that she had a difficult interview to face at school next day. The headmaster expected her to help him.

Secretly she wondered who was going to help *her*.

The bout of hysteria was alien to her nature. It was not like her to be so unrestrained. She wondered if she was going mad. Was that what he was trying to do? Drive her mad? More than once he'd threatened to have her committed to the local asylum. People would be even more sorry for him then. He would enjoy that. He would be the patient, long-suffering husband. She could imagine him never missing a visiting time. He would bring flowers and sweets. No expense would be spared then.

Her insomnia had returned. She would eat secretly, fearfully, sometimes sneaking out of bed to do so in the middle of the night. She worried about her health. She took bouts of palpitations and worried that there was something wrong with her heart. She did not fear a heart attack, only helplessness, the dependence on Alec that might result from it. The need to defend herself against him grew until it became the most urgent and the most secret purpose in her life. Half of her felt it too neurotic, too foolish, too ridiculous to speak of. The other half felt certain that it was only too horrifyingly, terrifyingly true.

Sometimes when he nagged at her as she was struggling to cope with the depressing chaos of the back shop, her need to defend herself, her instinct for survival prompted her to think murderous thoughts. She went beyond wishing him dead. She thought of ways to bring the blessed state about. She saw herself administering poison. Madeleine Smith had poisoned her lover with arsenic. But where in reality did one obtain such a thing? The very next morning after her bout of hysteria, he was whining on and on, and on and on, while she was cutting a loaf of bread, and she nearly raised the knife and plunged it into him. She was only stopped by the sudden and unexpected thought of Annalie. She had not thought of her for a very long time. Too many more urgent and more pressing matters closer to home had taken up her attention. She stood motionless, the knife halfway through the loaf.

'Have you gone to sleep or something?' Alec said. 'Do you hear what I'm saying? You're mad. That's what's up with you. If you just saw yourself . . .'

She stared across at him through her ragged fringe. She could quite easily kill him. It was then the realization came to her that anyone could be capable of murder if pushed far enough. It made her think of Annalie in a different way. She saw, with painful honesty, that when

412

she'd gone to see Annalie in the prison she'd taken with her many prejudices and reservations and much lack of understanding. She'd loved Annalie but as a strange, wild creature or as an erring child. She'd loved her because she needed someone to belong to and someone to love her. In her secret heart of hearts though, she'd been appalled at what Annalie had done. She had tried to justify it by insisting it was self-defence. Perhaps it was. But she'd looked at that wild-eyed creature and in her heart she'd been appalled. She had believed then that someone who could commit such a violent deed was fundamentally different from ordinary, normal, decent human beings. She had been willing to be loyal to such a person, so strong had been her need to belong to someone. Now she saw her mother in a deeper, more compassionate way. She understood.

'Are you going to stand there like a dummy for ever?' Alec said. 'Am I never going to get a bit of bread for my breakfast?'

She returned her attention to the knife and finished cutting the loaf. Then she sat quietly drinking her tea. Yes, murder would be easy. She felt irrevocably locked into one course of action. Unless something else could be done. Unless she could find some other means of escape. It was her nature to stubbornly work at something until she succeeded. But she could not succeed in her marriage. She had never been one to gravitate naturally towards change. Yet something had to change. She needed to be secure with one person in one place. She needed to know who and where she was. She needed to belong. Did she belong here?

The confrontation she had to face that day in the headmaster's office seemed the last straw. She felt on a roller coaster of distress. Yet she behaved outwardly as normal. She had become shabby and neglected-looking with her frayed cardigans and down-at-heel shoes, but she still appeared calm and quietly in control. A sensible, dependable sort of person she was thought of at school. A good teacher. The sort of person you could trust your children with.

The interview with Mr and Mrs McGinty was to take place in the afternoon when the primary were finishing for the day. Elizabeth said goodbye to her class and went along to the headmaster's office. He was bracing himself behind his desk. Elizabeth sat down on a chair he'd placed ready at one side of his desk. Two other chairs sat in front.

Mr and Mrs McGinty had the build of a couple of gorillas, and Mr Hunter had expressed a hope to Elizabeth before they arrived that they didn't become physical.

'If that happens, Mrs Harper, you lift the phone and dial 999 for the police while I deal with the pair of them.'

'Yes, Mr Hunter.'

The McGintys arrived looking tense, aggressive, suspicious-eyed. They were ready for trouble.

'You'll have met Mrs Harper,' Mr Hunter began. 'Gerald's teacher.'

'Aye.' Mrs McGinty flung the word out as a challenge.

'Well,' Mr Hunter pressed on, 'Mrs Harper and I have been having a serious talk about Gerald's progress. Or rather to be perfectly frank, Gerald's lack of progress. Mrs Harper, as I'm sure you appreciate, is an excellent teacher and she has devoted much time and patience to helping Gerald. I too have coached him and tested him. And, I'll come right to the point, we have both decided that Gerald will have to be transferred to the special school.'

'Oh here!' A most unexpected transformation came over Mr and Mrs McGinty. 'That's great, so it is.' They smiled fondly at each other. Then Mrs McGinty beamed round at Mr Hunter and Elizabeth. 'That's where we met!'

414

Elizabeth thought she was going to take hysterics again. She didn't dare look at Mr Hunter. How he managed to proceed and give them further details of the transfer before showing them out she did not know.

When he returned he let out a loud guffaw of laughter and she sat for a few minutes with her palm clutched over her mouth, fighting for control. It was strange how the relief from confrontation with the McGintys didn't make her feel any better. Hysteria still clung to her all the way back to the shop. She was shivering with it. She felt this time she really was going mad.

CHAPTER 52

God and the doctor we like adore,
But only when in danger, not before.
The danger o'er, both are alike requited,
God is forgotten and the doctor slighted.

The words jingled in Hector's mind. It was a verse his
grandfather had often recited. His grandfather had
been a minister like his son after him. They'd wanted
and expected Hector to be the third generation of
clergy but he had disappointed them. No, it was more
than that. Both his father and his grandfather had been
outraged.

'An actor? An actor? You wish to be an actor?'

It was strange thinking of them now as he floated in
and out of consciousness. They sounded so much like
actors themselves, especially when they spoke in such
ringing tones and with such dramatic gestures from the
pulpit. They were wonderful performers and it was
because of them and their powerful resounding delivery
that the seeds of his ambition had been sown.

His grandfather had not only been at the opening of
the Glasgow Royal Infirmary, but at the laying of the
foundation stone on 19 May 1792.

Hector wasn't sure if it was in the ambulance or
when he'd arrived that someone had mentioned the
Royal Infirmary. Or whether it was in the ambulance
or later that he'd received the injection of morphia that
had made him feel so dreamy. Anyway he remembered
his grandfather. He heard the booming voice tell of the
great ceremonial occasion of the laying of the founda-
tion stone.

After the service in St Andrew's Church a procession

416

led by city dignitaries walked up Saltmarket and High Street to the Old Castle Yard opposite Provand's Lordship, Glasgow's oldest house where Mary Queen of Scots was reputed to have written the fatal Casket Letters.

'Ah, my boy,' his grandfather told him, 'if only you'd been there to witness the scene.'

Hector smiled. He could see his grandfather's tall inspiring figure before him now.

'Thousands of spectators were gathered to watch the stone being laid in that traditional area of sanctuary surrounding the cathedral where this great infirmary now stands. On this very site once stood the Archbishop's castle.'

Hector caught a blurred glimpse of a ward and then a nurse appeared to bend over him. On her uniform was an oval badge. Inside the oval was the serpent of Aesculapius coiled round a Scottish thistle and below was the motto, *Auspice Caelo*. Hector smiled. *Auspice Caelo*: Favoured by Heaven.

He had been favoured in so many ways. First of all he had been born here in this oldest and most historic area of Glasgow. He felt the city had soaked into his bones. He was part of its roots. He felt proud of it. There was a tough bouncy resilience about the place that he admired. There was a largesse about its people that warmed his heart towards them. Who better to illustrate the resilience and generosity of spirit of the Glasgow man than Professor Jardine and his small band of dedicated men who, in a stormy era of world-shaking events, were determined to build this great infirmary?

It had pierced Hector's imagination when his grandfather told him the French Revolution was at its height at the time. And in Scotland many people were mourning the death of Bonnie Prince Charlie. Robert Burns was in his early thirties and Sir Walter Scott was a young man studying law.

417

How vividly alive Grandfather had made history appear to him. Everything had seemed so fascinating. His grandfather had told of how Joseph Lister had introduced antiseptic treatment in this very infirmary. At first Lister had been made a fool of by other surgeons. They were in the habit of operating garbed in the Prince Albert coat. They threaded needles with silk and stuck them in their coat lapels until needed. Their knives were held in their teeth when not in use. But they had come round to Lister's way of thinking eventually. It had taken Grandfather a long time to come round to accepting that his grandson was destined to be an actor, not a minister.

Grandfather and Father had united in opposing his ambition. So strong was their opposition that he'd had to leave home without their blessing. They had only come round thanks to Sally. Dear Sally. She had been so much more talented than him although she would never countenance such an admission. She had been so loyal, so supportive, so generous-hearted. Was it any wonder she had won a place in his grandfather's and father's hearts?

'If only my mother had been alive,' he often told her. 'How she would have loved you too.'

His chest heaved with the sorrow of losing his so dearly beloved wife and he opened his eyes hoping against hope to see her. But still, there was only the starched nurse, the tightly tucked bedmats and the strong smell of Lysol.

He and Sally had been so close. Yet at the same time they had respected each other's space and privacy. Often they were separated for weeks while they worked on different tours but their separation only made their coming together again all the more precious. Oh, such a delight! There never had been the slightest jealousy in any form or any mistrust, or any negative emotion to spoil their love and friendship. They had been good friends. Often they'd talked well into the night, catching up on all the news and theatrical gossip after they'd been on separate tours.

Her illness had been a terrible blow but she'd borne it without complaint.

'It has brought us even closer together,' she'd said.

He had nursed her for as long as possible. Then she had been taken into the Royal. Had she been in this very same part of the infirmary? Was he in the medical department as she had been? He liked to think that somehow she was close to him in spirit, and then began to realize that she was. It was a beautiful peaceful sensation. He felt so lucky. He had been favoured in his birthplace. He had been favoured in having wonderfully strong characters as antecedents. He had been favoured in love. For a moment or two another tempestuous, disturbing ghost troubled him, made his mind become searching and anxious, his breath catch in his throat.

Then, thankfully, the peace returned. He was a happy man.

CHAPTER 53

It had been a great sing-song at Mrs Rafferty's. Mr
Briggs from the top flat had given his accordion big
licks, really belted it out, he had. The whole crowd of
them had sung to high heavens. And laugh? Mrs
Rafferty had never had such a good time for years.
She'd laughed so much she'd wet herself. There had
been such a rabble of noise they hadn't heard the
battering at the door at first. It turned out it was an
air-raid warden who'd heard the singing and had come
to tell them the all-clear had gone two hours ago.
Laugh? They nearly split their sides. Even Granny
MacAndrish laughed, and she was usually the one who
complained. She had gone to the Mahoneys' lobby in
the next close during the last raid. Her complaint there
was that a priest had come to sprinkle holy water
around and she'd got soaked. What she'd called that
priest, and to his face too, couldn't be repeated.

They were still laughing as Mrs Rafferty was saying
goodnight and seeing them out.

'Good morning,' they corrected her.

Then suddenly Annalie came bursting in on the
scene, coat flying open, hair looking as if she'd been
dragged backwards through a bush, eyes sticking wildly
out of her head.

'I've been everywhere,' she cried out. 'At home. All
our friends. All round the streets. Everywhere.'

'Hush, hen. Come on in. Try and calm yourself.' Mrs
Rafferty shut the door and led the distraught Annalie
into the kitchen. 'Now sit yourself down. I'll pour you
a cup of tea. I've one made.'

'No, I don't need tea. I had tea at Flo's. Where can

I find a phone? Who has a phone? I can't think. I must phone around the hospitals. Oh my God, Mrs Rafferty, if anything's happened to him . . .'

'Now, just calm yourself. There'll be a perfectly simple explanation, I'm sure. But if you must phone, well – one of the shops would probably have a phone but they won't be open for a while yet. The paper shop would be the first, I suppose. Or the dairy.'

'The police. Why didn't I think of that before?'

'You're that upset, hen.'

'Or a first-aid post. They might have one. But definitely the police. I must dash along to the police station.'

'Wait a minute, hen.' Mrs Rafferty caught her in full flight. 'I'm coming with you. You've been running about long enough on your own.'

'Thanks, Mrs Rafferty. They'll phone for me, won't they?'

'Of course they will, hen.' She struggled into her coat and tied a headsquare under her chin. 'I've got another scarf if you want something over your head.'

'No, it doesn't matter. I had a hat earlier. I don't know what I've done with it. I'm not bothered about myself. I just want to know that Hector's all right.'

'Come on then.'

It was a terrible carry-on, as Mrs Rafferty told everybody afterwards. The police had been very good and phoned the Royal Infirmary first and that's where they'd found him. Annalie would have run all the way to the infirmary if Mrs Rafferty and Constable McDougal had allowed it. They had to physically restrain the distracted woman until a taxicab arrived. Then the car had barely drawn up outside the infirmary gates when Annalie leapt out and raced into the building. Mrs Rafferty, puffing and panting and flesh wobbling out of control, caught up in the corridor where a nurse and a white-coated doctor were struggling to bar Annalie's way.

421

'I don't believe you,' Annalie kept repeating, her voice climbing rapidly into hysteria. 'I want to see my husband.'

'I cannot allow you to go into the ward in such a state,' the doctor insisted. 'I have other patients to consider. Come to my office, Mrs Bellamy, and I'll give you something to calm you.'

'Maybe you'd better do what the doctor tells you, hen.' Mrs Rafferty tried to put a comforting arm around Annalie but was violently shaken off.

'I don't believe you. Hector can't be dead.'

The doctor turned to Mrs Rafferty and said quietly, 'Mr Bellamy died a few minutes before you arrived.'

'No!' Annalie broke free and disappeared into the ward, leaving the swing door whamming noisily behind her.

Tears filled Mrs Rafferty's eyes. 'Oh dear, is this not terrible? The poor wee lassie.'

'Bring her to my office,' the doctor said. 'Nurse will help you.'

It had been a harrowing job to tear Annalie away from Hector. She clung to his body like a madwoman, her moaning and wailing rising to a crescendo of screams. Eventually she had to be heavily sedated and driven in the doctor's car back to Mrs Rafferty's place.

That's where she was now. The doctor called in regularly and she was still under medication. But now it was for severe depression.

'I'm that worried about her,' Mrs Rafferty told Flo as she poured her out a cup of tea.

'Aren't we all,' Flo agreed.

'She just sits through in that room staring out the window. She never says a word unless I speak to her.'

'Do you think it would do any good to get her back to her own place?'

'What? With all the memories of him there? Not to mention her Aunty Murn and her daddy and her wee brothers. She's lost them all out of that house. Poor lassie.' Mrs Rafferty's eyes filled with tears. 'I don't know what to do for her.'

'You've been marvellous, hen.' Flo patted Mrs Rafferty's hand. 'You've always been a good friend to her.'

'And her to me,' Mrs Rafferty said. 'But it's just not like her, this. She's always been such a rare wee fighter.'

'Och, I know, but she was awful fond of that man. And what with one thing and another she's had more to cope with than most. There was what happened with her wean as well, remember.'

'Wee Betty,' Mrs Rafferty sighed. 'I mind her fine. I used to nurse her on my knee. She had lovely big dark eyes just like her mammy.'

'Aye,' Flo said, sighing along with her.

Suddenly Mrs Rafferty brightened with hope. 'Here Flo, what if I got Betty to come and see her mammy? That would do the trick, eh?'

'But . . .' Flo looked puzzled. 'Do you know where she is? I'm sure Annalie doesn't.'

'No. But surely I could find out if I tried.'

'Glasgow's a big place, hen. And she might not even be in Glasgow by now.'

Mrs Rafferty scratched absently at one of her plump breasts. 'There must be a way. If we just think . . . Oh here, I tell you who will know.'

'Who?'

'That woman who took her in. Her man was wee Betty's father. The rotten pig got Annalie in the family way when she was just a wee lassie working as a maid in his house.'

'Do you think . . .?' Flo didn't look at all certain. 'Anyway, how's that going to help? I mean, even if you had the nerve to go and ask them, how do you know they'd even give you the time of day? Nobs like them haven't any time for the likes of us.'

'I've got to do something, Flo.'

'Well, better you than me, hen.'

'Would you stay here with Annalie while I go? I worry about leaving her in the house by herself.'

'You mean now?'

'If I put it off I'll lose what wee bit nerve I have. If you go through and get her attention off the window she won't notice me slipping out. Poor lassie, she sits there as if she's hoping to see Hector coming striding along the road. He was a big fine-looking man, wasn't he?'

Flo sighed. 'He was that. Do you know where to go, hen?'

'Och aye. Many's the time Annalie told me about the place. Monkton House it's called and it's on Queen's Drive. I'll get the tram along.'

She buttoned on her grey bell-tent of a coat (made from an ex-RAF blanket) and tied on her tartan-checked headsquare.

'Well, that's me,' she said. 'Wish me luck, hen.'

'All the very best,' Flo said. 'I'll away through and see what I can do with Annalie.'

Mrs Rafferty felt nervous but her apprehension did not stem from any belief that Christina Monkton would be nasty to her. Or Adam Monkton for that matter. He had done wrong in getting Annalie in the family way, but these things happened all the time to lassies working in big houses. They fell for the men and the men fell for them and Bob's your uncle! There would never be any question of marriage, of course. How often had she said to Annalie at the time, 'You're living in cloud-cuckoo-land, hen. He'll never marry you.'

'He loved me,' Annalie had insisted, long after they had parted.

'They all say that, hen.'

'If he had known about my baby he would never have married Christina Gillespie. It would have been different.'

'Listen, hen,' Mrs Rafferty told her. 'Half the weans running about Glasgow are weans like yours. Have you ever heard of a master marrying a maid? Now tell me, have you?'

They had sat in silence for a moment and then Annalie said, 'He was different.'

'No he wasnae, hen. The quicker you realize that the better you'll get on. You've your own life to live.'

She'd told her that again. Only the other day.

But this time all Annalie had said was, 'What life?'

Mrs Rafferty felt certain that if she could get Annalie and wee Betty, as she'd always thought of her, together then without any doubt Annalie would perk up and have a good reason for living again. That hopeful, cheerful certainty sped her on her way to Queen's Park. It was only when she arrived at Queen's Drive and saw the big imposing villa that her heart quailed. Not because of anything the Monktons might or might not say to her, but at her own temerity in approaching such an elevated place and having the cheek to expect such important folk to have anything to do with her. She felt ashamed. She prepared to apologize for herself. Only her desperation to help her friend forced her feet to approach the back door of the house. (She would never have dreamt of sullying the front door with her presence.)

A maid opened the back door and immediately said, 'We haven't got any rags today.'

Mrs Rafferty tried to look earnest and respectable. 'No, hen, I've come about wee Betty.'

'Wee Betty?' The maid looked – as Mrs Rafferty told Flo later – fair flummoxed. 'Who's wee Betty?'

'If I could have a quick word with Mrs Monkton. I wouldn't take long. Please, hen,' she added, ashamed that she'd nearly forgotten her manners.

'Mrs Monkton?' the maid echoed incredulously. Then another voice called from the nether region.

'Agnes, who is it?'

'Somebody wants to see Mrs Monkton, Mrs Fullerton. Will I bring her in?'

'Yes, of course, girl.'

Mrs Fullerton, who was obviously the cook, was hurriedly tidying her apron when Mrs Rafferty entered the kitchen, but she stopped in fury and amazement when she saw the plump figure in the shapeless blanket of a coat.

'And here was me thinking it was somebody who should have come in the front door!'

'Oh, I'd never dream . . .' Mrs Rafferty modestly protested. 'No, hen, I just want a wee word with Mrs Monkton. Or here —' her face suddenly brightened '— maybe you'd know and that would save me bothering her.'

'Know what?' Mrs Fullerton looked as if she could hardly credit what was going on.

'About wee Betty.'

'Who on earth . . .'

'That's what I said,' interrupted the maid.

'Oh here.' Mrs Rafferty apologetically sucked in her lips. 'Annalie used to give me a row about that. Calling her Betty, I mean. Her name is Elizabeth. Annalie always used to say her name was Elizabeth Gordon then. That was when she was just a wee wean. But when she was growing up here she was Elizabeth Monkton.'

The cook and the maid exchanged looks. In a quieter, more cautious voice the cook said, 'What about her?'

'Well you see, hen, that's what I wanted to talk to Mrs Monkton about. You know who I mean?'

'Yes.'

'But do you know where she is?'

'No. And even if I did I wouldn't tell you. Agnes, show this person out.'

Mrs Rafferty had a sudden tragic vision of Annalie

426

sitting at the window in the Gorbals. It strengthened her resolve. Let the toffs say what they liked or do what they liked. She wasn't budging.

'I'm not budging,' she said. 'Until I speak to Mrs Monkton.'

'Don't be ridiculous,' Mrs Fullerton said. 'Get out of my kitchen at once.'

'I'm not budging.' Mrs Rafferty decided she might as well be hung for a sheep as a lamb and sat down at the kitchen table.

'What are you going to do?' Agnes asked Mrs Fullerton.

The cook hesitated for a minute and then said, 'Bring me a clean apron. I'll go up and tell Mrs Monkton what's happened. Let her worry about it. I've got a dinner to make.'

CHAPTER 54

Mrs Rafferty weakly trembled from the top of her tartan-scarfed head to the toes of her scuffed brown shoes. Even her teeth shivered in her mouth. Never in her life had she seen such imposing surroundings. Even the air was different, warm, sweetly perfumed. Crossing the spacious hall she felt as if she was treading on hallowed ground.

The cook sank her further into wretched self-consciousness with a supercilious look peppered with disgust before opening another door and leading her shrinking, apologetic figure into a luxurious room.

'The person I told you about, madam,' the cook announced.

'Thank you, Mrs Fullerton, that will be all,' Christina Monkton said.

Mrs Rafferty clutched desperately at her string shopping bag. Inside bulged her old black purse; she didn't own a handbag.

'I'm awful sorry to bother you, hen,' she began in desperation, 'but I'm that worried about Annalie, you see.'

'Annalie Gordon has nothing to do with me.'

'Oh, she's not Annalie Gordon now.' Mrs Rafferty immediately brightened. She always enjoyed a harmless gossip. 'Oh, not for a long time, hen. No, she's Annalie Bellamy now. But Hector, that was her man, died with his heart. A fine big man he was too . . .'

'I am not in the slightest interested in Annalie Gordon or Bellamy or whatever she's called now. I'm a very busy woman. Please state your business as briefly as possible.'

428

'Oh.' Mrs Rafferty was deflated again. 'I'm that sorry, hen. It's just I'm worried about her and I thought if I found wee Betty, I mean Elizabeth, that might help her, you see.'

'No, I don't see.'

'We all need our own flesh and blood when we're in trouble and I just thought . . .'

'If Elizabeth had wanted to get in touch with her she would have done so long ago.'

'The lassie did try. I remember how she asked around but none of us let on. We thought it best at the time. Annalie didn't want to see her then. She just wanted to hide away. The poor soul was so ashamed about the killing and the trial and everything.'

'I'm not surprised.'

'But it's different now.'

Christina raised a cool brow. 'Is it?'

'Oh aye, hen. With losing her man, the poor soul's that down. She needs all the help she can get. Me and her friends have tried our best but it's no use.'

A silence followed in which Mrs Rafferty gazed in anguish at the elegantly lounging figure in the glistening pearls and french-grey afternoon dress. The dress looked, as she told Flo much later, as if Mrs Monkton had been poured into it and 'I wouldn't be a bit surprised if that frock cost more than what would keep the pair of us for a week.'

Now she waited for Christina Monkton to say something helpful. But all Christina Monkton said was, 'Well?'

'You see we was hoping you'd be the one to know where wee Betty, I mean Elizabeth, is.'

'I am no longer in contact with my stepdaughter.'

'Maybe so, hen, but you'll surely know where she is.'

Christina Monkton glanced at her watch. 'You have wasted enough of my time. I must ask you to leave.' She leaned forward to press the bell to summon the maid but before she could do so, desperation once more overcame Mrs Rafferty.

'I'm not leaving here,' she cried out, 'until I've got wee Betty's address.'

And feeling faint with horror at the thought of her own temerity, she sat down.

Elizabeth gazed around the back shop. It was early morning. The sun was shining. In its misty rays dust motes floated. Cardboard boxes piled high. Bilious brown mountains. Elizabeth couldn't remember where she'd put her clothes. The mountains pressed in on her. High and hard and insurmountable. They crushed into her mind, squeezing out thought. More and more, she was feeling like this, grinding to a halt, struggling to force her mind to function. Alec was out at the toilet. She had been standing like this in her nightdress when he left. She mustn't still be glued to the same spot and still in her nightdress when he returned.

One thing at a time. One step at a time. She started fumbling her way between the mountains from one side of the room to the other. Eventually her feet found her clothes. They were in a neat little pile on the floor in the corner.

She couldn't remember if she'd washed. One thing at a time. One step at a time. Carefully, methodically, she pulled on one garment after the other. She noticed her hands had a slight tremble. Alec mustn't see her trembling. She hid her hands in the pockets of her cardigan.

She couldn't remember if she'd made breakfast. Then as if reading her mind Alec came in the side door from the close and said, 'I haven't time for breakfast now. There's people standing in the close mouth waiting for me to open. If you were any use you'd have been up hours ago and had it ready. It's not as if I expected a big fry-up. A slice of sausage or fried egg on a roll was

430

all I wanted. Now I'll have to start a hard day's work on nothing. You're getting worse. Do you know that? How you get on at that school I don't know. You're worse than useless. And you're stupid into the bargain. If you just saw yourself standing there like a stupid halfwit.'

He stomped through to the front shop and she could hear him jerking at the big bolts and bars of the door. Then the key scraped rustily in the lock. She didn't know how she was managing at the school. At the same time she believed it was being at the school every day that preserved her sanity. Or what there was left of it. Sometimes she thought she was helped by her inborn stubbornness. She had this capacity for putting her head down and holding on. At other times she wondered if the stubbornness was just prolonging her agony.

She had no doubts, however, that being at school among the children was her lifeline. As long as she could keep hanging on, keep well enough to keep going to the school, she'd be all right.

She couldn't remember if she'd prepared her school work. A cold sweat made her tremble again. If her work became affected ... If she lost her job ...

One thing at a time. One step at a time. She found the small cardboard case in which she kept her papers. Then she found her coat. She slipped quietly out of the side door, through the close, and away. She always felt like running after she got out. She had to use great restraint. Recently she had been having strange worrying experiences outside. On several occasions she had found herself on the tram or even having arrived at the Good and the Bad without any recollection whatsoever of how she got there. These blank spaces in time frightened her.

She clung to her school routine and the cheerful normality of the children and the parents she often came in contact with, especially on parent-teacher nights. There the progress or problems of the children could be discussed with their mothers. (Most of the fathers were away in the forces.)

As often as not it was the problems of the mothers that dominated the discussions. Elizabeth listened to them sympathetically and that seemed in most cases to be enough. Even if she never uttered a word, afterwards Jimmy's or Sandra's or Alice's or Johnny's mother would say gratefully, 'Here, thanks very much, hen. You've been a great help as usual. I feel a lot better now. You're a wee gem, so you are.'

After these nights working late at the school, going back to the shop was even more of an ordeal. She'd try to delay the evil hour. Once she walked all the way, arriving very late and exhausted to face an outraged Alec.

'I was nearly sending for the police. You could have fallen in the river or jumped in, for all I knew.'

'For all you cared, you mean.'

It was an unusual sign of bitterness. Usually she didn't say anything.

The mountain would crush into her mind. Overshadowing it. All she could do was persevere. Try to keep going. One thing at a time. One step at a time. And all the time knowing that one day she might not be able to take that first step.

CHAPTER 55

'Is there something wrong, hen?' Jimmy Brown's mother stopped beside Elizabeth who had been standing motionless for some time at the school gates.

Elizabeth gazed at her wide-eyed. 'Yes there is, Mrs Brown. You'll think I'm mad but . . . I don't think I can go home.'

'I don't think you're mad at all, hen. Now, you just come along with me. I'll make you a nice cup of tea and you'll tell me what's up. I'll soon get you sorted out.'

Elizabeth allowed herself to be led none too gently along Garngad Road to the cobbled hill of Cobden Street, one of four side streets which ran off Garngad Road. Mrs Brown lived in a bottom flat in one of the tall black tenements. She was a bustling woman who was in the habit of driving all before her, and at high speed. As well as meeting her at the parent-teacher evenings, Elizabeth had been visited many times by Mrs Brown at the school. Not to complain – quite the reverse. 'You're a walkin' wonder with that wean,' she often said, meaning her Jimmy. 'That McLeish woman never listened to me when I told her my Jimmy was highly sprung. Now he's doing that well at his lessons.' Mrs Brown always ignored the rule that parents must not visit teachers direct but always through the headmaster.

'Och him!' She brushed Mr Hunter aside. 'What's he got to do with anything?'

'Come on in, hen,' she said now. 'Jimmy, you go out and play, son. I'll fling you out a piece and jam in a minute.'

Elizabeth felt dazed and more than a little ashamed.

She felt she was letting herself and everyone else down. This was not the way a teacher was expected to behave. Her heart sank at the thought of what Miss McLeish would say if she knew. Even Miss Pringle would be shocked at such weakness, such fraternization. But there was nothing she could do about it. She felt physically ill. Even her mind had ground to a halt.

'Now hen –' Mrs Brown plumped herself down at the table beside Elizabeth '– drink up your tea and just let it all pour out.'

Elizabeth put her hand over her mouth for fear of hysterics again.

'You can trust me, hen,' Mrs Brown went on. 'I'm a decent woman. Not like some of the hairies around here. Why can't you go home, hen? Let me guess. It's some bloody pig of a man.'

'I can't stand it any longer,' Elizabeth blurted out. 'Especially since the house was bombed and we've been living in the back shop. I can't cope any more. I don't know what I'm going to do. If I just could get a place of my own. Oh, you don't know how I long for a place of my own.'

'Right,' Mrs Brown said. 'You drink up that tea and then we'll go along and see Orange Annie.'

'Orange Annie?'

'She's the factor for this street. All she'll want to know is what foot you kick with.'

'What foot?'

'You know – Protestant or Catholic.'

'Protestant, but . . .'

'That's all right then.'

'I don't understand. I mean do you think . . . You can't mean . . .'

'Listen, hen, if you can give her a wee backhander – key money she calls it – you're in.'

'But in where?'

'Och, there's always some place going. Somebody

434

dying or moving one way or another. Now you come to mention it, there's Biddy Maxton going down to London. Her man was killed out in the desert or someplace and she's going down to live with her sister. Now, wait a minute, hen, was that last week or next week? Time flies and you don't know where you are half the time. Anyway, Orange Annie'll tell us. On you come.'

More dazed than ever Elizabeth allowed Mrs Brown to grip her arm and lever her firmly out of the house, along the street and up another close. The cobbled slope of the street was thick with children enjoying the long summer's evening. Crowds of them were sitting on the kerb staring glassy-eyed at a busker playing spoons on his knees, head and hands, in time to an accordion.

Humming cheerily to the accordionist's tune, Mrs Brown rattled the letter box and a sound of shuffling feet could be heard coming along the lobby. Then the door opened to reveal a tall reed of a woman with a Woodbine hanging from the corner of her mouth. Her eyes were shrewd and narrow and permanently creased against the drifting cigarette smoke.

'Aye,' she said, appraising Elizabeth from head to toe.

'Annie this is Mrs Harper, Jimmy's teacher. A right wee gem but she's got a f— pig of a man and she wants shot of him.'

Elizabeth's natural reticence was shaken to its roots. 'Mrs Brown, I really don't think...'

Mrs Brown blithely ignored the interruption. 'She's looking for a bolt hole, and I told her about Biddy's place. It's not taken yet, is it? She's okay for key money, aren't you, hen?'

'Well, yes but...'

'And she's a Proddie.'

Annie stood aside. 'Come in.'

Once in the kitchen piles of newspapers and other

odds and ends were lifted from a couple of chairs and flung on the floor. But it was Mrs Brown who extended the invitation to sit down.

'She leaves at the end of the week,' Annie said.

'Is that okay, hen?' Mrs Brown turned to Elizabeth.

'You mean I could get the house?'

'It's a room and kitchen,' Annie said.

Elizabeth was trembling. Everything was moving too quickly. She had a sinking feeling she might be doing the wrong thing. She seemed always to be doing the wrong thing in her personal life. A sense of failure depressed her. She wasn't sure if she wanted the house. It would only bring more problems. Living in the same area with her pupils and their families might undermine her respect and authority for a start.

'Aye, a room and kitchen would be fine,' Mrs Brown answered for Elizabeth. 'Now, tell her the rent and what key money you want, Annie.'

'I didn't expect', Elizabeth mumbled, 'anything to happen right away like this. I . . . I find it difficult to take in.' She put her hands up to her temples. There seemed to be two screwdrivers, one on either side of her head twisting further and further into her brain.

'The poor soul,' Mrs Brown said to Annie. 'She's at her wits' end. I found her standing like a stoockie at the school gate. See f— men!'

'Aye,' Annie said. She was obviously a woman of few words.

Elizabeth had trained the children in her care never to use bad language in her presence. (And, she hoped, in nobody else's presence either.) She knew that many, although not all, parents were in the habit of swearing, but out of respect for her or her position as a teacher they refrained from cursing in front of her. This admirable self-control had been no doubt helped by Elizabeth's shocked silences and reproving stares.

Mrs Brown had always been an exception. Mrs

Brown cheerfully ignored shocked silences and reproving stares. Or never noticed them.

Elizabeth tried to think when Mrs Brown now said, 'What choice have you got, hen? I'll tell you. You take this wee room and kitchen or you go back to your back shop with your pig of a man. Now' – she raised a protesting hand – 'you don't need to tell me what he's like . . .' (Although in fact Elizabeth had no intention of telling anybody what Alec was like.) 'You don't need to tell me,' Mrs Brown repeated. 'Haven't I got a pig of my own? Drinks like a bloody fish.'

'Aye,' Annie said, lighting another cigarette off the one in her mouth.

Mrs Brown's mention of the back shop reminded Elizabeth of all the horrors of it and her feelings of being trapped in it. And all the fears that beset her there. She knew she couldn't go back. Not without hope of escape.

'I feel most fortunate in getting this opportunity,' Elizabeth managed at last. 'I appreciate your kindness. The kindness of both of you. Indeed I feel quite overwhelmed . . .'

'Tell her the rent and the key money, Annie,' Mrs Brown repeated. 'Now,' she said after that had been duly arranged, 'come on. We'll have a gander at it. Biddy won't mind.'

'You mean look at the house?' Elizabeth said as Mrs Brown caught her by the elbow and whipped her to her feet. 'But the poor woman's recently been bereaved, you said.'

'Her and a million others, hen. No, she's a nice wee soul, Biddy. She won't mind. Keeps that place clean as a new pin. This is your lucky day, hen. You might have got a place like a midden. The places I could show you around here!' She was bustling Elizabeth towards the door and it was with some difficulty that Elizabeth managed to twist round in mid-flight to thank the factor.

'Aye,' Annie said, watching them leave through her grey cloud of cigarette smoke.

Out in the street another busker was doing a soft-shoe shuffle on a plywood board over which he'd sprinkled a layer of sand.

And from the back yard of the close they now entered came the lusty strains of a man singing 'No Surrender'.

'See him?' laughed Mrs Brown. 'He's a right two-faced bastard. In the other three streets next to here there's a wee Ireland. You know, mostly Papes. And there he belts out nothing but Irish songs. Here we are, hen.'

She rattled loudly at the letter box of an upstairs door while humming snatches of 'No Surrender'. The door was opened by a small pale-faced woman severely dressed in black with a jet brooch at her throat. Her brown hair was drawn back into a bun at the nape of her neck.

'Hello, hen,' Mrs Brown greeted her cheerily. 'This is Mrs Harper . . .' (Elizabeth braced herself for another shocking revelation. Thankfully none came.) 'She's going to be moving in here at the end of the week. How about a wee gander round, hen?'

'Only if it's convenient,' Elizabeth added hastily.

The woman smiled. 'Yes, of course. Come in.'

The house smelled of lavender wax polish. Everything glowed and gleamed and sparkled. Biddy led them first into the front room which had a double window looking down on to the sloping Cobden Street, and a set-in-the-wall bed. A rug graced the front of the mauve-tiled fireplace. In the empty grate a pink paper fan was propped open. Furniture consisted of a drop-leaf table and four chairs with gold-coloured plush seats and backs, and a sideboard. Biddy opened a cupboard door to show a walk-in cupboard.

'My man put that rail in for our clothes and the shelf above it for hats and suitcases and things. He was very good with his hands.'

438

'What a splendid idea,' Elizabeth said. 'I mean, it's very useful. I'm so sorry about what's happened.'

'Och well,' Mrs Brown said, 'it's an ill wind that doesn't bring somebody some good. I was just saying to her' – she jerked a thumb towards Elizabeth – 'it's her lucky day.'

'I hope you'll be happy here,' Biddy said. 'My man and I were happy here. He was proud of this place.'

Elizabeth admired the woman's quiet dignity and wished there was something she could say, some way she could comfort her.

She touched Biddy's arm. 'Rest assured, I'll appreciate it and take very good care of it.'

Biddy smiled. 'Come through to the kitchen. Nothing much here as you can see,' she remarked as they passed through the shoe box of a hall. 'Except that. It looks like a wee sideboard, doesn't it? It's actually the coal bunker. My man shifted it from the kitchen and sanded the wood and polished it up. You'd never guess, would you? And it saves so much dust and mess in the kitchen. That high shelf was always there. I've never used it. It was too high for me to get up to. I don't like heights.'

The kitchen was no different in layout from any other tenement kitchen except it was minus the coal bunker, which helped give the small room a more spacious look.

'I'm taking everything,' Biddy said. 'Except the two mattresses and this table and those chairs. My sister's not married and she's been on her own in the family house since Mum and Dad died. The house down there's pretty full of stuff as it is but I've told her I want to hang on to my front-room table and chairs and my good sideboard.'

'You're quite right,' Elizabeth said. 'And I'll be glad of the kitchen table and chairs. I'll pay you for them, of course.'

'Och, they're not worth anything,' Biddy said. 'Just plain scrubbed wood.'

439

'Here, Biddy,' Mrs Brown laughed. 'You should never look a gift horse in the mouth, hen. Take the money!'

'I'll have to go to the bank,' Elizabeth explained. 'Will tomorrow do?'

'Yes, of course. But I really didn't expect anything.'

'What'll you give her?' Mrs Brown wanted to know.

'I don't know about these things,' Elizabeth said worriedly. 'What would be fair? Two or three pounds?'

'Good gracious!' Biddy gasped. 'That's far too much. I'll be perfectly happy with a pound. I'm leaving that old kettle and frying pan as well and I certainly don't want anything for them. I'd just be throwing them out.'

And so it was arranged. Outside again Elizabeth said goodbye to Mrs Brown and went dazedly on her way back to the shop, and Alec.

Mrs Brown had said, 'Do you think you can manage now, hen? You're welcome to stay with me until Biddy moves. The only thing is my man might try to get in the wrong bed. There's no telling what the f— bastard'll do when he's drunk.'

Elizabeth had declined the offer and assured Mrs Brown that she felt much better now that she knew she'd some place to go to on Saturday. The thought of freedom, a safe place of her own, kept bubbling up inside her like hysterical laughter. She felt unhinged. For one thing, she shrank from telling Alec. She didn't feel able to cope with his fury, his derision or his self-pity. Her nerves had long since stretched far beyond endurance. She didn't know how to unstretch them. Her mind told her that the flat in Cobden Road was her good and blessed escape for which she should be truly grateful. Yet her emotions still longed for the ultimate security of freeing herself from Alec altogether. Getting rid of him, rubbing him out, making him disappear for ever. So tied was she in misery with him she could not conceive of ever truly escaping from his obsessive, destructive influence. She knew that if she

said, 'I have a place of my own' or 'I am leaving you'
he would somehow spoil the magic, the illusory happiness, and she would sink helplessly into the pit again.
Already she did not believe the words to be true.

She arrived at the shop and saw Alec smiling his shy
half smile. She went through to the dark, cluttered back
shop with its iron-barred window. She thought: One
thing at a time. One step at a time.

CHAPTER 56

Mrs Rafferty eventually confessed to Annalie, 'I hope you'll not be angry with me, hen, but I was that worried about you.'

'There's no need,' Annalie said dully.

'There is so. You haven't been yourself for ages. I had to do something. I thought if I could find wee Betty and bring the pair of you together, it might help.'

Annalie made no comment and so Mrs Rafferty pressed on, 'I went to the Monktons.'

'Oh, Mrs Rafferty,' Annalie sighed. 'I know you mean well but I can imagine you got short shrift there.'

'As a matter of fact she was quite nice.'

'Christina Monkton?' Annalie shrugged. 'Of course, you think everybody's nice. That's because you're so nice yourself.'

'Well, maybe she didn't greet me like a bosom pal. But then why should she, hen? The thing was I told her what I'd come for. You should have heard me.' Mrs Rafferty sucked in her lips. 'Oh, I don't know to this day how I could have been so cheeky. I said I wasn't leaving the house until I found out where wee Betty was. I was that desperate, you see. I was up to high doh as well. I've never seen such a palace of a place. Fancy wee Betty being brought up in a place like this, I thought. But it wasn't my cup of tea, hen. I didn't feel at home.'

'Did she tell you?'

Mrs Rafferty was cheered to see the slight lift of interest in Annalie's manner.

'Yes, she did, hen. And I went right there.'

'Where?'

'Govan. Her man has a shop.'

'I remember Elizabeth said her husband was a businessman.'

Mrs Rafferty hesitated. 'It's only a wee shop, hen. It's not even as big as Hurley's.'

'Oh?' Annalie looked puzzled.

'And they live in the back. He took me through so that we could talk in private. Her man, Alec, they call him. Alec Harper.'

'In the back?'

'Aye. Oh, the poor thing. I don't know how wee Betty stood it for so long. Especially being used to such a palace of a place. I couldn't have stood thon myself, Annalie. It was all cluttered with boxes and dear knows all what. You couldn't have swung a cat in there. There was no comforts, no comforts at all for the poor lassie.'

Annalie was galvanized into life. 'For God's sake, did you see her? Is she all right?'

'Yes, well, no. Well I don't rightly know, hen.'

'What do you mean, you don't know?' Annalie shouted.

'Now calm down, Annalie. The truth is he didn't know where she was. She'd walked out on him, he said. And I can't say I blame her, he seemed an awful self-pitying jessie of a man, the way he was going on. All he seemed to be caring about was himself. He said he didn't have a clue that she was going to disappear like that. She'd absolutely no reason to, he said. Out of the blue, he said. She'd left a note but there wasn't an address on it. Said their marriage was over and she didn't ever want to see him again or have anything at all to do with him. She'd always had a cruel streak, he said. But I don't believe that of wee Betty, do you?'

'Of course not. I hope you told the shit what you thought of him.'

'Well no, I didn't, hen. I was that taken aback with that awful place and the thought of wee Betty living

443

there. It was worse than my place down the dunny in Commercial Road. At least my place had a fire and a bit of floor space to move about in. There wasn't even the comfort of a fire in that back shop.'

'Did Elizabeth work in the shop?'

'No. I asked him and he said no. He'd always had to struggle along by himself. I can't stand a moaning minnie of a man like that, can you? Remember my Patrick, Annalie? A fine figure of a man, eh? A real man. Did you ever see him, working on the roads, stripped to the waist . . .?'

'Oh, Mrs Rafferty, she needs me. I hope and pray she's all right.' Annalie was burning with life and energy now.

'You'll find her, hen. Don't you worry,' Mrs Rafferty said happily.

'I'll go and see the shit.' Annalie jumped to her feet. 'He must know, I'll make him tell me.'

'Wait a minute, hen. There's no point in rushing into things and getting yourself all upset. Just let's think for a minute. Didn't you tell me that wee Betty was a teacher before she got married?'

'Yes, why?'

'Well, maybe she went back to it. Every place is crying out for women to go back to work now. There's big posters about it.'

Annalie's face glowed. Her eyes sparkled. 'You're right, Mrs Rafferty. That's a wonderful idea. There's a real chance that's just what's she's done. I'll go to Bath Street to the Education Offices first thing tomorrow. Oh, I wish they were open now. I'd run all the way there. Why do offices have to close so early?'

Mrs Rafferty laughed. 'I don't know, hen. But first thing tomorrow's better. Then if they give you the name of a school, you'll have time to catch the school before it shuts.'

'My poor baby.' Annalie paced the floor, wringing

her hands. 'God knows what she might have suffered. Might still be suffering.'

'Try to be patient, Annalie. Take one of your tablets. You're not going to be any use to the lassie if you're all upset.'

'I don't want tablets. I want to be able to think. Where can she be? Even if she's still teaching. Where can she be living?'

'One thing at a time. If you find out she's teaching, you'll find out which school and they'll give you her address. In fact,' Mrs Rafferty realized, 'the Education Offices should have her home address, that's if she's still teaching.'

'She will be. She must be. How else could she make a living?'

Mrs Rafferty sighed. 'Och, hen, there's a war on, remember. What them posters actually say is, "Women of Britain, Come into the Factories", I suppose they mean munition factories. She could have gone there.'

'What? Elizabeth? Never. You didn't see her grown up, Mrs Rafferty. She was a lady,' Annalie said proudly. 'Dignified and gentle spoken, and so well educated, of course. She couldn't rough it in munitions.'

Mrs Rafferty sighed again. 'I'm afraid the poor soul *has* been roughing it, hen. I can't see you getting a wink of sleep tonight, Annalie.'

'Oh never mind me.' Annalie flapped an impatient hand. 'I'm all right.' Then something occurred to her. 'Except I don't think I've any money. I'll need cash for bus fares, and what if Elizabeth needs money?'

'Don't worry, hen,' Mrs Rafferty said. 'I've never touched your sick benefit. It's all behind the clock there.'

'But that was for my keep.' Annalie was aghast. 'Mrs Rafferty, don't tell me you've been keeping me for nothing. You can't afford to do things like that.'

'Och, my family are awful generous to me, hen. I

didn't need anything from you. And many's the time you've helped me in the past.'

'Oh, Mrs Rafferty, I feel terrible. What have I been thinking about – sitting here all this time feeling sorry for myself?'

'No, hen, you've been ill.'

She had been staying with Mrs Rafferty for months now, ever since Hector's death. Unable to face going back to live in her own house or just not interested enough to move back to it, it now occurred to her that her house might be a haven for Elizabeth. For both of them. She was glad and grateful now that her friends had rallied round and completely redecorated the room and kitchen, even changed the curtains and bedcovers, in an effort to tempt her to start a new life in it. Then a terrible thought came to torment her. What if Elizabeth had not forgiven her for deserting her not only once, but twice? She remembered the eager excited face in the crowd the day she had been released from prison. Elizabeth had wanted her then, perhaps needed her then, and she had hidden away from her own daughter.

'God forgive me. God forgive me.' She tore at her hair and cried to high heaven.

'Nobody can help being ill.' Mrs Rafferty was not over-anxious, or even surprised by this dramatic outburst. She'd known Annalie a long time.

'What if Elizabeth hasn't forgiven me? What if she hides away from me?'

'Now, now, there's no use crossing bridges before you come to them.'

Mrs Rafferty was right. She couldn't sleep. By morning she was like a wild thing, dark-eyed, white-faced and unruly-haired. Mrs Rafferty had to be unusually firm.

'Now you listen to me, Annalie. You're not going to be a bit of use to your lassie like this. You sit down there and drink your tea and eat your porridge.'

Annalie had done as she was told and then had to run to the sink to throw up.

'Oh dearie me,' Mrs Rafferty said. 'You're an awful lassie.'

Annalie managed a wry smile. 'Some lassie. Haven't you seen my grey hairs?'

'You haven't grey hairs,' Mrs Rafferty scoffed. 'Your hair's still as black as a raven.'

'You're needing new specs. But never mind. I don't care now if all my hair falls out. I don't care about anything as long as Elizabeth's all right.'

She was waiting at the door of the Education Offices in Bath Street before they opened and lost no time in pestering everyone until she was given answers to her desperate queries. The relief was wonderful when she learned that yes, Mrs Harper was teaching. She was at present on the roll of St Rollox School in Garngad Road. But the home address she was furnished with was of the shop in Govan.

From Bath Street she made her way as quickly as possible to Garngad and was taken aback to find that it looked a more run-down and tougher district than the Gorbals. The school was easy enough to find on the main road and, running now, she forced her way through the doors into the building. Seeing a cleaner in a sackcloth apron coming along the corridor carrying a zinc bucket, she hurried towards her.

'Could you tell me where Mrs Harper's classroom is?'

'There's no classes in today,' the cleaner said. 'Your head must be away with the fairies, hen. This is Saturday.'

'Shit!' Annalie cried out. 'Isn't there anyone here I can talk to? Do you know where I can find Mrs Harper?'

'Not me, hen. All my work's done when there's nobody here. I don't know many of the teachers.

Especially not nowadays. I used to when my Bert was young. Now, what was the name of his teacher?'

'Isn't there anybody else at all?'

'The jannie should be somewhere around. A right grumpy old bugger he is, though. You'll be lucky if you get the time of day from him. But here, wait a minute, hen. Now that I come to mention old grumpy-guts, his grouse today was that the headmaster had come in. He'd forgotten some papers he needed to work on over the weekend or something. Mind you, the jannie has a point, in a way. This place is never shut now. I mind before the war this place shut all July and August for the holidays. Now it's open every day and even during the night. If it's not air-raid wardens, its fire-watchers, if it's not fire-watchers, it's . . .'

'For God's sake,' Annalie said in a fever of impatience, 'where's the headmaster's room?'

'Okay, keep your shirt on. It's just along there. The name's on the door.'

When his door burst open Mr Hunter turned in surprise from his search through untidy mountains of papers on his desk. He was even more taken aback at the vision of luxurious black curls and flashing dark eyes and the dashing figure in scarlet dress and beret.

'Good morning, Miss . . .?'

'Mrs . . . Mrs Bellamy.'

'Mrs Bellamy, do have a seat. What can I do for you? You're not one of our mothers, are you? I'm sure I would have remembered . . .' He felt he would have been more likely to have seen her on the stage or on the silver screen than in Garngad. She was not a young woman, but a startlingly beautiful one nevertheless.

'I'm the mother of one of your teachers, Mrs Harper.'

'Really?' He was all the more astonished. Yet there was a similarity in the unusual flecks of violet in the eyes and the colour of the hair. But that was all. Even the hair was different. This woman's hair was a riot

448

of waves and curls. Mrs Harper's hair was straight and clung close to her head, and she had a fringe that always looked too long and rather raggedly cut. Mrs Harper dressed quietly. In fact you could pass Mrs Harper and never notice her. This woman would never go unnoticed.

'Mrs Harper is an excellent teacher,' he said.

'I want her address. It's urgent.'

'Ah! I don't know about that.'

'What do you mean, you don't know about that?' Annalie flashed angrily back at him. 'You must know her address.'

'I do, dear lady, I do.'

'Well?'

'Mrs Harper asked me, indeed begged me, not to divulge her address.'

'All right, damn you. I'll come back on Monday and go to her class and see her there.'

Mr Hunter shook his head. 'I'm afraid that won't be possible.'

'Why won't it be possible? You can't stop me.'

'The point is, Mrs Bellamy, she is off sick. I'm afraid she's had a bit of a breakdown – caused by marital problems, I suspect. Anyway, the poor woman needs a complete rest, the doctor said. But I'm hoping we'll have her back soon.'

'Give me her address, please.'

'The trouble is, I feel if I did that I would be breaking my word. I gave my solemn word to Mrs Harper, indeed the poor woman was in such a state, she made me swear on the Bible, that I would not divulge where she was to anyone.'

'She would be thinking of her shit of a husband, can't you see?'

Mr Hunter stiffened. There was a lack of self-discipline about Mrs Bellamy that he strongly disapproved of. He liked to run a tight ship and this woman, startlingly beautiful though she was, did not fit comfortably into his scheme of things.

'I suspect that could be so,' he admitted warily.

'She needs me.' Suddenly Annalie burst into a wild storm of tears. She was literally howling like the proverbial banshee.

Mr Hunter was appalled, panic-stricken. Hysterical women frightened him. One thing he'd always liked about Mrs Harper was her gentle, well-balanced personality. Until the time of her unfortunate breakdown she had never given him a moment's worry. Even the last time he'd seen her she had not been hysterical – obsessive perhaps, and oddly furtive, but still quiet-spoken and circumspect. Not like this dreadful exhibitionist intent on causing such a noisy and outrageous scene.

'Very well, very well,' he cried out in desperation. 'If you'll just be quiet, I'll tell you.'

CHAPTER 57

It was 12 July, the anniversary of the Battle of the Boyne, and the day Orange Annie came into her own. Everybody had to whiten their window ledges and hang out flags and banners and pictures of King Billy on his horse, or Orange Annie would want to know why not. To really gain her approbation most people tried to hang up orange curtains as well. A huge banner was draped across the street from one side to another depicting King Billy on a skelly-eyed horse. It was a time of great celebration in Cobden Street and people frolicked crazily about and danced in the middle of the cobbled road and bawled out Orange songs. Too many toasts were drunk and fights flared up, here, there and everywhere. Until it looked as if the Battle of the Boyne was being fought all over again.

Annalie could hardly believe her eyes. The thought of gentle, ladylike Elizabeth living in among this rabble shocked her beyond words. The quicker she got her away from here the better. She would see about a job on tour right away and take Elizabeth with her. She could maybe get fixed up in one of the seaside towns. The fresh air would do Elizabeth good. She would see her agent immediately. He would be delighted. He'd had several things on his books for her recently but she hadn't been interested. Now she felt all her old energy and enthusiasm return. She remembered the thrill, the excitement, the applause. Then the winging of her thoughts stopped in mid-flight. Shame pulled her down. She must try to think from Elizabeth's point of view. Was that the right way to express love? For the first time in her life she was unsure. She must be sure this time. She had always believed that love was pushing everything to its limits. It was rushing in where angels feared to tread. It was blind unbridled passion. It was all or nothing at all.

For Elizabeth, if need be, she'd abandon all thoughts of the stage. She'd live here in Cobden Street, she'd devote the rest of her life to her daughter.

Again she struggled with herself and tried to find a safe path through the jungle of love. If there was such a thing? She didn't know. She who had always thought she'd known everything about love. She would have done anything for Adam Monkton. And did. She would have eaten him alive if she could. She had felt the same about Hector. She had been wildly passionate, fiercely jealous. How she'd hated Christina Monkton. How she'd fought to prevent Hector having any love scenes with any actress except her.

Hector had not been like that. Remembering Hector, not through the red-hot mists of passion, and passion lost, but just remembering Hector, she leaned up against the wall of Elizabeth's close in Cobden Street and closed her eyes.

Hector had loved her patiently, loyally. He always tried to see and do what was best for her. He had respected her space. He had never been jealous or possessive. He understood her. He trusted her. There had been about him – despite his dramatic outward appearance and behaviour – an undercurrent of strength and calm dependability. She had felt safe with Hector. She remembered that feeling now, standing in the strange close with a rabble of noise from the street blasting in with the draught. It was as if Hector was close to her again. It was as if they were standing together in the wings waiting to go on and play their parts on the stage. She could see him giving a grand sweeping gesture. He kissed her hand.

'My darling,' he said, 'this is your cue. Break a leg!'

Elizabeth was startled by the knocking on her door. For a moment she thought she was going to faint. She tried to tell herself that it would be Mrs Brown, but she knew it wasn't. Mrs Brown always rattled the letter box. She tried to tell herself that even if it was Alec, what had she to be afraid of? He had never laid a finger on her and she did not really believe he would ever be violent. He was not a violent man. No, she was as much afraid of herself as of him. She told herself that she was in a bad state of nerves and it was only her run-down nervous state that was making her feel as afraid as she did. *She* was the one who felt capable of violence. Alec would use other means. But her feelings were real nevertheless. She knew that you didn't need to use violence to destroy a person. A personality and its self-confidence could die, could be undermined, eroded, eaten away right down to its very roots. It was only a matter of time until a self-destruct mechanism took over and the body died too. She had thought that just by leaving Alec she would suddenly be all right. A magic transformation would take place overnight. A crippling burden would fly from her shoulders. She would suddenly be able to relax and sleep. Blessed sleep would come to blot everything out.

But none of these things had happened. If anything she had become worse. Fear had completely taken over. She had left her leaving too late. She felt so locked together with him. So firmly on an irreversible path to destruction. She had become too afraid to carry on with her normal work in case Alec came to the school. Her determination to survive was still strong – it was because of that she had become afraid to go out on the street in case she saw him watching for her, waiting for her. Eventually she had not been able to put her foot over the door. Mrs Brown and her other more immediate neighbours had been amazingly kind. They had taken turns to bring bowls of soup and cheery chat.

But their knocking on the door had only been another apprehension, another worry. At first she would not answer their knocks. She'd sit, as she was sitting now, shivering and sweating and angrily trying to tell herself to be sensible, at the same time knowing beyond all doubt she couldn't bear any more of Alec Harper. Enough was enough.

The knocking grew louder. Elizabeth took a deep breath and got up. Be sensible, she kept telling herself, be sensible. But when she reached the door she was in a state of physical collapse. Forcing herself, she opened it a crack.

'Darling,' Annalie said. 'It's all right. It's only me. I'm so glad I've found you. Can I come in?'

The door opened. Annalie went in and shut it behind her. Then she took Elizabeth in her arms and patted her back as she used to do when she was a child.

'It's all right, darling. Everything's all right now.'

'I . . . I can't believe it's you. How did you find me?'

'Never mind that. I have found you. That's all that matters. Now, come on, where's your manners, girl? Aren't you going to offer your mother a cup of tea?'

Elizabeth took another deep breath. 'It's really you,' she repeated half to herself as she walked towards the kitchen.

'Yes, it's really me. Here, let me do that.' Annalie took the kettle from Elizabeth and lit the gas ring. 'A nice wee place you've got here,' she said walking around with that special provocative hip-swinging way she had.

'It's all right. How strange it is to see you here.' A sudden anxiety came over Elizabeth. 'You haven't come from my husband, have you?'

'No. I took hysterics at the school. The headmaster was glad to give me your address to get rid of me. I hear your husband's a right shit. Do you take milk and sugar in your tea?'

454

'Just milk.' Elizabeth sank down on to a chair at the table and Annalie said:

'We've so much to learn about each other. So much to catch up on.'

'You're wearing a wedding ring.'

'I'm a widow now.'

'Are you still a dancer?'

'At my age? No, I've changed to acting. I enjoy it. I've my husband to thank for that. He was a wonderful actor. I wish you and Hector had met. You would have liked each other. Where's the teapot?'

Elizabeth pointed.

Annalie concentrated on making the tea for a minute or two then she said, 'So you're a teacher?'

'I haven't been working. I wonder now how I ever managed it. I wasn't much good. I tended to have what some of the other teachers call "fancy ideas".'

'So you had better ideas than some of those old fogies. So what? They're just jealous.'

Elizabeth gave a small smile. 'I'm glad you came.'

'You're a good teacher, Elizabeth. No, an excellent teacher. I've had that on good authority. I've been making enquiries. And don't you talk like that in the past tense as if your teaching days are finished.'

'I know you mean well, but I feel so shattered I just can't see myself ever managing to cope with any job again, especially teaching. It's such a very responsible job, you see. You've got to be the right type. You must be well balanced and in control. You can't take any negative or mixed-up feelings out on little children. They'll have enough to suffer when they grow up.'

'You sound as if you love them.'

'I do. Some people think the main thing you need for teaching in places like this is patience. But it's not, although you need that too. No, compassion is the main thing.'

'And you think you've lost that?'

Elizabeth looked shocked. 'Oh no.'

'Well then?'

'I feel so . . . nervous and overstrained.'

'I've got enough nerve and enough strength for both of us.'

Elizabeth sighed. 'Oh, Annalie.'

'Now, I'll stay here with you for a few days to feed you up and cheer you up. Or you can come to my place in the Gorbals. It's your life and your choice.'

'My life,' Elizabeth echoed bitterly. 'What have I made of my life? I should have enough strength on my own. But I haven't. I'm a useless weakling. A failure.'

'Nonsense. From what I've heard, you must have the strength of ten women to have put up with that shit you married and to have lived in that place for so long. Now, you're going to go back to that school – pronto. The best thing to do when you fall off a horse, or a trapeze, or lose your nerve on the stage, is to get right back on there again.'

She poured out two cups of tea and sat down at the table.

'There's no need for you to worry any more. I told you. We can stay together if you want us to stay together. But not for ever. You'll get shot of this man. Then one day you'll meet some other, better man to share your life with. And I'll have my work. I'm never in the one place for too long. Who knows what life has in store for both of us? But from now on, even if we're apart we'll always be together. Do you know what I mean?'

'You've changed.' Elizabeth gazed at her with interest. 'You look the same. But you've changed.'

'That's life.'

'So much has happened.'

'As I said, we've a lot of catching up to do, Elizabeth.' She gazed back at her daughter with matching earnestness. 'One thing you don't need to tell me because

456

I know it. You're not just the lady I once thought you were. You're a lovely woman. And you're a good teacher, Elizabeth. I'm proud of you.'

Elizabeth remembered the look of conviction in the dark eyes, and the strong, calm sincerity of the words when she took her first steps outside. When she braved her pupils again in the school of the Good and the Bad.

'You're a good teacher, Elizabeth. I'm proud of you.'

She would hang on to that. And to the children as they crowded round her, knowing only the best in her.

'I'm going to tell you a story,' she said.

DAUGHTERS AND MOTHERS

'The stylish work of a born storyteller'
– *Glasgow Evening Times*

Glasgow in 1945 is a gaunt, war-weary city of queues and coupons – yet it offers a new world of opportunity to the indomitable Rory Donovan. By turning her abundant energy and shrewd business skills to the flourishing black market, Rory can give her twins all the social advantages she so envied in her childhood friend Victoria. But Helena and Douglas soon pose the sort of problems money can't solve.

For Victoria, the war's end heralds her husband Matthew's move to London as an MP, while her daughter Amelia's self-destructive search for love has produced a child conceived at a drunken VJ Day celebration.

Then the past catches up with Rory and Victoria and shakes them to the core. The tragedy proves to be a turning point with far-reaching consequences for those they love and cherish . . .

Daughters and Mothers continues the sparkling saga of ambition and conflict that began in *Rag Woman, Rich Woman*.

'Marvellously rich and evocative novel of life in post-war Scotland' – *Western Mail, Cardiff*

'The flesh-and-blood characters in this page-turner seem as real as the folk in your own family' – *Sunday Post*

WOUNDS OF WAR

Glasgow in the sixties – where the legacy of war still lingers . . .

The war changed Joe Thornton so violently that Jenny is now afraid of her husband . . . Widowed by it, vain, silly, Hazel is adrift in the world, her props alcohol and her strong-minded daughter, Rowan . . . And Amelia's private war with her mother-in-law is still going on . . .

Their children have their own battles to fight: the civil rights movement for Rowan; Ban the Bomb for Harry Donovan and the Thorntons. And for all of them, there is the family battlefield.

But with the help of charismatic Rebecca, the three women find their painful way through friendship and new loves to their own kind of peace.

A WOMAN OF PROPERTY

It is 1915 and in the prosperous suburbs of Glasgow, Adam Monkton takes over as head of his family's building firm. He resents his wife, Christina who trapped him into marriage to escape her own oppressive upbringing. But his feelings begin to alter as she throws herself into property development and displays a surprising business acumen.

Meanwhile he is still strongly drawn to Annalie Gordon, the passionate, strong-willed servant girl who bore his first child. Struggling to survive in the slums of the Gorbals, she longs to be with the man she truly loves. But her rival is equally determined, and a woman of property . . .

'*A Woman of Property* is the latest chapter in the success story of Margaret Thomson Davis . . . a new spellbinder for you to read and enjoy' – *Evening Times*

AN ISLAND APART

Lillian Beckwith

Kirsty MacLennan is the cook-general at 'Islay', a respectable guest-house in a Scottish suburb. When her kindly employer retires, and the fractious Isabel takes her place, Kirsty decides it is time to leave – but where shall she go?

Her dilemma is unexpectedly solved by one of the guests – Islander Ruari MacDonald, who has come to the city to seek a bride. Accepting his proposal, Kirsty leaves her old life behind and takes up residence in the crofthouse on Westisle, an idyllic small island uninhabited but for the brothers Macdonald.

As Kirsty joyfully rediscovers her Hebridean roots, and adapts herself to the mysteries of marriage and the challenge of a rigorous new working routine, only one thing stands in her way: the silent, brooding presence of her brother-in-law . . .

A haunting story of love and loss, *An Island Apart* is one of Lillian Beckwith's most magical and elegiac evocations of Island life.

LIGHT A PENNY CANDLE

Maeve Binchy

'Thank heavens a thoroughly enjoyable and readable book'
– *The Times*

Evacuated from Blitz-battered London, genteel Elizabeth White is sent to stay with the boisterous Irish O'Connors. It is the beginning of an unshakeable bond between Elizabeth and Aisling O'Connor which will survive twenty turbulent years. Writing with warmth, wit and great compassion, Maeve Binchy tells a magnificent story of the lives and loves of two women, bound together in friendship.

A timeless bestseller.

'The most enchanting book I have read since *Gone With The Wind*.

'A marvellous novel which combines those rare talents of storytelling and memorable writing' – *Jeffrey Archer*

CROSS STITCH

Diana Gabaldon

Claire Randall is leading a double life. She has a husband in one century – and a lover in another . . .

On holiday with her husband just after the Second World War, she walks through a stone circle in the Scottish highlands and into a violent skirmish taking place in 1743.

A wartime nurse, Claire can deal with the bloody wounds that face her: it is harder to deal with the knowledge that she is in Jacobite Scotland and the carnage of Culloden is looming. Marooned amid the passion and violence, the superstition, the shifting allegiances and the fervent loyalties, Claire is in terrible danger from Jacobites and Redcoats – and from the shock of her own desire for a courageous renegade.

A passionate, unforgettable love story crossing two hundred years of Scottish history.

LAST GUESTS OF THE SEASON

Sue Gee

'A subtle and revealing look at human interaction . . . three stars' – *New Woman*

After years out of contact, Claire and Frances, once fellow students, meet again by chance. Both are now married, with children: impulsively, the families agree to go on holiday together.

The house in Portugal is set in a garden of lemon trees. Inside, it is cool and dark; outside, the valley shimmers in the heat and cicadas sing. In an atmosphere of watchfulness and longing, secrets are revealed whose intensity threatens to tear both families apart, and the night is full of terrors. As events move inexorably toward tragedy, no one sees who is to be the real victim.

Haunting and beautifully crafted, this is a novel which illuminates the darker side of family life and the salvation that is found in it.

'Careful, evocative writing full of touching observation' – *Woman's Journal*

THE WILDER SIDE OF LIFE

Diana Stainforth

She was a woman who seemed to have it all – until she chose to reject the illusion.

Francesca Eastgate appears to have it all – good looks, a blossoming career, a successful marriage and an immaculate home. But when charismatic ex-convict Jack Broderick appears on the scene, the illusion is soon shattered and her life thrown into turmoil.

Rejecting her oppressive husband William and flouting social convention, she escapes London's elegant Inns of Court – first to Broderick's dog track in Richmond and then to Las Vegas. There among the cut and thrust of the casinos and their poker tables, she learns to take control of her own life, and to decide where her heart really lies . . .

'I came to Las Vegas with nothing. It was sink or swim and I learnt to swim. This town gave me a fresh start. It taught me that I can survive on my own if I have to. It's made me strong.'

BESTSELLING FICTION AVAILABLE FROM ARROW

☐ An Island Apart	Lillian Beckwith	£3.99
☐ Dublin Four	Maeve Binchy	£3.99
☐ Light a Penny Candle	Maeve Binchy	£4.99
☐ The Lilac Bus	Maeve Binchy	£3.99
☐ Silver Wedding	Maeve Binchy	£3.99
☐ Victoria Line, Central Line	Maeve Binchy	£4.99
☐ Cross Stitch	Diana Gabaldon	£5.99
☐ Last Guests of the Season	Sue Gee	£4.99
☐ Friends and Other Enemies	Diana Stainforth	£4.50
☐ Indiscretion	Diana Stainforth	£3.99
☐ The Wilder Side of Life	Diana Stainforth	£4.99
☐ Daughters and Mothers	Margaret Thomson Davis	£4.99
☐ Rag Woman, Rich Woman	Margaret Thomson Davis	£4.99
☐ A Woman of Property	Margaret Thomson Davis	£4.99
☐ Wounds of War	Margaret Thomson Davis	£4.99

ARROW BOOKS, BOOKSERVICE BY POST, PO BOX 29, DOUGLAS, ISLE OF MAN, BRITISH ISLES

NAME _____

ADDRESS _____

_____

_____

Please enclose a cheque or postal order made out to Arrow Books Ltd, for the amount due and allow for the following for postage and packing.

U.K. CUSTOMERS: Please allow 75p per book to a maximum of £7.50

B.F.P.O. & EIRE: Please allow 75p per book to a maximum of £7.50

OVERSEAS CUSTOMERS: Please allow £1.00 per book.

Whilst every effort is made to keep prices low it is sometimes necessary to increase cover prices at short notice. Arrow Books reserve the right to show new retail prices on covers which may differ from those previously advertised in the text or elsewhere.